WORKS ISSUED BY

THE HAKLUYT SOCIETY

THE TRAVELS OF IBN BAṬṬŪṬA

A.D. 1325–1354

VOL. II

SECOND SERIES

No. CXVII

ISSUED FOR 1959

HAKLUYT SOCIETY

PATRON

H.R.H. THE DUKE OF GLOUCESTER, K.G., P.C., K.T., K.P.

COUNCIL AND OFFICERS, 1961

PRESIDENT

Sir ALAN BURNS, G.C.M.G.

VICE-PRESIDENTS

Professor E. G. R. TAYLOR, D.Sc.
J. A. WILLIAMSON, Esq., D.Litt.
Professor D. B. QUINN
J. N. L. BAKER, Esq., M.A., B.Litt.

COUNCIL (WITH DATE OF ELECTION)

W. E. D. ALLEN, Esq., F.S.A. (1961)
K. R. ANDREWS, Esq., Ph.D. (1958)
Professor C. F. BECKINGHAM (1958)
Professor C. R. BOXER, F.B.A. (1960)
EILA M. J. CAMPBELL, M.A. (1958)
G. R. CRONE, Esq., M.A. (1961)
E. S. DE BEER, Esq., Hon. D.Litt., (1961)
Professor G. S. GRAHAM (1960)
Professor C. C. LLOYD (1958)
Sir HARRY LUKE, K.C.M.G., D.Litt. (1961)
J. W. S. MARR, Esq., M.A., B.Sc. (1960)
G. P. B. NAISH, Esq. (1960)
Royal Geographical Society (General Sir JAMES MARSHALL-CORNWALL)
Lieut.-Cdr D. W. WATERS, R.N. (1959)
Sir RICHARD WINSTEDT, K.B.E., C.M.G., F.B.A., D.Litt., Hon. LL.D. (1959)
D. P. J. WOOD, Esq., Ph.D. (1959)

TRUSTEES

J. N. L. BAKER, Esq., M.A., B.Litt.
E. W. BOVILL, Esq., F.S.A.
Sir GILBERT LAITHWAITE, G.C.M.G., K.C.B., K.C.I.E., C.S.I.

TREASURER

F. B. MAGGS, Esq.

HON. SECRETARY

R. A. SKELTON, Esq., B.A., F.S.A., F.R.Hist.S.,
British Museum, London, W.C.1

HON. SECRETARIES FOR OVERSEAS

Australia: G. D. RICHARDSON, Esq., The Public Library of N.S.W., MacQuarie Street, Sydney, N.S.W.
Canada: Professor J. B. BIRD, McGill University, Montreal.
New Zealand: C. R. H. TAYLOR, Esq., M.A., Alexander Turnbull Library, Wellington, N.Z.
South Africa: DOUGLAS VARLEY, Esq., South African Library, Cape Town.
U.S.A.: W. M. WHITEHILL, Esq., Ph.D., F.S.A., Boston Athenaeum, 10½ Beacon Street, Boston, Massachusetts.

PUBLISHER AND AGENT FOR SALE AND DISTRIBUTION OF VOLUMES

CAMBRIDGE UNIVERSITY PRESS, Bentley House, 200 Euston Road, London, N.W.1.

Arab deep-sea dhow, Persian Gulf
Photograph by Commander Alan Villiers

THE TRAVELS OF IBN BAṬṬŪṬA

A.D. 1325-1354

Translated with revisions and notes
from the Arabic text edited by
C. DEFRÉMERY and B. R. SANGUINETTI

by

H. A. R. GIBB

VOL. II

REPRINTED BY
ARCHIVAL FACSIMILES LIMITED
with the permission of the Hakluyt Society
1995

FIRST PUBLISHED BY
THE SYNDICS OF THE CAMBRIDGE UNIVERSITY PRESS
Bentley House, 200 Euston Road, London N.W.1
American Branch: 32 East 57th Street, New York, N.Y. 10022

for the Hakluyt Society

1962

REPRINTED 1995 BY
ARCHIVAL FACSIMILES LIMITED
The Old Bakery, Banham, Norfolk, NR16 2HW

ISBN 1 85297 043 X

Printed in Great Britain by Antony Rowe Limited
Chippenham, Wiltshire

CONTENTS

LIST OF ILLUSTRATIONS AND MAPS .. .. *page* viii

FOREWORD TO VOLUME TWO ix

CHAPTER VI. SOUTHERN PERSIA AND 'IRAQ .. 271

Ibn Baṭṭūṭa travels from al-Najaf to Wāsiṭ, 271; visits the Rifā'ī convent at Umm 'Ubaida, 273; anecdote on the Ḥaidarīs in India, 274; goes on to al-Baṣra, 275; description of the city, 276; its monuments and sanctuaries, 277; sails to al-Ubulla and 'Abbādān, 280; to Māchūl, 283; rides to Rāmiz, 283; to Tustar, 284; to Īdhaj, 287; the Atābek of the Lurs, 288; funeral ceremonies at his court, 290; Ibn Baṭṭūṭa visits the atābek, 293; goes on to Iṣfahān, 294; Suhrawardī affiliation, 297; travels to Yazdikhāṣ and Shīrāz, 298; description of Shīrāz and its people, 299; Shaikh Majd al-Dīn, 300; his embroilment with Sultan Khudābandah, 302; Sultan Abū Isḥāq, 306; his conflict with Muẓaffar Shāh, 308; his ambition and generosity, 310; anecdotes on the generosity of the Sultan of Dihlī, 311; sanctuaries at Shīrāz, 313; Shaikh Ibn Khafīf, 314; other sanctuaries at Shīrāz, 316; journey to Kāzarūn, 319; hospice of Shaikh Abū Isḥāq, 319; Ibn Baṭṭūṭa goes on to Zaidāni, al-Ḥuwaiza', and al-Kūfa, 321; description of the city, 322; Bi'r Mallāḥa and al-Ḥilla, 324; sanctuary of the 'Master of the Age', 325; al-Karbalā', 325; Baghdād, 326; poems on the city, 327; its bridges and baths, 329; Western bank, 331; Eastern bank, 332; tombs of the caliphs and saints, 334; Sultan Abū Sa'īd, 335; fate of Dimashq Khwāja, 337; flight of al-Jūbān and his sons, 338; Abū Sa'īd's murder by Baghdād Khātūn, 340; dissolution of his kingdom, 341; description of his *maḥalla*, 342; Ibn Baṭṭūṭa visits Tabrīz, 344; returns to Baghdād, 345; passes Sāmarrā, 346; goes on to al-Mawṣil, 347; the city and its sanctuaries, 348; its governor, 350; Jazīrat Ibn 'Omar, 350; Naṣībīn, 351; Sinjār, 352; Dārā and Mārdīn, 352; the sultan of Mārdīn, 353; anecdote on its qāḍī, 354; Ibn Baṭṭūṭa returns to Baghdād, 355; joins the pilgrim caravan to Mecca, 355; pilgrimages of A.H. 727, 728 and 729, 356; outbreak in the sanctuary, 358.

CHAPTER VII. SOUTHERN ARABIA, EAST AFRICA, AND THE PERSIAN GULF .. .. .. *page* 360

Ibn Baṭṭūṭa leaves Mecca for Judda, 360; embarks on a *jalba*, 361; is driven ashore on the African coast, 362; travels with the Bujāh to Sawākin, 363; sails to Ḥalī, 364; the ascetic Qabūla, 364; the sultan of Ḥalī, 365; Ibn Baṭṭūṭa sails to al-Ahwāb, 366; rides to Zabīd, 366; its inhabitants and scholars, 367; Aḥmad b. al-'Ojail, 367; journey to Ta'izz, 368; the sultan of al-Yaman, 369; visit to Ṣan'ā', 371; 'Adan, 371; its trade and merchants, 372; Ibn Baṭṭūṭa sails to Zaila', 373; to Maqdashaw, 373; customs of its merchants, 374; its sultan, 375; voyage to Manbasa and Kulwā, 379; the sultan of Kulwā, 380; return voyage to Ẓafāri, 382; its produce, 383; inhabitants, 383; hospices, 385; description of the betel tree, 387; use of betel, 387; the coco-palm, 388; uses of the coconut, 388; the sultan of Ẓafāri, 390; Ibn Baṭṭūṭa sails to Ḥāsik, 391; to Maṣīra, 394; to Ṣūr, 394; his adventurous walk to Qalhāt, 394; description of Qalhāt, 396; Ṭībī, 397; Nazwā, 397; the Ibāḍīs and their customs, 398; the sultan of 'Omān, 398; description of Hurmuz Island, 400; its sultan, 401; journey to Khunju Bāl, 404; perils of the desert, 404; Kawristān, 405; Lār, 405; hospice of Shaikh Abū Dulaf at Khunj, 406; Qais, 407; pearl-fisheries, 408; Baḥrain, 409; al-Quthaif, 410; Hajar, 410; Yamāma, 410; pilgrimage of A.H. 732, 411; poisoning of Baktumūr and Amīr Aḥmad, 411.

CHAPTER VIII. ASIA MINOR AND SOUTH RUSSIA .. 413

Ibn Baṭṭūṭa leaves Mecca to go to India, 413; sails to 'Aidhāb, 413; travels to Cairo and al-Lādhiqīya, 414; sails on a Genoese vessel to 'Alāyā, 415; virtues of Asia Minor and its people, 416; the sultan of 'Alāyā, 417; Anṭāliya, 417; the Akhīs and their customs, 418; the sultan of Anṭāliya, 421; journey to Burdūr, Sabarta and Akrīdūr, 421; the sultan of Akrīdūr, 422; Qul Ḥiṣār and its sultan, 424; Lādhiq, 425; its akhīs, 426; its sultan, 427; journey to Ṭawās, Mughla, and Mīlās, 428; the sultan of Mīlās, 429. Ibn Baṭṭūṭa then goes to Qūniya, 430; the *futuwwa*, 430; Mawlānā Jalāl al-Dīn, 430; the sultan of al-Laranda, 432; journey to Nakda and Qaisarīya, 432; Sīwās, 434; the amīr Artanā, 435; Amāsiya, 436; Sūnusā, 436; Kūmish, 436; Arzanjān, 437; Arz al-Rūm, 437; return to Birgī, 438; its sultan, 439; anecdote on a Jewish doctor, 443; and a meteorite, 443; Tīra, 444; Ayā Sulūq, 444; Yazmīr,

445; its governor 'Omar Bak, 445; Maghnīsīya, 447; Barghama, 448; Balī Kasrī, 449; Burṣā, 449; its sultan 'Othmān Bak, 451; Yaznīk, 452; Makaja, 454; Saqarī river, 454; Kāwiya, 454; Yanija, 455; Kainūk, 456; Muṭurnī, 457; Būlī, 459; Garadai Būlī, 460; Burlū, 461; Qaṣṭamūniya, 461; its sultan, Sulaimān Pādshāh, 462; hospice [at Tashköprü], 464; Ṣanūb, 465; exploits of Ghāzī Chalabī, 466; voyage to Karsh, 468; landing in Dasht-i Qifjaq, 469; Kaffa, 470; al-Qiram, 471; waggons, 472; customs of the Turks, 473; journey to Azāq, 475; ceremonies there, 476; Turkish horses, 478; journey to Māchar, 479; respect shown to wives by Turks, 480; Bish Dagh and return to Māchar, 481; Sultan Muḥammad Ūzbak, 482; his public ceremonial, his khātūns, 483; the principal khātūn, 486; the second khātūn, 487; the third khātūn, 488; the fourth khātūn, 488; the sultan's daughter, 489; his sons, 489; journey to Bulghār, 490; the Land of Darkness, 491; festival at Bish Dagh, 492; journey to al-Ḥājj Tarkhān, 496; Ibn Baṭṭūṭa sets out for Constantinople with the third khātūn, 498; journey to Surdāq, 499; Bābā Salṭūq, 499; entry into Greek territory, 500; reception of the khātūn, 502; approach to Constantinople, 504; entry, 504; Ibn Baṭṭūṭa's audience of the Emperor, 505; description of the city, 506; the Great Church, 506; monasteries, 511; the ex-king Jirjis, 512; the qāḍī of Constantinople, 513; departure and journey to al-Ḥājj Tarkhān, 514; to al-Sarā, 515; description of al-Sarā, 515; preparations for the journey to Khwārizm, 517.

BIBLIOGRAPHY .. .. *page* 518

APPENDIX: A Provisional Chronology of Ibn Baṭṭūṭa's Travels in Asia Minor and Russia 527

LIST OF ILLUSTRATIONS AND MAPS

Arab deep-sea dhow. Persian Gulf .. .. .. *frontispiece*

Fig. 1. Ibn Baṭṭūṭa's itineraries in Southern Persia and 'Iraq .. .. *preceding page 271*

2. Baghdād in the fourteenth century .. .. *page* 330

3. Ibn Baṭṭūṭa's itineraries in Southern Arabia, East Africa and the Persian Gulf .. *facing page* 361

4. Anatolia and the Black Sea, showing Ibn Baṭṭūṭa's itineraries .. .. .. *following page 412*

5. Constantinople = ... *page* 507

FOREWORD TO VOLUME TWO

As Ibn Baṭṭūṭa moves further and further out of the central lands of the Middle East, it becomes progressively more difficult to follow up his travels in detail. For Egypt, Syria and the Ḥijāz there are extensive contemporary materials, historical and biographical, which enable the annotator to check his statements with relative assurance. To the reader who is interested only in the travel narrative this may seem to be superfluous or misguided effort, and indeed the translator hopes that the narrative may be read by some with pleasure for its own sake, and without too much critical questioning. But these travels have also served, and will continue to serve, as a major source for the political, social and economic life of large regions of Asia and Africa; if then this translation is to meet these needs in any adequate degree, it becomes an imperative task to check every significant detail as far as possible. In particular, it must be established with reasonable certitude whether Ibn Baṭṭūṭa is speaking at first-hand or at second-hand, whether he visited the cities that he describes, and when.

To establish these facts, the only two instruments available are the internal consistency of the narrative and the concordant or contradictory statements of approximately contemporary sources. If additional justification be needed for recourse to the second, it is amply furnished by the disconcerting situation revealed by study of the first. Ibn Baṭṭūṭa is not overly concerned with chronology, and his dating for some of the journeys recorded in this volume is impossible to reconcile with some of the facts that he mentions. It would still be premature, however, to attempt to impose a precise chronology upon them. The same principle has been followed, therefore, as in the first volume. The author's own chronology has been retained in the text, and discrepancies are pointed out in the footnotes. In addition, in chapters VII and VIII, where Ibn Baṭṭūṭa gives precise dates, the footnotes give alternative dates, on the provisional assumptions that the travels in chapter VII are to be placed in 1329 instead of 1331–2, and those in chapter VIII in 1331–2 instead of 1333–4. The question will be fully discussed in the terminal essay; for the present, the arguments for these assumptions have been set out in an article entitled *Notes sur les voyages d'Ibn Battuta en Asie Mineure et en Russie*, in *Mélanges Lévi-Provençal*, to be published in Paris, 1962; this is reprinted in a revised English version as an Appendix to the present volume.

The biographical works and chronicles utilized in the first volume are of little assistance for checking detail in this second volume, except, occasionally, the *Durar al-Kāmina* of Ibn Ḥajar. Substitutes of approximately equal value are available, however, only for Shīrāz and al-Yaman. The contemporary Persian chronicles of the Mongol kingdom in Persia and al-'Irāq are far from equalling the Egyptian and Syrian chronicles in range and density of detail, and for East Africa and Anatolia only the scrappiest materials are available. Such as they are, however, they all supply on occasion useful facts and synchronisms, as will be shown in the footnotes to the relevant passages. In a few instances, the task of annotation has been lightened by articles on and annotated translations of sections of Ibn Baṭṭūṭa's travels, and by studies relating to individual regions in which his data are utilized or discussed.

The most serious question raised by some of the travel narratives in the present volume is not, however, that of their chronology but that of their veracity. In some passages relating to South-eastern Persia it will be seen that he either anticipates his later journeys in 1347–8 or confuses an earlier with a later journey. On the other hand, the extensive excursion to the eastern provinces which he interpolates in his travels in Asia Minor raises the gravest doubts. With even more assurance it can be asserted that the journey that he claims to have made to the trading centre of Bulghār on the middle Volga is fictitious. This is followed by a journey through the South Russian steppes to and from Constantinople, which some critics have regarded as equally fictitious. The present translator, for his part, is convinced that it is genuine, and that it fits without difficulty into a revised chronology.

As in the preceding volume the text of the edition of Defrémery and Sanguinetti has been taken as the basis of the translation. The variant readings recorded by the editors have been duly noted, and occasionally adopted, and a few obviously erroneous readings have been corrected. In addition, the entire text has been compared with one of the Paris manuscripts (no. 2289), which is a somewhat careless copy of what seems to have been a good original. It would have been ridiculous to burden the footnotes with the numerous errors of the copyist, but in several passages the manuscript has supplied valid alternative readings and a few corrections and vocalizations not noted in the French edition.

In conclusion, the translator acknowledges with gratitude the assistance willingly given by many colleagues and friends in elucidating problems posed by the text, in drawing attention to studies and articles in diverse journals, and lending copies of some otherwise inaccessible. Special acknowledgement is due to Professor Omeljan Pritsak for his assistance in the elucidation of many Old Turkish terms, to the Bibliothèque Nationale in Paris for supplying photostatic copies of considerable sections of MSS. 2289 and 2291, and to those reviewers of the first volume who have contributed corrections and additions to its annotation. It is hoped to assemble these in a cumulative list at the conclusion of the work.

ABBREVIATIONS

BSOAS	*Bulletin of the School of Oriental and African Studies*, London.
Dozy	R. P. A. Dozy, *Supplément aux dictionaires arabes*.
Durar	*al-Durar al-Kāmina*. By Ibn Ḥajar al-ʿAskalānī.
E.I.	*Encyclopaedia of Islam*.
E.I.[2]	*Ibid.*, second edition.
GJ	*Geographical Journal*, London.
JA	*Journal Asiatique*, Paris.
JRAS	*Journal of the Royal Asiatic Society*, London.
Manhal	*al-Manhal al-Ṣāfī*. By Ibn Taghrībirdī.
Selections	*Ibn Baṭṭūṭa's Travels in Asia and Africa*. Translated and selected by H. A. R. Gibb.
'Omari	*Bericht über Anatolien*. By al-ʿUmarī, edited by F. Taeschner.
Yāqūt	*Muʿjam al-Buldān*. By Yāqūt al-Rūmī.
Zetterstéen	*Beiträge zur Geschichte der Mamlūkensultane in den Jahren* 690–741 *der Hiǵra*. Edited by K. V. Zetterstéen.

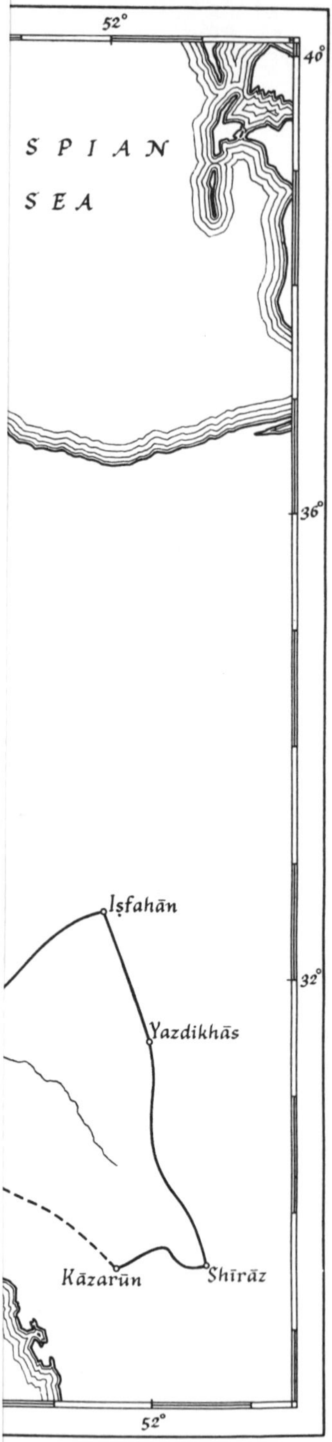
52°
40°
S P I A N
S E A
36°
Iṣfahān
32°
Yazdikhās
Kāzarūn
Shīrāz
52°

CHAPTER VI

Southern Persia and 'Iraq

AFTER we had enjoyed the privilege of visiting [the tomb 1
of] the Commander of the Faithful 'Alī (peace be on him),[1] the caravan went on to Baghdād. But I set out for al-Baṣra, in company with a large troop of the Khafāja Arabs, who are the occupants of that country.[2] They are very powerful and violent, and there is no way to travel in those regions save in their company, so I hired a camel through the commander of that troop, Shāmir b. Darrāj al-Khafājī. We set out from Mashhad 'Alī (peace be on him) and halted [first] at al-Khawarnaq,[3] the seat of al-Nu'mān b. al-Mundhir and his ancestors, the kings of the house of Mā' al-Samā'. It is still inhabited, and there are remains of vast domes, lying on a wide plain on a canal derived from the
Euphrates. From there we went on, | and alighted at a place 2
called Qā'im al-Wāthiq, where there are vestiges of a ruined village and a ruined mosque, of which nothing but the minaret remains.[4] On resuming our journey, our way lay alongside the Euphrates by the place known as al-'Idhār, which is a water-logged jungle of reeds, inhabited by nomad Arabs called al-Ma'ādī.[5] They are brigands, of the Rāfiḍī sect.

1 At al-Najaf (Mashhad 'Alī), see vol. I, pp. 256–7.

2 The Khafāja are a branch of the powerful tribe of 'Uqail. In the tenth century they migrated from al-Ḥasa to the region of Kūfa, where they are still established; see *Encyclopaedia of Islam*, s.v., and Max Freiherr von Oppenheim, *Die Beduinen* (Wiesbaden, 1952), III, 128, 180.

3 Al-Khawarnaq was a famous pre-Islamic palace, one mile east of al-Najaf. It is usually attributed to the early Arab kings of al-Ḥīra (more particularly to al-Nu'mān b. Imru'ul-Qais, d. *c.* 418, not al-Nu'mān b. al-Mundhir, d. *c.* 602) or to the Persian king Bahrām Gūr, d. 438. Although maintained as a residence by the Arab governors of al-Kūfa in the seventh and eighth centuries, it has completely disappeared, and this is apparently the last mention of it.

4 I have found no other reference to this place.

5 Al-'Idhār, a vague term meaning 'marginal land between the cultivation and the desert', is usually applied to the region south of al-Kūfa, but here

They came out upon a party of poor brethren who had fallen behind our troop, and stripped them of everything down to their shoes and wooden bowls. They fortify themselves [as it were] with this jungle and are able to defend themselves in it against all attacks. Savage beasts also inhabit this jungle, in large numbers. Our journey through this 'Idhār took three days' march, and thereafter we arrived at the city of Wāsiṭ.

The City of Wāsiṭ.[6] It has fine quarters and an abundance of orchards and fruit trees, and is famed for its notable men, the living teachers among whom furnish a way to the Good and
3 the tombs of the dead furnish lessons for meditation. | Its inhabitants are among the best people in al-'Irāq—indeed, the very best of them without qualification. Most of them can recite the Holy Qur'ān from memory and are expert in the art of its melodious recitation with the correct reading. All those in the country who wish to learn this art come to them, and in the caravan of al-'Irāq with which we travelled there were a number of students who had come for the purpose of learning the manner of reciting the Qur'ān from the shaikhs in this city. It has a large and magnificent college with about three hundred cells, where strangers who have come to learn the Qur'ān are lodged; this college was built by the shaikh Taqī al-Dīn b. 'Abd al-Muḥsin al-Wāsiṭī,[7] who is one of its principal citizens and jurists. To each student in it he gives a set of clothing every year and supplies money for his expenses every day, and he himself sits in the college with his brothers and his associates to teach the Qur'ān. I met him and he showed me hospitality and supplied me with provisions of dates and money.

---

apparently to the marshlands. Since Wāsiṭ lies 115 miles east of al-Najaf, the indications given by Ibn Baṭṭūṭa for his journey are quite inadequate. The name Ma'ādī is an earlier form of Ma'dān, by which the marsh-dwellers are still known; see Oppenheim, *Die Beduinen*, III, 477 ff.

[6] Wāsiṭ, on the Dujaila (still in the fourteenth century the main channel of the Tigris; see Mustawfī, *Nuzhat al-Qulūb*, trans. G. Le Strange (Leyden-London, 1919), 53, 207), was founded by al-Ḥajjāj, governor of al-'Irāq under the Umayyad caliphs, about 703, as the 'midway' garrison town between al-Kūfa and al-Baṣra, each about fifty leagues distant. On the modern examination of the site see Fu'ad Safar, *Wasit* (Baghdād, 1945). Its fame as a centre of learning at this time is confirmed by the number of scholars known as al-Wāsiṭī.

[7] 'Abd al-Raḥman b. 'Abd al-Muḥsin al-Wāsiṭī (d. 1343/4), author of a biography of Shaikh Aḥmad al-Rifā'ī (see the following note).

When | we halted at the city of Wāsiṭ the caravan stopped 4
outside it for three nights in order to trade. This gave me the opportunity of visiting the grave of the saint Abu'l-'Abbās Aḥmad al-Rifā'ī, which is at a village called Umm 'Ubaida, one day's journey from Wāsiṭ.[8] I asked the shaikh Taqī al-Dīn to send someone with me to conduct me to it, and he sent with me three Arabs of the Banū Asad,[9] who are the occupants of that region, and mounted me on one of his own horses. I set out at noon and after spending that night in the enclosure of the Banū Asad we arrived at the hospice at noon on the following day. It is a vast convent in which there are thousands of poor brethren. Our visit coincided with the arrival of the shaikh Aḥmad Kūjak, the grandson of the Friend of God Abu'l-'Abbās al-Rifā'ī, whose tomb we had come to visit.[10] The shaikh had come from his place of residence in the land of Rūm [Anatolia] in order to visit his grandfather's tomb, and it was to him that the headship of the hospice had descended. |

When the afternoon prayers had been said, drums and 5
kettle-drums were beaten and the poor brethren began to dance. After this they prayed the sunset prayer and brought in the repast, consisting of rice-bread, fish, milk and dates. When all had eaten and prayed the first night prayer, they began to recite their *dhikr*, with the shaikh Aḥmad sitting on the prayer-carpet of his ancestor above-mentioned, then they began the musical recital. They had prepared loads of firewood which they kindled into a flame, and went into the midst of it dancing; some of them rolled in the fire, and others ate it in their mouths, until finally they extinguished

[8] Shaikh Aḥmad b. 'Alī al-Rifā'ī (d. 1183), founder of the widespread Rifā'ī fraternity of ṣūfīs; see *E.I.*, s.v. al-Rifā'ī. The term Aḥmadīya, used by Ibn Baṭṭūṭa, was later dropped to avoid confusion with the Egyptian order of Shaikh Aḥmad al-Badawī (d. 1276). Umm 'Ubaida (or 'Abīda), now called Shaikh Aḥmad Rifā'ī, lies about 30 miles south-east of Wāsiṭ.

[9] One of the most famous Arab tribes, established in al-'Irāq since the Arab conquest. Since the twelfth century they have occupied the area along the Euphrates west and north-west of its junction with the Tigris; *E.I.*^{2}, s.v., and Oppenheim, *Die Beduinen*, III, 450–7.

[10] This Aḥmad Kuchuk ('the Lesser') is described on p. 463 below as a son of Tāj al-Dīn; the latter is presumably the great-great-grandson of Shaikh Aḥmad who died in 1304 (Ibn Kathīr, *al-Bidāya wa'l-Nihāya*, Cairo, n.d., XIV, 35). Aflākī (tr. Huart, II, 366) reports a meeting at Amasya between Shaikh Aḥmad Kuchuk and the Mevlevi shaikh 'Ārif (d. 1320).

it entirely. This is their regular custom and it is the peculiar characteristic of this corporation of Aḥmadī brethren. Some of them will take a large snake and bite its head with their teeth until they bite it clean through.[11] |

6 *Anecdote.* I was on one occasion at a place called Afqānbūr in the district of Hazār Amrūhā, which is at a distance of five nights' journey from Dihlī, the capital of India.[12] We had encamped there on a river called the river of al-Sarw.[13] This was in the season of the *shakāl* (*shakāl* in their language meaning rain[14]), which falls at the time of the summer heats. The river was coming down in flood from the mountains of Qarājīl. Now everyone who drinks from it, whether man or beast, dies because of the falling of the rain on poisonous grasses. We stayed by this river for four days without anyone going near it. There came to me there a company of poor brethren who had iron rings on their necks and arms, and whose chief was a coal-black negro. They belonged to the corporation known as the Ḥaidarīya[15] and they spent one night with us. Their chief asked me to supply him with fire-
7 wood | that they might light it for their dance, so I charged the governor of that district, who was 'Azīz known as al-Khammār (an account of him will be given later), to furnish it. He sent about ten loads of it, and after the night prayer they kindled it, and at length, when it was a mass of glowing coals, they began their musical recital and went into that fire, still dancing and rolling about in it. Their chief asked me for a shirt and I gave him one of the finest texture; he put it on

[11] The thaumaturgic practices of the Rifā'īya have always been notorious; cf. E. W. Lane, *Modern Egyptians* (London, 1836), ch. X. They are said to have been introduced only in the Mongol period, about a century after Shaikh Aḥmad's death.

[12] I.e. the division of Amroha, on whose harvests Ibn Baṭṭūṭa had been given an assignment (see vol. III, p. 436, Arabic). The village of Afghanpūr, now Aghwānpūr, 5½ miles south-east of Tughluqābād, one of the 'four cities' of Delhi (*The Rehla of Ibn Battuta*, Mahdi Husain (Baroda, 1953), 54, n. 2), can hardly be the place mentioned here.

[13] Spelled incorrectly *Surūr* in the printed text; cf. vol. III, 437 (Arabic). The modern name of the river is Sarjū (*Rehla*, 145, n. 2). Qarājīl is the name traditionally given to the Himalayas in the Arabic and Persian texts.

[14] Evidently from Sanskrit *varṣakāla*, 'monsoon season', rendered as *barshakāl* by al-Bīrūnī, *India*, Hyderabad, 1958, p. 170.

[15] A ṣūfī fraternity related to the Qalandarīs (see vol. I, p. 37, n. 108), founded by Quṭb al-Dīn Ḥaidar of Zāwa (see vol. III, p. 79, Arabic).

and he began to roll about in the fire with it on and to beat the fire with his sleeves until it was extinguished and dead. He then brought me the shirt showing not a single trace of burning on it, at which I was greatly astonished.

After making the visitation of the shaikh Abu'l-'Abbās al-Rifā'ī (God give us good of him) I returned to the city of Wāsiṭ and found that the company that I was with had already started out, but I overtook them on the way. We alighted at a water-point called al-Hadhīb, then continued our journey and alighted in Wādi'l | Kurā', where there was 8
no water, then after a further march in a place called al-Mushairib.[16] From there we went on and camped in the vicinity of al-Baṣra, and on resuming our march we entered the city of al-Baṣra on the forenoon of the following day.

The city of al-Baṣra.[17] We alighted at the *ribāt* of Mālik ibn Dīnār.[18] As I approached the city I had remarked at a distance of some two miles from it a lofty building as tall as a castle. I asked what it was and was told that it was the mosque of 'Alī ibn Abī Ṭālib (God be pleased with him). Al-Baṣra was in former days so widely settled and so vast in extent that this mosque was in the centre of the town, whereas now it is two miles outside it. Likewise from this mosque to the old wall that encircled the town it is about the same distance, so that the mosque stands midway between the old wall and the present city.[19]

The city of al-Baṣra is one of the metropolitan cities of al-'Irāq, renowned throughout | the whole world, spacious in 9

[16] None of these stations seems to be identifiable on modern maps. Mustawfī (see n. 6 above) gives the regular stations from Wāsiṭ to al-Baṣra as Nahrabān, Fārūth, Dair al-'Ummāl, and Ḥawānīt, the total distance being forty farsakhs (p. 166).

[17] The original city of al-Baṣra, on the site of modern Zubair, was abandoned in the twelfth century, and the later mediaeval city lay two miles further east, being linked to the Shaṭṭ al-'Arab by a canal. The palm-groves of the region have always been celebrated, and remain so. The general layout of the ancient city and sites are studied by L. Massignon, 'Explication du Plan de Basra', in *Westöstliche Abhandlungen Rudolf Tschudi überreicht* (Wiesbaden, 1954), 154–74.

[18] See below, p. 279, n. 34.

[19] The Arabic historians attribute the Great Mosque at al-Baṣra, not to 'Alī, but to Ziyād (d. 676), governor under Mu'āwiya. According to al-Harawī (81; trans. 187), the minaret and south wall only were ascribed to 'Alī. The remains of the mosque lie to the East of the old town of Zubair; L. Massignon, 'Plan de Basra', 155, Plan I.

area and elegant in its courts, remarkable for its numerous fruit-gardens and its choice fruits; blessed with an abounding portion of plenty and of fruitfulness, since it is the meeting place of the two seas, the salt and the fresh.[20] No place on earth exceeds it in quantity of palm-groves, so that the current price of dates in its market is fourteen 'Irāqī pounds to a dirham, their dirham being one-third of the *nuqra*.[21] The qāḍī there, Ḥujjat al-Dīn, sent me a hamper of dates that a man could scarcely carry; I sent them to be sold and they fetched nine dirhams, three of which were taken by the porter as the charge for carrying them from the house to the market. There is manufactured there from dates a honey called *sailān*, which is sweet and like jalap.[22]

Al-Baṣra is composed of three quarters. One of them is the quarter of Hudhail, and its chief is the worthy shaikh 'Alā al-Dīn ibn al-Athīr, a generous and distinguished scholar, who showed me hospitality and sent me clothes and money. |
10 The second quarter is the quarter of Banū Ḥarām, whose chief is the noble sayyid Majd al-Dīn Mūsā al-Ḥasanī, a bountiful and meritorious man, who [also] showed me hospitality and sent me dates, *sailān* and money. The third quarter is the quarter of the Persians, the chief of which is Jamāl al-Dīn ibn al-Lūkī.[23]

The people of al-Baṣra are of generous nature, hospitable to the stranger and readily doing their duty by him, so that no stranger feels lonely amongst them. They hold the Friday prayers in the mosque of the Commander of the Faithful

[20] An allusion to a Qur'ānic phrase, e.g., 'He it is Who hath sent forth the two seas, this one sweet and fresh, that salt and bitter, and Who set between them a barrier and ban inviolable' (sūra xxv. 53).

[21] The standard silver dirham of account; see vol. I, p. 223, n. 141.

[22] *Sailān* (or more precisely *sayalān*) means 'a flowing'; its use in the sense of 'date-honey' does not seem to be attested elsewhere.

[23] Ḥudhail and Banu Harām were among the old quarters of al-Baṣra, named after Arab tribes; the former is mentioned by a writer in 1142, in a description of the city which strikingly resembles that of Ibn Baṭṭūṭa (Ibn Haukal, *Opus Geographicum*, 2nd ed. (Leiden, 1938) I, 237); the latter acquired literary fame from the 48th *maqāma* of al-Ḥarīrī. The quarter 'of the Persians' is not mentioned elsewhere, to my knowledge, but Rashīd al-Dīn mentions a quarter called *al-Shūka* (? *al-Shawka*), containing a hospice for travellers, college, and hospital; *Letters of Rashid al-Dīn Faḍl Allah*, ed. M. Shafi (Lahore, 1947), 14. The three governors have not been identified, and the name of the third is variously transcribed in the manuscripts.

'Alī (God be pleased with him) which I have already mentioned; it is closed after that and they do not visit it except on Fridays. This is one of the finest of mosques. Its court is of immense extent and paved with red pebbles which are brought from Wādi'l-Sibā'.[24] There is preserved in it the copy of the Holy Qur'ān which 'Othmān (God be pleased with him) was reading when he was killed, and the stain of the blood is still
on the leaf which contains | the word of God Most High 'And 11
God will suffice thee against them, for He is the Hearer, the Knower'.[25]

An anecdote, for reflection. I was present one day at the Friday service in this mosque and when the preacher rose and recited his discourse he committed in it many gross errors of grammar. I was astonished at his conduct and spoke of it to the qāḍī Ḥujjat al-Dīn, who said to me 'In this town there is not a man left who knows anything of the science of grammar'. Here is a lesson for men to reflect on—magnified be He who changes all things and inverts all conditions. This Baṣra, to whose inhabitants fell the mastery in the science of grammar, from whose soil sprang its trunk and its branches, and from whose people arose its leader whose primacy is undisputed—the preacher in this town cannot deliver a Friday discourse according to its rules for all his efforts![26] |

This mosque has seven minarets, one of them the minaret 12
which shakes, or so they say, when the name of 'Alī ibn Abī Ṭālib (God be pleased with him) is mentioned. I climbed up to this minaret from the top of the roof of the mosque, accompanied by one of the inhabitants of al-Baṣra, and I found in one angle of it a wooden hand-grip nailed into it, resembling the handle of a builder's trowel. The man who was with me placed his hand on that hand-grip and said 'By right

[24] Six miles north of Zubair, as mentioned below, slightly to the north of the present station of Shu'aiba Junction.

[25] 'Othmān, the third caliph, was murdered in al-Madīna in 655 by mutinous troops from Egypt, while engaged (according to tradition) in reading the Qur'ān. A number of mosques claimed the possession of this relic. The verse quoted is part of sūra ii. 137.

[26] The rules of Arabic grammar were systematized at al-Baṣra in the eighth century, and it was the 'School of al-Baṣra' which set the universally acknowledged standards of correct classical usage. The 'leader' referred to is the Persian Sībawaih (d. *c.* 796), who composed the first comprehensive work on the subject and was reputedly buried in Shīrāz; see *E. I.*, s.v. (For *dawbihi* in the printed text read *darbihi*.)

of the head of the Commander of the Faithful 'Alī (God be pleased with him), shake,' and he shook the hand-grip, whereupon the whole minaret quivered. I in my turn placed my hand on the hand-grip and said to him 'And I say "By right of the head of Abū Bakr, the successor of the Apostle of God (God give him blessing and peace), shake,' and I shook the hand-grip and the whole minaret quivered. They were astonished at this. The people of al-Baṣra are followers of the Sunna and the Community, and no one who does as I did has anything to fear from them, but if anything like this were to happen at Mashhad 'Alī [Najaf] or Mashhad al-Ḥusain [Karbalā'] or at al-Ḥilla or al-Baḥrain or Qumm or Qāshān
13 or Sāwa or Āwa | or Ṭūs, whoever did it would perish, because they are fanatical Shī'ites.[27]

Ibn Juzayy says 'I have seen in the city of Barshāna, in the valley of al-Manṣūra in the land of al-Andalus (God protect her),[28] a minaret which shakes without having mentioned to it the name of any of the Caliphs or anyone else. It is the minaret of the principal mosque there, of no very ancient construction, and it is about the finest minaret that you could see for beauty of appearance, proportions and height, without any inclination or deviation. I climbed it once in company with a number of people, and some of those who were with me grasped the sides of its topmost part and shook them so that the whole tower quivered, until I made signs to them to stop shaking it and they stopped.' (To return).

Description of the Blessed Sanctuaries at al-Baṣra. One of them is the tomb of Ṭalḥa ibn 'Obaidallāh, one of the Ten [to whom Paradise was promised] (God be pleased with
14 them). It is inside the city and has a dome over it | and an adjacent mosque and convent in which food is served to all comers. The people of al-Baṣra venerate it very highly, and rightly so. There is also the tomb of al-Zubair ibn al-'Awwām,

[27] Ibn Baṭṭūṭa's uncompromising Sunni loyalties have already been demonstrated in vol. I, pp. 83, 93, etc. The cities mentioned were all noted centres of Shī'ism and the term translated 'fanatical Shī'ites' is in the original 'Rāfiḍī extremists'. The Persian geographer Mustawfī (*c.* 1340) also mentions the trembling of the minaret at the oath by 'Alī, 'for although it is indeed a matter contrary to reason, yet in respect of any miracle wrought by 'Alī, the Commander of the Faithful, reason does not enter' (*Nuzhat al-Qulūb*, trans. 45).

[28] Purchena, on the Rio Almanzora, 58 km. north of Almeria.

the disciple of the Apostle of God (God give him blessing and
peace) and the son of his parental aunt (God be pleased with
them both). It is outside al-Baṣra and has no dome, but has a
mosque and a convent in which food is served to travellers.[29]
Also the grave of Ḥalīma of the tribe of Sa'd, the foster-
mother of the Apostle of God (God be pleased with her), and
by her side the grave of her son, the foster-brother of the
Apostle of God (God give him blessing and peace).[30] Then the
grave of Abū Bakra, the companion of the Apostle of God
(God give him blessing and peace) which has a dome over it.[31]
About six miles from al-Baṣra, near Wādi'l-Sibā', is the grave
of Anas ibn Mālik, the servant of the Apostle of God (God
give him blessing and peace),[32] but it cannot be visited except
in a large company because of the number of wild beasts and
its uninhabited state. Furthermore there is | the grave of 15
al-Ḥasan ibn Abi'l-Ḥasan al-Baṣrī, the chief of the generation
of Followers (God be pleased with him),[33] and the tombs of
Muḥammad ibn Sīrīn, Muḥammad ibn Wāsi', 'Utba the lad,
Mālik ibn Dīnār, Ḥabīb al-'Ajamī, and Sahl ibn 'Abdallāh al-
Tustarī (God be pleased with them all).[34] Over each of these

[29] Ṭalḥa and al-Zubair, two of the inner circle of Muḥammad's Companions, opposed 'Alī's assumption of the caliphate and were defeated by 'Alī at the battle of 'the Camel' outside al-Baṣra in 656, both being killed in in the battle. Their tombs still exist, that of Ṭalḥa near the Great Mosque, and that of al-Zubair in the town named after him; see L. Massignon, 'Plan de Basra', 157, Plan II.

[30] These tombs are not mentioned in other sources.

[31] Abu Bakra (d. 672), an Abyssinian slave emancipated by Muḥammad. His descendants formed one of the notable families of al-Baṣra for over a century; see *E.I.*², s.v.

[32] Anas b. Mālik (d. 710) was, as a young boy, the personal servant of Muḥammad, and the last survivor of the Companions; see *E.I.*, s.v.

[33] Al-Ḥasan al-Baṣrī (642–728), the most famous of the early Muslim ascetics; see *E.I.*, s.v. and L. Massignon, *Essai sur les origines du lexique technique de la mystique musulmane* (Paris, 1922), 152–79. His tomb is still preserved; Massignon, 'Plan de Basra', 157, Plan II.

[34] Muḥammad b. Sīrīn (d. 728), a celebrated Traditionist; see *E.I.*, s.v. Muḥammad b. Wāsi' (d. 738), an early ascetic; see al-Hujwīrī, *Kashf al-Maḥjūb*, trans. R. A. Nicholson (London, 1911), 91–2. 'Utba b. Abān, called *al-Ghulām* ('the deacon') because of his assiduity in religious exercises, was killed in battle with the Greeks near al-Miṣṣīṣa: al-Iṣfahānī, *Hilyat al-Auliyā'* (Cairo, 1936), VI, 226–38; Mālik b. Dīnār (d. *c.* 747), a companion of al-Ḥasan al-Baṣrī; al-Hujwīrī, trans., 89. Ḥabīb al-'Ajamī was a disciple of al-Ḥasan al-Baṣrī: al-Hujwīrī, trans., 88–9. Sahl b. 'Abdallāh al-Tustarī (d. 886 or later) was the founder of a famous school of Islamic mysticism: al-Hujwīrī, trans., 139–40, 195–210.

tombs is a tombstone with the name of the person buried there and the date of his death inscribed upon it. All of these are inside the old wall, and are today about three miles distant from the town. In addition, there are there the graves of a vast number of the Companions and Followers who found martyrdom on the day of the Camel.

16 The governor | of al-Baṣra at the time of my arrival there was named Rukn al-Dīn al-'Ajamī of Tawrīz,[35] and he showed me hospitality and made gifts to me. Al-Baṣra is on the banks of the Euphrates and Tigris, and there is high tide and low tide there just as there is in the Wādī Salā and elsewhere in the country of the Maghrib.[36] The channel of salt water which comes up from the Sea of Fārs is at a distance of ten miles from the town, and at high tide the salt water overpowers the sweet but at low tide the sweet water overpowers the salt. The inhabitants of al-Baṣra draw this water for use in their houses and for this reason the saying goes that their water is brackish.

Ibn Juzayy remarks: It is for the same reason that the air of al-Baṣra is unhealthy and that the complexions of its inhabitants are yellowish and sallow, to such an extent that they have become proverbial. A certain poet said when a citron was brought in front of the Ṣāḥib:[37]

A citron here amongst us shows
the image of the lachrymose. |
17 So God hath clothed in sickly hue
the slaves of love—the Baṣrans too!

(To return.) Thereafter, from the strand of al-Baṣra, I embarked in a *sumbuq*, that is a small boat,[38] for al-Ubulla. The distance between them is ten miles, through an uninterrupted succession of fruit gardens and overshadowing palmgroves both to right and left, with traders sitting in the

[35] Not identified.

[36] Wādī Salā is the estuary of the river now called Bou Regreg, between the cities of Rabāṭ and Salā (Sallee). The 'channel of salt water' is the southern end of the Shaṭṭ al-'Arab.

[37] 'The Ṣāḥib' is the traditional designation of Ismā'īl b. 'Abbād (d. 995), vizier of the Buwaihid princes of Western Persia, and a noted patron of literature.

[38] A small high-prowed vessel with a mast for a lateen sail, illustrated in Alan Villiers, *Sons of Sinbad* (London, 1940), 2–3.

shade of the trees, selling bread, fish, dates, milk and fruit. Between al-Baṣra and al-Ubulla there is the cell of Sahl ibn 'Abdallāh of Tustar; and when those travelling in the vessels draw level with it you may see them drinking from the water of the river which faces it and praying at the same time, in order to profit by the blessing of this saint (God be pleased with him). The sailors in this country row standing up.[39]

Al-Ubulla was in former times a great city, frequented by merchants from India and Fars, but it fell into decay and is now a village,[40] though it preserves traces of palaces | and 18
other buildings which indicate its former greatness. Here we embarked on the channel which comes up from the Sea of Fārs in a small ship belonging to a man from al-Ubulla named Mughāmis. It was after sunset when we sailed and in the early morning we reached 'Abbādān, a large village on a salt marsh, with no cultivation but containing many mosques and cells and hermitages for devotees.[41] It is three miles from the strand.

Ibn Juzayy remarks: 'Abbādān was a township in former times, but it is barren, grain is not grown on it and has all to be imported, and water also is scarce in it. A certain poet said of it:

> Who will tell my friends in Andalus that I
> Dwell in 'Abbādān, at earth's remotest shore?
> Desolatest spot that ever met my eye—
> Only that its fame I wanted to explore. |
> Every sip of water there you have to buy, 19
> Every crust of bread's a prize to wrangle o'er.[42]

(To return.) On the shore of 'Abbādān there is a hermitage

[39] For *yaḥrifūna* and other variants in the MSS. read *yajdifūna*. For Sahl b. 'Abdallāh see above, p. 279, n. 34.

[40] Al-Ubulla (Apologos) occupied the site of the 'Ashar quarter of modern Baṣra, on the Shaṭṭ al-'Arab. It was the chief port at the head of the Persian Gulf until the foundation of al-Baṣra by the Arabs in 639.

[41] 'Abbadān, formerly an island between the estuaries of the Tigris and the Kārūn (Dujail), hence called in Persian *Miyān Rūdān* ('Between the Rivers'), became celebrated as a religious centre when it was selected as a retreat by the disciples of al-Ḥasan al-Baṣrī (see above, p. 279, n. 33) in the eighth century; see *E.I.*², s.v. and al-Harawī, *Guide des Lieux de Pèlerinage* (Damascus, 1957), 191, who also mentions the sanctuary of al-Khiḍr. For the association of al-Khiḍr with Ilyās (Elijah) see below, p. 466, n. 193.

[42] The sense and provenance of the verse obviously require *tahādā* to be taken in its Spanish-Arabic sense; see Dozy, s.v.

which is called after the name of al-Khiḍr and Ilyās (peace be upon them), and alongside it a convent inhabited by four poor brethren with their children, who maintain the service of the hermitage and the convent and subsist on private charity. Everyone who passes by them gives them alms. The men of this convent told me that there was at ʿAbbādān a devotee of great merit, living entirely alone. He used to come down to this sea once a month and catch there enough fish for a month's provision, and would not be seen again until the end of the next month. This had been his custom for many years. When we reached ʿAbbādān I had no other care than to seek him out, so while those who were with me were occupied in prayers in the mosque and cells, I went off in search of him.
20 I came to a mosque in a ruinous condition | and found him praying in it, so I sat down beside him. He shortened his prayer, and after pronouncing the benedictions took my hand and said to me 'May God grant you your desire in this world and the next'. I have indeed—praise be to God—attained my desire in this world, which was to travel through the earth, and I have attained in this respect what no other person has attained to my knowledge. The world to come remains, but my hope is strong in the mercy and clemency of God, and the attainment of my desire to enter the Garden.

When I came back to my companions and told them what had happened to me with this man and indicated his place to them, they went to see him, but they could not find him nor come to any information about him and they were filled with amazement at this incident. We returned in the evening to the convent and put up in it for the night. After the last night-prayer one of the four poor brethren came into our room. It was the custom of this brother to go into ʿAbbādān every
21 night and light the lamps in the mosques, after which | he returned to his convent. When he reached ʿAbbādān [that evening], he found the devotee, who gave him a fresh fish, saying to him, 'Take this to the guest who came today'. So the poor brother said to us as he came in, 'Which of you saw the Shaikh today?' I replied, 'It was I who saw him' and he said, 'He says to you "This is your hospitality-gift".' I thanked God for that and the poor brother cooked that fish for us and we all ate of it. I have never tasted better fish. For a

moment I entertained the idea of spending the rest of my life in the service of this shaikh, but I was dissuaded from it by the pertinacity of my spirit.

On the next morning we resumed our sea-voyage, making for the town of Māchūl. It was a habit of mine on my travels never, so far as possible, to retrace any road that I had once travelled over.[43] I was desirous of making for Baghdād in al-ʻIrāq, and a man at al-Baṣra advised me to travel to the country of the Lūrs, and from there to ʻIrāq al-ʻAjam and
then on to ʻIrāq al-ʻArab, and I followed | his advice. Four 22
days later we reached the town of Māchūl, a small place on the coast of this channel which we have described as coming out of the Sea of Fārs.[44] Its ground is saline, without trees or vegetation, and it has an immense bazaar, one of the largest of its kind. I stayed there only one day and after that I hired from some merchants who bring grain from Rāmiz to Māchūl a mount for my conveyance. We travelled for three nights across open country inhabited by Kurds in hair-tents, who are said to be Arabs by origin,[45] and then reached the town of Rāmiz, a fine city with fruit-trees and rivers.[46] We lodged there with the qāḍī Ḥusām al-Dīn Maḥmūd, in whose company I found a man of learning, religion, and piety, of Indian
origin, called Bahā' | al-Dīn. His name was Ismāʻīl and he 23
was one of the sons of the shaikh | Bahā' al-Dīn Abū Zakarīyā of Multān,[47] and had studied under the shaikhs of Tawrīz and other places. I stayed only one night in the town of Rāmiz, after which we continued our journey for three nights more across a plain where there are villages inhabited by Kurds. At the end of each stage of this journey there was a hospice at

[43] This explains many of the strange groupings of cities in his narrative.

[44] Now Bender Maʻshur, at the head of Khor Mūsā, east of the delta. Ibn Baṭṭūṭa is obviously mistaken in describing it as on the same 'channel' as the Shaṭṭ al-ʻArab.

[45] The routes in this region were infested by bedouins already in the tenth century; P. Schwarz, *Iran im Mittelalter*, IV (Leipzig, 1921), 334. In the thirteenth century there was a large immigration of Kurdish and related tribes (including some Arabs of the ʻOqail tribe) from northern Syria into this area; see *E.I.*, s.v. Lur.

[46] Rāmiz is the shortened form of Rām(a) Hurmuz, a Sasanian foundation some 90 miles east of Bender Maʻshūr.

[47] Abū Zakarīyā is an error for Zakarīyā; Bahā' al-Dīn (1183–1267), a Khurasanian by origin, was the leading representative of the Suhrawardī order in India (see vol. III, p. 102, Arabic).

which every traveller was supplied with bread, meat and sweetmeats. Their sweetmeats are made with grape-syrup mixed with flour and ghee. In each hospice there is a shaikh, a prayer-leader, a muezzin, and a servitor for the poor brethren, together with slaves and servants who cook the food.

I came next to the city of Tustar, which is situated at the edge of the plain in the dominion of the Atābek and the beginning of the mountains—a large city, splendid and flourishing, with noble orchards and superb gardens, and possessed of rare attractions and well-stocked markets.[48] It is of ancient foundation, having been captured by Khālid b. al-Walīd, and
24 it is after this city that Sahl b. ʿAbdallāh is called. | It is encircled by the river called al-Azraq, which is a marvel, unsurpassed in its clearness and exceedingly cold during the hot season.[49] I have never seen any river as blue except the river of Balakhshān.[50] The city has a single gate by which travellers can enter, called *darwāza Disbūl, darwāza* meaning in their language 'gate', but it has other gates leading down to the river.[51] On both banks of the river, there are orchards and water-wheels; the river itself is deep and over it, leading to the travellers' gate, there is a bridge upon boats like the bridges of Baghdād and al-Ḥilla.[52]

[48] Tustar, the Arabic form of Shushtar, situated on a cliff on the east bank of the Kārūn river, 90 miles north of Bender Maʿshūr, and 70 miles northwest of Rāmhurmuz; see *E.I.*, s.v. Shuster, and L. Lockhart, *Famous Cities of Iran* (London, 1939), 86–95, with plates and sketch-plan. It was captured by the Arabs under Abū Mūsā al-Ashʿarī in 642, after a long siege in which the city was defended by the Persian general Hurmuzān; L. Caetani, *Annali dell'Islam* (Milan, 1911), IV, 454–9. Since Īdhaj, Ibn Baṭṭūṭa's next stop (and the capital of 'the Atābek'), lies only 40 miles north of Rāmhurmuz, he seems to have taken a curiously zigzag route.

[49] Al-Azraq (i.e. Blue River) is the Kārūn, usually called Dujail in the mediaeval texts. It is divided immediately above Tustar into two branches, the eastern branch being an artificial canal, called Masrūqān, which flows past the east side of the city; see *E.I.*, s.v. Kārūn.

[50] The river of Balakhshān (i.e. Badakhshān) is an affluent of the Oxus, called by the mediaeval geographers Dirghām and in modern times Kokcha; see vol. III, p. 82 (Arabic).

[51] Mustawfī (trans., 108) mentions four gates. The spelling Disfūl and Dispūl (for the more usual Dizbūl) is found also in the contemporary *Letters of Rashīd al-Dīn.*

[52] The earlier geographer al-Maqdisī also mentions the bridge of boats at Tustar. At a later period it was replaced by a bridge built upon the dam (see next note). By 'deep', I suspect that Ibn Baṭṭūṭa means that the river flows far below the town.

Ibn Juzayy remarks: It is of this river that a certain poet has said:

> See Tustar's water-fence[53]
> With wondrous art dispense
> The streams that it impounds
> To all the thirsty grounds.
>
> So will a mighty prince
> Engross his subjects' pence,
> Then parcel them away
> Upon his soldiers' pay. |

There is an abundance of fruits at Tustar, commodities are 25
plenteously available, and its bazaars have not their equal in attraction. Outside the city there is a venerated tomb to which the inhabitants of those regions come on pilgrimage and make vows. It has a convent where a number of poor brethren lodge, and the people there assert that it is the tomb of Zain al-'Ābidīn 'Alī b. al-Ḥusain b. 'Alī b. Abī Ṭālib.[54] I stayed in the city of Tustar at the college of the pious shaikh and versatile imām, Sharaf al-Dīn Mūsā, son of the pious shaikh and learned imām Ṣadr al-Dīn Sulaimān, who is descended from Sahl b. 'Abdallāh. The shaikh is a man of generous qualities and outstanding merits, who combines knowledge and religion, saintly life and munificence. He has a college and a convent, the servitors of which are slaves of his, four in number, Sumbul, Kāfūr, Jawhar and Surūr. One of them administers the endowments of the convent, the second lays out whatever is required of expenditure on each
day, | the third is the servitor of the table for visitors and 26
supervises the distribution of food to them, and the fourth is

[53] The weir of Tustar, traditionally built by the Roman emperor Valerian and his troops during their captivity there, 260–7 (and hence called in Persian *Band-i Qaisar*, 'Caesar's Dam'), was a dam about 400 yards in length across the Kārūn, behind which the river-bed was paved with square blocks, from which it derived its Arabic name *Shādharwān* (from Persian *shādorwān* = 'figured carpet'). The weir provided not only the head of water for the Masrūqān canal (see above, n. 49), but also for another canal, called Mināw, which was led off above the dam through a tunnel under the citadel of the city, and thence irrigated the lands to the southward.

[54] 'Alī Zain al-'Ābidīn, the fourth Imām of the Shī'ites, died in al-Madīna *c.* 711 and was buried there (Harawī, 93; trans., 211). Al-Harawī, however (98; trans., 222), mentions at Tustar the tomb of Muḥammad, son of the sixth Imām, Ja'far al-Ṣādiq.

the superintendent of the cooks, water-carriers and domestics. I stayed with him for sixteen days and I have never seen anything more admirable than his organization nor more lavish than the supply of food at his table. There was put before each man enough to supply four persons: pilaff of rice flavoured with pepper and cooked in ghee, fried chickens, bread, meat and sweetmeats.

This shaikh is one of the handsomest of men in figure and most upright in conduct. He preaches to the public after the Friday prayer in the cathedral-mosque, and when I attended his preaching-session all the preachers whom I had seen previously in the Ḥijāz, Syria, and Egypt sank in my estimation, nor have I ever met his equal. I was present with him one day in a garden of his on the bank of the river where there was a
27 gathering of the doctors and the notables of the city, | and the poor brethren came from every direction. He served them all with food, then led them in the mid-day prayer and, after the Qur'ān-readers had recited in front of him, chanting in a manner that brought tears to the eyes and with moving and stirring modulations, he rose up to preach and admonish. He delivered a discourse with solemnity and dignity, making extempore use of all kinds of learning, interpretations of the Book of God, citation of the traditions of the Apostle of God, and dissertation upon their meanings. When he had finished, bits of paper were thrown to him from all sides, for it is a custom of the Persians to jot down questions on scraps of paper and throw them to the preacher, who answers them. When these scraps of paper were thrown to him, he collected them all in his hand and began to answer them one after the other in the most fascinating and elegant manner.[55] It was then time for the ‘aṣr prayer, so he led the congregation in the prayers and then they retired. His assembly was an assembly of learning, admonition and blessed power, the penitents
28 presented themselves one after the other, | and he took the pledge from them and clipped their forelocks.[56] They were

[55] The same practice is related of many other scholars; see, for example, Ibn Jubair's account of Ibn al-Jawzī at Baghdād (222; trans. Broadhurst, 231). This Sharaf al-Dīn Mūsā has not been identified.

[56] In the Qur'ān (sūra xcvi. 16) the forelock is called 'lying, sinful'; the clipping of the forelock is thus presumably a symbol of renunciation of falsehood and error.

fifteen men of the student class who had come from al-Baṣra for this purpose, and ten men of the general population of Tustar.

Anecdote. When I entered this city I was attacked by a fever, for visitors to these countries in the hot season generally suffer from fever, as happens also in Damascus and other cities which have abundant waters and fruits. The fever attacked my companions also and one of them died, a shaikh whose name was Yaḥyā al-Khurāsānī. The shaikh [of whom I have spoken] paid the costs of his preparation for burial with all that a dead man needs, and prayed over him. I left there also one of my companions called Bahā al-Dīn al-Khatanī, and he died after my departure. During my illness I
had no | appetite for the dishes which were prepared for me in 29
his college. The faqīh Shams al-Dīn al-Sindī, one of the students there, mentioned a certain dish to me and I fancied it and paid him some dirhams. He had that dish cooked for me in the bazaar and brought it to me and I ate of it. When this was told to the Shaikh he was cut to the quick and came to see me and said 'How can you do this and have food cooked in the bazaar? Why did you not order the servants to prepare for you what you fancied?' He then had them all called and said to them 'Whatever he asks for from you in the way of food and sugar and so on, bring it to him and cook for him whatever he wishes', and he impressed this on them in the most emphatic way—God reward him with good.

We set out from the city of Tustar, travelling for the space of three nights through towering mountains, at each stage there being a hospice like those already described, and came
to the city of Īdhaj, also called | Māl al-Amīr,[57] the capital of 30
the sultan Atābek. On my arrival there I met with its shaikh of shaikhs, the learned and pious Nūr al-Dīn al-Kirmānī, who has the supervision of all the hospices (which these people call by the term *madrasa*). The Sultan venerates him and comes to visit him, and so also the officers of state and the chief men of the capital visit him morning and evening.

[57] Now called Mālamīr, on a tributary of the Kārūn river. This name, meaning 'the amīr's estate', is explained by Schwarz (IV, 336) as connected with the fact that the 'Abbāsid caliph al-Mahdī (775–85) was born here, but is more probably of later origin. It was at this time the capital of the principality of the Greater Lur (see below, n. 59).

He received me honourably and hospitably and lodged me in a hospice by the name of al-Dīnawarī, where I stayed for some days. My arrival was at the period of the summer heats;[58] we used to pray the night prayers and then lie down to sleep on the top of the roof of the hospice and descend to the hospice itself in the early morning. I had in my company twelve poor brethren including an imām, two skilled reciters of the Qur'ān and a servitor so that we made a well-organized party.

Account of the king of Īdhaj and Tustar. The king of Īdaj at
31 the time of my entry into it | was the sultan Atābek Afrāsiyāb,
son of the sultan Atābek Aḥmad,[59] *atābek* being with them a title common to every king who rules that country,[60] and the country itself is called the country of the Lūrs.[61] This sultan succeeded his brother Atābek Yūsuf, and Yūsuf succeeded his father Atābek Aḥmad. The Aḥmad just mentioned was a pious king; I have heard from a trustworthy person in his country that he established four hundred and sixty hospices in his territories, forty four of them in the capital Īdhaj. He divided the revenue of his territories into three parts, one third of it for the upkeep of the hospices and colleges, one third for the pay of his troops, and one third for his own ex-

[58] This statement, repeating a remark already made relating to his stay at Tustar, is difficult to reconcile with his later statement (below, p. 297) that he was in Iṣfahān on 14 Jumādā II = 7 May 1327, in consequence of which his stay at Mālamīr can only be dated to the first half of April. It would seem, however, from what follows that he has confused details of this visit with his second visit in 1347, when he presumably passed through Mālamīr on his way from Iṣfahān to Tustar (vol. IV, p. 312, Arabic).

[59] Here again Ibn Baṭṭūṭa is confused. As pointed out by the French translators, Afrāsiyāb (II), son of Aḥmad, reigned 1340–56. Not only so; but since the reigning Atābek in 1327 was in fact Aḥmad (1298–1333), it is curious that Ibn Baṭṭūṭa should report his actions only on hearsay 'from trustworthy persons'. On the Greater Lur or Hazāraspid dynasty and its relations to the Īlkhāns see B. Spuler, *Die Mongolen in Iran*, 2nd ed. (Berlin, 1955), 161–3, and *E.I.*, s.v. Lur.

[60] *Atābek* was the title given by the Seljuk sultans to the 'tutors' of the young princes to whom the government of a province was allotted. Since several Atābeks founded dynasties of their own, the title came to be commonly given to mediatized princes; in this instance it is said to have been granted by the 'Abbāsid caliph al-Nāṣir (see below, p. 326, n. 180) to Hazārasp, the first of this line of princes (*c.* 1203–52).

[61] The Lurs are an Iranian people with some mixture of immigrant elements; see *E.I.*, svv. Lur and Luristān. The Hazāraspid princes apparently belonged to the Bakhtiyārī, one of the four main tribes of Lurs.

penditure and the upkeep of his household, slaves and servants. From this money he used to send a gift to the king of al-'Irāq every year, and often went to visit him in person. I observed from my own experience that of the pious foundations that preserve his name in his country the majority are amid | lofty mountain-ranges; but roads [to them] have been 32
hewn out of the rocks and stones and have been made so level and so wide that transport animals can climb them with their loads. These mountains extend for a distance of seventeen days' journey in length and ten days' in breadth, and they are exceedingly high, in continuous chains one after the other, and cut through by rivers. The trees on them are oaks, from the flour of which they make bread. At each station in these mountains there is a hospice, which they call the 'college', and when the traveller arrives at one of these colleges he is given a sufficient supply of food for himself and fodder for his beast, whether he asks for it or not. For it is their custom that the college servitor comes, counts all those who have alighted at it, and gives each one of them two cakes of bread, with meat and sweetmeats. All this comes out of the sultan's endowments for its upkeep. The sultan Atābek Aḥmad was a self-mortifying and pious man, as | we have 33
said, and used to wear a hair-shirt beneath his clothes next his skin.

Anecdote. The sultan Atābek Aḥmad once went to visit the king of al-'Irāq, Abū Sa'īd. One of the king's courtiers told him that the Atābek was coming into his presence wearing a cuirass, for he thought that the hair-shirt which was beneath his outer garments was a cuirass. So the king ordered them to test this in some familiar manner, in order to find out what truth there was in it. One day when the Atābek came into his presence, the amīr al-Jubān, the chief of the amīrs of al-'Irāq, and the amīr Suwaita, the amīr of Diyār Bakr, and the shaikh Ḥasan, who is the present sultan of al-'Irāq,[62] came up to him and took hold of his garments as though they were jesting with him in a playful mood and found the hair-shirt

[62] For al-Jūbān (i.e. Choban) see below, p. 337, and Shaikh Ḥasan, p. 341. Suwaita is the amīr Nuṣrat al-Dīn Sūtāy Noyon, who served under Hulagu, was appointed governor of Diyār Bakr in 1313 (also of Moṣul and Sinjār), and died in 1332: *Durar*, II, 178–9; *Letters of Rashīd al-Dīn*, 40; Ḥāfiẓ-i Abrū, *Chronique*, trans. K. Bayani (Paris, 1936), 36.

underneath his robes. When the sultan Abū Sa'īd saw this he rose up and came to him, embraced him and, making him sit by his side, said to him *San Aṭā*, which means in Turkish
34 'You are my father'. He returned to him the value of | his present many times over and wrote for him a *yarligh*, that is a rescript,[63] to the effect that neither he nor his sons should henceforth require of him any gift.

In that same year he died, and his son Atābek Yūsuf ruled for ten years,[64] and after that his brother Afrāsiyāb. When I entered the city of Īdhaj I wished to see this sultan Afrāsiyāb, but that was not easily come by as he goes out only on Fridays, owing to his addiction to wine. He had one son and one only, who was his designated heir, and who fell ill at this time. On a certain night one of his servants came to me and made enquiries of me about myself; when I told him he went away and came back later after the sunset prayer, bringing with him two great platters, one with food and the other with fruit, and a pouch containing money. Accompanying him were musicians with their instruments and he said to them 'Make music, so that these poor brethren will dance and
35 pray for the Sultan's son.'[65] I said to him 'My associates | have no knowledge of either music or dancing,' but we prayed for the sultan and his son, and I divided the money among the poor brethren. In the middle of the night we heard cries and lamentations, for the sick boy had died.

On the following morning the shaikh of the hospice and [some of] the townsfolk came into my room and said 'All the principal men of the city, qāḍīs, faqīhs, sharīfs and amīrs, have gone to the Sultan's palace for the [ceremony of] condolence, and it is your duty to go along in company with them.' I refused to go, but when they insisted with me and I had no alternative but to go, I set out with them. I found the audi-

[63] *Yarligh* was a term employed by the Mongols to denote a patent stamped with the sovereign's seal; see Yule's *Marco Polo*, I, 352.

[64] There is some confusion again here, since Aḥmad died in 1333, and Choban was killed in 1328. Yūsuf's accession is variously dated in 1330 and 1333, but he may have been co-regent for some years, since in the *Letters* (255) of Rashīd al-Dīn (executed in 1318) he is already called 'Atābek Yūsuf Shāh, king of Luristan'.

[65] An interesting indication that the use of music was by this time regarded as a typical feature of darwīsh rituals.

ence hall[66] in the sultan's palace filled with men and youths —slaves, sons of princes, viziers and soldiers—all wearing sacks of coarse cloth[67] and horses' saddle-cloths; they had put dust and straw on their heads and some of them had cut off their forelocks. They were divided into two groups, one group | at the top end of the hall and another at its lower end, 36
and each group would advance towards the other, all beating their breasts with their hands and crying *khūndikārimā*, which means 'Our master'.[68] The spectacle that I witnessed there was an appalling thing and a disgraceful sight, the like of which I have never encountered.

Anecdote. A strange thing that happened to me that day was that, when I entered, I saw that the qāḍīs, the khaṭībs and the sharīfs had taken up positions with their backs to the walls of the hall. The place was crammed with them on all sides, some of them weeping, some pretending to, some with eyes fixed on the ground, and all of them wearing on top of their robes unbleached lengths of rough cotton stuff, not properly tailored and inside out, with the face of the cloth next their bodies.[69] Each one of them also had on his head a bit of rag or a black veil. They continue to do the same | until 37
forty days have passed, this being for them the end of the period of mourning, and thereafter the sultan sends a complete set of clothing to every one who has done so.

When I saw all parts of the audience-hall crowded with people I looked right and left, searching for a place to seat myself. Then I saw there a dais, raised above the ground about a span; at one corner of it there was a man, apart from the crowd, sitting there, and wearing a woollen robe like the felt coat which the poor people in that country wear on days of rain or snow and on journeys. So I went up to where this man was; my companions fell back behind me when they saw

[66] Ibn Baṭṭūṭa here uses the characteristic Maghribī term *mishwar* (literally 'council chamber'), rarely found in the East.

[67] *Talālīs*, the long sacks used for grain and other heavy goods; see Dozy, s.v. tillīs. For saddle-cloths cf. Aflākī (see p. 430, n. 67), I. 72.

[68] *Khūndikār* (*Khūndigār*) is derived, like the classical Persian *Khāwandagār*, from *Khudāwand* = 'lord, master'; *-mā* is the suffix 'our'.

[69] The wearing of garments inside out was a regular ceremonial practice in prayers for rain (*istisqā'*; see *E.I.*, s.v.), and was sporadically adopted also as a sign of mourning. The other customs which so scandalized Ibn Baṭṭūṭa appear to have been peculiar to the Lurs.

me going towards him and were amazed at my action, whereas I had no knowledge at all of what he was. I mounted the dais and gave the word of greeting to the man; he returned my greeting and raised himself from the ground as if he in-
38 tended to rise, a gesture which they call 'half-rising', | and I sat down in the corner opposite him. Then I observed that the people present had fixed their eyes on me, everyone of them; I was surprised at them, and I looked at the faqīhs and shaikhs and sharīfs, all with their backs to the wall behind the dais. One of the qāḍīs made a sign to me that I should come beside him, but I did not do so, and then I began to suspect that the man was the sultan. At the end of an hour or so, the chief shaikh Nūr al-Dīn al-Kirmānī, whose name we have mentioned above, came forward, mounted the dais and saluted the man; he rose up to him, and the shaikh then sat down between me and him; thereupon I knew for certain that the man was the sultan. Next, the bier was brought in, surrounded by citron lemon and orange trees, the branches of which they had loaded with their fruits, the trees themselves being carried by men, so that the bier seemed to be a moving orchard, with torches on tall lances carried before it, and candles likewise. Prayers were recited over it, and those present went out with it to the burial-ground of the kings,
39 which is at a place | called Halāfīhān, four miles distant from the city.[70] There is there a large *madrasa* [hospice], through which the river runs; inside it there is a mosque in which the Friday service is held, and outside it a bath, and the whole place is surrounded by a large fruit-garden. At this hospice food is served to all comers and goers.

I was unable to go with them to the burial-ground because of the distance to the place, so I returned to the madrasa [where I was lodged]. Some days later the sultan sent to me the messenger who had brought the hospitality-gift previously, to invite me to visit him. So I went with the messenger to a gate called the Cypress Gate and we mounted a long flight of steps, finally reaching a room which was uncarpeted, on account of the mourning that they were

[70] This place is probably to be identified with Kal'a-i Madrasa, 12 miles north of Mālamīr (in which case 'four miles' is possibly an error for 'four farsakhs').

observing at the time. The sultan was sitting on a cushion, with two goblets in front of him which had been covered up, one of gold and the other of silver. There was in the chamber a green prayer-rug; | this was laid out for me near him, and I 40
sat down on it. No one else was in the room but his chamberlain, the faqīh Maḥmūd, and a boon companion of his, whose name I do not know. He put questions to me about myself and my country, and asked me about al-Malik al-Nāṣir and the land of al-Ḥijāz, and I answered him on these points. At this juncture there came in a great faqīh, who was chief of the doctors of the law in that country, and the sultan said to me 'This is Mawlānā Fāḍil', for in all the lands of the Persians a faqīh is never called by any title other than *mawlānā*,[71] and is so addressed by the sultan and everyone else. The sultan then began to recite the praises of the faqīh just mentioned, and it became clear to me that he was under the influence of intoxication, for I had already learned of his addiction to wine. Afterwards he said to me in Arabic (which he spoke well), 'Speak'. I said to him 'If you will listen to me, I say to you "You are the son of the sultan Atābek Aḥmad, who was noted for piety and self-restraint, and there is nothing to be laid against you as | a ruler but this",' and I pointed to the 41
two goblets. He was overcome with confusion at what I said and sat silent. I wished to go but he bade me sit down and said to me, 'To meet with men like you is a mercy.' But then I saw him reeling and on the point of falling asleep, so I withdrew. I had left my sandals at the door but I could not find them, so the faqīh Maḥmūd went down in search of them, while the faqīh Fāḍil went to look for them inside the chamber, found them in a window-embrasure there, and brought them to me. His kindness shamed me, and I began to apologise to him, but at that he kissed my sandals, placed them on his head, and said 'God bless you. What you said to our sultan no one could say but you. I sincerely hope, by God, that this will make an impression on him.'

[71] Literally 'our master', from which is derived the common Persian and Indian term *mullah* for a professional religious teacher or jurist. Ibn Baṭṭūṭa may have noted the point because the same term (or the corresponding form *Mawlāya*, 'my master') was already becoming exclusively applied in Morocco to the sultans (cf. vol. I, p. 2) and finally became, in the form *Moulay*, part of the ruler's title.

A few days later came my departure from the city of Īdhaj. I stopped at the *madrasa* of the sultans, where their graves are, and stayed there for some days, and the sultan
42 sent me | a number of dinars [as a farewell gift], with a like sum for my companions. For ten days we continued to travel through the territories of this sultan amidst lofty mountains, and on each night we would halt at a *madrasa* where food was served.[72] Some of these *madrasas* are in cultivated country, and some have no cultivation in the vicinity at all, but everything that they require is transported to them. On the tenth day we halted at a *madrasa* by the name of Madrasa Kirīwā'lrukh, which marks the end of the territories of this king.[73]

We travelled on from there across a well-watered plain belonging to the province of the city of Iṣfahān, and thereafter reached the town of Ushturkān, a pleasant township, with numbers of running streams and orchards, and possessed of a very fine mosque intersected by the river.[74] From this place we went on to the city of Fīrūzān, which is a small town with
43 streams, trees and orchards.[75] We arrived there | after the hour of afternoon prayer, and found that its population had gone out to escort a funeral. Behind and before the bier they had lit torches, and they followed it up with fifes and singers, singing all sorts of merry songs. We were astonished at this behaviour of theirs. After spending one night there, we passed on the following morning through a village called Nablān;[76] this is a big village on a broad river, beside which there is a mosque of the utmost beauty. One goes up to it by a flight of steps, and it is surrounded by orchards.

We travelled on for the whole of this day between orchards and streams and fine villages with many pigeon-towers, and after the time of the 'aṣr prayer we reached the city of Iṣfahān, also called Iṣpahān, in Persian 'Irāq.[77] The city of Iṣfahān is

[72] As late as the nineteenth century, the road from Mālamīr to Iṣfahān was still called 'the Atābek's road' (*jadde-i atābeg*); Schwarz, IV, 937, n. 2.

[73] Probably *Girīw al-Rukhkh*, 'neck of the rukh' (Schwarz, *ibid.*). It is identified with the modern Kahvarukh in Chārmaḥāll.

[74] Ushturkān (? '[place] of camels') is not attested elsewhere.

[75] Six farsakhs from Iṣfahān; Schwarz, V, 648.

[76] Probably an error for Lunbān, a large village close to the city; Schwarz, V, 655. The river is the Zāyanda-rūd (Zinde-rūd), the river of Iṣfahān.

[77] The main city of Iṣfahān was at this time somewhat to the east of the present city, as the city has gradually shifted westwards (Schwarz, V, 623–4).

one of the largest and fairest of cities, but it is now in ruins for the greater part, as the result of the feud there between the Sunnīs and the Rāfiḍīs, which continues to rage between them still to the present day, so that they never cease to | fight.[78] It is rich in fruits, among them being apricots of un- 44
rivalled quality which they call *qamar al-dīn*; the people there dry these apricots and preserve them, and their kernels when broken open disclose a sweet almond.[79] Others of its products are quinces that are unequalled for goodness of taste and size, delicious grapes, and the wonderful water-melons whose like is not to be found in the world, except for the water-melons of Bukhārā and Khawārizm. Their rind is green, and the inside is red; they are preserved as dried figs are preserved in the Maghrib, and are exceedingly sweet. When anyone is not used to eating them, they relax him on his first experience of them—and so indeed it happened to me when I ate them at Iṣfahān.

The people of Iṣfahān have fine figures and clear white skins tinged with red; their dominant qualities are bravery and pugnacity, together with generosity[80] and a strong spirit of rivalry between them | in procuring [luxurious] viands. 45
Some curious stories are told of this last trait in them. Sometimes one of them will invite his friend and will say to him, 'Come along with me for a meal of *nān* and *mās*'—that is bread and curdled milk in their language; then, when his friend goes along with him, he sets before him all sorts of wonderful dishes, with the aim of outdoing him by this [display]. The members of each craft appoint one of their own number as headman over them, whom they call the *kilū*,[81] and so do the leading citizens from outside the ranks of the

[78] This was apparently a continuation of the feuds between rival Sunnī schools (Ḥanafī/Shāfi'ī) for which Iṣfahān was noted in earlier centuries, and whose violence had laid parts of the city in ruins even before the Mongol conquest (Schwarz, V, 607–8).

[79] See vol. I, p. 91, n. 92; p. 117, n. 178.

[80] This is not the prevailing view in either mediaeval or modern times; cf. for the former Schwarz, V, 603, 616, n. 5, and for the latter, E. G. Browne, *A Year among the Persians*, 3rd ed. (London, 1950), 214: 'The character which they bear among the Persians is not altogether enviable, avarice and niggardliness being accounted their chief characteristics.'

[81] *Kulū*, 'headman', 'market superintendent'; the term is sometimes found at this period attached to a personal name as a title (Ḥasan Kulū, etc.); see Qāsim Ghanī, *Tā'rīkh-i 'Aṣr-i Ḥāfiẓ* (Tehran, n.d.), 57, 230 ff.

craftsmen. One company [for example] will be composed of young bachelors. These companies try to outdo one another and invite one another to banquets, displaying all the resources at their disposal and making a great show in regard to the dishes and everything else. I was told that one company of them invited another, and cooked their viands with lighted candles, then the second company returned the invitations and cooked their viands with silk. |

46 My lodging at Iṣfahān was in a convent which is attributed to the shaikh 'Alī b. Sahl,[82] the disciple of al-Junaid. It is held in great veneration and is visited by the people of those regions, who seek to obtain blessing by visiting it. Food is served in it to all wayfarers, and it has a magnificent bath, paved with marble, and with *qāshānī* tiles[83] on its walls. It is endowed for the service [of God], so that nothing is required of any person in order to enter it. The shaikh of this convent was a pious and scrupulous devotee Quṭb al-Dīn Ḥusain, son of the pious shaikh, the friend of God, Shams al-Dīn Muḥammad b. Maḥmūd b. 'Alī, known as al-Rajā.[84] His brother was the scholar and jurisconsult Shihāb al-Dīn Aḥmad. I stayed with the shaikh Quṭb al-Dīn in his hospice for fourteen days, and what I saw of his zeal in religious exercises and his affection for the poor brethren and the distressed and his humility towards them filled me with admiration. He went to
47 great lengths in | honouring me, showed me generous hospitality, and presented me with a fine set of garments. At the very hour of my arrival at the convent he sent me food and three of those water-melons which we have mentioned already, and which I had not seen nor eaten previously.

A Grace of this Shaikh's. One day he came to visit me in the part of the hospice where I was staying. This place looked out over a garden belonging to the shaikh, and on that day his garments had been washed and spread out in the garden to

[82] A famous ascetic, died in Iṣfahān 919/920; his tomb is still in existence and visited in the northern section of the city. For al-Junaid, the most famous exponent of 'orthodox' Ṣūfism, who died in Baghdād in 910, see *E.I.*, s.v.

[83] On *Qāshānī* tiles see vol. I, p. 256, n. 42, and on the town of Qāshān, Schwarz, V, 568–70.

[84] Not identified, but of a notable family of scholars in Iṣfahān (see Ibn al-Ṣābūnī *Takmilat al-Ikmāl*, Baghdad, 1958, 145–6).

dry. Among them I saw a white tunic with a lining, [of the
kind] called by them *hazārmīkhī*.[85] I admired it and said to
myself 'This is the kind of thing that I was wanting.' When
the shaikh came into my room, he looked out towards the
garden and said to one of his servants 'Fetch me that
hazārmīkhī robe,' then when they brought it, he put it upon
me. I threw myself at his feet, kissing them, | and begged him 48
to clothe me also with a skull-cap from his head, and to give
me the same authorization in [transmitting] this that he had
received from his father on the authority of the latter's
shaikhs. He invested me with it accordingly on the fourteenth
of Latter Jumādā in the year 727[86] in his convent afore-
mentioned, as he had been invested with it by his father
Shams al-Dīn and his father had been invested with it by
his father Tāj al-Dīn Maḥmūd, and Maḥmūd by his father
Shihāb al-Dīn 'Alī al-Rajā, and 'Alī by the Imām Shihāb
al-Dīn Abū Ḥafṣ 'Omar b. Muḥammad b. 'Abdallāh al-
Suhrawardī,[87] and 'Omar had been invested by the great
shaikh Ḍiyā' al-Dīn Abu'l-Najīb al-Suhrawardī, and Abu'l-
Najīb by his paternal uncle, the Imām Waḥīd al-Dīn 'Omar,
and 'Omar by his father Muḥammad b. 'Abdallāh, known as
'Amawaih, and Muḥammad by the shaikh Akhū Faraj al-
Zinjānī, and Akhū Faraj by the shaikh Aḥmad al-Dīnawarī,
and Aḥmad by the Imām | Mamshād al-Dīnawarī, and Mam- 49
shād from the shaikh, the seer of the truth, 'Alī b. Sahl al-
Ṣūfī, and 'Alī from Abu'l-Qāsim al-Junaid, and al-Junaid
from Sarī al-Saqaṭī, and Sarī al-Saqaṭī from Dā'ūd al-Ṭā'ī,
and Dā'ūd from al-Ḥasan b. Abi'l-Ḥasan al-Baṣrī, and al-
Ḥasan b. Abi'l-Ḥasan al-Baṣri from the Commander of the
Faithful, 'Alī b. Abī Ṭālib.

Ibn Juzayy comments: In this manner did the shaikh

[85] Literally '[garment] of a thousand wedges', the darwīsh robe made of numbers of 'patches' or small pieces; see vol. I, p. 80, n. 47.

[86] 7 May 1327. What follows is the chain of authorities by which Ibn Baṭṭūṭa was affiliated into the Suhrawardī order, acquiring thereby valuable connections for some of his future journeys.

[87] Shihāb al-Dīn 'Omar (d. 1234) was the founder of the Suhrawardī order, one of the most widespread religious congregations in the eastern Islamic world. The family claimed descent from the second caliph, 'Omar b. al-Khaṭṭāb, and the founder's tomb is still preserved in the mother-convent of the order at Baghdād. For the early links in this chain of authorities, see below, p. 335, n. 210, and for al-Ḥasan al-Baṣrī, above, p. 279, n. 33.

Abū 'Abdallāh [Ibn Baṭṭūṭa] cite this chain of authorities.
But it is a matter of common knowledge that Sarī al-Saqaṭī
was the disciple of Ma'rūf al-Karkhī, and Ma'rūf was the
disciple of Dā'ūd al-Ṭā'ī; likewise that between Dā'ūd
al-Ṭā'ī and al-Ḥasan there was Ḥabīb al-'Ajamī. In regard to
Akhū Faraj al-Zinjānī, it is known only that he was the
disciple of Abu'l-'Abbās al-Nihāwandī, and that al-Nihāwandī was the disciple of Abū 'Abdallāh ibn Khafīf, that Ibn
Khafīf was the disciple of Abū Muḥammad Ruwaim, and
Ruwaim the disciple of Abu'l-Qāsim al-Junaid. As for
50 Muḥammad b. | 'Abdallāh 'Amawaih, he it was who was the
disciple of the shaikh Aḥmad al-Dīnawarī 'the Black', without any intervening person; but God knows best. The person
who became the disciple of Akhū Faraj al-Zinjānī was
'Abdallāh b. Muḥammad b. 'Abdallāh, the father of Abu'l-
Najīb.

(To return). We set out thereafter from Iṣfahān with the
object of visiting the shaikh Majd al-Dīn at Shīrāz,[88] which is
ten days' journey from there. We came to the town of Kalīl,
three nights' journey from Iṣfahān; it is a small town, with
running streams, gardens and fruit-trees.[89] I saw apples being
sold in its bazaar at fifteen 'Irāqī pounds for a dirham, their
dirham being the third of a nuqra. We alighted there at a hospice
which was founded by the headman of this town, known as
Khwāja Kāfī, a man of considerable wealth, whom God had
assisted to spend it in the way of good works, such as the
giving of alms, the foundation of hospices, and the provision
of food for the wayfarers. We continued our journey from
51 Kalīl on the same day and | came to a large village called
Surmā'[90] where there is a hospice, supplying food to all
comers and goers, founded by the same Khwāja Kāfī.

From there we journeyed to Yazdukhāṣ, a small town substantially built, and with a fine bazaar; the congregational mosque in it is a marvel, built of stone and with arcades of stone also.[91] the town is on the edge of a valley, in which are

[88] For Majd al-Dīn al-Shārāzī, see below, pp. 300–6.

[89] Not known otherwise and apparently misplaced; see the following note.

[90] Surmā' is two days' journey *south* of Yazdikhwāst; Browne, *A Year among the Persians*, 254.

[91] Yazdikhwāst, built on a precipitous rock. Browne (*op. cit.*, 245–8) describes the town, but saw no arcades at the mosque.

its orchards and its streams. In its outskirts there is a *ribāṭ* in which travellers are lodged; it has an iron gate and is of the utmost strength and impregnability, and inside it there are shops where everything that travellers may need is on sale. The *ribāṭ* was founded by the amīr Muḥammad Shāh Īnjū, the father of the sultan Abū Isḥāq, king of Shīrāz.[92] At Yazdukhāṣ there is made the cheese called Yazdukhāṣī, |
which has not its equal for goodness of flavour; the weight of 52
each of such cheeses is from two to four ounces. We went on from there by way of the Dasht al-Rūm,[93] which is open country inhabited by Turks, and then travelled to Māyīn,[94] a small town with many streams and orchards and fine bazaars. Most of its trees are walnuts.

From there we travelled to the town of Shīrāz, which is a city of solid construction and wide range, famous in repute and high in esteem; it has elegant gardens and gushing streams, sumptuous bazaars and handsome thoroughfares; and is densely populated, substantial in its buildings, and admirable in its disposition.[95] Those engaged in each craft occupy the bazaar particular to that craft, no outsiders mixing with them. Its inhabitants are handsome in figure and clean in their dress. In the whole East there is no city except Shīrāz which approached Damascus in the beauty of its
bazaars, fruit-gardens and rivers, | and in the handsome 53
figures of its inhabitants. It is situated in a plain, surrounded by orchards on all sides and intersected by five streams; one of these is the stream known as Rukn Ābād, the water of which is sweet, very cold in summer and warm in winter, and gushes out of a fountain on the lower slope of a hill in those parts called al-Qulai'a.[96]

[92] See below, p. 306. *Ribāṭ* here has its original sense of fortified convent or khān.

[93] Various desert areas on this road are called *dasht* ('wilderness'), but no other reference has been found to this name ('wilderness of the Anatolians').

[94] Fourteen farsakhs north of Shīrāz: Schwarz, I, 26; III, 182; Mustawfī, trans., 176.

[95] For the mediaeval descriptions of Shīrāz, see Schwarz, II, 43 ff., and A. J. Arberry, *Shīrāz* (Norman, Oklahoma, 1960).

[96] Ruknābād acquired enduring literary fame through the poems of the Shīrāzī poet Ḥāfiẓ (d. 1389): see *E.I.*, s.v.; E. G. Browne, *A Literary History of Persia* (Cambridge, 1920), III, 271–311. Its source lies a few miles north of the city, but the name Qulai'a ('small fort') does not seem to be attested elsewhere. See also Arberry, *Shīrāz*, p. 51.

The principal mosque of Shīrāz, which is called the 'ancient mosque',[97] is one of the largest of mosques in area and most beautiful in construction. Its court occupies a wide expanse paved with marble, and is washed down every night during the summer heats. The leading inhabitants of the city assemble in this mosque every night and pray the sunset and night prayers in it. On its northern side is a gate known as the Ḥasan gate, leading to the fruit market, which is one of the most admirable of bazaars and to which I for my part would give the preference over the bazaar of the Courier Gate at Damascus.[98] |

54 The people of Shīrāz are distinguished by piety, sound religion, and purity of manners, especially the women. These wear boots, and when out of doors are swathed in mantles and head-veils, so that no part of them is to be seen, and they are [noted for] their charitable alms and their liberality. One of their strange customs is that they meet in the principal mosque every Monday, Thursday and Friday, to listen to the preacher, sometimes one or two thousand of them, carrying fans in their hands with which they fan themselves on account of the great heat, I have never seen in any land an assembly of women in such numbers.

On my entry into the city of Shīrāz I had no desire but to seek out the shaikh, the qāḍī, the imām, the pole of the saints and solitaire of the age, noted for his evident 'graces', Majd al-Dīn Ismā'īl b. Muḥammad b. Khudhādād (*Khudhādād* meaning 'gift of God').[99] I arrived at the madrasa, called after him the Majdīya, in which is his residence, it being in fact his
55 own foundation, | and went in to visit him with three of my companions. I found there the men of law and principal in-

[97] The 'ancient mosque' (*al-jāmi' al-'atīq*) of Shīrāz was built by the Ṣaffārid prince of Sijistān, 'Amr b. Laith (879–900), who held Fārs as part of his dominions at various times.

[98] The Ḥasan Gate is not mentioned in the contemporary Persian works on Shīrāz. For the Courier Gate at Damascus, see vol. I, p. 131.

[99] Majd al-Dīn, whose correct name was Ismā'īl b. Yaḥyā b. Ismā'īl, was born in 1272/3 and died in 1355. His grandfather (d. 1268) and father (d. 1307) were both qāḍīs at Shīrāz. See Subkī, *Ṭabaqāt al-Shāfi'īya* (Cairo, n.d.), VI, 83–4; Junaid Shīrāzī, *Shadd al-Izār* (Tehran, 1327 Sh.), 423–6. According to al-Subkī, Majd al-Dīn was first appointed as qāḍī at the age of fifteen (presumably as substitute for his father) and held the office for seventy-five years(?).

habitants of the city awaiting him; then he came out to attend the afternoon prayer, having with him Muḥibb al-Dīn and 'Alā al-Dīn, the sons of his uterine brother Rūḥ al-Dīn, one of them on his right and the other on his left—they being his substitutes in his office as qāḍī, on account of his weak sight and advanced age.[100] When I saluted him, he embraced me and took me by the hand until he came to his prayer-mat, then let go my hand and signed to me to pray alongside him, and I did so. After he had prayed the afternoon prayer, there was read before him part of the book of the Lanterns (*al-Maṣābīḥ*) and of the *Shawāriq al-Anwār* of al-Ṣaghānī,[101] and his two substitutes informed him of the suits which had come up before them. The notables of the city came forward to salute him, as was their custom with him morning and evening, and then he asked me about myself and how I had come, and questioned me | about the Maghrib, Egypt, 56
Syria and al-Ḥijāz, to all of which I answered. He gave orders for my lodging to his servants, who lodged me accordingly in a very small chamber in the madrasa.

On the following morning there came to visit him the envoy of the king of al-'Irāq, the sultan Abū Sa'īd, namely Nāṣir al-Dīn al-Darqandī, one of the chief amīrs and of Khurāsān by origin.[102] When he came before the qāḍī, he removed his cap —which they call *kulā*[103]—from his head, kissed the qāḍī's

[100] In 1327 Majd al-Dīn was about fifty-five years of age, and this description can apply only to Ibn Baṭṭūṭa's later visit to Shīrāz (see n. 118 below) in 1347. In 1327 also, his substitutes were apparently his brothers Sirāj al-Dīn Mukram (d. 1332) and Rūḥ al-Dīn Isḥāq (d. 1355 also) (Junaid Shīrāzī, 426–8), and only at a later date would Mukram's son Muḥibb al-Dīn Muḥammad and Isḥāq's son 'Alā' al-Dīn Muḥammad have officiated as his substitutes.

[101] Al-Ḥasan b. Muḥammad al-Ṣaghānī, Ḥanafī traditionist and grammarian, born at Lahore in 1181 and d. at Baghdād in 1252. His most celebrated work was *Mashāriq* (not *Shawāriq*) *al-Anwār*, a rearrangement of the standard works of Tradition by al-Bukhārī and Muslim (see vol. I, p. 144, n. 289; p. 154, n. 319); *Maṣābīh al-Sunna* was another famous compilation of traditions from the same and other reputed collections of Prophetic *Ḥadīth* made by al-Baghawī (d. 1122) (see *E.I.*², s.v.).

[102] Of the several Dilqandī's in the contemporary records, the most likely to fit this passage is 'Imād al-Dīn Nāṣir b. Muḥammad (d. 1345), who was both an amīr and a sharīf (al-'Azzawī, *Ta'rīkh al-'Irāq baina Iḥtilālain* (Baghdād, 1936), II, 51); but another amīr al-Dilqandī, 'Alī b. Ṭālib, was governor of Kūfa until 1333 (*ibid.*, 35).

[103] Persian *kulāh*.

foot, and sat down before him holding one of his own ears with his hand. This is the regular usage of the amīrs of the Tatars in the presence of their kings. Now this amīr had come with about five hundred mounted men, his mamlūks, servants, and companions; but he encamped outside the city and came in to the qāḍī's residence with only five persons, and entered his chamber entirely alone, in deference to him. |

57 *Narrative of the reason of their esteem for this Shaikh, which is an example of manifest grace.*[104] The [late] king of al-'Irāq, the sultan Muḥammad Khudābandah,[105] had as an associate, while yet in his state of infidelity, a doctor of law of the Imāmī sect of the Rāfiḍīs called Jamāl al-Dīn Ibn Muṭahhar.[106] When this sultan embraced Islām and the Tatars were converted by his conversion, he showed even greater esteem for this faqīh; the latter consequently gave him a beguiling view of the Rāfiḍīs and its superiority over the other [Islamic schools]. He expounded to the sultan the history of the Companions and of the Caliphate, persuaded him to believe that Abū Bakr and 'Omar were [only] viziers of the Apostle of God and that 'Alī, being the son of his paternal uncle and his son-in-law, was the [true] heir to the Caliphate,[107] and represented this to him in terms with which he was familiar, i.e. that the kingship which he himself possessed was his only by inheritance from his ancestors and kinsmen
58 —taking advantage of the short time | since the sultan had been living in infidelity and his lack of knowledge of the principles of the Faith. The sultan, accordingly, gave orders that the people should be forced to [subscribe to] the Rāfiḍī doctrines, sent rescripts to that effect to the two 'Irāqs, Fārs, Ādharbāijān, Iṣfahān, Kirmān and Khurāsān, and despatched envoys to the various cities.[108] The first cities to

[104] The following narrative is the most elaborate version of a famous story, not related in detail elsewhere; but both al-Subkī and Junaid Shīrāzī (see above, n. 99) refer to Majd al-Dīn's being 'thrown to the dogs and the lions' or 'imprisoned with ravening beasts and wild dogs'.

[105] Also called Öljaitu, reigned 1304–16; see below, p. 335.

[106] Jamāl al-Dīn al-Ḥasan b. Yūsuf al-Ḥillī (1251–1325), one of the most celebrated Shī'ite theologians; *Durar*, II, 71–2.

[107] For the refusal of the Shī'ites to recognize the first three Caliphs, see vol. I, p. 93, n. 98

[108] This was in 1310. See on this whole episode B. Spuler, *Die Mongolen in Iran*, 190–1.

which these orders were brought were Baghdād, Shīrāz, and Iṣfahān. As for the people of Baghdād, the inhabitants of the Bāb al-Azaj quarter, who are all adherents of the Sunna and for the most part followers of the school of the Imām Ibn Ḥanbal,[109] refused to submit to them, and declared that they would 'neither hear nor obey'. On the [following] Friday they came with their weapons to the congregational mosque, where the sultan's envoy was, and when the khaṭīb mounted the mimbar [to deliver the formal address], they surged up towards him—some twelve thousand men in all, armed, who constituted the garrison of Baghdād and its most notable citizens—and swore an oath to him that if he should change the customary *khuṭba* or add to it or subtract from it in any way[110] | they would kill him and kill the sultan's envoy and 59
submit themselves thereafter to what God willed. For the sultan had commanded that the names of the Caliphs [Abū Bakr, 'Omar and 'Othmān] and of the other Companions of the Prophet should be removed from the *khuṭba* and that there should be mentioned in it no names but that of 'Alī and his followers, such as 'Ammār (God be pleased with him).[111] But the khaṭīb was afraid of being killed, and he delivered the accustomed *khuṭba*.

The people of Shīrāz and of Iṣfahān acted in the same way as the people of Baghdād. So the envoys returned to the king and gave him an account of what had happened in regard to this matter. Whereupon he ordered the qāḍīs of the three cities to be fetched, and the first of them who was brought was the qāḍī Majd al-Dīn, the qāḍī of Shīrāz, the sultan being at that time at a place called Qarābāgh, which is his summer residence.[112] When the qāḍī arrived, the sultan gave orders that he should be thrown to the dogs which he had there—

[109] For Bāb al-Azaj, see the sketch-plan of Baghdād below, p. 330. Ibn Baṭṭūṭa rightly describes it as a stronghold of Ḥanbalism.

[110] For the general contents of the formal *khuṭba* at the Friday congregational prayers, see vol. I, p. 232.

[111] 'Ammār b. Yāsir, a vigorous partisan of 'Alī, was killed in the battle of Ṣiffīn between 'Alī and Mu'āwiya, the governor of Syria, in 657; see *E.I.*[2], s.v.

[112] In the mountains, north of the Aras river; see P. Clavijo, *Embassy to Tamerlane*, trans. G. Le Strange (London, 1928), 362 and map II. The Mongol Īlkhāns maintained the nomadic habit of migrating to the highlands for their summer camp (*āylagh*); see *E.I.*, s.v. Yāilā.

these are enormous dogs, with chains on their necks, and
trained to eat human beings. When anyone is brought to be
delivered to the dogs, he is set at liberty and without chains
60 in a wide plain; | those dogs are then loosed on him, so they
overtake him, tear him to pieces, and eat his flesh. But when
the dogs were loosed on the qāḍī Majd al-Dīn and reached
him, they fawned on him and wagged their tails before him
without attacking him in any way.

On being informed of this, the sultan went out from his
residence, bare-footed, prostrated himself at the qāḍī's feet,
kissing them, took him by the hand and placed upon him all
the garments that he was wearing. This is the highest mark of
distinction which a sultan can confer in their usage. When he
bestows his garments in this way upon some person, this
action constitutes an honour for the latter and for his sons
and his descendants, which they inherit generation after
generation so long as these garments last or any part of them,
the most honourable garment in this respect being the
trousers. When the sultan had bestowed his garments on the
61 qāḍī Majd al-Dīn, he took his hand, | led him into his resi-
dence, and commanded his wives to show him reverence and
profit by his blessing. The sultan also renounced the doctrine
of the Rāfiḍīs and sent rescripts to his territories to the effect
that their inhabitants should conform to the doctrine of the
followers of the Sunna and the Community.[113] He made a
magnificent gift to the qāḍī and sent him back to his country
with every mark of esteem and veneration. Among the gifts
which he made to him were one hundred of the villages of
Jamakān, which is a [valley like a] trench between two
mountains, twenty-four farsakhs in length and traversed by
a great river, with the villages ranged on both sides of it.[114]

[113] That Öljaitu did not in fact entirely renounce his Shīʿite sympathies is proved by his coinage. Sunnism, although henceforth tolerated, was not officially re-established until the accession of Abū Saʿīd in 1316; Spuler, *Die Mongolen in Iran*, 190–1.

[114] The Ribāt of Jam(a)kān is placed by Mustawfī (trans., 176) 5 farsakhs south of Kavār and 6 farsakhs north of Mīmand, i.e., near the modern Zanjīrān. Ibn Baṭṭūṭa has apparently confused the name with that of Ṣīmkān, a district 6 farsakhs in length lying midway between Mīmand and Kārzin drained by a right-bank affluent of the Sakkan (Mānd) river, since on his return journey in 1347 (vol. IV, p. 311, Arabic) he places Jamakān between these two places: cf. Schwarz, III, 71–2. Mīmand, to the east of

This is the finest place in the [region of] Shīrāz, and among its larger villages, which are equal in size to towns, is Maiman; this belongs to the qāḍī of whom we have been speaking.[115] One of the curious things about this place called Jamakān is that the half of it which is contiguous with Shīrāz—namely, for the distance of twelve farsakhs—is exceedingly cold. The snow falls there and the majority of the trees are walnuts. But the other half, which | is contiguous to the land of Hunj 62 Ubāl and the country of al-Lār,[116] on the way to Hurmuz, is exceedingly hot, and there the majority of the trees are date palms.

I had a second opportunity to meet the qāḍī Majd al-Dīn at the time when I left India. I went to visit him from Hurmuz, to gain the blessing of a meeting with him, in the year 48.[117] It is thirty-five days' journey from Hurmuz to Shīrāz. When I entered his chamber (though he had then become too weak to walk) and saluted him, he recognized me, rose up to welcome me, and embraced me. My hand happened to touch his elbow, and [I felt] his skin clinging to the bone without any flesh between them. He lodged me in the same madrasa where he had lodged me the first time. I visited him one day and found the king of Shīrāz, the sultan Abū Isḥāq (who will be mentioned shortly), sitting in front of him, holding his own ear in his hand. This is the height of good manners amongst them, and all the people do so when they are seated in presence of the king. I went | on another occasion to see him 63 in the madrasa, but found its gate closed. When I asked after the reason for this, I was told that there had been a dispute between the mother and the sister of the sultan over some inheritance, and that he had referred it to the qāḍī Majd al-

---

Fīrūzābād, is Ibn Baṭṭūṭa's Maiman. His division of the valley into a hot region and a cold region probably derives from the traditional division of Fārs into the *Garmsīr* ('Hot Lands') and *Sardsīr* ('Cold Lands'), originally a south-north division, but later on distinguishing the coastal lowlands from the interior highlands (see G. Le Strange, *Lands of the Eastern Caliphate* (Cambridge, 1905), 249).

[115] According to the Persian *Guide to Shīrāz* (Bahman Karīmī, *Rāhnumāyi Āthār-i Tārīkh-i Shīrāz* (Tehran, 1327 Sh.), 55), the township of Mīmand was constituted by Tāshī Khātūn (below, p. 307, n. 121) a *waqf*-endowment for the tomb-mosque called Shāh Chirāgh (below, p. 313, n. 135), and still is so.

[116] See below, p. 405.

[117] Began 13 April 1347. See vol. IV, p. 311 (Arabic) and the following note.

Dīn. So both of them came down to him in the madrasa, pleaded their cases before him, and he gave judgment between them in accordance with the Divine Law. The people of Shīrāz do not call him 'the qāḍī', but speak of him only as *Mawlānā a'ẓam* [that is 'Our most venerated master'] and actually write the same in the documents of registration and contracts in which his name has to be mentioned. The last time that I saw him was in the month of Second Rabī' in the year 48. His lights gave illumination to me and his blessed power has procured blessings for me, God profit us by him and those like him!

Account of the Sultan of Shīrāz. The sultan of Shīrāz at the
64 time of my entry | was the distinguished king Abū Isḥāq, son
of Muḥammad Shāh Īnjū.[118] His father named him Abū Isḥāq after the shaikh Abū Isḥāq al-Kāzarūnī[119]—God profit us by him! He is one of the best of sultans, handsome in figure and conduct and form, of generous character and good moral qualities, humble in manner yet a man of power, with an army numbering more than fifty thousand Turks and Persians. His most favoured supporters are the people of Iṣfahān; on the other hand, he places no trust in the people of Shīrāz, will not take them into his service, nor admit them to intimacy, nor permit any man of them to carry arms, because they are men of bravery and great courage, and audacious against kings. Whosoever of them is found with a weapon in his hand is punished. I myself once saw a man being dragged by the *jandārs* (that is the police troops) to the *ḥākim* [chief of police], after they had tied his hands to his neck. I asked what he had done, and was told that there had
65 been found | in his hand a bow during the night. So the sultan

[118] This paragraph can only relate to Ibn Baṭṭūṭa's second visit to Shīrāz in July 1347. Abū Isḥāq's grandfather Muḥammad Shāh (called Ṭakhṭākh by Rashīd al-Dīn, *Letters*, 168) was administrator for the Mongol Īlkhāns of the crown domains (*injū* in Mongol) in Fārs, and hence called Ṭakhṭākh Injū. His son Maḥmūd Shāh Injū asserted his independence in Shīrāz in 1325, and was presumably the 'Sultan' of Shīrāz in 1327. He was executed in January 1336, and succeeded by his eldest son Mas'ūd, who was forced to surrender Shīrāz to Pīr Ḥusain, grandson of Choban, in 1339/40. The latter was driven out two years later by his nephew Malik Ashraf, and only on Ashraf's withdrawal in 1342/3 did Abū Isḥāq, the youngest son of Maḥmūd Shāh, assume the royal title: see Spuler, *Die Mongolen in Iran*, 327–9; *Ta'rīkh-i Guzīda*, ed. E. G. Browne (Leiden-London, 1910), 630, 637.

[119] See below, p. 319.

of whom we are speaking has made a practice of holding down the men of Shīrāz and favouring the Iṣfahānīs over them, because he is afraid that they may make an attempt on his life.

His father Muḥammad Shāh Īnjū was governor of Shīrāz on behalf of the king of al-'Irāq, and was a man of upright conduct and beloved by the citizens. When he died, the sultan Abū Sa'īd appointed in his place the shaikh Ḥusain, the son of al-Jūbān, the chief of the amīrs (an account of him will be given later), and sent him with a large body of troops. So he arrived at Shīrāz, took possession of it, and seized its revenues. Now Shīrāz is one of the greatest cities of the world in yield of revenue; al-Ḥājj Qiwām al-Dīn al-Tamghājī, who was the intendant of revenues in it,[120] told me that he had contracted to farm them for ten thousand silver dinars a day, the value of which in the currency of the Maghrib is two thousand five hundred gold dinars. When the amīr Ḥusain, after staying in the city for some time, prepared | to rejoin the king of al-'Irāq he arrested Abū Isḥāq, 66
the son of Muḥammad Shāh Īnjū, together with his two brothers Rukn al-Dīn and Mas'ūd Bak and his mother Ṭāsh Khātūn,[121] intending to carry them off to al-'Irāq so that they should be put to the question for their father's riches. When, however, they reached the centre of the bazaar at Shīrāz, Ṭāsh Khātūn unveiled her face (she had been wearing a veil out of shame at being seen in such a condition, for it is the custom of the Turkish women not to cover their faces) and called on the men of Shīrāz to come to their aid, saying, 'Is it thus, O men of Shīrāz, that I am to be carried away from amongst you, I who am so-and-so the wife of so-and-so?' Thereupon one of the woodworkers, named Pahlawān[122]

[120] Ḥājjī Qiwām al-Dīn is a well-known figure, owing to his patronage of the poet Ḥāfiẓ. He was confidant (sometimes called vizier) of Abū Isḥāq Injū, and died in 1353 (Qāsim Ghanī, 145–6). *Ṭamghāchī*, apparently the ethnic of Ṭamghāch (a term of political geography, probably identified at this time with Eastern Turkestan), seems in this instance to mean 'Keeper of the Seal' (*ṭamgha*). Mustawfī (trans., 114) gives the revenues from Shīrāz as 450,000 dinars, whereas those from Baghdād were about 800,000 (trans., 43). For Ḥusain b. Choban, see above, n. 118.

[121] Properly Ṭāshī Khātūn, as in other sources and in the dedication of a Qur'ān as *waqf* at Shīrāz, where she is called 'the supreme Khātūn, queen of the Sulaimānī kingdom, Tāshī Khātūn' (Qāsim Ghanī, 77, n. 1; see also another version of this story in the *Anonym of Iskander*, Tehran, 1957, 162).

[122] For this title see vol. I, p. 249, n. 2.

Maḥmūd (I saw him in the bazaar when I came to Shīrāz), rose up and said 'We shall not let you go out of our town, nor accept any such thing.' The people supported him in his declaration, and the whole body of them rose up, came in with
67 their weapons, killed | many of the troops, seized the moneys [which were being taken to al-'Irāq] and set free the woman and her sons. The amīr Ḥusain and those with him fled, and came before the sultan Abū Sa'īd in a discomfited condition. The sultan then gave him a powerful body of troops and commanded him to return to Shīrāz and to take such measures towards its inhabitants as he saw fit. When the news of this reached its people, they realized that they were powerless to resist him, so they sought out the qāḍī Majd al-Dīn and besought him to prevent the effusion of blood on both sides and that a reconciliation should be effected. He went out accordingly to the amīr Ḥusain. The amīr dismounted from his horse for him and saluted him, and a peaceful agreement was reached. The amīr Ḥusain encamped that day outside the city, and on the following day its inhabitants went out to
68 welcome him in the most beautiful order; they decorated | the city and lit a great number of candles, and the amīr Ḥusain entered with great pomp and ceremony, and observed the most generous conduct towards them.

Then, when the sultan Abū Sa'īd died and his line was extinguished, and when every amīr seized what was in his hands, the amīr Ḥusain became afraid that the people [of Shīrāz] would make an attempt on his life and removed himself from them. The sultan Abū Isḥāq made himself master of it, as well as Iṣfahān and the land of Fārs, this amounting to [an area of] a month and a half's march. Having [thus] a powerful military force at his disposal, his ambition incited him to take possession of the neighbouring lands, and he began with the nearest of them. This was the city of Yazd, a fine, clean city with magnificent bazaars, perennial streams and verdant trees, whose population are merchants of the Shāfi'ite rite.[123] So he laid siege to it and captured it, but the amīr Muẓaffar Shāh, son of the amīr Muḥammad Shāh b.

[123] Note that Ibn Baṭṭūṭa here describes Yazd (for which see Schwarz, I, 19–20; L. Lockhart, 58–64), although he nowhere mentions having visited it at any time.

Muẓaffar, shut himself up in a castle six miles from the city, a forbidding fortress encompassed by sands.[124] When Abū Isḥāq went on to besiege him in it, the amīr Muẓaffar displayed a courage transcending the natural order of things and such as has never been heard of. He would fall upon the camp
of the sultan Abū Isḥāq | in the night, kill at will, burn the 69
bivouacs and encampments, and return to his fortress, yet nothing could be done to get the upper hand of him. One night he fell upon the sultan's enclosure, killed a number there, seized ten of his pedigree horses, and returned to his fortress. Thereupon the sultan commanded that on every night five thousand horsemen should ride out and lay ambushes for him. They did so, and when he made a sortie as usual with a hundred of his associates and fell upon the camp, the men in ambush surrounded him and the [rest of the] troops came up in successive parties, yet he fought them off and got safely back to his castle, while none of his associates were captured but one man. This man was brought to the sultan Abū Isḥaq, who put a robe of honour on him, and sent by him a safe-conduct for Muẓaffar, in order that he should come to him. Muẓaffar refused to do so, but there followed an exchange of correspondence between them. For an affection for him had grown up in the heart of the sultan Abū Isḥāq
through witnessing his bold actions, and he said | 'I should 70
like to see him, and when I have seen him I shall withdraw and leave him.' Accordingly the sultan took up a position outside the castle while Muẓaffar took up his stance in its gateway and saluted him. The sultan then said to him 'Descend, on guarantee of safety,' but Muẓaffar replied 'I have made a vow to God that I should not come down to you until you for your part enter my castle, and thereafter I shall come out to you.' The sultan said to him 'I accept the condition,' and entered in with ten of his intimate companions.

[124] On the Muẓaffarids of Yazd see *E.I.*, s.v. They were an Arab family from Khurāsān, the head of which at this time was Mubāriz al-Dīn Muḥammad (1300–64), son of Muẓaffar (d. 1314). Muḥammad seized Yazd in 1318 and Kirmān in 1340. The conflict between him and Abū Isḥāq, and the latter's unsuccessful siege of the castle of Maibūd, is reported also in *Tā'rīkh-i Guzīda* (645–6), but without date or mention of his son Muẓaffar Shāh. Muḥammad subsequently captured Shīrāz (1353) and replaced the Injūid family by his own; Abū Isḥāq fled, but was captured and executed in May 1356 (*ibid.*, 674).

When he reached the gate of the fortress, Muẓaffar dismounted, kissed his stirrup, and walking before him on foot led him into his apartment, where the sultan partook of his food. Muẓaffar then went out with him on horseback to the camp, and there the sultan bade him sit by his side, placed his own robes on him, and made him a large present of money. It was agreed between them that the *khuṭba* should be recited in the name of Abū Isḥāq[125] and that the province should belong to Muẓaffar and his father, and the sultan returned to his own country. |

71 The sultan Abū Isḥāq had at one time conceived the ambition to build a vaulted palace like the Aywān Kisrā,[126] and ordered the inhabitants of Shīrāz to undertake the digging of its foundations. They set to work on this, each corporation of artisans rivalling every other, and carried their rivalry to such lengths that they made baskets of leather to carry the earth and covered them with lengths of embroidered silk. They did the same with the panniers and sacks on the donkeys, and some of them made mattocks[127] of silver and lit quantities of candles. When they were digging they would put on their best garments and fasten silk aprons round their waists, while the sultan would watch their work from a balcony he had [there]. I saw this edifice, which had then reached the height of about thirty cubits from the ground. When its foundations were laid the inhabitants of the city were freed from service on it, and labourers began to work on it for wages. Several thousands of them were collected for
72 that purpose, | and I heard from the governor of the city that the greater part of its revenues was spent on this building. The officer charged with it was the amīr Jalāl al-Dīn ibn al-Falakī al-Tawrīzī, one of the great [amīrs], whose father was a substitute for the vizier of the sultan Abū Sa'īd, named 'Alī Shāh Jīlān.[128] This amīr Jalāl al-Dīn al-Falakī had

[125] I.e., that Abū Isḥāq should be recognized as his suzerain.

[126] Aywān Kisrā ('The Hall of Chosroes') is the Perso-Arabic name of the great Sasanid palace at Ctesiphon, the vaulted hall of which is still to be seen a few miles below Baghdād.

[127] One MS. reads 'a lantern' (*fanūs*) for 'mattocks' (*fu'ūs*).

[128] Al-Falakī is apparently an error for al-Qūhakī; 'Izz al-Dīn Qūhakī, governor of Fārs, was appointed substitute (*nā'ib*) of Tāj al-Dīn 'Alī Shāh (see below, p. 345, n. 249) in 1312 (Spuler, *Die Mongolen in Iran*, 287, n. 4;

a brother, a distinguished man named Hibat Allāh and entitled Bahā' al-Mulk; he joined the service of the king of India at the same time as I did, and along with us came also Sharaf al-Mulk Amīr Bakht. The king of India gave robes of honour to us all and appointed each one to a service appropriate for him, assigning to us a fixed stipend and a gift, as we shall relate in due course.

This sultan Abū Isḥāq wished to be compared to the king of India just mentioned for his munificence and the magnitude of his gifts, but 'How distant are the Pleiads from the clod!' The largest | of Abū Isḥāq's gifts that we heard tell of was 73
that he gave the Shaikh-Zāda al-Khurāsānī,[129] who had come to him as an envoy from the king of Harāt, seventy thousand dinars, whereas the king of India never ceased to give many times more than that to persons from Khurāsān and elsewhere in numbers beyond reckoning.

Anecdote. As one instance of the extraordinary dealings of the king of India with the Khurasanians, there came to his court one of the doctors of the law from Khurāsān, of Harāt by family, but he lived in Khwārizm, called the amīr 'Abdallāh. The Khātūn Turabek, wife of the amīr Qutludumūr, the ruler of Khwārizm,[130] had sent him as bearer of a gift to the king of India of whom we are speaking. The king accepted the gift and gave in return one many times its value, which he sent to her. But the envoy of hers whom we have mentioned chose to remain at his court, and the king enrolled him among his familiars. One day, he said | to this 74
man, 'Go into the treasury and take out of it as much gold as you are able to carry.' So he went to his house and came back with thirteen bags; he then filled each one of these as full as it would hold, tied each bag to one of his limbs (for he was a powerful man), and rose up with them. When he got outside the treasury, he fell and was unable to rise; whereupon the sultan gave orders to weigh the amount that he had carried

346). Tawrīz was the popular pronunciation for Tabriz; see Yule's *Marco Polo*, I, 74–6.

[129] *Shaikh-zāda* is an Arabic-Persian formation, meaning 'son of the Shaikh', adopted by or used of descendants of celebrated doctors. In his account of the court of Delhi, Ibn Baṭṭūṭa mentions several other such Shaikh-zādas.

[130] For Qutlūdumūr and his wife Turabak see vol. III, p. 9 (Arabic).

out. It amounted to thirteen maunds, in the maunds of Dihlī, each one of which is twenty-five Egyptian *raṭls*.[131] The king ordered him to take it all, and he took it and went off with it.

A similar anecdote. On one occasion Amīr Bakht, entitled Sharaf al-Mulk al-Khurāsānī (the same man as was mentioned previously), felt indisposed at the capital of the king of India. The king came to visit him, and as he entered Amīr Bakht
75 wished to get up, but the king swore that | he should not come down from his *kat* (*kat* meaning a bed[132]). A seat, which they call a *mūra*,[133] was placed for the sultan and he sat down on it. He then called for gold and a balance and when they were brought he commanded the sick man to sit on one of the pans of the balance. Amīr Bakht then said, 'O Master of the World, had I known that you would do this, I should have put on many clothes.' The sultan replied, 'Put on now all the clothes that you have.' So he put on his garments intended for wear in cold weather, which were padded with cotton-wool, and sat on the pan of the balance. The other pan was filled with gold until it tipped down, when the king said 'Take this and give it in alms for your recovery,' and left him.

Another analogous anecdote. The jurist 'Abd al-'Azīz al-Ardawīlī, who had studied the science of Tradition at Damascus and made a profession of it, came to join his service, and
76 the king fixed his stipend | at a hundred silver dinars a day (this being the equivalent to twenty-five gold dinars [of the Maghrib]). This jurist came to his audience one day, and the sultan asked him about a certain *ḥadīth*. He reeled off so many *ḥadīths* to him on that subject, that the sultan, delighted with his powers of memory, swore to him by his own head that he should not leave the audience hall until he (the sultan) took what action towards him he thought proper. The sultan then descended from his seat, kissed his feet, and commanded a golden tray to be brought. This tray resembles

[131] The Egyptian *raṭl* was of two standards, 450 grammes and 500 grammes; since the *mann* ('maund') of Delhi is evaluated at 15·284 kilogrammes, Ibn Baṭṭūṭa evidently implies the latter (see W. Hinz, *Islamische Masse und Gewichte* (Leiden, 1955), 22, 29).

[132] Urdu *khaṭ*.

[133] Urdu *Moṛha*.

a small bowl, and he ordered that a thousand gold dinars should be put into it. The sultan then took this into his own hand, poured the coins over him, and said. 'These are yours and the tray as well.' On [another] occasion a man of Khurāsān known as Ibn al-Shaikh 'Abd al-Raḥmān al-Isfarāyinī,[134] whose father had settled in Baghdād, came to his court, and the sultan gave him fifty thousand silver dinars, and quantities of horses, slaves and robes of honour. We shall have many stories to relate of this king when we describe the land of India, and we have brought these in here only because, as
we have already mentioned, | the sultan Abū Isḥāq wanted to 77
be likened to him in respect of his gifts—whereas, although he was generous and of eminent merit, he could not be classed with the king of India in generosity and open-handedness.

Account of some of the sanctuaries at Shīrāz. One of these is the mausoleum of Aḥmad b. Mūsā, the brother of al-Riḍā 'Alī b. Mūsā b. Ja'far b. Muḥammad b. 'Alī b. al-Ḥusain b. 'Alī b. Abī Ṭālib (God be pleased with them); it is a sanctuary highly venerated by the people of Shīrāz, who visit it in order to obtain blessing by him and make their petitions to God by his virtue. Ṭāsh Khātūn, the mother of the sultan Abū Isḥāq, built over it a large college and hospice, in which food is supplied to all comers, and Qur'ān-readers continually recite the Qur'ān over the tomb.[135] The Khātūn makes a practice of coming to this sanctuary on the eve of every |
Monday, and on that night the qāḍīs, the doctors of the law, 78
and sharīfs assemble [there]. Shīrāz is of all cities in the world the one which most abounds in sharīfs; I heard from trustworthy persons that the number of sharīfs in it who are in receipt of stipends is more than fourteen hundred, counting both children and adults. Their Naqīb is 'Aḍud al-Dīn al-Ḥusainī. When these persons are assembled in this blessed sanctuary, they 'seal' the Qur'ān[136] by reading from copies,

[134] 'The Shaikh 'Abd al-Raḥmān' converted the first of the Mongol Īlkhāns (Takudar, renamed Aḥmad) to Islam, was sent by him on a mission to Egypt to announce his conversion, but was detained in Damascus until his death in 1285; Ibn al-'Imād, *Shadharāt al-Dhahab* (Cairo, n.d.), V, 381.

[135] The tomb-mosque of Aḥmad b. Mūsā, the brother of the eighth Imām of the Shī'ites, was constructed by order of Ṭāshī Khātūn in 1343/4, and is locally known as Shāh Chirāgh. The mosque was rebuilt in 1506 and later, but the college or hospice no longer exists (Junaid Shīrāzī, 289–92).

[136] See vol. I, p. 153, n. 318.

and the readers recite [it] with beautiful modulations. Food, fruit and sweetmeats are brought in, and when those present have eaten, the homiletic preacher delivers a sermon. All this takes place from after the midday prayer until the night prayer, while the Khātūn occupies an upper chamber with a grilled window which overlooks [the nave of] the mosque. To end with, kettledrums, fifes and trumpets are sounded at the gate of the tomb, exactly as is done at the gates of kings.

Another of the sanctuaries of Shīrāz is the mausoleum of the imām and pole, the saint Abū 'Abdallāh b. Khafīf, who is
79 known by them | [simply] as 'the Shaikh'.[137] He is the paragon of the whole land of Fārs, and his mausoleum is highly venerated by them; they come to it morning and evening, and rub their hands on it [for a blessing]. I myself saw the qāḍī Majd al-Dīn come to it on visitation and kiss it. The Khātūn comes to this sanctuary on the eve of every Friday. Over it [has been built] a hospice and a college, and the qāḍīs and doctors of the law assemble there and go through the same ceremony as at the tomb of Aḥmad b. Mūsā. I myself was present at both places [on the occasion of these gatherings]. The tomb of the amīr Muḥammad Shāh, father of the sultan Abū Isḥāq, is contiguous to this tomb.

The shaikh Abū 'Abdallāh b. Khafīf occupies a high rank among the saints and is widely celebrated. It was he who revealed the track of the mountain of Sarandīb in the island of Ceylon in the land of India.[138] |

80 *A miracle of this shaikh.* It is related that on one occasion

[137] Abū 'Abdallāh Muḥammad b. Khafīf, known as *al-Shaikh al-Kabīr*, (d. 982 and buried in the main cemetery) was the founder of orthodox Sufism in Shīrāz; see Junaid Shīrāzī, 38–46, and the biography of the shaikh by Abu'l-Ḥasan al-Dailamī, *Sīrat-i Ibn al-Ḫafīf aṣ-Ṣīrāzī*, ed. A. Schimmel (Ankara, 1955); also Arberry, *Shīrāz*, 61–85.

[138] For the track of Adam's Peak in Ceylon, see *Selections*, 258–9 (vol. IV, 179–82 Arabic). The story that follows is not found in any of the score or so of surviving biographical notices of the saint (see the editor's Introduction to the *Sīrat*, cited in the preceding note) and apparently derives from the traditional stories and legends of the sailors in the Persian Gulf. It is possible, however, that the tradition of his visit or visits to Ceylon may be founded on fact; but the Arabic epitaph found in Ceylon dated A.H. 337 = A.D. 949 of an unknown personage named Khālid b. Abū Tha'laba (?) (E. Combe *et al.* (edd.) *Répertoire chron. d'épigraphie arabe* (Cairo, 1931), III, no. 1435), although it contains ṣūfī phraseology, cannot be directly connected with him, except possibly through the name Abū Tha'laba (cf. *Sīrat*, 211).

he set out for the mountain of Sarandīb, accompanied by about thirty poor brethren. They were assailed by hunger on the way to the mountain, in an uninhabited locality, and lost their bearings. They asked the shaikh to allow them to catch one of the small elephants, which are exceedingly numerous in that place and are transported thence to the capital of the king of India. The shaikh forbade them, but their hunger got the better of them; they disobeyed his instruction and, seizing a small elephant, they slaughtered it and ate its flesh.[139] The shaikh, however, refused to eat it. That night, as they slept, the elephants gathered from every direction and came upon them, and they went smelling each man and killing him until they had made an end of them all. They smelled the shaikh too, but offered no violence to him; one of them took hold of him, wrapped its trunk round him, set him | on its 81
back, and brought him to the place where there was some habitation. When the people of the place saw him [thus], they were astonished at it, and went out to meet him and find out all about him. Then the elephant, as it came near them, seized him with its trunk, and lifted him off its back down to the ground in full view of them. These people then came up to him, touched the fringes of his robe [for a blessing] and took him to their king. [There] they made known the story of his adventure—[all of] them being infidels—and he stayed with them for some days. That place lies on a *khawr* called 'Bamboo Khawr', *khawr* meaning 'river'. In the same place there is a pearl fishery,[140] and it is recounted that the shaikh, one day during his stay there, dived in the presence of their king and came out with both hands closed. He said to the king 'Choose what is in one of them.' The king chose what was in his right hand, whereupon he passed over to him what it contained. They were three stones of | ruby, un- 82
equalled [in quality], and they are still in the possession of their kings, [set] in their crown and inherited by them in succession.

I visited this island of Ceylon. Its people still remain in a

[139] In spite of the celebrated dictum of Sa'dī (*Gulistān*, ed. J. Platts (London, 1874), i, 3; see p. 318, n. 145 below): 'The sheep is clean but the elephant is carrion', there appears to be no general agreement among Muslims that elephant flesh is forbidden.

[140] See vol. IV, p. 177 (Arabic).

state of infidelity, yet they hold the poor brethren of the Muslims in great respect, lodge them in their houses and give them food, and these Muslims will be in their rooms amidst their wives and children, contrary to [the practice of] all the other infidels of India. For these never admit Muslims to their intimacy, nor give them to eat or to drink out of their vessels, although at the same time they neither act nor speak offensively to them. We were compelled to have some of them cook flesh for us, and they would bring it in their pots and sit at a distance from us. They would bring banana leaves and put rice on them—this is their regular food—and they would pour over it *kūshān*,[141] which is a meat sauce, and go away; after we had eaten of this, what we left over would be eaten by the
83 dogs and the birds. If | any small child who had not reached the age of reason ate any of it, they would beat him and give him cow dung to eat, this being, so they say, the purification for that act.

Among the sanctuaries at Shīrāz is the mausoleum of the virtuous shaikh, the pole, Rūzbihān al-Baqlī, one of the great saints.[142] His tomb is in a congregational mosque, in which [the Friday prayers and] the *khuṭba* are held. It is in the same mosque that the qāḍī Majd al-Dīn mentioned above (God be pleased with him) performs his prayers. In this mosque I attended his lectures on the book of the *Musnad* of the Imām Abū 'Abd Allāh Muḥammad b. Idrīs al-Shāfi'ī.[143] He stated [his chain of authorities as follows] 'We received the tradition on it from Wazīra, daughter of 'Omar b. al-Munajjā, who said: We received the tradition from Abū 'Abd Allāh al-Ḥusain b. Abū Bakr b. al-Mubārak al-Zubaidī, who had it from Abu'l-Ḥasan al-Makkī b. Muḥammad b. Manṣūr b.
84 'Allān al-'Urḍī who | had it from the qāḍī Abū Bakr Aḥmad b. al-Ḥasan al-Harashī, from Abu'l-'Abbās b. Ya'qūb al-Aṣamm, from al-Rabī' b. Sulaimān al-Murādī, from the Imām Abū 'Abd 'Allāh al-Shāfi'ī'. I attended also the lec-

[141] See below, p. 376.

[142] Rūzbihān b. Abū Naṣr al-Baqlī (whose name is variously corrupted in the MSS.), 1128–1209, was of Dailamite origin; see Junaid Shīrāzī, 243–7, and L. Massignon 'La vie et les Oeuvres de Rûzbehân Baqlî', in *Studia Orientalia Ioanni Pedersen dicata* (Copenhagen, 1953), 236–49.

[143] I.e. a collection of the Traditions of the Prophet cited by al-Shāfi'ī (see vol. I, p. 43, n. 126) in his legal works, made by his pupil Abū Ja'far al-Naysābūrī. For the *Mashāriq al-Anwār* see above, p. 301, n. 101.

tures of the qāḍī Majd al-Dīn in this same mosque on the book *Mashāriq al-Anwār* of the Imām Raḍī al-Dīn Abu'l-Faḍā'il al-Ḥasan b. Muḥammad b. al-Ḥasan al-Ṣaghānī, on the authority of his hearing it from the shaikh Jalāl al-Dīn Abū Hāshim Muḥammad b. Muḥammad b. Aḥmad al-Hāshimī al-Kūfī, in his transmission of it from the imām Niẓām al-Dīn Maḥmūd b. Muḥammad b. 'Omar al-Harawī from the author of the book.

Another of the sanctuaries at Shīrāz is the tomb of the virtuous shaikh Zarkūb,[144] over which [there is built] a hospice for the provision of food. All of these sanctuaries are inside the city, and so also are most of the graves of its inhabitants. For if | the son or the wife of one of them dies, he 85
prepares a tomb for him [or her] in one of the chambers of his house and buries him there. He furnishes the chamber with reed mats and carpets, places a great number of candles at the head and feet of the deceased, and makes a door from the chamber towards the lane [outside the house] and an iron grille. From this door there enter the Qur'ān-readers, who recite with beautiful modulations, and there are not in the whole inhabited world any whose recitation of the Qur'ān is more beautifully modulated than the inhabitants of Shīrāz. The members of the household look after the tomb, cover it with carpets, and light lamps over it, so that the deceased person is, as it were, still present [with them]; and it was told me that they prepare every day the deceased person's portion of food and give it away in alms on his behalf.

Anecdote. I was passing one day through one of the bazaars in the city of Shīrāz when I saw there a mosque, substantially built and handsomely carpeted. Inside it there were copies of the Qur'ān, placed in | silken bags laid upon a rostrum. On 86
the northern side of the mosque was a cell with a grille opening in the direction of the bazaar, and there [sat] an old man, of handsome appearance and garments, with a Qur'ān before him, in which he was reading. I saluted him and sat down facing him, and, after he had asked me where I came from and I had replied to him, I questioned him on the subject of

[144] 'Izz al-Dīn Mawdūd b. Muhammad al-Dhahabī (d. 1265), an associate of Shaikh Aḥmad al-Rifā'ī (see above, p. 273, n. 6) and of Shaikh Rūzbihān al-Baqlī; see Junaid Shīrāzī, 310–15.

his mosque. He told me that it was he who had built it and endowed it with the revenues from a number of properties, for the maintenance of Qur'ān-readers and others, and that this cell in which I had sat down with him was the site of his grave, if God should decree his death in that city. He then lifted a carpet which was underneath him, and [there was] the grave, covered over with planks of wood. He showed me also a chest, which was at the other side of him, and said 'In this chest is my shroud and the spices for my burial, and some money that I earned by hiring myself to dig a well for a
87 saintly man, and when he paid me | this money I put it aside to meet the expenses of my interment, and any of it left over is to be distributed in alms.' I was astonished at what he told me and made ready to withdraw, but he adjured me to stay and served me with food in that place.

Among the sanctuaries outside Shīrāz is the grave of the pious shaikh known as al-Sa‘dī, who was the greatest poet of his time in the Persian language and sometimes introduced Arabic verses into his compositions.[145] It has [attached to it] a hospice which he had built in that place, a fine building with a beautiful garden inside it, close by the source of the great river known as Rukn Ābād. The shaikh had constructed there some small cisterns in marble to wash clothes in. People go out from the city to visit his tomb, and they eat from his table,[146] wash their clothes in that river and return
88 home. | I did the same thing at his tomb—may God have mercy upon him. In the neighbourhood of this hospice is another hospice, with a madrasa adjoining it. These two are built over the tomb of Shams al-Dīn al-Simnānī,[147] who was an amīr and faqīh at the same time and was buried there by his own testamentary indication.

[145] The Persian poet Sa‘dī (Mushrif al-Din Muṣliḥ b. ‘Abdallāh al-Sa‘dī), d. 1292, author of the famous 'Rose Garden' (*Gulistān*) and other poetical works. The almost contemporary Junaid Shīrāzī, author of *Shadd al-Izār* (461–2) also exalts his eminence as a Ṣūfī, endowed with 'miraculous graces' (*karāmāt*), and mentions the hospice, which supplied food to 'great and small, birds and beasts'. The tomb has remained in existence, although somewhat neglected until recently (Browne, *A Year among the Persians*, 307), but the adjoining buildings have disappeared; Arberry, *Shīrāz*, 112–38.

[146] I.e. eat food prepared and supplied at his hospice.

[147] Muḥammad b. al-Ḥasan b. ‘Abd al-Karīm, formerly Grand Qāḍī of Simnān (*Letters of Rashīd al-Dīn*, 27–9).

In the city of Shīrāz, one of the principal faqīhs is the sharif Majīd al-Dīn, a man of astonishing generosity.[148] He often gives away everything that he possesses and the very clothes that he is wearing, and puts on an [old] patched robe that he has. The chief men of the city come to his house to visit him, and then they find him in this condition and give him [new] clothes. His pension from the sultan is fifty silver dinars a day.

Then followed my departure from Shīrāz with the object of visiting the grave of the pious shaikh Abū Isḥāq al-Kāzarūnī, at Kāzarūn, which is at a distance of two days' journey from Shīrāz.[149] We encamped on the first day in the territory of the Shūl, who are a body of Persians living in the open country[150] and amongst whom there are a number of devotees. |

A Grace of one of these [*devotees*]. One day I was in a certain 89
mosque in Shīrāz, and had sat down to recite the Book of God (High and Mighty is He) after the midday prayer. It came into my mind that I should like to have a copy of the Holy Book so that I might read from it. At the same moment there entered a young man, who came up to me and said in a powerful voice 'Take'; I raised my head towards him, and he cast in my lap a copy of the Holy Book and left me. I recited the whole Book that day and waited for him in order to return it to him, but he did not come back to me. Afterwards I made enquiries about him and was told 'That was Buhlūl the Shūlī,' but I never saw him again.

We arrived in Kāzarūn in the evening of the second day and went to the hospice of the shaikh Abū Isḥāq (God benefit us by him), where we passed that night.[151] It is their

[148] Not identified.

[149] Fifty-five miles (20 farsakhs) to the west of Shīrāz; Schwarz, III, 196.

[150] A tribe, probably of Kurdish origin, who were driven out of Luristān in the twelfth century and occupied the region north and north-west of Shīrāz, as far south as Dasht-i Arzhan. The name is preserved in the village of Shūl, 33 miles north-north-west of Shīrāz, and the district of Shūlistān (*E.I.*, s.v. Shūlistān).

[151] Abū Isḥāq Ibrāhīm b. Shahriyār al-Kāzarūnī (963–1035), a pupil of Ibn al-Khafīf (above, p. 314, n. 137), founded a missionary order whose members played an active role from Anatolia to Southern India and China (cf. vol. IV, pp. 89, 103, 279, Arabic). His tomb still exists in Kāzarūn. See F. Meier, *Die Vita des Scheich Abū Isḥāq al-Kāzarūnī* (Leipzig, 1948), Intro.

custom to serve to every visitor, whoever he may be, *harīsa* made from flesh, wheat and ghee,[152] and eaten with thin
90 breadcakes; and they will not let any visitor to them | proceed on his journey without staying as their guest for three days, and disclosing his wants to the shaikh who [resides] in the hospice.[153] The shaikh tells these to the poor brethren attached to the hospice (these exceed a hundred in number, some of them married, others who are celibate, having renounced the goods of this world), and they then 'seal' the Qur'ān, perform the *dhikr*, and pray on his behalf at the tomb of the shaikh Abū Isḥāq, when his want is satisfied by God's goodwill.

This shaikh Abū Isḥāq is highly venerated by the people of India and China. Travellers on the Sea of China make a practice when the wind turns against them and they fear pirates, of making vows to Abū Isḥāq, and each one of them sets down in writing the obligation he has undertaken in his vow. Then, when they come safely to land, the servitors of the hospice go on board the ship, take the inventory, and exact [the amount of] his vow from each person who has pledged himself.[154] There is not a ship that comes from China or
91 from | India but has thousands of dinars in it [vowed to the saint], and the agents on behalf of the intendant of the hospice come to take delivery of that sum. There are some poor brethren who come to beg alms of the shaikh; each of these receives a written order for some amount, sealed with the shaikh's device (this is engraved on a silver die, and they put the die into red wax and apply it to the order so that the mark of the stamp remains upon it), to this effect: 'Whoso has in his possession [moneys dedicated under] a vow to the

[152] *Harīsa* is a kind of gruel composed of pounded wheat or other cereals, sometimes mixed with pounded meat. It was a dish especially associated with the Ṣūfīs; al-Maqdisī, *Descriptio Imperii Moslemici*, 2nd ed. (Leiden, 1906), III, 44.

[153] Another contemporary eye-witness reports that every morning about a thousand persons, men and women, came to the 'table of the Shaikh', and each received from the servitors at the convent a bowl with *harīsa*, oil, and bread; *Vita*, Intro., 69.

[154] On the role of Abū Isḥāq as the protector of travellers by sea, cf. *Vita*, Intro., 69–71, where there is quoted also the text of a document from the superior of the mother-convent delivered to a member of the order, authorizing the payment to him of sums from the vows and other alms due to the saint.

Shaikh Abū Isḥāq, let him give thereof to so-and-so so much,' the order being for a thousand or a hundred [dirhams], or some intermediate or smaller sum, according to the standing of the poor brother concerned. Then, when the mendicant finds someone who has in his possession anything under vow, he takes from him and writes for him a receipt for the amount on the back of the order. The king of India once vowed ten thousand dinars to the Shaikh Abū Isḥāq, and when the news of this reached | the poor brethren of the hospice, one 92
of them came to India, took delivery of the money, and went back with it to the hospice.

We travelled next from Kāzarūn to the city of al-Zaidānī [i.e. the two Zaids], which is called by this name because it contains the grave of Zaid b. Thābit and the grave of Zaid b. Arqam, both of them of the Anṣār, and Companions of the Apostle of God (God's blessing and peace upon him).[155] It is a beautiful town, with abundant fruit-gardens and streams, fine bazaars, and exquisite mosques. Its people are of upright conduct, trustworthy, and strict in religious observance. To this town belonged the qāḍī Nūr al-Dīn al-Zaidānī; he had migrated to join the people of India, and was appointed as qādī in that country in the Maldive Islands. These are a large number of islands, the king of which was Jalāl al-Dīn Ṣāliḥ, and he married this king's sister. An account of the king will be given later, and of his daughter Khadīja,[156] who was invested with the kingdom in these islands after him, and it was there that the abovementioned qāḍī | Nūr al-Dīn 93
died.

We travelled on from there to al-Ḥuwaizā', a small town inhabited by Persians, four nights' journey from al-Baṣra,

[155] Zaidān is described as a village between Arrajān (now Behbehān) and Dawraq (now Fellāḥīya), one day's march from the latter and less than three days' from Arrajān (Schwarz, IV, 384–5). It would seem therefore to have been on or near the Jarrāhī river, to the north of Bandar Ma'shūr, and near Ibn Baṭṭūṭa's route from the latter to Rāmiz (p. 283 above). The Arabic dual form is apparently an error on his part, the ending *-ān* being probably an instance of the usage (mentioned by Yāqūt, *Mu'jam al-Buldān*, s.v. al-Baṣra) of adding *-ān* to the name of the person after whom a place is named. In any case, Zaid b. Thābit died in al-Madīna in 665 (al-Harawī, 94; trans., 213), and Zaid b. Arqam died in al-Kūfa in 683 (Ibn Sa'd, *Kitāb al-Ṭabaqāt al-Kabīr* (Leiden, 1909), VI, 10).

[156] Vol. IV, pp. 110 ff. (Arabic); see *Selections*, 241 ff.

and five nights' from al-Kūfā.[157] To this town belongs the pious shaikh and devotee Jamāl al-Dīn al-Ḥuwaizā'ī, shaikh of the Sa'īd al-Su'adā convent in Cairo.[158] Then we travelled on, making for al-Kūfa, through a wilderness in which there is no water except at a single place called al-Ṭarfāwī.[159] We reached this place on the third day of our journey, then after the second day of our arrival at it we came to the city of al-Kūfa.[160]

The city of al-Kūfa. She is one of the metropolitan cities of al-'Irāq, distinguished among them by superior prerogative; the place of abode of Companions and followers, habitation of scholars and saints, and capital city of 'Alī b. Abī Ṭālib,
94 Commander of the Faithful.[161] But | desolation has gained the mastery over her, by reason of the hands of violence which have been extended towards her, and her disordered state is due to the beduins of Khafāja who live in the vicinity, for they rob on her highway.[162] The town is unwalled and its buildings are of brick; its bazaars are pleasant, dried dates and fish being the chief commodities sold in them, and its principal mosque is a great and noble cathedral mosque with seven naves[163] supported by thick pillars of dressed stones,

[157] Al-Ḥuwaizā' or al-Ḥawīza lies in a marshy plain seventy miles north of Muḥammara (Khurramshahr), described by Mustawfī (trans., 108) as a famous hunting-ground and a centre of the Mandaeans. The vizier Rashīd al-Dīn in his *Letters* (179) refers to the success of his efforts to restore the prosperity of al-Ḥawīza, which had become 'the lair of lions and haunt of highwaymen', by settling Lurs, Kurds and Arabs on its lands, some twenty years before this time.

[158] Already mentioned in vol. I, p. 58.

[159] Ibn Baṭṭūṭa must have crossed the Tigris at some point between Ḥuwaizā' and al-Kūfa. 'Through a wilderness' suggests a route westward to some point on the old course of the Tigris. The waterpoint of al-Ṭarfāwī cannot now be identified.

[160] Al-Kūfa, a few miles north of Najaf, was founded by the Arabs in 638, after their conquest of al-'Irāq from the Sasanid Persians, as one of their two garrison-cities, the other being al-Baṣra. For the surviving traces of the mediaeval city, see L. Massignon, 'Explication du Plan de Kufa,' in *Mélanges Maspéro* (Cairo, 1935), III, 337–60.

[161] The fourth Caliph, nephew and son-in-law of the Prophet, who transferred the capital of the Arab empire to al-Kūfa in 656. This paragraph reproduces with little change the description of al-Kūfa by Ibn Jubair 211–12; trans. Broadhurst, 219–21).

[162] See above, p. 271, n. 2.

[163] Ibn Jubair says more precisely 'five naves on the southern (*qibla*) side and two on the other sides'. The architecture of this mosque (rebuilt in 670) is discussed by K. A. C. Creswell, *Early Muslim Architecture* (Oxford, 1932), I, 36–7.

which were prepared in sections, set one on top of the other and the interstices filled with molten lead, and of immense height. In this mosque there are [a number of] sacred relics. One of them is a chamber alongside the miḥrāb, on the right as one faces the qibla; it is said that [Abraham] al-Khalīl (God's blessing upon him) had in that spot a place of prayer. Close by it is a miḥrāb [in a space] enclosed by bars made of teak and raised [above the level of the floor]; this is the miḥrāb of 'Alī b. Abī Ṭālib (God be pleased with him). It was in this spot that he was cut down by the accursed Ibn Mul-
jam,[164] and the people made a point of praying | in it.[165] 95
In the corner, at the [western] end of this colonnade, is a small mosque, also enclosed by bars of teak; this is said to be the spot at which the furnace boiled up[166] at the time of Noah's (peace be upon him) flood. Behind it, outside the mosque, is a chamber that they assert to be the house of Noah (peace be upon him), and in line with it [another] chamber that they assert to be the cell of Idrīs (peace be upon him).[167] Adjoining this is an open space, extending along the southern wall of the mosque, which is said to be the place of building of the ark of Noah (peace be upon him); and at the far end of this space is the house of 'Alī b. Abī Ṭālib (God be pleased with him) and the chamber in which he was washed [after his death]. Adjoining this is a chamber, and this also is said to be the house of Noah[168] (peace be upon him); but God knows best what truth there is in all of this.

On the eastern side of the mosque there is a chamber, raised above the ground and feached by steps, in which is the grave of Muslim b. 'Aqīl b. Abī Ṭālib[169] (God be pleased with
him), and in its vicinity, outside the mosque, | the grave of 96

[164] One of the sectaries called Khārijites, who avenged the massacre of a large body of the sectaries by 'Alī's army at al-Nahrawān in 658 by striking 'Alī with a sword in this mosque in 660.

[165] Ibn Jubair adds 'weeping and supplicating'.

[166] A quotation from Qur'ān, xi, 40; xiii, 27, reflecting a Talmudic interpretation of the biblical 'fountains of the deep' as pouring out boiling water from a furnace or cauldron.

[167] Commonly identified in Muslim tradition with the biblical Enoch; see *E.I.*, s.v.

[168] Ibn Jubair says 'of the daughter of Noah'.

[169] Muslim b. 'Aqīl, a nephew of 'Alī, was sent as the agent of his cousin al-Ḥusain to Kūfa in 680, and was there seized and executed; see *E.I.*, s.v.

'Ātika and Sukaina, the daughters of Ḥusain[170] (peace be upon him). As for the governor's castle at al-Kūfa, which was built by Sa'd b. Abī Waqqāṣ[171] (God be pleased with him), nothing is left of it but the foundations. The Euphrates is at a distance of half a farsakh from al-Kūfa, to the east of the town, and is bordered by groves of date palms, crowded together and each adjoining the other. To the west of the cemetery of al-Kūfa I saw a spot that was of dense blackness in a white plain; I was told that it is the grave of the accursed Ibn Muljam, and that the people of al-Kūfa come every year with loads of firewood and light a fire over the site of his grave for seven days. In its vicinity is a dome which, I was told, is over the grave of al-Mukhtār b. Abī 'Obaid.[172]

We then resumed our journey and halted [for the night] at Bi'r Mallāḥa, a pretty town in the midst of palm-groves.[173] I encamped outside it, and would not enter the place, because its inhabitants are Rāfiḍīs. We went on from there next
97 morning and alighted in the city of al-Ḥilla, which is | a large town, situated perpendicularly along the Euphrates, which is on the east side of it.[174] It has fine markets, stocked with both natural produce and manufactured goods, and a large number of habitations and palm groves encompassing it both inside and out, the houses of the town lying among the groves. It has also a great bridge fastened upon a continuous row of boats ranged from bank to bank, the boats being held in place both fore and aft by iron chains attached on either bank to a huge wooden beam made fast ashore.

The inhabitants of this city are all of them Imāmīs [Shī'ites] of the 'Twelver' sect, and are divided into two factions, one known as 'the Kurds' and the other as 'men of

[170] For Sukaina, see vol. I, p. 142, n. 282; *E.I.*, s.v. No mention of her sister 'Ātika has been found in any of the historical sources.

[171] See vol. I, p. 255, n. 38; *E.I.*, s.v.

[172] The leader of a popular Shī'ite rising in Kūfa in 685, killed in battle with the forces of Ibn al-Zubair (see vol. I, p. 179, n. 85; see also *E.I.*, s.v.).

[173] Literally 'Saline Well', the reputed site of the tomb of Ezekiel, identified by the Muslims with the Qur'ānic prophet Dhu'l-Kifl (cf. al-Harawī, 76; trans., 174) and now called Kifl.

[174] Al-Ḥilla ('The Settlement') was founded by the Shī'ite Arab shaikh Sadaqa b. Mazyad in 1102, as the capital of a minor Arab principality in Lower 'Irāq. Thanks to its bridge, it became an important station on the route from Baghdād to the Ḥijāz.

the Two Mosques'. Factional strife between them is never
interrupted, and fighting is always going on. Near the principal bazaar in this town there is a mosque, over the door of
which a silk curtain is suspended. They call this 'the Sanctuary
of the Master of | the Age'.[175] It is one of their customs that 98
every evening a hundred of the townsmen come out, carrying
arms and with drawn swords in their hands, and go to the
governor of the city after the afternoon prayer; they receive
from him a horse or mule, saddled and bridled, and [with this
they go in procession] beating drums and playing fifes and
trumpets in front of this animal. Fifty of them march ahead
of it and the same number behind it, while others walk to
right and left, and so they come to the Sanctuary of the
Master of the Age. Then they stand at the door and say 'In
the name of God, O Master of the Age, in the name of God
come forth! Corruption is abroad and tyranny is rife! This is
the hour for thy advent, that by thee God may divide the
true from the False.' They continue to call in this way,
sounding the trumpets and drums and fifes, until the hour of
the sunset prayer; for they assert that Muḥammad b. al-
Ḥasan | al-'Askarī entered this mosque and disappeared from 99
sight in it, and that he will emerge from it since he is, in their
view, the 'Expected Imam'.

The city of al-Ḥilla was [later] seized, after the death of the Sultan Abū Sa'īd, by the amīr Aḥmad b. Rumaitha, son of Abū Numayy, the amīr of Mecca.[176] He ruled it for several years and made a good governor, praised by the people of al-'Irāq; but eventually the shaikh Ḥasan, the sultan of al-'Irāq, defeated him, tortured him, put him to death, and seized all the wealth and treasures which were in his possession.

We travelled from there to the city of al-Karbalā', the

[175] A Shī'ite term for the Twelfth or 'Expected' Imām, Muḥammad, son of the eleventh Imām (d. 873); see *E.I.*, s.v. Kā'im al-Zamān. (For the other sanctuary of the Expected Imām at Sāmarrā, see below, p. 346.) The following invocation to him is based on Qur'anic themes (sūras xxx. 41, and v. 25; reading *fayafruqa* for *faya'rifa* in the printed text).

[176] Aḥmad b. Rumaitha had been appointed amīr of the Arabs in al-'Irāq by Sultan Abū Sa'īd about 1330, with his seat at al-Ḥilla. In 1336 he declared his independence and seized al-Kūfa, but was defeated and killed by Shaikh Ḥasan in 1339; see al-'Azzāwī, II, 35–6.

sanctuary of al-Ḥusain b. 'Alī (peace be upon both).[177] It is a small town, surrounded by palm groves and watered from the Euphrates. The sanctified tomb [of al-Ḥusain] is inside the town, and beside it is a large college and a noble hospice, in which food is supplied to all wayfarers.[178] At the gate of the Mausoleum stand chamberlains and guardians, without whose leave no person may enter. [The visitor] kisses the
100 august threshold, which is of silver. Over | the sanctified tomb there are [hanging] lamps of gold and silver, and upon its doors there are silken curtains. The inhabitants of this town [also] are divided in two factions, the 'sons of Rakhīq' and the 'sons of Fāyiz',[179] and fighting goes on interminably between them; yet they are all Imāmīs and trace their descent from one ancestor, and in consequence of their disorders this city has fallen into ruins. We travelled on from there to Baghdād.

The City of Baghdād, city of the Abode of Peace and capital of al-Islām, of illustrious rank and supreme pre-eminence, abode of Caliphs and residence of scholars. Abu'l-Ḥasan Ibn Jubair (God be pleased with him) has said:[180] 'And this illustrious city, although she still remains the capital of the 'Abbāsid Caliphate, and centre of allegiance to the Imāms of Quraish, yet her outward lineaments have departed and nothing remains of her but the name. By comparison with her former state, before the assault of mis-
101 fortunes upon her and the fixing of the eyes | of calamities in her direction, she is as the vanishing trace of an encampment or the image of the departing dream-visitant. There is no beauty in her that arrests the eye, or summons the busy passer-by to forget his business and to gaze—except the Tigris, which lies between her eastern and western [quarters] like a mirror set off between two panels, or a necklace ranged between two breasts; she goes down to drink of it and never

[177] The site of the battle in 680 in which al-Ḥusain was killed by the troops of al-Kūfa; see vol. I, p. 46, n. 140.

[178] On the mosque of al-Karbalā' see *E.I.*, s.v. Mashhad Ḥusain.

[179] No other reference to these factions, nor to the factions at al-Ḥilla, has been traced.

[180] Ibn Jubair visited Baghdād in 1184, during the Caliphate of al-Nāṣir (1180–1225). The city itself, however, was not destroyed on its capture by the Mongols in 1258, and, as noted below, Ibn Baṭṭūṭa's account is drawn largely from that of Ibn Jubair.

suffers thirst, and views herself by it in a polished mirror that never suffers rust; and between her air and her water feminine beauty is brought to its flowering.'

Ibn Juzayy remarks: One would imagine that Abū Tammām Ḥabīb b. Aws[181] had witnessed with his own eyes what befell her in the end, when he said of her:

Over Baghdād is stationed death's loud herald—
Weep for her, then, weep for time's rapine there!
Erstwhile, upon her stream by war imperilled,
When in her streets its flames were briefly bated, |
Men hoped her happy fortunes reinstated. 102
Now all their hopes have turned to dull despair!
Since she, from youth to eldritch age declined,
Has lost the beauty that once charmed mankind.

Many persons have composed verses in her praise and have celebrated her charms at length, and finding the subject to admit of spacious discourse have enlarged on it profusely and in pleasing fashion. Of her said the imām and qāḍī Abū Muḥammad 'Abd al-Wahhāb b. 'Alī b. Naṣr al-Mālikī al-Baghdādī[182] [in verses] which my father (God's mercy on him) recited to me many times:

The fragrance of the Baghdād breeze
Bids my fond heart by her to stay,
Though contraried by fate's decrees;
Then how shall I depart today,
When both delights commingle there—
The airy and the debonair?

Concerning her also he says (God have mercy on him and be pleased with him): |

Salute Baghdad in every habitation, 103
And due from me is doubled salutation.
No, not in hate, I swear, did I depart,
For both her shores are graven on my heart.

[181] Abū Tammām, celebrated Syrian-Arab poet (d. 846), especially noted for his ponderous and involved style. In the fourth line, I read *ḥīnan* for *ḥusnan*.

[182] He emigrated to Egypt towards the end of his life and died there in 1031; al-Khaṭīb al-Baghdādī, *Ta'rīkh Baghdād* (Cairo, 1931), XI, 31–2.

She cramped me sore for all her spaciousness,
And fortune never granted me redress,
Like one beloved whom I would fain draw nigh
While she, evasive, willed the contrary.

And of her he says again, angrily repudiating her [in verses] which my father (God's mercy on him) recited to me many a time:

Baghdād for men of wealth has an ever-open door
But short and narrow shrift is all she gives the poor.
The livelong day I roamed through all her lanes and lands,
As lorn as the Qur'ān in a free-thinker's hands.

Concerning her the qāḍī Abu'l-Ḥasan 'Alī b. al-Nabīh[183] says, in the course of an ode: |

104 Over 'Irāq from afar a fulgent moon she descried,
On through the darkness she pressed into a noonday's glare.
Sweetly around her the breeze the scents of Baghdād diffused,
But for her journey's fatigue she could have flown in that air!
Gardens she called to her mind amid the pastures of Karkh,
Streams ever limpid, and verdant glades that are never sere,
Flowers from the hills of Muḥawwal she plucked, and at the Tāj
Saw from its portals a splendour of sunlight flare.

The following verses were composed by a woman of Baghdād in recollection of the city:

O for Baghdād, and O for its 'Irāq!
For its gazelles with witchery in their eyes,
For where beside the stream they swaying walk
With faces that like crescent moons arise
Above the blackness with their necklets starred,
As if their gently-nurtured qualities
Had stirred the passion of the 'Udhrite bard![184] |
105 Such beauties might I with my soul redeem
That shine for all time in her sunlit gleam!

[183] Ibn al-Nabīh (d. 1222) was a secretary (not qāḍī) in the Ayyūbid chancery (C. Brockelmann, *Geschichte der arabischen Litteratur* (Weimar, 1898), I, 261–2). The verses quoted describe a journey on his she-camel. Karkh was the main sector of west Baghdād and al-Muḥawwal a village on its western outskirts; the Tāj was the great palace of the Caliphs on the east bank.

[184] Reading *khuliqa* for *khuluqu*. For the love-poetry called 'Udhrite see vol. I, p. 253, n. 23.

(Resumes). There are two bridges at Baghdād, made fast in the same manner as we have mentioned in describing the bridge of the city of al-Ḥilla.[185] The population are continually crossing them, night and day, men and women; indeed they find in this unending pleasure.[186] Of mosques in Baghdād in which the *khuṭba* is pronounced and the Friday services are held there are eleven, eight of them on the west bank and three on the east bank. As for the other mosques, they are very numerous, and so too are the colleges, although these have fallen into ruin. The bath-houses in Baghdād [also] are numerous; they are among the most sumptuous of baths, and the majority of them are painted and plastered with pitch, so that it appears to the spectator to be black marble. This pitch is brought from a spring between al-Kūfa and al-Baṣra, from which it flows continuously and gathers
at its sides | like black clay; it is shovelled up from there and 106
transported to Baghdād.[187] In each of these bath-houses there are a large number of cubicles, each one of them floored with pitch and having the lower half of its wall [also] coated with it, and the upper half coated with a gleaming white gypsum plaster; the two opposites are thus brought together in contrasting beauty. Inside each cubicle is a marble basin fitted with two pipes, one flowing with hot water and the other with cold water. A person goes into one of the cubicles by himself, nobody else sharing it with him unless he so desires. In the corner of each cubicle is another basin for washing in, and this also has two pipes with hot and cold [water]. Every one on entering is given three towels; one of them he ties round his waist on going into [the cubicle], the second he ties round his waist on coming out, and with the
third he dries the water | from his body. I have never seen 107

[185] See above, p. 324. The two bridges at this time were the old bridge at the northern end of the Tuesday Market (Sūq al-Thalathā') and one from the vicinity of the former Tāj palace to the suburb of Qurayya.

[186] The phrase is taken from Ibn Jubair, who, however, uses it of the continual crossing of the river by ferry.

[187] The two preceding sentences also are taken, slightly abbreviated, from Ibn Jubair, but the details that follow are independent. The site of the spring of pitch 'between al-Kūfa and al-Baṣra' is not defined in any known source, and it seems more probably that the bitumen was obtained from the well-known seepages at Hīt (on the Euphrates) or al-Qayyāra (on the Tigris; see below, p. 347).

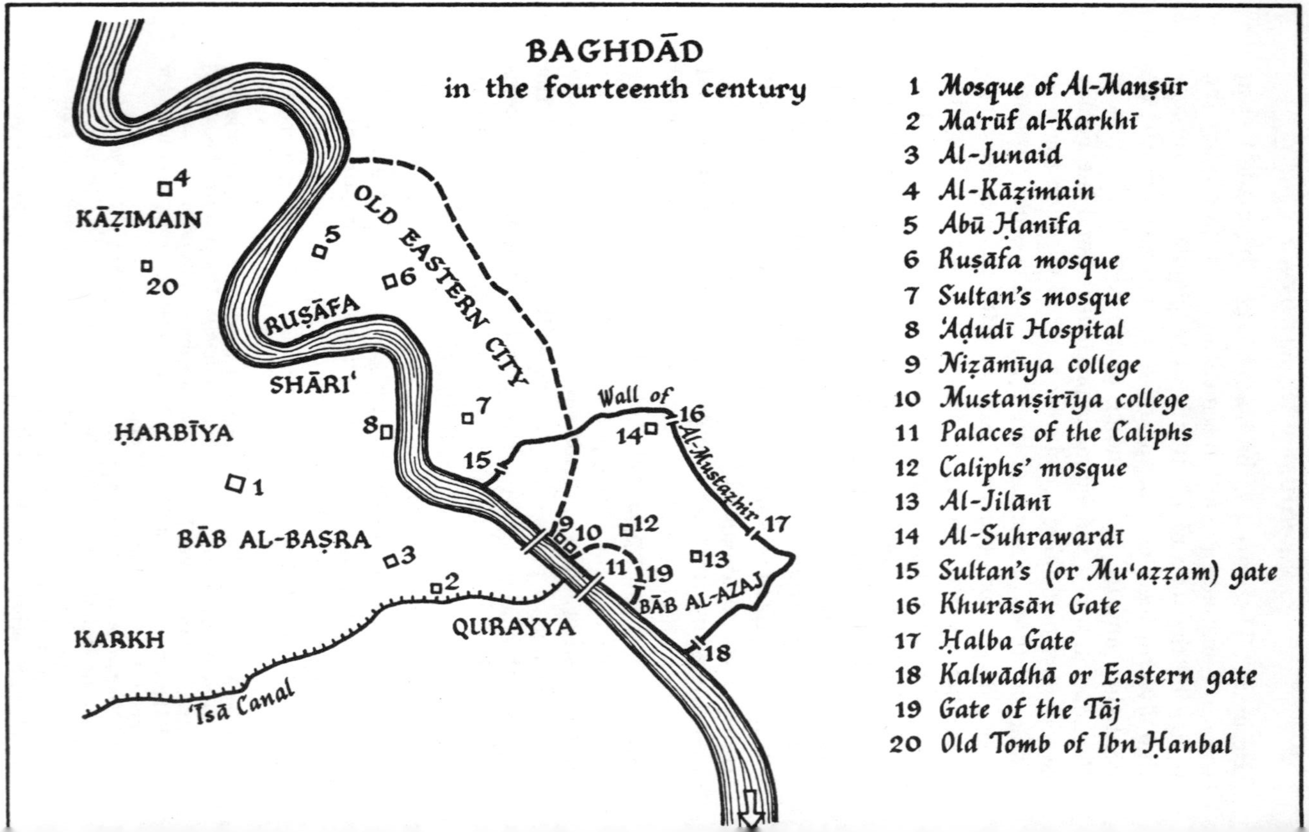
BAGHDĀD
in the fourteenth century
KĀẒIMAIN
ḤARBĪYA
BĀB AL-BAṢRA
KARKH
QURAYYA
SHĀRI'
RUṢĀFA
OLD EASTERN CITY
Wall of Al-Mustaẓhir
BĀB AL-AZAJ
'Īsā Canal
1 Mosque of Al-Manṣūr
2 Ma'rūf al-Karkhī
3 Al-Junaid
4 Al-Kāẓimain
5 Abū Ḥanīfa
6 Ruṣāfa mosque
7 Sultan's mosque
8 'Aḍudī Hospital
9 Niẓāmīya college
10 Mustanṣirīya college
11 Palaces of the Caliphs
12 Caliphs' mosque
13 Al-Jīlānī
14 Al-Suhrawardī
15 Sultan's (or Mu'aẓẓam) gate
16 Khurāsān Gate
17 Ḥalba Gate
18 Kalwādhā or Eastern gate
19 Gate of the Tāj
20 Old Tomb of Ibn Ḥanbal

such an elaboration as all this in any city other than Baghdād, although some [other] places approach it in this respect.

Account of the Western side of Baghdād.[188] The western side of the city was the one first built, but is now for the most part in ruins. In spite of that, there still remain of it thirteen quarters, each quarter like a city in itself, with two or three bath-houses, and in eight of them there are cathedral mosques. One of these quarters is that [called] Bāb al-Baṣra [i.e. Baṣra Gate];[189] it contains the mosque of the Caliph Abū Ja'far al-Manṣūr (God's mercy on him). The Māristān [Hospital] lies between the quarter of Bāb al-Baṣra and the quarter of al-Shāri', on the Tigris; it is a vast edifice in ruins, of which only the vestiges remain.[190] On this western side there are several sanctuaries: the tomb of Ma'rūf al-Karkhī (God be pleased with him),[191] in the quarter of Bāb | al-Baṣra; on 108
the road to Bāb al-Baṣra a superbly constructed mausoleum inside of which is a tomb with a broad sepulchral stone carrying the inscription 'This is the grave of 'Awn, a son of 'Alī b. Abī Ṭālib';[192] on this side also the tomb of Mūsā al-Kāẓim b. Ja'far al-Ṣādiq, the father of 'Alī b. Mūsā al-Riḍā, and beside it the tomb of al-Jawād—both of these tombs are

[188] This paragraph is based on Ibn Jubair also, but revised in view of the changes resulting from the Mongol conquest in 1258. It was on the western bank that al-Manṣūr built his new capital, the famous 'Round City' of Baghdād, in 756. Its site lay between Bāb al-Baṣra and Ḥarbīya, but the only surviving monument of it at this time was the Great Mosque of al-Manṣūr. See K. A. C. Creswell, *A Short Account of Early Muslim Architecture* (London, 1958), 163–82. Also Fig. 2, no. 1.

[189] So called because it was the suburb outside the southern or Baṣra Gate of the Round City.

[190] The Hospital was built by the Buwaihid prince 'Aḍud al-Dawla in 979 on the site of the site of the former Khuld ('Paradise') palace of the early 'Abbāsid Caliphs, and was still in operation at the time of Ibn Jubair; see G. Le Strange, *Baghdad during the Abbasid Caliphate* (Oxford, 1900), 103–5. Also Fig. 2, no. 8.

[191] A celebrated ṣūfī, d. 816, and venerated as one of the protectors of the city. The tomb is still a prominent landmark on the west bank; see Fig. 2, no. 2.

[192] Ibn Sa'd (III, 12) mentions 'Awn among the sons of 'Alī, but he is otherwise unknown (Ibn Jubair mentions another son, Mu'īn, along with 'Awn, but no other reference to him has been found), and al-Harawī does not mention the tomb. Le Strange (*Baghdad*, 352) conjectures that it may be the monument now called the tomb of the Lady Zubaida (wife of the caliph Hārūn al-Rashīd; see vol. I, p. 243, n. 215), who was buried in al-Kāẓimain.

inside the sepulchral chamber and surmounted by a platform veneered with wood which is covered with plaques of silver.[193]

Account of the Eastern side of Baghdād.[194] This eastern part of Baghdād has magnificent bazaars and is splendidly laid out. The largest of its bazaars is one called the Tuesday bazaar, in which each craft [occupies a section] by itself.[195] In the centre of this bazaar is the wonderful Niẓāmīya College, the splendour of which is commemorated in a number of proverbial phrases, and at the end of it is the Mustanṣirīya College, named after the Commander of the Faithful |
109 al-Mustanṣir bi'llāh Abū Ja'far, son of the Commander of the Faithful al-Ẓāhir, son of the Commander of the Faithful al-Nāṣir.[196] All four schools are included in it, each school having a [separate] *īwān*,[197] with its own mosque and lecture room. The teacher takes his place under a small wooden canopy, on a chair covered with rugs; he sits [on this] in a grave and quiet attitude, wearing robes of black and his [black] turban, and with two assistants on his right and left, who repeat everything that he dictates. This same system is followed in every formal lecture of all four sections. Inside this college there is a bath-house for the students and a chamber for ablutions.

On this eastern side there are three mosques in which the

[193] Mūsā b. Ja'far (d. 799) and his grandson Muḥammad b. 'Alī b. Mūsā al-Jawād (d. 835), the seventh and ninth Imāms of the Shī'ites, from whose sanctuary the Shī'ite suburb of al-Kāẓimain ('the two Kāẓims') took its name; see Fig. 2, no. 4.

[194] The eastern city grew up originally around the suburb of Ruṣāfa, but fell into ruin from the effects of war and floods. In 1095 the caliph al-Mustaẓhir enclosed the suburbs surrounding the Caliphs' palaces with a new wall, and the area so enclosed survived the Mongol conquest and remained for many centuries the main 'city' of Baghdād.

[195] The Tuesday Market (*Sūq al-Thalathā'*) ran parallel to the river between the quarter of the Caliphs' palaces and the main bridge.

[196] The Niẓāmīya College, founded by Niẓām al-Mulk, vizier of the Seljuk sultans Alp Arslān and Malikshāh, in 1065, was the most famous of Islamic colleges in the Middle Ages; see *E.I.*, s.v. Madrasa, and Fig. 2, no. 9. It was originally a Shāfi'ite college exclusively. The Mustanṣirīya was built by the caliph al-Mustanṣir in 1234, and the building (recently restored) still stands (Fig. 2, no. 10). The inclusion of all four Sunnī schools in this college was an innovation.

[197] *Īwān* (from Persian *līwān*) means a vaulted hall at the end or side of a central court.

Friday prayers are held. One is the Caliphs' mosque, which is adjacent to the palaces and residences of the Caliphs.[198] It is a large cathedral mosque, containing fountains and many lavatories for ablutions and baths. | I met in this mosque the 110
shaikh, the learned and pious imām, the doyen of traditionists in al-'Irāq, Sirāj al-Dīn Abū Ḥafṣ 'Omar b. 'Alī b. 'Omar al-Qazwīnī,[199] and attended his lectures in it on the entire *Musnad* of Abū Muḥammad 'Abdallāh b. 'Abd al-Raḥmān b. al-Faḍl b. Bahrām al-Dārimī,[200] this being in the month of Rajab the Solitary in the year 727.[201] He said: 'We were instructed in it by the pious woman shaikh and traditionist Sitt al-Mulūk Fāṭima, daughter of the notary Tāj al-Dīn Abu'l-Ḥasan 'Alī b. 'Alī b. Abu'l-Badr, who said: We were instructed by the shaikh Abū Bakr Muḥammad b. Mas'ūd b. Bahrūz al-Ṭayyib al-Māristānī, who said: We were instructed by Abu'l-Waqt 'Abd al-Awwal b. Shu'aib al-Sinjārī al-Ṣūfī, who said: We were instructed by the imām Abu'l-Ḥasan 'Abd | al-Raḥmān b. Muḥammad b. al- 111
Muẓaffar al-Dā'ūdī, who said: We were instructed by Abū Muḥammad 'Abdallāh b. Aḥmad b. Ḥamawaih al-Sarakhsī, who had it from Abū 'Imrān 'Īsā b. 'Omar b. al-'Abbās al-Samarqandī, from Abū Muḥammad 'Abdallāh b. 'Abd al-Raḥmān b. al-Faḍl al-Dārimī'.

The second cathedral mosque is the Sultan's mosque, which is situated outside the town,[202] and in proximity to it are palaces designated as the Sultan's. The third cathedral mosque is that of al-Ruṣāfa, which is about a mile from the Sultan's mosque.[203]

[198] The palaces of the Caliphs occupied a large area, enclosed by its own wall, on the bank of the river, roughly in the centre of the space enclosed by the wall of al-Mustaẓhir; see Le Strange, *Baghdad*, 263 ff. Also Fig. 2, nos. 11, 12.

[199] A celebrated teacher of Tradition, d. 1349; *Durar*, III, 180.

[200] The *Musnad* (or *Sunan*) of al-Dārimī (d. 869) is a highly reputed collection of Prophetic Tradition, although not included in the six 'canonical' collections.

[201] 23 May–21 June 1327. See above, p. 297 and n. 86.

[202] In the former Mukharrim quarter, to the north of al-Mustaẓhir's wall (Fig. 2, no. 7). The palaces of the sultans were situated between this and the river.

[203] Al-Ruṣāfa was the suburb built around the palace of al-Mahdī, the third 'Abbāsid caliph (775–85), on the left bank, opposite the Round City of his father al-Manṣūr; see Le Strange, *Baghdad*, 187–98. Also Fig. 2, no. 6.

Account of the Tombs of the Caliphs at Baghdad and of the Tombs of Scholars and Devotees which it contains. The tombs of the 'Abbāsid caliphs (God be pleased with them) are in al-Ruṣāfa, and over each of these tombs is the name of its occupant.[204] Among them are the graves of al-Mahdī, of al-
112 Hādī, of al-Amīn, | of al-Mu'taṣim, of al-Wāthiq, of al-Mutawakkil, of al-Muntaṣir, of al-Musta'īn, of al-Mu'tazz, of al-Muhtadī, of al-Mu'tamid, of al-Mu'taḍīd, of al-Muktafī, of al-Muqtadir, of al-Qāhir, of al-Rāḍī, of al-Muttaqī, of al-Mustakfī, of al-Muṭī', of al-Ṭā'i', of al-Qā'im, of al-Qādir, of al-Mustaẓhir, of al-Mustarshid, of al-Rāshid, of al-Muqtafī, of al-Mustanjid, of al-Mustaḍī, of al-Nāṣir, of al-Ẓāhir, of al-Mustanṣir, and of al-Musta'ṣim—who was the last of them. It was from him that the Tatars captured Baghdād by the sword; they slaughtered him some days after their occupation, and [even] the name of the 'Abbāsid Caliphate ceased to be associated with Baghdād. This was in the year 654.[205]

In the vicinity of al-Ruṣāfa is the grave of the Imām Abū Ḥanīfa (God be pleased with him).[206] Over it there is a great dome, and a hospice at which food is served to all comers. In
113 the city of Baghdād today there is no hospice | in which food is supplied except this hospice—Magnified be he who brings destruction and change to all things.[207] Near it is the grave of the Imām Abū 'Abdallāh Aḥmad b. Ḥanbal (God be pleased with him).[208] There is no dome over it, and it is said that a dome was built over his grave on several occasions, but it was then destroyed by the decree of God Most High. His grave is

[204] This list of tombs of all the 'Abbāsid caliphs in roughly chronological order from 775 to 1258 (omitting only Hārūn al-Rashīd, al-Ma'mūn and al-Qā'im's successor al-Muqtaḍī) is highly suspect. al-Harawī's list, compiled about 1200, mentions only the tombs of ten caliphs (down to al-Mustanjid) at al-Ruṣāfa, and of four on the west bank (73–4; trans., 163–4; cf. also Le Strange, *Baghdad*, 194, note).

[205] The correct date is 656 = 1258.

[206] The tomb-mosque still exists in the suburb called (in honour of him) al-Mu'aẓẓam (Fig. 2, no. 5). Abū Ḥanīfa (d. 767) was the eponymous founder of the 'Irāqī school of law, called after him the Ḥanafī school; see *E.I.*[2], s.v.

[207] I.e. 'Marvel at this change in human affairs'.

[208] The founder of the Ḥanbalī school of law, d. 855. The original tomb, on the west bank (Fig. 2, no. 20) was washed away by floods, and the site was transported at some unknown date to the east bank; see al-Harawī, trans., 164, n. 8.

held in great veneration by the inhabitants of Baghdād, most of whom follow his school. Near it is the grave of Abū Bakr al-Shiblī, one of the imāms in the practice of Ṣūfism (God's mercy on him),[209] and the graves of Sarī al-Saqaṭī, Bishr al-Ḥafī, Dā'ūd al-Ṭā'ī, and Abu'l-Qāsim al-Junaid (God be pleased with them all).[210] The people in Baghdād have one day in each week for the visitation of one of these shaikhs, and a day following it for another shaikh, and so on until the end of the week. In Baghdād there are [also] many graves of devotees and scholars (God Most High be pleased | with them). 114 In this eastern part of Baghdād there are no fruits, but all fruit is transported to it from the western part, because it is there that the gardens and groves are.

My arrival at Baghdād coincided with the presence in it of the king of al-'Irāq, so let us speak of him here.

Account of the Sultan of the Two 'Irāqs and of Khurāsān, namely the illustrious sultan Abū Sa'īd Bahādur Khān (*Khān* in their language meaning 'king'),[211] son of the illustrious sultan Muḥammad Khudābandah—he was the one of the [line of] kings of the Tatars who was converted to Islam.[212] His name is differently pronounced; some say Khudhābandah, with *dh*, but as to *bandah* there is no dispute. The interpretation of the name according to the latter pronunciation is 'Abdallāh [i.e. slave of God], because *Khudhā* in

[209] Died 946/7; his tomb is still preserved in al-Mu'aẓẓam; see al-Harawī, 74; trans., 165.

[210] All four of these tombs were situated on the west bank, and still are (see Fig. 2, no. 3), except that of Bishr al-Ḥāfī, which has been transferred to the east bank. Bishr (d. 841), Sarī (d. 871), and al-Junaid (d. 910) are all celebrated saints of the ṣūfī school of Baghdād; Dā'ūd al-Ṭā'ī (d. 781) was the link between them and the early school of ascetics (see the chain of authorities on p. 297 above), but is believed to have died in al-Kūfa.

[211] Abū Sa'īd (b. *c.* 1304, reigned 1316–35) was, as explained below, the last of the direct line of Mongol Khāns of Persia and al-'Irāq, descended from Chingiz Khān. *Bahādur* is a Mongol word (*bagatur*) meaning 'brave, hero', and was assumed as a title by Abū Sa'īd in 1319 after breaking a revolt of several amīrs.

[212] Khudābandah's proper name was Öljaitu-Buqa (meaning 'Good Augury' in Mongol), but according to Ḥāfiẓ-i Abrū (trans., p. 4) this was later changed to Timur and then to Kharbandah, following a Mongol custom of changing a child's name to protect him against the evil eye. Öljaitu was born in 1282, and succeeded his brother Ghāzān Khān in 1304. He was not, however, the first of the Ilkhāns to adopt Islam, since both Aḥmad Takudar (1282–4) and Ghazan (1295–1304) were Muslims.

115 Persian | is the name of God (High and Mighty is He) and *bandah* is 'servant' or 'slave' or words to that effect. It is said also that it is really Kharbandah, *khar* in Persian meaning 'ass', so that his name according to this means 'servant of the ass'. What a world of difference there is between these two statements! But yet it is this latter name that is the best known, and the former was the name to which he changed it out of religious zeal. It is said that the reason why he was called by this latter name is that the Tatars name a new-born child after the first person to enter the house after its birth; when this sultan was born the first person to enter was a mule-driver, whom they call *kharbandah*, so he was given this name. Kharbandah's brother in turn [was called] Qāzghān, which the people pronounce Qāzān. *Qāzghān* means a cooking pot, and the story goes that he was given this name because, when he was born, a slave girl entered carrying a cooking pot.[213]

116 It was this Khudhābandah who | embraced Islam—we have previously related the story of this, and how he attempted to compel the people to adopt the Rāfiḍī doctrine after his conversion, and the story of his relations with the qāḍī Majd al-Dīn.[214] When he died, there succeeded to the kingdom his son Abū Sa'īd Bahādur Khān. He was an excellent and a generous king. He became king while of tender age, and when I saw him in Baghdād he was still a youth, the most beautiful of God's creatures in features, and without any growth on his cheeks. His vizier at that time was the amīr Ghiyāth al-Dīn Muḥammad, son of Khwāja Rashīd;[215] his father was one of the emigrant Jews, and had been appointed vizier by the sultan Muḥammad Khudhābandah, the father of Abū Sa'īd. I saw both [the sultan and his vizier] one day on the Tigris in a launch (which they call *shabbāra*, and is like

[213] *Qāzghān* or *qazghān* is Turkish for 'cauldron', and colloquially pronounced *qazān* (or with a Persian accent *ghazān*), but in contemporary sources the two names are clearly distinguished.

[214] See above, p. 302.

[215] According to Ḥāfiẓ-i Abrū (who calls him a man of rare distinction, learning, and knowledge of affairs) Ghiyāth al-Dīn was not appointed to the vizierate until after the death of Dimashq Khwāja (on 24 August 1327). His father Faḍl Allāh Rashīd al-Dīn (b. 1247, executed 1318) is deservedly famous both as an administrator and as a historian. Ghiyāth al-Dīn was himself executed in 1336 along with Abū Sa'īd's successor Arpa Khān.

a *sallūra*);[216] in front of him was Dimashq Khwāja, son of the amīr al-Jūbān who held the mastery over Abū Sa'īd, and to right and left of him were two *shabbāras*, carrying musicians and dancers. | I was witness to one of his acts of generosity on 117
the same day; he was accosted by a company of blind men, who complained to him of their miserable state, and he ordered each one of them to be given a garment, a slave to lead him, and a regular allowance for his maintenance.

When the sultan Abū Sa'īd succeeded, being a young boy, as we have mentioned, the chief of the amīrs, al-Jūbān, gained control over him[217] and deprived him of all powers of administration, so that nothing of sovereignty remained in his hands but the name. It is related that on the occasion of one of the festivals Abū Sa'īd needed ready money to meet some expenses, but having no means of procuring it he sent for one of the merchants, who gave him what money he wished. Things went on in this way until one day his father's wife Dunyā Khātūn[218] came into his chamber and said to him: 'If *we* were men, we should not let al-Jūbān and his son continue to behave in this way.' He asked her what she meant by these words, and she said to him: | 'The conduct of 118
Dimashq Khwāja, the son of al-Jūbān, has reached the point of dishonouring your father's wives. Last night he passed the night with Ṭughā Khātūn, and he has sent to me saying "Tonight, I shall pass the night with you".[219] The only thing to be done is to assemble the amīrs and troops, and then when he goes up to the citadel incognito to spend the night there, you can seize him. As for his father, God will suffice to deal with him.' Al-Jūbān was at that time absent in Khur-

[216] A *shabbāra* is a kind of barge with an elevated cabin, used by princes and notables; see H. Kindermann, *'Schiff' in Arabischen* (Zwickau, 1934), s.v., and for the *sallūra*, *ibid.*, 41.

[217] Choban, of the Sulduz tribe of Mongols, was the grandson of Turan-noyon, one of Hulagu's generals. He was married successively to the two daughters of Öljaitu Khudābandah, Dawlandī, mother of his son Jalū Khān (see below, p. 328), and after her death to Sāṭī Beg, mother of Ṣūrghān (killed in 1346). He was thus the brother-in-law of Abū Sa'īd, as well as commander-in-chief of the armed forces.

[218] Daughter of the Artukid (Turkish) prince of Mārdīn, al-Malik al-Manṣūr Najm al-Dīn Ghāzī; see below, p. 353.

[219] This appears to be a popular elaboration of an intrigue between Dimashq Khwāja and Qonqotai, a favourite concubine of Öljaitu Khān; see Ḥāfiẓ-i Abrū, (trans., 97), and cf. Spuler, *Die Mongolen in Iran*, 124.

āsān.[220] The affront to his honour roused Abū Sa'īd to anger; he spent the night laying plans for action, and when he learned that Dimashq Khwāja was in the citadel he commanded the amīrs and the troops to encircle it on every side. The next morning Dimashq came out, accompanied by a soldier called al-Ḥājj al-Miṣrī, and found a chain stretched across the gate of the citadel and fastened with a lock, so that he could not go out on horseback. Al-Ḥājj al-Miṣrī struck the chain with his sword, and after he had cut it through they came out to-
119 gether, only to be surrounded | by the troops. One of the amīrs of the private guard,[221] named Miṣr Khwāja, and a eunuch named Lu'lu' attacked Dimashq Khwāja and killed him; they brought his head to the king Abū Sa'īd and threw it before his horse's feet, for this is what they customarily do with the heads of their chief enemies. The sultan gave orders to pillage his house and to kill all those of his attendants and mamlūks who put up a fight.

The news of this reached al-Jūbān while he was in Khurāsān. With him were his sons, Amīr Ḥasan, who was the eldest, Ṭālish and Jalū Khān, who was the youngest—he was the son of the sister of the sultan Abū Sa'īd, his mother Sāṭī Beg being the daughter of the sultan Khudhābandah[222]—and also the regiments and garrison troops of the Tatars. They agreed together to fight against the sultan Abū Sa'īd and marched towards him, but when the two armies met the Tatars deserted to their sultan and left al-Jūbān without
120 support. When | he saw this he turned in his tracks, fled to the desert of Sijistān, and took refuge in its depths. He decided to join the king of Harāt, Ghiyāth al-Dīn, in order to gain his protection and find security in his city, since he had put the latter in his debt by previous good services. His two sons Ḥasan and Ṭālish disagreed with him over this plan, arguing that Ghiyāth al-Dīn was not a man of his word, since he had betrayed Fīrūz Shāh after he fled to him for

[220] Choban was in command of an expedition against the troops of the Chagatāy-Khān Tarmashīrīn (see vol. III, pp. 31 ff., Arabic), who had invaded Khurāsān. The following account of the death of Dimashq Khwājah and the fate of his father Choban is substantially confirmed by the contemporary Persian sources.

[221] Ibn Baṭṭūṭa here uses the Egyptian term *khāṣṣikīya*; see vol. I, p. 30.

[222] There is a slight error here; see above, n. 217.

refuge, and had put him to death.[223] But al-Jūbān would not hear of anything but joining Ghiyāth al-Dīn, so his two sons separated from him, and he went on, accompanied by his youngest son, Jalū Khān. Ghiyāth al-Dīn came out to welcome him, dismounted before him, and brought him into the city on guarantee of safety; but a few days later treacherously killed him and his son with him, and sent their heads to the sultan Abū Sa'īd. As for Ḥasan and Ṭālish, they proceeded to Khwārizm and made their way to the sultan Muḥammad Ūzbak;[224] he received them hospitably and took them under his protection, until certain actions | of theirs made it neces- 121
sary to kill them and he put them to death. Al-Jūbān had a fourth son, whose name was al-Dumurṭāsh; he fled to Egypt, where al-Malik al-Nāṣir received him honourably and offered him [the governorship of] Alexandria, but he refused to accept it, saying 'All that I want is troops to fight Abū Sa'īd with'.[225] He was [the kind of man that] when al-Malik al-Nāṣir sent a robe to him, he gave the person who brought it to him a more handsome robe, out of despite for al-Malik al-Nāṣir, and he behaved in a manner which made it necessary to kill him, so al-Malik al-Nāṣir put him to death and sent his head to Abū Sa'īd. We have already related in a previous narrative the story about him and about Qarāsunqūr. When al-Jūbān was killed, his corpse and that of his son were brought [to Mecca] and taken to the 'Standing' at 'Arafāt [during the Pilgrimage]; they were then carried to al-Madīna to be buried in the mausoleum which al-Jūbān had made for himself near the mosque of the Apostle of God (God bless and give him peace). But this was prevented, and he

[223] Ghiyāth al-Dīn Kurt, prince of Herāt, succeeded his father Fakhr al-Dīn Kurt in 1310 and died 1328/9. As shown by the parallel sources, Ibn Baṭṭūṭa has confused both the Kurt prince and his victim. The Oirat Nawrūz, son of Arghūn, governor of Khurāsān (d. 1278), was appointed commander-in-chief by Ghāzān Khān in 1295; he befriended Fakhr al-Dīn Kurt and had him appointed prince of Herāt, but when Nawrūz himself fell out with Ghāzān Khān in 1297 and fled to Herāt, Fakhr al-Dīn was compelled to surrender him. See Ḥāfiz-i Abrū, tr. K. Bayani, 104–5.

[224] See below, pp. 482 sqq.

[225] Timurtāsh b. Choban had been appointed governor of Anatolia in 1316. He declared himself independent in 1321 and extended his domains into south-western Anatolia. For his flight to Egypt after the death of Choban and execution there, see vol. I, p. 109, n. 158.

was buried in the Baqī'.[226] It was al-Jūbān who had the water brought to Mecca (God Most High ennoble her).[227]

122 When the sultan Abū | Sa'īd had become sole master in the kingdom he decided to marry al-Jūbān's daughter; she was named Baghdād Khātūn and was one of the most beautiful of women. She was married to the Shaikh Ḥasan, the same who became master of the kingdom after the death of Abū Sa'īd, he being the son of the sultan's paternal aunt.[228] On the sultan's order he divorced her, and Abū Sa'īd married her and she became the most favoured of his wives.[229] Among the Turks and the Tatars their wives enjoy a very high position; indeed, when they issue an order they say in it 'By command of the Sultan and the Khātūns'. Each khātūn possesses several towns and districts and vast revenues, and when she travels with the sultan she has her own separate camp. This khātūn gained an ascendancy over Abū Sa'īd, and he preferred her to all the other [wives]. She continued to enjoy this position for [almost] the whole period of his life; but he subsequently married a woman called Dilshād,[230] whom he loved with a violent passion, and neglected Baghdād Khātūn. |
123 She became jealous in consequence, and administered poison to him in a kerchief, with which she wiped him after conjugal relations. So he died, and his line became extinct, and his amīrs seized the provinces for themselves, as we shall relate. When the amīrs learned that it was Baghdād Khātūn who had poisoned him they resolved to kill her. The Greek slave Khwāja Lu'lu', who was one of the principal and senior

[226] According to *Durar*, I, 542 (where the personal character of Choban is highly praised), this was done on the orders of the Sultan of Egypt, al-Malik al-Nāṣir. For Baqī' al-Gharqad see vol. I, p. 179.

[227] Choban had in 1325 restored the old conduit of Zubaida (see vol. I, p. 243, n. 215) which had been allowed to fall into disrepair, with the result that good water became abundant and cheap in Mecca during the Pilgrimage, and plentiful enough to grow vegetables in the city (*Chroniken der Stadt Mekka*, ed. F. Wüstenfeld (Leipzig, 1859), II, 428–9; IV, 248).

[228] See below, p. 341.

[229] According to *Durar*, I, 480, Choban had prevented Abū Sa'īd from marrying Baghdād Khātūn. After her marriage with Abū Sa'īd, she used to ride in a magnificent cortege of Khātūns (cf. below, pp. 343–4) and to wear a sword round her waist.

[230] Dilshād was the daughter of Dimashq Khwāja, and during the reign of her subsequent husband Shaikh Ḥasan enjoyed undisputed authority; *Durar*, II, 101–2.

amīrs, took the initiative in this; he came to her while she was in the bath-house and beat her to death with his club. Her body lay there for some days, with only her pudenda covered with a piece of sacking. The Shaikh Ḥasan became independent in the kingdom of 'Irāq al-'Arab, and married Dilshād, the wife of the sultan Abū Sa'īd, exactly as Abū Sa'īd had done in marrying his wife.

Account of those who seized power over the kingdom after the death of the sultan Abū Sa'īd. Among those was the Shaikh Ḥasan, the son of his paternal aunt,[231] whom we have just mentioned; he seized | the whole of 'Irāq al-'Arab. The others 124
were: Ibrāhīm Shāh, son of the amīr Sunaita,[232] who seized al-Mawṣil and Diyār Bakr; the amīr Artanā,[233] who seized the territories of the Turkmens, known also as the land of the Rūm; Ḥasan Khwāja b. al-Dumurṭāsh b. al-Jūbān,[234] who seized Tabrīz, al-Sulṭānīya, Hamadān, Qumm, Qāshān, al-Rayy, Warāmīn, Farghān,[235] and al-Karaj; the amir Ṭughaitumūr,[236] who seized part of the territories of Khurāsān; the amīr Ḥusain,[237] son of amīr Ghiyāth al-Dīn, who seized Herāt and the greater part of the territories of Khurāsān; Malik Dīnār,[238] who seized the lands of Makrān and Kīj;

[231] Called Shaikh Ḥasan the Greater (or the Elder), of the Jalā'ir tribe of Mongols, governor of Anatolia in the latter part of Abū Sa'īd's reign, occupied Tabrīz in 1336; after losing this to Ḥasan b. Timurtāsh (see below, n. 234), he occupied Baghdād in 1339 and maintained his rule in al-'Irāq until his death in 1356. Ibn Baṭṭūṭa omits the brief reign of Arpa Khān, and other descendants of Hulagu or of Chingiz Khān who were fleetingly recognized as Sultans. For the confused history of this period, see Spuler, *Die Mongolen in Iran*, 127–37.

[232] Ibrāhīm Shāh, son of Sūtāy (see above, p. 289, n. 62), is recorded as having occupied Mosul in 1342/3; *Durar*, II, 221.

[233] See below, p. 435.

[234] Known as Shaikh Ḥasan the Lesser; he had remained in Anatolia after his father's flight (see above, p. 339, n. 225), revolted against Shaikh Ḥasan al-Jalā'irī in 1338, proclaimed Abū Sa'īd's sister Sāṭī Beg sultan, and occupied the provinces mentioned until murdered by his wife in 1343.

[235] This is probably Farāhān (mentioned by Mustawfī, trans., 73, along with Karaj), a valley 50–60 miles south-east of Hamadān. Karaj was the upper part of the same valley; see Le Strange, *Lands*, 197–9.

[236] Ṭughāy-Timūr, a descendant of Chingiz Khān's brother, set up as independent prince in Khurāsān in 1336, after the death of Arpa Khān; killed in warfare with the Serbedārs (see vol. III, p. 64, Arabic), in 1351/2.

[237] Ḥusain b. Ghiyāth al-Dīn Kurt, reigned 1331/2–1369/70: see above, p. 339, n. 223; Spuler, *Die Mongolen in Iran*, 155–61.

[238] Probably Ghiyāth al-Dīn Dīnār, of a local noble house in Makrān, related by marriage to the princes of Hormuz (see J. Aubin, 'Les Princes d'Ormuz

Muḥammad Shāh b. Muẓaffar, who seized Yazd, Kirmān, and Warqū;[239] the king Quṭb al-Dīn Tamahtan, who seized
125 Hurmuz, Kīsh, al-Qaṭīf, | al-Baḥrain and Qalhāt; the sultan Abū Isḥaq (whom we have mentioned previously), who seized Shīrāz, Iṣfahān, and the kingdom of Fārs, this [extending over] a space of forty-five days' journey; the sultan Afrāsiyāb Atābek, who seized Īdhaj and other territories, and whom we have mentioned previously.[240]

Let us return now to the matter that we were dealing with. I left Baghdād after this in the *maḥalla* of the sultan Abū Sa'īd,[241] on purpose to see the ceremonial observed by the king of al-'Irāq in his journeying and encamping, and the manner of his transportation and travel. It is their custom to set out with the rising of the dawn and to encamp in the late forenoon. Their ceremonial [on setting out] is as follows: each of the amīrs comes up with his troops, his drums and his standards, and halts in a position that has been assigned to him, not a step further, either on the right wing or the left wing. When they have all taken up their positions and
126 their ranks are set in perfect order, | the king mounts, and the drums, trumpets and fifes are sounded for the departure. Each of the amīrs advances, salutes the king, and returns to his place; then the chamberlains and the marshals move forward ahead of the king, and are followed by the musicians. These number about a hundred men, wearing handsome robes, and behind them comes the sultan's cavalcade. Ahead of the musicians there are ten horsemen, with ten drums carried on slings round their necks, and five [other] horsemen

du XIIIe au XVe siecle' in *J A* (Paris, 1953) 102, 138, Table I). Kīj (or Kīz), which is always associated with Makrān in the mediaeval texts, is the Kej (Kech) valley in the middle course of the Dasht river, now in Baluchistan. It was five days' journey (about 160 miles) east of the chief port of Makrān at Tīz, 8 miles north of Chahbar; see T. H. Holdich, 'Notes on Ancient and Mediaeval Makran,' in *GJ* (London, 1896), VII, 387–405 and map.

[239] Warqū was a local pronunciation of Abarqūh (Abarqūya), 80 miles south-west of Yazd, on the main route to Shīrāz; Schwarz, I, 17–18.

[240] For Muḥammad Shāh b. Muẓaffar, see above, p. 309, n. 124; for Quṭb al-Dīn Tahamtan, below, p. 401; for Abū Isḥāq, above, p. 306; and for Afrāsiyāb, above, p. 288.

[241] The *maḥalla* was the mobile camp of the Mongol khāns; cf. below, p. 482. According to Ḥāfiz-i Abrū (trans., 96), Abū Sa'īd left Baghdād 'in the spring' of this year, i.e. most probably in May.

carrying five reed-pipes,[242] which are called in our country *ghaiṭas*. They make music with these drums and pipes and then stop, and ten of the musicians sing their piece; when they finish it those drums and pipes play [again], and when they stop, ten others sing their piece, and so on until ten pieces are completed, whereupon the encampment takes place. On the sultan's right and left during his march are the great amīrs, who number about fifty, and | behind him are the standard- 127
bearers, drums, fifes and trumpets, then the sultan's mamlūks, and after them the amīrs according to their ranks. Each amīr has his own standards, drums and trumpets. The organization of all this is supervised by the amīr jandār,[243] who has a large corps [under his command]. The punishment of anyone who lags behind his unit and his corps is that his boots are taken off, filled with sand, and hung round his neck. He walks on his bare feet until finally, on reaching the encampment, he is brought before the amīr [jandār], thrown face downwards on the ground, and beaten with twenty-five lashes on his back; whether he be of high degree or low degree, they except no one from this [punishment].

When they encamp, the sultan and his mamlūks occupy a camp by themselves, and each of his khātūns occupies a separate camp of her own, each | of them also having her own 128
imām, muezzins, Qur'ān-readers, and bazaar. The viziers, secretaries and officials [of the finance department][244] encamp separately, and each amīr also has his own camp. They all present themselves for duty after the afternoon prayer, and are dismissed after the last evening prayer, [returning to their camps] with torches carried before them. When the hour of departure comes, the great drum is beaten,[245] fol-

[242] Arabic *ṣurnāyāt*. The *ṣurnāy* is not a flute (*nāy*) but a reed-pipe or oboe, with a wooden tube. For the varieties of this instrument, including the Moroccan *ghaiṭa*, see H. G. Farmer, *Turkish Instruments of Music in the Seventeenth Century* (Glasgow, 1937), 23–6.

[243] *Jāndār* (Persian = 'arms-bearer') was the term for ushers at the court, who acted also as a bodyguard and as executioners. *Amīr jāndār* (spelled *jandār* by Ibn Baṭṭūṭa) may thus be loosely translated 'chief of the bodyguard'.

[244] *Ahl al-ashghāl*, literally 'employees', is apparently used here in the Moroccan sense of *ashghāl* as 'fiscal administration'; see Dozy, s.v. shughl.

[245] The 'great drum' (called in Mongol *kūrgā*) was one of the royal insignia: see Yule's *Marco Polo*, I, 339 f.; H. G. Farmer in *E.I.*, Supplement, s.v. Ṭabl Khāna.

lowed by the beating in succession of the drums of the chief khātūn, who is the queen, then of the other khātūns, then of the vizier, then of those of the amīrs all at once. Then the amīr of the advance guard rides off with his troops, followed by the khātūns, then the sultan's baggage and baggage-animals and the baggage of the khātūns, then another amīr with a troop under his command to prevent persons from intruding in between the baggage and the khātūns, and finally the rest of the army.

I travelled in this *mahalla* for ten days, and thereafter accompanied the amīr 'Alā al-Dīn Muḥammad, one of the
129 great and distinguished amīrs, to the town of Tabrīz.[246] | We arrived at the city of Tabrīz after ten days' journey, and encamped outside it in a place called al-Shām.[247] At that place is the grave of Qāzān, king of al-'Irāq, and alongside it a fine madrasa and a hospice in which food is supplied to all wayfarers, consisting of bread, meat, rice cooked in ghee, and sweetmeats. The amīr arranged for my lodging in this hospice, which is situated among rushing streams and leafy trees. On the following morning I entered the city by a gate called the Baghdād Gate, and we came to an immense bazaar called the Qāzān bazaar, one of the finest bazaars I have seen the world over.[248] Each trade has its own location in it, separate from every other. I passed through the jewellers' bazaar, and my eyes were dazzled by the varieties of precious stones that I saw; they were [displayed] in the hands of beautiful slave-
130 boys, wearing rich robes | and their waists girt with sashes of

[246] 'Alā al-Dīn was later in this year appointed joint-vizier, and subsequently controller of finances. Abū Sa'īd was on his way to Sulṭānīya (the new capital built by Öljaitu, 65 miles west of Qazwīn and 190 miles south-west of Tabrīz), about 400 miles from Baghdād by Hamadān. The point at which Ibn Baṭṭūṭa left the *mahalla* would then be somewhere in the vicinity of Hamadān (280 miles from Baghdād).

[247] Shām was a new suburb built by Ghāzān Khān outside the second wall of the city, called in Persian histories Ghāzānīya, and by Rashīd al-Dīn (*Letters*, 207) Shām-i Ghāzān. Ghāzān's tomb is described by Mustawfī (see the next note) as constructed of 'lofty edifices such as are not to be seen in the whole land of Īrān'; see also A. U. Pope (ed.), *A Survey of Persian Art* (London, 1939), II, 1045–6.

[248] Tabrīz was at this time at the height of its prosperity as the entrepôt between Europe and the Mongol empire. The contemporary Persian geographer Mustawfī (trans., 78–83) elaborates on its size, magnificence, products, and wealth, but does not mention a 'Baghdād Gate' in his list of gates in either wall. See also Yule's *Marco Polo*, I, 74–6.

silk, who [stood] in front of the merchants exhibiting the jewels to the wives of the Turks, while the women were buying them in large quantities and trying to outdo one another. What I saw of all this was a scandal—may God preserve us from such! We went into the ambergris and musk bazaar [also] and saw the like of this again, or worse. Afterwards we came to the cathedral mosque, which was founded by the vizier 'Alī Shāh, known by the name of Jīlān.[249] Outside it, to the right as one faces the *qibla*, is a college, and to the left is a hospice. The court of the mosque is paved with marble, and its walls are faced with [tiles of] *qāshānī*, which is like *zalīj*;[250] it is traversed by a canal of water, and it contains all sorts of trees, vines and jasmines. It is their custom to recite every day, after the afternoon prayer, the sūras *Yā-Sīn*, *Victory*, and *'Amma*[251] in the court of the mosque, and | the people of the city gather [there] for the ceremony. 131

We spent one night in Tabrīz. On the following morning the amīr 'Alā al-Dīn received the order of the sultan Abū Sa'īd to rejoin him, so I returned along with him, without having met any of the scholars of Tabrīz. We continued our journey until we reached the sultan's *maḥalla*, where this amīr told the sultan about me and introduced me into his presence. He asked me about my country, and gave me a robe and a horse. The amīr told him that I was intending to travel to the noble Ḥijāz, whereupon he gave orders for me to be supplied with provisions and mounts in the pilgrim caravan[252] accompanying the *Maḥmil*, and wrote instructions to that effect on my behalf to the governor of Baghdād, Khwāja Ma'rūf.[253] I returned therefore to the city of Baghdād, and

[249] Tāj al-Dīn 'Alī-Shāh Jīlān was appointed joint-vizier with Rashīd al-Dīn in April 1312, compassed the latter's execution in 1318, and died in 1324 (the only vizier of the Īlkhāns to die in his bed). His immense mosque, built outside the Narmiyān quarter, dominated the city, and its ruins survive under the name of the *Arg* or citadel; see Pope, II, 1056–61; IV, plates 377–9.

[250] See vol. I, p. 256, n. 42.

[251] Sūras xxxvi, lxvii, and lxxviii of the Qur'ān.

[252] The Arabic term *sabīl* is defined as 'a pilgrim caravan conducted by an *amīr ḥājjī* and in which food, mounts, and everything needed by the pilgrims are supplied to them without charge'; Juwayni, *Ta'rīkh-i Jahān-gushā* (Leyden-London, 1916), II, 96, n. 5. For the *maḥmil* see vol. I, p. 58, n. 181.

[253] Khwāja 'Izz al-Dīn Ma'rūf is mentioned as governor of Baghdād in 1336; al-'Azzāwī, I, 523.

received in full what the sultan had ordered for me. As there still remained more than two months before the time for the departure of the caravan,[254] I thought it a good plan to journey to al-Mawṣil and Diyār Bakr to see those districts, and
132 then return to | Baghdād when the caravan was due to set out, and go on to the noble Ḥijāz.

So I went out from Baghdād to a station on the canal of Dujail, which is derived from the Tigris and waters a large number of villages.[255] We halted next, after two days' journey, at a large village called Ḥarba,[256] [in] a wide and fertile [tract]. Journeying on from there, we halted at a place on the bank of the Tigris near a fort called al-Maʿshūq;[257] the fort is built on the Tigris and on the eastern bank opposite it is the city of Surra-man-rā'a, also called Sāmarrā. Some people call it Sām Rāh, which means in Persian 'The road of Sām', *rāh* being 'road'.[258] This city has fallen into ruins, so that nothing is left of it but a fraction. It has an equable climate and is strikingly beautiful in spite of its decay and the effacement of its monuments. Here too there is a sanctuary of the 'Master of the Hour', as at al-Ḥilla.[259] |

[254] This would imply that he returned to Baghdād before the end of June 1327.

[255] This and the following sections as far as Naṣībīn are abridged from Ibn Jubair's narrative, with the exception of the reference to the Shīʿite sanctuary at Sāmarrā and two paragraphs relating to Moṣul.

Dujail canal was taken off from the west bank of the Tigris below Sāmarrā, and rejoined it at Baghdād. The northern road on the right bank followed this canal from the Ḥarbīya quarter in west Baghdād.

[256] The chief town in the district called Maskin, on the Dujail canal, about 50 miles north of Baghdād.

[257] Originally a palace built on the west bank of the Tigris opposite Sāmarrā by the caliph al-Muʿtamid (870–92), later converted into a fort, and now known as al-ʿĀshiq: see al-Yaʿqūbī, *Bibl. Geographorum arabicorum*, VII, 268; Alois Musil, *The Middle Euphrates* (New York, 1927), 53.

[258] *Surrā man rā'a* ('Rejoiced is the beholder') was the official designation of the city when it was the capital of the ʿAbbāsid caliphs (from 835 to 890). This is evidently a play upon an older name (in Assyrian *surmarrate*, in Syriac *sumara*), and the common designation as Sāmarrā is ingeniously explained as a punning correction of the official name to *Sā'a man rā'a* ('Grieved is the beholder'), after the abandonment and ruin of the city. *Sām-rāh* is a parallel Persian adaptation, Sām being one of the heroes of the Persian epic cycle. For the history of Sāmarrā see E. Herzfeld, *Geschichte der Stadt Samarra* (Hamburg, 1948).

[259] This is the sanctuary, still venerated by the Shīʿites, in which the Twelfth or 'Expected' Imām is said to have gone into concealment. It is

After one day's journey from there we reached Takrīt,[260] a 133
large city with spacious environs, fine markets and many mosques, and whose inhabitants are distinguished by goodness of disposition. The Tigris is on the northern [261] side of the city, and it has a well-fortified castle on the bank of the river. The city itself is of ancient construction and protected by a wall, which surrounds it. From there we journeyed two stages and came to a village called al-'Aqr, on the bank of the Tigris.[262] At its upper end there is a hill, on which there stood formerly a fort, and at its lower end is the khān known as Khān al-Ḥadīd, a powerful building with towers. From this place there is a continuous sequence of villages and cultivation to al-Mawṣil.

Continuing our journey we halted at a place called al-
Qayyāra,[263] near the Tigris. At this place | there is a patch of 134
black land in which are springs that exude pitch, and tanks are constructed for it to collect in. When you see it, it looks like clay on the surface of the ground, deep black in colour, glistening, soft and with a good smell. Round these tanks is a large black pool, covered by a kind of thin scum, which the pool deposits on its edges, and it also becomes pitch. In the vicinity of this place there is a large spring, and when they wish to transport the pitch from it, they light over it a fire, which dries up what watery moisture there is at that spot; then they cut it up into slabs and transport it. We have already mentioned the spring of the same kind which is between

---

known as *Ghaibat al-Mahdī*: see Herzfeld, 286–9; al-Harawī, 72; trans., 159–60. For the similar sanctuary at al-Ḥilla see above, p. 325.

[260] On the west bank of the Tigris, thirty miles north of Sāmarrā, and noted for its fortress, which guarded the approach to central 'Irāq from the north. See *E.I.*, s.v.; F. Sarre and E. Herzfeld, *Archäologische Reise in Mesopotamien* (Berlin, 1911), 219–22; III, plate 29.

[261] Ibn Baṭṭūṭa here quietly corrects an apparent error in Ibn Jubair, who has 'southern'. The citadel itself was situated on a sandstone bluff at the northern end of the town, 'defended landwards by a deep moat and accessible only by secret steps cut in the rock and leading from the heart of the citadel to the water's edge' (S. Lane-Poole, *Saladin* (London–New York, 1898), 3).

[262] The site of the Assyrian city of Kartukulti-ninurta, 64 miles north of Takrīt.

[263] '(The place) abounding in pitch', still noted for its seepages of bitumen, 32 miles south of Moṣul.

al-Kūfa and al-Baṣra.[264] We continued our journey from these springs for two stages, and thereafter arrived at al-Mawṣil.

The city of al-Mawṣil.[265] It is an ancient and prosperous
135 city, and its citadel | known as al-Ḥadbā' is imposing in appearance and famed for its impregnability, surrounded by a wall of solid construction, strengthened by massive towers.[266] Adjoining it are the buildings of the Sultan's palace and separating these two [complexes of buildings] from the town is a broad street, extending in length from the upper part of the town to its lower end. The town itself is encircled by two stout walls, no less, close-set with towers, and inside the walls there are chambers, one above the other, circularwise in its inner face. In no city walls have I seen its like except the wall round the city of Dihlī, the capital of the king of India.[267]

Al-Mawṣil has a large suburb, containing mosques, bath-houses, warehouses and bazaars, and in it there is a cathedral mosque on the bank of the Tigris, round which there are iron lattices, and adjoining it platforms overlooking the Tigris, of
136 the utmost beauty | and skill in construction.[268] In front of the mosque is a hospital. Inside the city there are two cathedral mosques, one ancient[269] and the other modern.[270] In the court of the modern mosque is a cupola, inside which there is an octagonal basin of marble supported by a marble column;

[264] P. 329 above.

[265] Founded *c.* 642 by the Arabs as a garrison-city, on the site of a fortified monastery on the west bank of the Tigris; see *E.I.*, s.v.

[266] The citadel and fortifications were reconstructed by the atābeg Zankī (1127–44) and his successors, and were not destroyed in the Mongol invasions. *Al-Ḥadbā'* means 'the hump-backed', a poetical designation corresponding to *al-Shahbā'* for the citadel of Aleppo; cf. vol. I, p. 95, n. 105; p. 101, n. 132, and below, p. 353.

This was the old citadel, situated to the north of the later Turkish citadel (*Ich Qal'a*), whose ruins still stand at the northern end of the city.

[267] See vol. III, p. 148 (Arabic).

[268] The 'Red Mosque', built by the governor Mujāhid al-Dīn in 1180. According to Ibn Jubair he founded the hospital also. On the mosque see A. Sioufi in *Sumer* (Baghdad, 1955), XI, 177–88.

[269] The Umayyad mosque, enlarged by Marwān II (744–50); see A. Sioufi in *Sumer* (Baghdad, 1950), VI, 211–19.

[270] The mosque of Nūr al-Dīn, known as the Great Mosque, built in 1170–2 and recently restored. In the following sentence Ibn Baṭṭūṭa again corrects Ibn Jubair, whose text implies that the cupola and fountain were in the ancient mosque.

the water spouts out of this with force and impetus, rises to the height of a man, and then falls down, providing a beautiful spectacle. The *qaisārīya*[271] of al-Mawṣil is very fine; it has iron gates and [the interior] is encircled by shops and chambers, one upon the other, of skilful construction.

In this city is the sanctuary of the prophet Jirjīs[272] (upon him be peace); there is a mosque over it, and the tomb is in an angle of it, to the right as one enters. This lies between the new mosque and the gate of the bridge. We had the privilege of visiting his tomb and of praying in his mosque, and to God Most High be the praise. There too is the hill of Yūnus (upon
whom | be peace) and at about a mile from it the spring 137
called by his name.[273] It is said that he commanded his followers to purify themselves at it, after which they ascended the hill and he prayed, and they with him, whereupon God averted the chastisement [of the city] from them. In its vicinity is a large village, near which is a ruined site said to be the site of the city known as Nīnaway [Nineveh], the city of Yūnus (upon whom be peace). The remains of the encircling wall are still visible, and the positions of the gates which were in it are clearly seen. On the hill there is a large edifice and a convent with numerous chambers, cells, lavatories and water-channels, the whole being enclosed by a single gate. In the centre of the convent is a chamber over which there is a silk curtain, and with a door inlaid [with precious metals]. It is said that this was the place on which Yūnus (on whom be peace) stood [when he prayed], and the miḥrāb of the mosque in this convent is said to have been the cell in which he per-
formed his devotions (peace be upon him). The inhabitants | of 138
al-Mawṣil come out to this convent on the eve of every Friday to perform their devotions in it. They are distinguished by

[271] For the *qaisarīya* or main bazaar see vol. I, p. 97, n. 115.

[272] The mausoleum of Jirjīs (St George) is still preserved, in the quarter called after him Bāb al-Nabī ('Prophet's Gate'); see F. Sarre and E. Herzfeld, II, 236–8.

[273] The sanctuary of Jonah is prominently situated (on the site of an older Christian sanctuary) on a hill east of the Tigris (probably the remains of the ziggurat of Nineveh), formerly called Tell Tawba ('the hill of repentance'); al-Harawī, 70; trans., 156. The surrounding village is now known as Nabī Yūnus. The spring still exists, on the outer side of the second eastern rampart of Nineveh (al-Harawī, trans., 156, n. 4); in Ibn Jubair's time there was a mosque adjoining it.

noble and generous dispositions, gentleness of speech, virtue, affection for the stranger and care for him.

The governor of the city at the time of my visit to it was the virtuous Sayyid and Sharīf 'Alā al-Dīn 'Alī, son of Shams al-Dīn Muḥammad, known by the sobriquet of Ḥaidar, and a man of generosity and distinction.[274] He lodged me in his own dwelling and paid for all my expenses and maintenance during the period of my stay with him. He has to his credit many benefactions and famous acts of munificence, and the sultan Abū Sa'īd used to hold him in high honour, and set him in authority over this city and its dependencies.[275] He rides out in an impressive cavalcade of his mamlūks and troops, and the leading men of the city and principal citizens come to salute him in the morning and the evening. He is a man of courage and one who inspires respect. His son, at the time of writing this, is in the royal city of Fez, the place of settlement of strangers, asylum of the dispersed, goal of the
139 homagers—God increases her | in glory and splendour by the felicity of the days of our Master, the Commander of the Faithful [i.e. Sultan Abū 'Inān], and guard her regions and her provinces!

We then set out from al-Mawṣil and halted at a village called 'Ain al-Raṣad,[276] on a river over which there is a permanent bridge, and where there is a large khān. Journeying on, we halted at a village called al-Muwailiḥa, and from there alighted at Jazīrat Ibn 'Omar, a large and beautiful city surrounded by the river [Tigris], which is the reason why it is called Jazira ['island'].[277] The greater part of it is in ruins. It has a good bazaar and an ancient mosque, built of stone and

[274] Perhaps to be identified with Malik 'Alī b. Muḥammad-Shāh b. Malik Pahlawān, of the Rawwādī Kurdish family of Mimlān, formerly atābegs of Tabrīz (*Letters of Rashīd al-Dīn*, 128–9).

[275] Reading *mā ilaihā* with three MSS.; see Dozy, s.v. ilā.

[276] Located by Ibn Jubair less than a day's journey from Moṣul, with al-Muwailiḥa half a day's journey further on. 'Ain al-Raṣad is probably therefore to be identified with Kizlek Köprü, 25 miles north-west of Mosul, and al-Muwailiḥa more tentatively in the vicinity of Tell Uwaināt, 22 miles north-west of Kizlek Köprü.

[277] Cizre on Turkish maps, 90 miles north-west of Moṣul; see *E.I.*, s.v., and Le Strange, *Lands*, 93–4. In place of this, Ibn Jubair has a village called Judāl, one stage from al-Muwailiḥa and one day's journey from Naṣībīn.

of solid workmanship, and the city wall also is built of stone. Its inhabitants are of upright character and friendly towards strangers. On the day that we stayed there we saw Jabal al-Jūdī, which is mentioned in the Book of God as that on which there came to rest the ship of Noah (on him be peace); it is a lofty and high-soaring mountain.[278]

We travelled on two stages from there | and reached the 140
city of Naṣībīn, which is an ancient city of middling size, most of it now fallen into ruin.[279] It is situated in a wide and open plain, in which there are flowing streams, thickly planted orchards, trees ranged in order and abundance of fruits. In this town there is manufactured a rose-water which is unequalled for perfume and sweetness. Round it there runs like a bracelet a river which wells out from springs in a mountain close by and is divided into several channels, so that it threads through its orchards. One branch of it enters the town, flows through the streets and dwellings, cuts through the court of its principal mosque, and empties into two basins, one of them in the middle of the court [of the mosque] and the other at the east gate. In this city there is a hospital and two colleges, and its inhabitants are upright, pious, sincere and trustworthy. Abū Nuwās[280] spoke truly in saying: |

Pleasant to me was Naṣībīn once on a day, and I to her— 141
Would that my lot in this world were Naṣībīn.

Ibn Juzayy remarks: People characterize the city of Naṣībīn by badness of water and unhealthy climate,[281] and on this one of the poets has said:

[278] Sūra, xi. 46. The sentence is quoted from Ibn Jubair's account of his stay at Judāl. Jabal Jūdī (Cudi daği on Turkish maps) is a range 25 miles east of Jazīrat ibn 'Omar, rising to over 6,000 feet, backed by a higher range to the north-east rising to over 12,000 feet. For the Mesopotamian background of this identification with the site of Noah's ark, see *E.I.*, s.v. Djūdī.

[279] Sixty miles west of Jazīrat ibn 'Omar. The paragraph is abridged from Ibn Jubair, who also quotes the verses of Abū Nuwās.

[280] See vol. I, p. 61, n. 195. The point of the verses is the play on the name of the city and the Arabic word *naṣībī*, 'my share').

[281] The unwholesome climate and water of Naṣībīn are remarked also by Max von Oppenheim, *Vom Mittelmeer zum Persischen Golf* (Berlin, 1900), II, 36. Mustawfī (trans., 105) states that its roses are 'the finest throughout all the lands of Īrān'.

How strange that thing in Naṣībīn
Which seems all ailments to invite!
Never red rose in her is seen,
And even cheeks are deathly white.

Thereafter we travelled to the city of Sinjār,[282] which is a large town with an abundance of fruits and trees, and permanent springs and streams, built at the foot of a mountain, and resembling Damascus in the number of its streams and gardens. Its cathedral mosque is a famous place of blessing; it is stated that prayer made in it is answered, and it is encircled and traversed by a running stream. The inhabitants of Sinjār are Kurds, and are brave and generous. One of those
142 whom | I met there was a pious shaikh and devotee, the ascetic 'Abdallāh al-Kurdī, one of the great shaikhs and endowed with miraculous powers. It is stated of him that he eats only after fasting for forty days, and then breaks his fast only with half a cake of barley bread. I met him in a hermitage on top of the mountain of Sinjār,[283] when he prayed on my behalf and provided me with some silver pieces which I kept in my possession until I was despoiled by the Indian infidels.

We travelled from there to the city of Dārā, which is an ancient and large place, white in appearance, and with an imposing castle, but now in ruins and totally uninhabited.[284] Outside it there is an inhabited village in which we made our stay. Journeying on from there we came to the city of Mārdīn, a great city at the foot of a hill, one of the most beautiful, striking and substantially-built cities in [the lands

[282] This is obviously misplaced, as the next place mentioned, Dārā, lay about 15 miles north-west of Naṣībīn. Sinjār (Balad) lies at the foot of a low range 80 miles west of Moṣul: see Le Strange, *Lands*, 98; Sarre and Herzfeld, I, 202–4; II, 307 ff.

[283] Al-Harawī (trans., 142) mentions a sanctuary 'at the top of Sinjār' associated with 'Alī b. Abī Ṭālib; it was destroyed during the Mongol invasion, but later rebuilt.

[284] Dārā was the great frontier fortress of Byzantium against Sasanid Persia, and Ibn Baṭṭūṭa correctly describes it as completely ruined. See al-Harawī, trans., 143, n. 8; E. Sachau, *Reise in Syrien und Mesopotamien* (Leipzig, 1183), 395–8. As its buildings were of black stone (*Bibl. Geog. Arab.*, III, 140), his (and Ibn Jubair's) adjective 'white' is perhaps to be taken as 'glistening'.

of] Islam, | and with the finest bazaars.[285] Here there are manufactured the fabrics called by its name from the wool known as *mar'izz* [i.e. goat's hair]. It has a soaring castle, one of the most famous fortresses, on the summit of its hill. 143

Ibn Juzayy remarks: This castle of Mardīn is called al-Shahbā', and it is to it that the poet of al-'Irāq, Ṣafī al-Dīn 'Abd al-'Azīz b. Sarāyā al-Ḥillī[286] refers in his stanza:

> Leave wide-bosomed Ḥilla's halls,
> Skew the camels from Zawrā',
> Halt not in hunched Moṣul's walls,
> Lo, the lightning of Shahbā'
> Sears the demon of time's haps. |

The fortress of Aleppo also is called al-Shahbā'. This poem in stanza form is a gem, composed as a panegyric of al-Malik al-Manṣūr, the sultan of Mārdīn.[287] He was a generous [prince] and widely famed; he ruled in it for some fifty years, survived to the reign of Qāzān, king of the Tatars, and became allied by marriage to the sultan Khudhābandah through [the marriage of the latter to] his daughter Dunyā Khātūn.[288] 144

Account of the Sultan of Mārdīn at the time of my visit. He is al-Malik al-Ṣāliḥ, son of al-Malik al-Manṣūr (whom we have just now mentioned), and inherited the kingdom from his father. He is a man of widely famed generosity; there is none more open-handed than he in the land of al-'Irāq, Syria and Egypt; and poets and poor brethren come to visit him and he makes them munificent gifts, following the example of his father. He was visited by Abū 'Abdallāh Muḥammad b. Jābir al-Andalusī al-Marwī, the blind [poet], to recite a

[285] One of the most famous fortresses in Western Asia, which even the Mongols and Timur were unable to storm: see generally *E.I.*, s.v.; Sachau, 404–7.

[286] The most famous 'Irāqī poet of the time, d. 1349. The stanza is built on the poetical names for al-Ḥilla (*al-Faiḥā'*), Baghdād (*al-Zawrā'*, see vol. I, p. 121, n. 193), Moṣul (*al-Ḥadbā'*, see above, p. 348), and *al-Shahbā'*. For the similarly-named citadel of Aleppo, see vol. I, p. 95.

[287] Ghāzī b. Qarā Arslān, of the Artuqid dynasty (see *E.I.*[2], s.v. Artukids), d. 1312, succeeded by his son Shams al-Dīn Ṣāliḥ (after the death of the latter's brother), reigned 1312–64: *Durar*, III, 216–17; II, 202. Al-Malik al-Ṣāliḥ also is eulogized in a number of poems by Ṣafī al-Dīn al-Ḥillī.

[288] See above, p. 337.

panegyric, and gave him twenty thousand dirhams. To his
145 credit [also] are works of charity, | colleges, and hospices for the supply of food. He has a vizier of high distinction, namely the learned imām, unique scholar of the time, and solitaire of the age, Jamāl al-Dīn al-Sinjārī; he studied in the city of Tabrīz and under the great scholars [of the past generation]. His Grand Qāḍī is the accomplished imām Burhān al-Dīn al-Mawṣilī, who claims descent from the shaikh and saint Fatḥ al-Mawṣilī.[289] This qāḍī is a man of sound religion, scrupulosity and virtue; he dresses in coarse garments of woollen cloth, which are not worth ten dirhams apiece, and wears a turban of the same kind. He often holds his judicial sessions in the courtyard of a mosque, outside the college, in which he used to perform his devotions; and anyone seeing him who did not know him would think him to be one of the qāḍī's servants or assistants.

Anecdote. It was told me that a certain woman came up to
146 this qāḍī as he was coming out | of the mosque, and not knowing him she said to him 'O shaikh, where is the qāḍī sitting?' He said to her 'What do you want of him?' She replied 'My husband has beaten me, and, besides, he has another wife and does not make a fair division [of time] between us. I have summoned him before the qāḍī, but he has refused, and I am a poor woman and have nothing that I can give to the qāḍī's men so that they may bring him to his tribunal.' He said to her 'And where is your husband living?' She replied 'In the village of al-Mallāḥīn, outside the town.' Then he said to her 'I shall go with you to him myself,' and when she exclaimed 'But truly, by God, I have nothing that I can give you' he said 'And I would not take anything from you in any case,' then added 'Go on [ahead] to the village and wait for me outside it, for I shall be following you.' So she went on as he had ordered her, and waited for him, and he came up to her there, having no one at all with him, for it was his habit never to allow anyone to follow him. She brought him then to the house of her husband, who, on seeing him
147 said to her, 'What is this ill-favoured shaikh | who is accompanying you?' Then the qāḍī said 'Indeed, by God, I am so, but give satisfaction to your wife.' When the argument grew

[289] None of these persons has been identified.

prolonged, other people came up and, recognizing the qāḍī, saluted him. The man was overcome with fear and confusion, but the qāḍī said to him, 'Don't be upset. Put your affair with your wife to rights,' so the man gave her satisfaction and the qāḍī gave them enough for their needs that day and went off. I met this qāḍī and he gave me hospitality in his house.

I then set out to return to Baghdād, and on reaching the city of al-Mawṣil, which we have mentioned above, I found its pilgrim caravan outside the town, proceeding to Baghdād. Among them was a pious woman devotee called the Sitt Zāhida, a descendant of the Caliphs, who had gone on pilgrimage many times and used to fast assiduously. I saluted her and placed myself under her protection. She had with her a troop of poor brethren who were in her service. On this
journey | she died (God have mercy on her); her death took 148
place at Zarūd[290] and she was buried there.

When we arrived at Baghdād I found the pilgrims making preparations to set out, so I sought out its governor, Ma'rūf Khwāja, and asked him for the things that the sultan had ordered for me. He assigned me the half of a camel-litter and provisions and water for four men, writing out an order to that effect for me, then sent for the commander of the pilgrim caravan, who was the Bahlawān Muḥammad al-Ḥawīḥ,[291] and commended me to him. I already had an acquaintance with the latter which went back [to my journey from Mecca], but our friendship was strengthened by this and I remained under his protection and favoured by his bounty, for he gave me even more than had been ordered for me. As we left al-Kūfa I fell ill of a diarrhoea and they had to dismount me from the litter many times during the day; [during all this time] the commander [of the caravan] kept enquiring for me and giving instructions that I should be looked after. My illness continued until after I reached
Mecca, the sanctuary of God Most High | (may He exalt her 149
in honour and veneration). I made the [prescribed] circuits of the Holy House (God Most High ennoble it) on arrival, but I was so weak that I had to carry out the ordinances seated, so

[290] See vol. I, p. 253.
[291] See vol. I, p. 249, and below, p. 359, n. 310.

I made the circuits and the trottings between al-Ṣafā and al-Marwa[292] riding on the horse of the amīr al-Ḥawīḥ mentioned above.

We made the 'Standing' [at 'Arafāt] that year on a Monday,[293] and when we camped at Minā I began to feel relief and to recover from my malady. At the end of the Pilgrimage I remained as a 'sojourner' at Mecca [for the whole of] that year. In it [during this year] was the amīr 'Alā al-Dīn b. Hilāl, the inspector of the *dīwāns*, who was residing there for the construction of the hall of ablutions outside the druggists' [bazaar] by the gate of the Banū Shaiba.[294] In that same year there were among the Egyptians who 'sojourned' at Mecca a number of persons of note, including Tāj al-Dīn Ibn al-
150 Kuwaik, Nūr al-Dīn | the qāḍī, Zain al-Dīn Ibn al-Aṣīl, Ibn al-Khalīlī, and Nasir al-Din al-Asyuṭī.[295] I stayed that year in the Muẓaffariya College, and God healed me of my sickness. I led a most agreeable existence, giving myself up to circuits, pious exercises and frequent performances of the Lesser Pilgrimage.[296]

In the course of that year there arrived the pilgrims by way of Upper Egypt; with them came the pious shaikh Najm al-Dīn al-Uṣfūnī (this was the first of his Pilgrimages), the brothers 'Alā al-Dīn 'Alī and Sirāj al-Dīn 'Omar, sons of the pious shaikh Najm al-Dīn al-Bālisī, qāḍī of Cairo,[297] and a number of other persons. In the middle of Dhu'l-Qa'da there arrived the amīr Saif al-Dīn Yalmalak,[298] a man of eminent virtue, and in company with a number of the inhabitants of

[292] See vol. I, pp. 197–8, 205.

[293] For the 'Standing' at 'Arafāt see vol. I, p. 244, n. 78. The date in 727 was Monday, 26 October 1327.

[294] See vol. I, p. 206.

[295] Ibn al-Kuwaik is presumably Sirāj al-Dīn 'Abd al-Laṭīf b. Aḥmad al-Takrītī (1261–1334), a wealthy merchant of Alexandria, and the ancestor of a noted family of scholars: *Durar*, II, 405; IV, 24–5. Ibn al-Khalīl is 'Abdallāh b. Muḥammad b. Abū Bakr (d. 1375), a descendant of the caliph 'Othmān: *Durar*, II, 291; *Manhal*, no. 1336. The qāḍī Nūr al-Dīn is 'Alī b. 'Abd al-Nāṣir al-Sakhāwī (d. 1349), Mālikite Grand Qāḍī: *Durar*, III, 79; *Manhal*, no. 1596.

[296] For the Lesser Pilgrimage or '*Umra*, see vol. I, pp. 209, 234–5.

[297] Najm al-Dīn 'Abd al-Raḥmān b. Yūsuf (d. 1350), a noted devotee: *Durar*, II, 350, and cf. vol. I, p. 221. The qāḍī Najm al-Dīn is Muḥammad b. 'Oqail al-Bālisī (1262–1329), deputy of the Grand Qāḍī al-Qazwīnī (see vol. I, p. 132, n. 235); *Durar*, IV, 50.

[298] See vol. I., pp. 30–1.

Ṭanja, my own [native] town | (God guard her), including the 151
legist Abū 'Abdallāh Muḥammad, son of the qāḍī Abu'l-'Abbās, son of the qāḍī and khaṭīb Abu'l-Qāsim al-Jurāwī [?]; the legist Abū 'Abdallāh b. 'Aṭā'-Allāh; the legist Abū 'Abdallāh al-Ḥaḍarī; the legist Abū 'Abdallāh al-Mursī; Abu'l-'Abbās, son of the legist [v.l. qāḍī] Abū 'Alī al-Balansī; Abū Muḥammad b. al-Qābila; Abu'l-Ḥasan al-Biyārī; Abu'l-'Abbās b. Tāfūt; Abu'l-Ṣabr Ayyūb al-Fakhkhār ['the potter']; and Aḥmad b. Ḥakkāma. [There were also] of the inhabitants of Qaṣr al-Majāz the legist Abū Zaid 'Abd al-Raḥmān, son of the qādī Abu'l-'Abbās b. Khulūf, and of the inhabitants of al-Qaṣr al-Kabīr the legist Abū Muḥammad b. |
Muslim, Abū Isḥāq [v.l. Isḥāq b.] Ibrāhīm b. Yaḥyā, and his 152
son. There came also in the same year the amīr Saif al-Dīn Ṭuquzdumur, one of the Private Guard,[299] the amīr Mūsā b. Qaramān,[300] the qāḍī Fakhr al-Dīn,[301] inspector of the army and clerk of the mamlūks, al-Tāj Abū Isḥāq, and the Lady Ḥadaq,[302] the nurse of al-Malik al-Nāṣir. They distributed alms to all and sundry in the Holy Sanctuary, and the most liberal of them all in almsgiving was the qāḍī Fakhr al-Dīn.

Our 'Standing' [at 'Arafāt] took place that year on a Friday, of the year [seven hundred and] twenty-eight,[303] and at the conclusion of the Pilgrimage I remained as a 'sojourner' at Mecca (God Most High guard her) during the year twenty nine. In this year there arrived Aḥmad, son of the amīr Rumaitha, and Mubārak, son of the amir 'Uṭaifa, coming from al-'Irāq in company with | the amīr Muḥammad 153

[299] Ṭuquzdumur (d. 1345), twice son-in-law of al-Malik al-Nāṣir; *Durar*, II, 225' His pilgrimage in 1328 is confirmed in the Egyptian sources: Zetterstéen, 179.

[300] Bahā al-Dīn Mūsā, brother of Badr al-Dīn Maḥmūd, prince of Qaramān (see below, p. 432); his pilgrimage is mentioned also (but without date) by al-'Omarī (*Bericht über Anatolien*, ed. F. Taeschner (Leipzig, 1929), 29–30).

[301] 'Abdallāh b. Muḥammad (*c.* 1271–1333); he was responsible for certifying the construction work carried out by 'Alā al-Dīn on the aqueduct at Mecca in this year; *Durar*, II, 295.

[302] Tāj al-Dīn Abū Isḥāq has not been identified. The Lady Ḥadaq was the controller of al-Malik al-Nāṣir's *ḥarīm*; *Durar*, II, 7, where it is added that on this Pilgrimage 'she became proverbial for the amount of charity she distributed'.

[303] Friday, 14 October 1328, confirmed by *Chron. der Stadt Mekka*, II, 279.

al-Ḥawīḥ,[304] also the Shaikh Zāda al-Ḥarbāwī, and the shaikh Dāniyāl.[305] They brought large gifts of alms for the 'sojourners' and the inhabitants of Mecca on behalf of the sultan Abū Sa'īd, the king of al-'Irāq. In that year his name was included in the *khuṭba* after the name of al-Malik al-Nāṣir;[306] they also prayed for a blessing on him from the top of the pavilion of Zamzam; and after his name was mentioned that of the sultan of al-Yaman, al-Malik al-Mujāhid Nūr al-Dīn.[307] The amīr 'Uṭaifa was not in agreement with this, and sent his full brother Manṣūr to inform al-Malik al-Nāṣir of it, but Rumaitha ordered that Manṣūr should be brought back, and brought back he was. 'Uṭaifa sent him again by way of Judda, so that he finally did inform al-Malik al-Nāṣir of what had taken place.

We made the 'Standing' that year, i.e. twenty-nine, on a Tuesday[308] and at the end of the Pilgrimage I stayed on as a 'sojourner' at Mecca (God guard her) for the year thirty. During the pilgrimage season of that year there befel an
154 armed conflict between the amīr | of Mecca, 'Uṭaifa, and Āydumūr, the amīr jandār, [called] al-Nāṣirī.[309] The cause of this was that certain merchants among the Yamanites had goods stolen and complained about it to Āydumūr. Āydumūr said to Mubārak, the son of the amīr 'Uṭaifa, 'Produce these thieves.' He replied 'I have no knowledge of them, so how can I produce them? Moreover the people of al-Yaman are under our rule, and you have no authority over them. If anything is stolen from the people of Syria or Egypt, *then* demand restitution from me.' Whereupon Āydumūr shouted abuse at him, said to him 'You pimp, do you speak to me like this?' and struck him on the chest, so that he fell and his turban fell off his head. Mubārak was enraged, and his slaves equally so on his behalf; and when Āydumūr rode off to join

[304] For Rumaitha and 'Uṭaifa, amīrs of Mecca, see vol. I, 214–15; and for Muḥammad al-Ḥawīḥ above, p. 355.

[305] Dāniyāl b. 'Alī b. Yaḥyā al-Luristānī was one of the principal Persian shaikhs in Mecca and had been the Amīr Choban's agent for the restoration of the Lady Zubaida's aqueduct (see above, p. 340); *Chron. der Stadt Mekka*, II, 128.

[306] See vol. I, p. 248, where Ibn Baṭṭūṭa dates this in the previous year.

[307] See below, p. 369.

[308] Tuesday, 3 October 1329.

[309] This is an error for Saif al-Dīn Aldumur (see the following note).

his troops, Mubārak and his slaves overtook him, killed him, and killed his son as well.[310] Conflict then broke out in the sanctuary, where Amīr Aḥmad, uncle's son of al-Malik al-Nāṣir, was, and the Turks shot arrows and killed a woman who, it was said, | was egging the Meccans on to [join in] the 155
fighting. All of the Turks who were in the pilgrim caravan mounted their horses, as well as their commander Khāṣṣ Turk, but the qāḍī with the imāms and the 'sojourners' went out to them, carrying copies of the Qur'ān over their heads, and were able to make peace. The pilgrims went into Mecca, took what they possessed there, and returned to Egypt.

When the news of this reached al-Malik al-Nāṣir, he was cut to the quick and sent troops to Mecca. The amīr 'Uṭaifa and his son Mubārak took to flight, while his brother Rumaitha with his sons went out to Wādī Nakhla.[311] When the [Egyptian] troops arrived at Mecca, the amīr Rumaitha sent one of his sons to beg for a safe-conduct for himself and sons. They were granted this, whereupon Rumaitha came, carrying his shroud in his hand, before the commander.[312] He was given a robe of honour, Mecca was handed over to him, and the army returned to Cairo. Al-Malik al-Nāṣir (God's mercy on him) was a forbearing and generous-minded man.

[310] The murder of Aldumur and his son Khalīl on the day of the Festival is confirmed by *Durar*, I, 407 and several other sources. Two first-hand reports of the riot and massacre in the Sanctuary are contained in *Chron. der Stadt Mekka*, II, 279–80. According to al-Maqrīzī (*Al-Sulūk fi duwal al-Mulūk*, ed. M. M. Ziada (Cairo, 1942), II, pt. 2, 323–4), the conflict arose from orders sent by al-Malik al-Nāṣir to the amīr 'Uṭaifa to kill the leader of the 'Irāqī caravan, 'a man of Tabrīz called Muḥammad al-Ḥajīj' (evidently the same person as Ibn Baṭṭūṭa's Muḥammad al-Ḥawīḥ).

[311] See vol. I, p. 214, n. 111.

[312] According to the Mamlūk chronicle (Zetterstéen, 182) this detachment, commanded by Āytamush al-Ashrafī (*Durar*, I, 424), left Cairo at the end of November 1330. Ibn Baṭṭūṭa's statement is consequently not a first-hand account.

CHAPTER VII

Southern Arabia, East Africa and the Persian Gulf

156 I SET out at this time from Mecca (God Most High ennoble her) intending to travel to the land of al-Yaman, and came to Hadda,[1] which lies half way between Mecca and Judda. I then reached Judda, an old town on the sea coast, which is said to have been founded by the Persians.[2] Outside it there are antique cisterns, and in it are pits for water, bored in the solid rock and connected with each other in numbers beyond computation.[3] This year was one of little rain, so water was brought to Judda from the distance of a day's journey, and the pilgrims used to beg for water from the owners of the houses.

Anecdote. A strange thing happened to me in Judda. There stopped at my door a blind beggar led by a boy, to ask for
157 water. He saluted me, called me by my name | and took me by the hand, although I had no acquaintance with him, nor did he know me. I was astonished at his doing so; but next he grasped my finger with his hand and said 'Where is the *fatkha*?' (meaning the ring). Now, as I was going out from Mecca, I had been accosted by a certain poor brother, who asked me for alms, and as I had nothing with me at that time I handed him my ring. So when this blind man asked about it, I told him that I had given it to a poor brother, and he

[1] Eighteen miles west of Mecca, where the Judda road crosses the Wādī Fāṭima. For this name and that of the neighbouring Rutba, see Ibn al-Mujāwir, *Descriptio Arabiae Meridionalis*, ed. O. Löfgren (Leiden, 1951), I, 41.

[2] Ibn al-Mujāwir (I, 43–6) gives an account of the occupation and fortification of Judda (as the Arabic authors always write the name) by Persians after the destruction of Sīrāf (see below, p. 407, n. 138), and their later ejection by the local Arabs. Old Judda was about 10 m. S. of the present city.

[3] Cf. Ibn Jubair, 76; trans. Broadhurst, 71. Ibn al-Mujāwir gives a list of cisterns (I, 43–4).

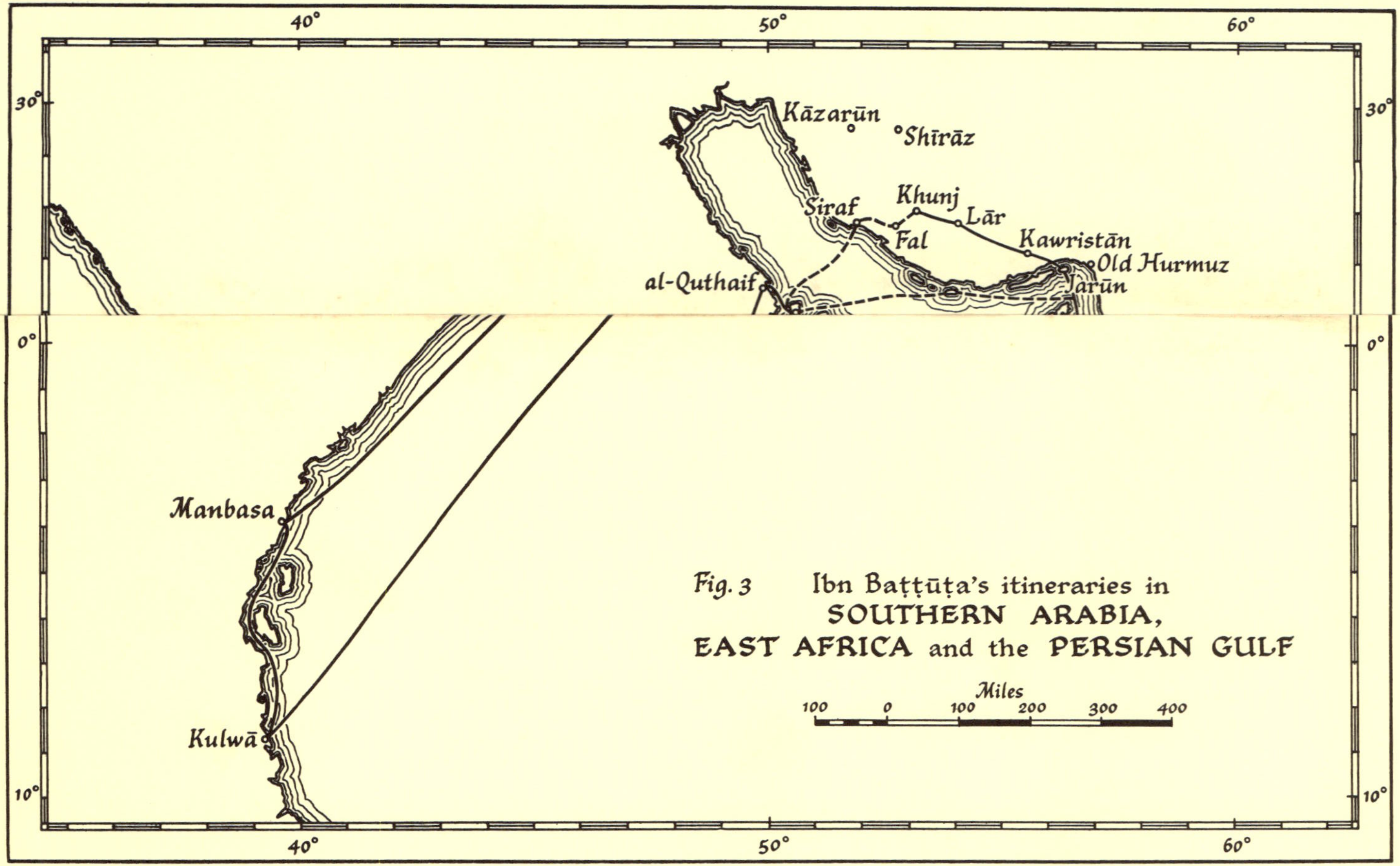

Fig. 3 Ibn Baṭṭūṭa's itineraries in SOUTHERN ARABIA, EAST AFRICA and the PERSIAN GULF

said 'Go back and look for it, for there are names written on it which contain a great secret.' Great was my astonishment at him and at his knowledge of all this—God knows best who and what he was.

In Judda there is a cathedral mosque called the Ebony Mosque,[4] known for its blessed power and in which prayer is answered. The governor in the city was Abū Ya'qūb b. 'Abd al-Razzāq, and its qāḍī and khaṭīb was the legist 'Abdallāh, a man from Mecca and a Shāfi'ite in rite. On Fridays, | when 158 the people assemble for the service, the muezzin comes and counts the number of residents of Judda at it. If they reach a total of forty, he holds the Friday *khuṭba* and prays with them, but if their number falls short of forty he prays a noon-prayer with four bowings, and no account is taken of those present who are not inhabitants of the town, however many they may be.[5]

We then embarked from Judda on a vessel that they call a *jalba*,[6] which belonged to Rashīd al-Dīn al-Alfī of al-Yaman, and of Abyssinia by origin. The sharīf Manṣūr b. Abū Numayy[7] embarked on another *jalba* and desired me to accompany him, but I did not do so on account of there being a number of camels with him in his *jalba*, and I was frightened of this, never having travelled by sea before. There were there a number of men of al-Yaman, who had placed their provisions and goods in *jalbas*, in preparation for the voyage. |

Anecdote. When we got on board, the sharīf Manṣūr 159

[4] Ibn Jubair says more precisely 'a mosque with two pillars of ebony wood'. The building was variously attributed to the second Caliph, 'Omar, or to Hārūn al-Rashīd.

[5] According to the Shāfi'ite school of law, the congregational prayer on Fridays is not valid unless attended by a minimum of forty Muslims. The local rule was abnormal only in disregarding the 'foreigners'.

[6] The *jalba* is described by Ibn Jubair (70–1; trans. Broadhurst, 65) as a wooden vessel, the planks of which are sewn together with thread made from coconut fibre (*qunbār*), caulked with slivers of datepalm wood, and smeared with castor or shark oil. The same traveller sharply criticizes the avarice of the owners of these boats in overloading them with pilgrims. (Broadhurst renders the word as *jilabah*, for which I know no authority. The Persian form is *galabat*, and the word is reflected in the English 'jolly-boat'.) See Kindermann, '*Schiff' in Arabischen*, 19.

[7] For Abū Numayy, sharīf of Mecca 1254–1301, and his descendants see vol. I, p. 214, n. 114. This Manṣūr was the brother of the amīrs of Mecca as mentioned above, p. 358.

ordered one of his slaves to fetch him an *'adīla* (that is half a camel-load) of flour and a cruse of ghee, taking them from the *jalbas* of the men of al-Yaman. When the man brought them to him, the merchants came to me weeping, stated to me that inside that *'adīla* there were ten thousand dirhams of silver, and begged me to speak to him, to send it back and take another instead. So I went to him and spoke to him on the matter, saying, 'The merchants have something inside this *'adīla.*' He replied 'If it is an intoxicant, I shall not return it to them, but if it is anything else they shall have it.' They opened the sack then and found the dirhams, so he gave it back to them, saying to me 'If it had been 'Ajlān, he would not have given it back,' 'Ajlān being the son of his brother Rumaitha; he had about that time entered the house of a Damascus merchant who was intending to go to al-Yaman, |
160 and had made off with most of what was in it. 'Ajlān is the amīr of Mecca at the present time, and he has reformed his conduct and shown himself just and upright.[8]

We then travelled on this sea with a favouring wind for two days, but thereafter the wind changed and drove us off the course which we had intended. The waves of the sea entered in amongst us in the vessel, and the passengers fell grievously sick. We continued in stormy weather until we emerged at a roadstead called Ra's Dawā'ir, between 'Aidhāb and Sawākin.[9] We landed there and found on the shore a hut of reeds, shaped like a mosque, and inside a large number of ostrich egg-shells filled with water, so we drank from these and cooked [some food].

I saw in that roadstead a marvellous thing. This is a channel something like a river-bed [which fills with water] flowing out from the sea. The people there would take a length of cloth, holding it by its ends, and bring it out filled
161 with fish, each about a cubit long, | which they call by the

[8] See vol. I, pp. 214–15, nn. 114, 116.

[9] As this roadstead was only two days' journey from Sawākin, it may most probably be identified with Mersā Darūr, in lat. 19° 50′ N., 43 miles from Sawākin (*Red Sea and Gulf of Aden Pilot* (London, Admiralty, 1900), 144). Water has to be brought to the shore from half a mile inland. The tidal arm mentioned below is, however, more probably the donga formerly at Mersā Shaikh Bārūd (or Barghūt), 14 miles to the southward (*ibid.*, 145), now engulfed in Port Sudan.

name of *būrī*.[10] These people then cooked and broiled a large quantity of them. A party of the Bujāh came to meet us; these are the inhabitants of that land, black in colour, with yellow blankets for clothes, and they tie round their heads red bands as broad as a finger.[11] They are hardy and brave fighters, their weapons being lances and swords, and they have camels which they call *suhb*, and on which they ride with saddles. We hired camels from them and travelled with them through a desert country with many gazelles. The Bujāh do not eat them, so they are sociable with human beings and do not flee from them.

After two days' travelling we came to an encampment of Arabs known as Awlād Kāhil,[12] who are intermingled with the Bujāh and know their speech. On the same day we reached the island of Sawākin. It is about six miles off the coast,[13] and has neither water, nor cereal crops, nor trees. Water is brought to it in boats, and on it there are cisterns | in which 162
rainwater is collected. It is a large island, and in it is [to be had] the flesh of ostriches, gazelles and wild asses; its inhabitants have goats also in large numbers, together with milk products and ghee, which is exported from it to Mecca. Their cereal is *jurjūr*, a kind of coarse grained millet, which is also exported to Mecca.

Account of its Sultan. The sultan of the island of Sawākin at the time of my coming was the Sharīf Zaid b. Abū Numayy. His father was the amīr of Mecca, and his two brothers were its amīrs after the [death of the] latter, namely 'Uṭaifa and Rumaitha, who have been mentioned previously. It came into his possession through the Bujāh, because they are his maternal relatives, and he has with him an armed force of the Bujāh, the Awlād Kāhil, and the Juhaina Arabs.[14]

[10] See vol. I, p. 35, n. 97, but it is questionable whether the same fish is meant here.

[11] Most of these details have already been mentioned by Ibn Baṭṭūṭa; see vol. I, p. 69.

[12] Commonly known as Kawāhla. They are of mixed origin, but claim that their eponymous ancestor Kāhil was a son or grandson of Fāṭima. See further A. Paul, *A History of the Beja Tribes of the Sudan* (Cambridge, 1954), 75.

[13] Ibn Baṭṭūṭa's memory has betrayed him here. Sawākin is one of two small islands, close to the mainland and within an almost land-locked bay.

[14] Juhaina was a southern Arab or Himyarite tribe, to which most of the Arab tribes in the Sudan claim to belong: see *E.I.*, s.v.; H. A. MacMichael, *History of the Arabs in the Sudan* (Cambridge, 1922).

We took ship from the island of Sawākin, making for the land of al-Yaman. No sailing is done on this sea at night
163 because of the large number of rocks in it. | They travel on it only from sunrise to sunset, then anchor and disembark, and at dawn they mount into the ship again. They call the captain of the ship the *rubbān*, and he remains constantly in the bow of the vessel to warn the steersman of rocks, which they call *nabāt*.[15] Six days after leaving the island of Sawākin we reached the city of Ḥalī, which is known [also] by the name of [Ḥalī] Ibn Ya'qūb;[16] he was one of the sultans of al-Yaman, and an inhabitant of it in former times. It is large and well-built, and inhabited by two Arab tribes, the Banū Ḥarām[17] and the Banū Kināna.[18] The congregational mosque of this city is one of the most beautiful of mosques and contains a congregation of poor brethren who devote themselves exclusively to religious exercises.

Among those was the pious shaikh, the devotee and ascetic Qabūla al-Hindī, one of the greatest of saints. His garments |
164 consist of a patched robe and a felt hat. He has a cell adjacent to the mosque, floored with sand and without even a rush mat or a rug in it. I saw nothing in the cell when I went to visit him, except a jug for ablutions and a table-mat of palm fibre, on which were some dry pieces of barley-bread and a little dish containing salt and marjoram. When anyone comes to visit him, he offers this to him, and his associates, hearing of the visitor, come, each one bringing what he has at hand without going to any effort or expense. After they have observed the afternoon prayers, they assemble before the

[15] The *rubbān* is the pilot, not the shipmaster (*nākhuda*); the two are distinguished in several narratives; see e.g. G. F. Hourani, *Arab Seafaring* (Princeton, 1951), 117. The word *nabāt*, literally 'plants', is apparently a seamen's term for reefs.

[16] Properly Ḥaly (with consonantal *y*), a large town on the highroad from Ṣan'ā' to Mecca, some 30 miles inland and 40 miles south-east of Qunfuda, in a district sufficiently fertile to produce three crops a year. The 'Son of Ya'qūb' attached to its name seems to be unknown. The port of Ḥalī is a small sheltered anchorage in the district now called 'Asīr, at 18° 31′ N., 41° 19′ E. (*Red Sea Pilot*, 295).

[17] A major segment of the south-Arabian tribe of Nahd (al-Hamdānī, *Ṣifat Jazīrat al-'Arab*, ed. D. H. Müller (Leyden, 1884), 116).

[18] An important north-Arabian tribe occupying the coastal area. Ḥaly was rebuilt by one of them towards the end of the thirteenth century (Ibn al-Mujāwir, 53), presumably by the Dhuwaib mentioned below.

shaikh for the *dhikr* until the sunset prayers, and when they have observed these each one then takes up his place for supplementary prayers. They continue in this exercise until the last evening prayers, and when they have observed these, they resume recitation of the *dhikr* until the first third of the night [has elapsed]. Thereafter they withdrew, but they return to the mosque at the beginning of the third third | and 165
engage in supplementary night-prayers until dawn, when they engage in devotions until the hour of sunrise prayers, after which they retire, but there are some of them who remain in the mosque until they pray the forenoon prayers. This is their practice continually, and indeed I should have wished to remain with them for the rest of my life, but my desire was not fulfilled—may God Most High overtake us by His grace and furtherance.

Account of the Sultan of Ḥalī. Its sultan was 'Āmir b. Dhuwaib, of the Banū Kināna, a man of eminent virtue [as well as] a man of letters and a poet. I travelled in his company to Judda (we had already made the Pilgrimage in the year 30), and when I came to his city he assigned me a lodging as his guest for some days. I embarked on a ship of his and reached the township of al-Sarja,[19] | a small town 166
inhabited by a body of the Awlād al-Hibā.[20] These are a company of merchants of al-Yaman, most of whom are inhabitants of Ṣa'dā'. They are men of generosity and openhandedness, and [make a practice of] supplying food to wayfarers, and assist pilgrims, transporting them in their vessels and giving them provisions from their own funds. They are indeed noted and famed for this, and God has multiplied their wealth and given them increase of His bounty and aided them to their work of charity; there is not upon the earth any who compare with them in this respect, except the shaikh Badr al-Dīn al-Naqqās, who lives in the town of al-

[19] A place named Sarja is mentioned as a halt on the Ṣan'ā'-Mecca road, ten stations before Ḥaly (al-Hamdānī, 188), but Ibn Baṭṭūṭa's port of call was Sharja, a township of grass huts with an anchorage in the vicinity of Luḥayya (al-Qalqashandī, *Ṣubḥ al-A'shā* (Cairo, 1915), V, 14; al-Khazrajī, *History of the Resuliyy Dynasty of Yemen*, trans. J. M. Redhouse, (Leyden-London, 1906–8), III, 148).

[20] Presumably the descendants of the sharīf 'Izz al-Dīn Hibā b. Faḍl, established in the town of Ṣa'dā on its capture by the Rasūlid sultan in 1254 (al-Khazrajī, II, 138, 145).

Qaḥma,[21] and has to his credit similar acts of generosity and munificence.

We stayed at al-Sarja only one night, enjoying the hospitality of these merchants, then continued our journey to the roadstead of al-Ḥādith,[22] where we did not land, thence on to the roadstead of al-Ahwāb,[23] and then [rode] to the city of Zabīd, a great city in al-Yaman.[24] Between it and Ṣan'ā' is a distance of forty farsakhs, and after Ṣan'ā' there is no
167 [place] in al-Yaman that is larger than it nor | whose population is wealthier. It lies amid luxuriant gardens with many streams and fruits, such as bananas and others, and is in the interior, not on the coast, and one of the capital cities of al-Yaman. It is a great and populous city, and contains groves of palms, orchards and running streams—[in fact] the pleasantest and most beautiful town in al-Yaman. Its inhabitants are courteous in manners, upright in conduct, and handsome in figure, and its women are of exceeding and pre-eminent beauty. This is the 'vale of al-Ḥuṣaib' of which it is related in certain Traditions that the Apostle of God (God bless and give him peace) said to Mu'ādh in his admonition [to him]: 'O Mu'ādh, when you come to the vale of al-Ḥuṣaib, quicken your pace.'[25]

The people of this city hold the famous [junketings called] *subūt al-nakhl*[26] in this wise. They go out, during the season

[21] Not al-Qaḥma in 'Asīr (between Ḥaly and Jīzān), but a township 9 miles north of Zabīd (Ibn al-Mujāwir, 236; cf. al-Khazrajī, III, 90).

[22] No other reference to this place has been found.

[23] Described by Ibn al-Mujāwir as 'the port for shipping from 'Adan', and said to have been constructed by a Persian merchant in 1138. Its exact location is unknown. The major port of Zabīd was Ghulāfiqa, 25 miles north-west of the city (*Red Sea Pilot*, 337, writes Khor Ghuleifaka).

[24] Zabīd was throughout the mediaeval centuries the capital of lowland Yaman and the main citadel of Sunnism (of the Shāfi'ī school) against the Zaidī Shī'ism (see below, p. 368, n. 29) of the highlands, centred on Ṣan'ā'.

[25] Mu'ādh b. Jabal was sent by Muḥammad as a missionary to the Yaman in 631 (see vol. I, p. 83, n. 58). Al-Ḥuṣaib is identified with Zābid in all interpretations of this Tradition, which continues: 'for there are women there who resemble the black-eyed maidens of Paradise.' Hence Ibn Baṭṭūṭa's remark on their 'exceeding beauty'; Ibn al-Mujāwir (246), however, says: 'Never have I seen in all of al-Yaman, dale or hill, a pretty face for eyes to dwell upon, nor any elegance, delicacy, grace, or sweetness among them.'

[26] These, literally 'Palm Saturdays', were a well-known feature of the social life of Zabīd. Redhouse (al-Khazrajī, III, 186, 197) calls them 'a local Saturnalia', and suggests that this was a pagan custom deriving from pre-Islamic times. Ibn al-Mujāwir (78–9) discreetly confirms the description,

of the colouring and ripening of the dates, | to the palm- 168
groves on every Saturday. Not a soul remains in the town, whether of the townsfolk or of the strangers. The musicians go out [to entertain them] and the bazaar folk sell fruit and sweetmeats. The women go out riding on camels in litters. Together with the exceeding beauty that we have already mentioned, they are virtuous and generous in character, and they have a predilection for the stranger and do not refuse to marry him, as the women of our country do. When he wishes to travel, his wife goes out with him and bids him farewell; and if there should be a child between them, it is she who takes care of it and supplies what is needed for it until its father returns. During his absence she makes no demands on him for maintenance or clothes or anything else, and when he is resident she is content with little from him for upkeep and clothes; But the women never leave their own town and would not consent to do so even if one of them were offered any sum that might be offered to her on condition that she should
leave | her town. 169

The scholars and doctors of the law in this country are upright, pious, trustworthy, generous, and of fine character. I met in the city of Zabīd the learned and pious shaikh Abū Muḥammad al-Ṣan'ānī, the jurist and accomplished ṣūfī Abu'l-'Abbās al-Abyanī, and the jurist and traditionist Abū 'Alī al-Zabīdī.[27] I placed myself under their protection; they received me honourably, and showed me hospitality, and I went into their palm-groves. In the company of one of them I met the jurist and learned qāḍī Abū Zaid 'Abd al-Raḥmān al-Ṣūfī, one of the eminent men of al-Yaman. Mention happened to be made in his presence of the ascetic and humble devotee Aḥmad b. al-'Ojail al-Yamanī, who was one of the greatest of men and of those favoured with miraculous powers.[28]

but asserts that the establishment of the palm-groves goes back only to the eleventh or twelfth centuries.

[27] None of these scholars have been identified. Al-Ṣan'ānī means 'belonging to Ṣan'ā' '; al-Abyanī means 'belonging to Abyan' or 'Ibyan' (the region 30 m. east of 'Adan); al-Zabīdī, however, is probably to be read al-Zubaidī (cf. al-Khazrajī, V, 136).

[28] Aḥmad b. Mūsā b. 'Alī 'Ojail (1212–91) was one of the celebrated jurists of his time in Arabia; see al-Khazrajī, I, 221–2, who, however, describes his eminence only as a jurist and makes no allusion to his alleged miraculous powers as a saint.

A miraculous grace. They relate that the jurists and leading men of the Zaidīya came once on visitation to the shaikh Aḥmad b. al-'Ojail. He sat awaiting them outside the hospice,
170 and his associates went to meet them | but the shaikh himself did not budge from his place. After they had saluted him and he had shaken hands with them and bidden them welcome, a discussion arose between them on the question of predestination.[29] They maintained that there is no predestined decree and that the [creature who is made] responsible for carrying out the ordinances of God creates his own actions, whereupon the shaikh said to them: 'Well, if the matter is as you say, rise up from this place where you are.' They tried to rise up but could not, and the shaikh left them as they were and went into the hospice. They remained thus until, when the heat afflicted them sorely and the blaze of the sun smote them, they complained loudly of what had befallen them, then the shaikh's associates went in to him and said to him 'These men have repented to God and recanted their false doctrine.' The shaikh then went out to them and, taking them by their hand, he exacted a pledge from them to return to the truth and abandon their evil doctrine. He brought him into his hospice, where they remained as his guests for three nights,
171 and then returned to | their own towns.

I went out to visit the grave of this saintly man, which is in a village called Ghassāna, outside Zabīd, and met his pious son Abu'l-Walīd Ismā'īl.[30] He received me hospitably and I spent the night with him. After visiting the shaikh's tomb, I stayed three nights [more] with him and set out in company with him to visit the jurist Abu'l-Ḥasan al-Zaila'ī. He is one of the great saints and leads the pilgrims from al-Yaman when they go on the Pilgrimage.[31] The inhabitants of that country, and its bedouins as well, hold him in great esteem and veneration. We came to Jubla,[32] a small and pretty town

[29] For the Zaidīs see vol. I, p. 182, n. 103. They shared the doctrine of the Mu'tazilite (or philosophical) school in asserting the freedom of the human will.

[30] Al-Khazrajī (IV, 422) dates the death of Ismā'īl b. Aḥmad b. 'Ojail in 1317. The village of Ghassāna was already at this time known as Bait al-Faqīh ('the Jurist's residence'), and is still called by that name.

[31] 'Alī b. Abū Bakr b. Muḥammad (1260–1332), of Abyssinian origin; al-Khazrajī, V, 54.

[32] Not on the direct route from Zabīd to Ta'izz, but 75 miles east-south-

with palms, fruit-trees and streams, and when the jurist Abu'l-Ḥasan al-Zaila'ī heard of the arrival of the shaikh Abu'l-Walīd he came out to meet him and lodged him in his hospice. I saluted him together with the shaikh, and we en-enjoyed a most agreeable residence with him for three days. When we left he sent one of the poor brethren with us and we proceeded to | the city of Ta'izz, the capital of the king of al- 172
Yaman. It is one of the finest and largest of the cities of al-Yaman. Its people are overbearing, insolent and rude, as is generally the case in towns where kings have their seats. It is composed of three quarters; one of them is the residence of the sultan, his mamlūks and courtiers, and the officers of his government, and is called by a name that I do not remember; the second is inhabited by the amīrs and troops and is called 'Udaina; the third is inhabited by the common people and contains the principal bazaar, and it is called al-Mahālib.[33]

Account of the Sultan of al-Yaman. He is the sultan al-Mujāhid Nūr al-Dīn 'Alī, son of the sultan al-Mu'ayyad Hizabr al-Dīn Dā'ūd, son of the sultan al-Muẓaffar Yūsuf b. 'Alī b. Rasūl.[34] His ancestor became widely known by the apellation of *Rasūl* ['Envoy'] because one of the 'Abbāsid caliphs sent him to al-Yaman to be a governor there, and later on | his sons gained the royal power for themselves. He 173
has an elaborate ceremonial in his sitting [for public audience] and his riding out. When I came to this city with the poor brother whom the shaikh and jurist Abu'l-Ḥasan al-Zaila'ī had sent to accompany me, he had sought out with me the Grand Qāḍī, the imām and traditionist Ṣafī al-Dīn al-Ṭabarī of Mecca;[35] we saluted him, and he bade us welcome and we

east of Zabīd, 40 miles north of Ta'izz, and a few miles south of modern Ibb. It was formerly the capital of the Ismā'īlī Ṣulaiḥid dynasty in al-Yaman.

[33] The first quarter was apparently called al-Mu'izzīya (al-Khazrajī, III, 138). 'Udaina was at the foot of the citadel (Ibn al-Mujāwir, 233). A quarter called al-Maḥālib does not seem to be otherwise attested (al-Maḥālib was a town on the site of modern Zaidīya, three farsakhs north of Wādī Surdūd (Ibn al-Mujāwir, 58–63), 80 miles north of Zabīd); perhaps the name stands here for Bāb al-Maḥālib.

[34] For the Rasūlid dynasty see vol. I, p. 203. Al-Malik al-Mujāhid Nūr Dīn reigned 1321–63, with some intervals of dethronement and imprisonment. Al-Mujāhid is a title, not to be literally translated as 'the warlike'.

[35] For the Ṭabarī family of Mecca see vol. I, p. 216, n. 119. But this member of the family is unknown, and the Grand Qāḍī of Ta'izz who died in 1342 was Jamāl al-Dīn Muḥammad b. Yūsuf al-Ṣabrī (*Durar*, IV, 310).

stayed in his house as guests for three nights. On the fourth day, which was a Thursday, the day on which the sultan sits in audience for the general public, the qāḍī presented me to him and I saluted him. The method of saluting him is that one touches the ground with his index-finger, then raises it to the head and says 'May God prolong thy majesty.' I did as the qāḍī had done; the qāḍī took his seat to the king's right, and on his command I sat in front of him. He then questioned me about my country, about our Master, the Commander of Faithful, the prince of liberality, Abū Sa'īd (God be pleased with him), and about the king of Egypt, the king of al-'Irāq, |
174 and the king of the Lurs, and I answered all the questions that he asked concerning them. His vizier was in his presence, and the king commanded him to treat me honourably and arrange for my lodging.

The ceremonial at the [public] session of this king is as follows, He takes his seat on a platform carpeted and decorated with silken fabrics; to right and left of him are the men-at-arms, those nearest him holding swords and shields, and next to them the bowmen; in front of them to the right and left are the chamberlain and the officers of government and the private secretary. The amīr jandār is in attendance on him, and the shāwūshes, who form part of the corps of jandārs, are stationed at a distance.[36] When the sultan takes his seat they cry with one voice *Bismillāh*, and when he rises they do the same, so that all those in the audience-hall know the moment of his rising and the moment of his sitting. When he has settled in his seat, each one of those persons whose custom it is to salute him enters, makes his salutation, and stands in
175 the place appointed for him on | the right and on the left. No person goes beyond his place or sits down, except those who are bidden to sit. The sultan says to the amīr jandār 'Command so-and-so to sit down,' whereupon the person so commanded to sit advances a little way from his place and sits down on a carpet there in front of those standing on the right and the left. The food is then brought, and it is of two sorts, the food of the commons and the food of the high officers. The

[36] For the amīr jandār, i.e. captain of the bodyguard, see above, p. 343. *Shāwūsh*, from the Turkish *chawush*, means an usher, herald, or more especially a man-at-arms belonging to the bodyguard.

superior food is partaken of by the sultan, the grand qāḍī, the principal sharīfs and jurists and the guests; the common food eaten by the rest of the sharīfs, jurists and qāḍīs, the shaikhs, the amīrs and the officers of the troops. The seat of each person at the meal is fixed; he does not move from it, nor does anyone of them jostle another. On exactly this same pattern is the ceremonial of the king of India at his meal, but I do not know whether the sultans of India took it over from the sultans of al-Yaman or | the sultans of al-Yaman took it over 176
from the sultans of India.

After I had remained for some days as the guest of the sultan of al-Yaman, during which he treated me generously and provided me with a horse, I took leave to continue my journey to the city of Ṣan'ā'.[37] It is the former capital of the country of al-Yaman, a large and well-constructed city, built with bricks and plaster, with many trees and fruits, and with a temperate climate and good water. It is a curious thing that the rain in the lands of India, al-Yaman and Abyssinia falls during the period of summer heat, and mostly during the afternoon of every day in that season, so that travellers make haste when the sun begins to decline, to avoid being caught by rain, and the womenfolk retire to their dwellings, because these rains are heavy downpours.[38] The whole city of Ṣan'ā' is paved and when the rain falls it washes and cleans all its streets. | The cathedral mosque of Ṣan'ā' is one of the finest 177
of mosques, and contains the grave of one of the prophets (peace be upon them).

I travelled from there next to the city of 'Adan, the port of the land of al-Yaman, on the coast of the great sea. It is surrounded by mountains and there is no way into it except from one side only.[39] It is a large city, but has no crops, trees, or water, and has reservoirs in which water is collected during the rainy season.[40] This water is at some distance from it and

[37] Ṣan'ā' lies 130 miles north of Ta'izz in a direct line, and the journey to it from Ta'izz and back involves a considerable detour.

[38] Ibn al-Mujāwir (159) says, speaking of the region of Ta'izz: 'Every afternoon there blows up a cold and bracing wind, after which the sky becomes clouded over and rain falls for an hour or two, then the sky clears.'

[39] Aden is about 85 miles south-east of Ta'izz, and somewhat further by road. The stages are enumerated by Ibn al-Mujāwir (155).

[40] For the famous reservoirs of Aden, see *E.I.*², s.v.

the bedouins often cut off the approach to it and prevent the townsfolk from obtaining it until the latter buy their consent with money and pieces of cloth. It is an exceedingly hot place, and is the port of the merchants of India, to which come great vessels from Kinbāyat [Cambay], Tānah, Kawlam [Quilon], Qāliqūt, Fandaraina, al-Shāliyāt, Manjarūr [Mangalore], Fākanūr, Hinawr [Honavar], Sindābūr [Goa], and other places. The merchants of India live there, and the merchants of Egypt also. The inhabitants of 'Adan are either
178 merchants or porters or fishermen. | The merchants among them have enormous wealth;[41] sometimes a single man may possess a great ship with all it contains, no one sharing in it with him, because of the vast capital at his disposal, and there is ostentation and rivalry between them in this respect.

Anecdote.[42] It was told me that one of them sent a slaveboy of his to buy for him a ram, and another of them sent a slaveboy for the same purpose. It happened that there was only a single ram in the bazaar on that day, so there ensued a contest for it between the two slaves, bidding against one another, until its price rose to four hundred dinars. Then one of them got possession of it and said, 'The sum of my wealth is four hundred dinars, and if my master gives me its price, good and well, but if not, I shall pay out of my own capital for it, and I shall have vindicated myself and defeated my rival.' He went off with the ram to his master, and when the
179 latter learned what had happened he freed him | and gave him a thousand dinars. The other returned to his master empty-handed, and he beat him, took his money and drove him out of his service.

I lodged in 'Adan with a merchant called Nāṣir al-Dīn al-Fa'rī. There used to come to his table every night about

[41] For the range and commodities of trade at Aden, cf. *The Suma Oriental of Tomé Pires* (London, Hakluyt Society, 1944), I, 15–17. The Kārimī or spice merchants of Egypt and al-Yaman were famous: see G. Wiet, 'Les marchands d'épices sous les Sultans mamlouks' in *Cahiers d'Histoire égyptienne* (Cairo, 1955), VII/2, 81–147; W. J. Fischel, 'The spice trade in Mamlūk Egypt' in *Journal of the Economic and Social History of the Orient* (Leiden, 1958), I/2, 157–74.

[42] The same story, in largely similar terms but about a particular fish (*ḍairāk*), is told by Ibn al-Mujāwir (98) to illustrate the rivalry of the rich merchants of Sīrāf in al-Yaman.

twenty of the merchants, and he had slaves and servants in still larger numbers. Yet with all this, they are men of piety, humility, uprightness and generous qualities, doing good to the stranger, giving liberally to the poor brother, and paying God's due in tithes as the Law commands. I met [also] in this city its pious qāḍī Sālim b. 'Abdallāh al-Hindī; the father of this man had been a slave, employed as a porter, but the son devoted himself to learning and became a master and leader [in the religious sciences]. He is one of the best and worthiest of qāḍīs. I stayed as his guest for some days.

I travelled from the city of 'Adan by sea[43] for four days, and arrived | at the city of Zaila', the city of the Barbara,[44] 180
who are a people of the negroes,[45] Shāfi'ites in rite. Their country is a desert extending for two months' journey, beginning at Zaila' and ending at Maqdashaw. Their cattle are camels, and they also have sheep which are famed for their fat. The inhabitants of Zaila' are black in colour, and the majority of them are Rāfiḍīs.[46] It is a large city with a great bazaar, but it is in the dirtiest, most disagreeable, and most stinking town in the world. The reason for its stench is the quantity of its fish and the blood of the camels that they slaughter in the streets. When we arrived there we chose to spend the night at sea in spite of its extreme roughness, rather than pass a night in the town, because of its filth.

We sailed on from there for fifteen nights and came to

[43] In view of the probable date for Ibn Baṭṭūṭa's arrival at Mogadishu (see below, n. 49), the beginning of his voyage is most probably to be placed at or after mid-January 1330 [1328].

[44] Zaila', on a sandy spit on the Somali coast due south of Aden (see *Red Sea Pilot*, 472), was included at this time in the Ethiopian kingdom of Awfāt or Ifāt; al-'Omarī, *L'Afrique moins l'Egypt*, trans. M. G. Demombynes (Paris, 1927), 5. In Egypto-Arabic usage the Somali regions are commonly called Jabart.

By the term *Barbara* the Arabic geographers apparently mean the Hamitic tribes who are neither Abyssinian (*Ḥabash*) nor negroes (*Zinj*), and more especially the Somalis, although Ibn Baṭṭūṭa here includes them among the negroes; see L. M. Devic, *Le Pays des Zendjs* (Paris, 1883), 51–2. The term itself probably came into Arabic from Greek (cf. *Periplus of the Erythraean Sea*, ed. W. H. Schoff (New York, 1912), 22–6, 56) and is ultimately derived from ancient Egyptian usage.

[45] Arabic *zinj* or *zanj*, a term ultimately derived from Persian or Sanskrit, probably in the language of the seamen of the Persian Gulf.

[46] I.e., Shī'ites, probably of the Zaidī sect.

Maqdashaw, which is a town of enormous size.[47] Its inhabitants are merchants possessed of vast resources; they own
181 large numbers of camels, | of which they slaughter hundreds every day [for food], and also have quantities of sheep. In this place are manufactured the woven fabrics called after it, which are unequalled and exported from it to Egypt and elsewhere.[48] It is the custom of the people of this town that, when a vessel reaches the anchorage, the *sumbuqs*, which are small boats, come out to it.[49] In each *sumbuq* there are a number of young men of the town, each one of whom brings a covered platter containing food and presents it to one of the merchants on the ship saying 'This is my guest,' and each of the others does the same. The merchant, on disembarking, goes only to the house of his host among the young men, except those of them who have made frequent journeys to the town and have gained some acquaintance with its inhabitants; these lodge where they please. When he takes up
182 residence with his host, the latter sells his goods for him | and buys for him; and if anyone buys anything from him at too low a price or sells to him in the absence of his host, that sale is held invalid by them. This practice is a profitable one for them.

When the young men came on board the vessel in which I was, one of them came up to me. My companions said to him 'This man is not a merchant, but a doctor of the law,' whereupon he called out to his friends and said to them 'This is the guest of the qāḍī.' There was among them one of the qāḍī's men, who informed him of this, and he came down to the beach with a number of students and sent one of them to me. I then disembarked with my companions and saluted him and his party. He said to me 'In the name of God, let us go to salute the Shaikh.' 'And who is the Shaikh?' I said, and he

[47] Mogadishu was founded in the tenth century as a trading colony by Arabs from the Persian Gulf, the principal group being from al-Ḥasā. The fidelity of Ibn Baṭṭūṭa's account of this place is remarked by M. Guillain, *Documents sur . . . l'Afrique orientale* (Paris, 1856), I, 286–90; II, 531, 539.

[48] The continuing importance of the cotton industry at Mogadishu is confirmed by Guillain (II, 531).

[49] Guillain (II, 548–9) indicates that (before the creation of the new port) the violence of the north-east monsoon in December and January made communication with the coast at Mogadishu practicable only in September-October and in and after February. For *sumbuqs* see above, p. 280.

answered, 'The Sultan,' for it is their custom to call the sultan 'the Shaikh'. Then I said to him 'When I am lodged, I shall go to him,' but he said to me, 'It is the custom that whenever there comes a jurist | or a sharīf or a man of re- 183
ligion, he must first see the sultan before taking a lodging.' So I went with him to the sultan, as they asked.

Account of the Sultan of Maqdashaw.[50] The sultan of Maqdashaw is, as we have mentioned, called only by the title of 'the Shaikh'. His name is Abū Bakr, son of the shaikh 'Omar; he is by origin of the Barbara and he speaks in Maqdishī, but knows the Arabic language. One of his customs is that, when a vessel arrives, the sultan's *sumbuq* goes out to it, and enquiries are made as to the ship, whence it has come, who is its owner and its *rubbān* (that is, its captain), what is its cargo, and who has come on it of merchants and others. When all of this information has been collected, it is presented to the sultan, and if there are any persons [of such quality] that the sultan should assign a lodging to him as his guest, he does so.

When I arrived with the qāḍī I have mentioned, who was called Ibn al-Burhān, an Egyptian | by origin, at the sultan's 184
residence, one of the serving-boys came out and saluted the qāḍī, who said to him'Take word to the intendant's office and inform the Shaikh that this man has come from the land of al-Ḥijāz.' So he took the message, then returned bringing a plate on which were some leaves of betel and areca nuts. He gave me ten leaves along with a few of the nuts, the same to the qāḍī, and what was left on the plate to my companions and the qāḍī's students. He brought also a jug of rose-water of Damascus, which he poured over me and over the qāḍī [i.e. over our hands], and said 'Our master commands that he be lodged in the students' house,' this being a building equipped for the entertainment of students of religion. The qāḍī took me by the hand and we went to this house, which

[50] The various Arab tribes occupied different quarters in Mogadishu (hence presumably its expansion), but recognized the supremacy of the tribe of Muqrī, who called themselves Qaḥṭānīs, i.e. south-Arabians, and furnished the qāḍī of the city. The sultanate seems to have emerged only towards the end of the thirteenth century, and the most noted of its sultans was this Abū Bakr b. Fakhr al-Dīn (see *Enciclopedia Italiana*, s.v. Mogadiscio). From Ibn Baṭṭūṭa's statement it would appear that the population was by now largely assimilated to the Somalis.

is in the vicinity of the Shaikh's residence, and furnished with carpets and all necessary appointments. Later on [the serving boy] brought food from the Shaikh's residence. With him came one of his viziers, who was responsible for [the care of] the guests, and who said 'Our master greets you and says
185 to you that you are heartily welcome.' He then set down | the food and we ate. Their food is rice cooked with ghee, which they put into a large wooden platter, and on top of this they set platters of *kūshān*.[51] This is the seasoning, made of chickens, fleshmeat, fish and vegetables. They cook unripe bananas in fresh milk and put this in one dish, and in another dish they put curdled milk, on which they place [pieces of] pickled lemon, bunches of pickled pepper steeped in vinegar and salted, green ginger, and mangoes. These resemble apples, but have a stone; when ripe they are exceedingly sweet and are eaten like [other] fruit, but before ripening they are acid like lemons, and they pickle them in vinegar. When they take a mouthful of rice, they eat some of these salted and vinegar conserves after it. A single person of the people of Maqdashaw eats as much as a whole company of us
186 would eat, as a matter of habit, | and they are corpulent and fat in the extreme.

After we had eaten, the qāḍī took leave of us. We stayed there three days, food being brought to us three times a day, following their custom. On the fourth day, which was a Friday, the qāḍī and students and one of the Shaikh's viziers came to me, bringing a set of robes; these [official] robes of theirs consist of a silk wrapper which one ties round his waist in place of drawers (for they have no acquaintance with these), a tunic of Egyptian linen with an embroidered border, a furred mantle of Jerusalem stuff, and an Egyptian turban with an embroidered edge. They also brought robes for my companions suitable to their position. We went to the congregational mosque and made our prayers behind the *maqṣūra*.[52] When the Shaikh came out of the door of the

[51] *Kūshān* is probably a term of the Persian Gulf seamen for seasonings of meat and vegetables, resembling curries, served with rice. The origin may be related to Persian *gūshtān*, glossed as 'meats and fruit pulps'.

[52] The enclosure in the congregational mosque reserved for the ruler; see vol. I, p. 127, n. 213.

maqṣūra I saluted him along with the qāḍī; he said a word of greeting, spoke in their tongue with the qāḍī, and then said in Arabic 'You are heartily | welcome, and you have honoured 187
our land and given us pleasure.' He went out to the court of the mosque and stood by the grave of his father, who is buried there, then recited some verses from the Qur'ān and said a prayer. After this the viziers, amīrs, and officers of the troops came up and saluted him. Their manner of salutation is the same as the custom of the people of al-Yaman; one puts his forefinger to the ground, then raises it to his head and says 'May God prolong thy majesty.'[53] The Shaikh then went out of the gate of the mosque, put on his sandals, ordered the qāḍī to put on his sandals and me to do likewise, and set out on foot for his residence, which is close to the mosque. All the [rest of the] people walked barefoot. Over his head were carried four canopies of coloured silk, with the figure of a bird in gold on top of each canopy.[54] His garments on that day were a large green mantle of Jerusalem stuff, with fine robes of Egyptian stuffs with their appendages (?)[55] under-neath it, and he was girt with a waist-wrapper | of silk and 188
turbaned with a large turban. In front of him were sounded drums and trumpets and fifes, and before and behind him were the commanders of the troops, while the qāḍī, the doctors of the law and the sharīfs walked alongside him. He entered his audience-hall in this disposition, and the viziers, amīrs and officers of the troops sat down in a gallery there. For the qāḍī there was spread a rug, on which no one may sit but he, and beside him were the jurists and sharīfs. They remained there until the hour of the afternoon prayer, and after they had prayed it, the whole body of troops came and stood in rows in order of their ranks. Thereafter the drums, fifes,

[53] See above, p. 370.

[54] Ibn Baṭṭūṭa does not call these by the name of the ceremonial parasol, *jitr*, the use of which had been apparently introduced by the Fāṭimid caliphs of Egypt and spread to all parts of the Muslim world. But apart from the fact of the four 'canopies' (*qibāb*), it is difficult to see how these differed from the parasols, especially as the latter too were often surmounted by the figure of a bird.

[55] All MSS. but one apparently read *ṭarūḥātihā* (see the French editors' note on p. 455); if this is correct, *ṭarūḥa* probably means something like 'veil' or 'attachment', but the term seems not to be attested elsewhere, and I suspect a copyist's error for *maṭrūzāt* = *muṭarrazāt*, 'embroideries'.

trumpets and flutes are sounded; while they play no person moves or stirs from his place, and anyone who is walking stands still, moving neither backwards nor forwards. When the playing of the drum-band comes to an end, they salute
189 with their fingers as | we have described and withdraw. This is a custom of theirs on every Friday.

On the Saturday, the population comes to the Shaikh's gate and they sit in porticoes outside his residence. The qāḍī, jurists, sharīfs, men of religion, shaikhs and those who have made the Pilgrimage go in to the second audience-hall, where they sit on platforms prepared for that purpose. The qāḍī will be on a platform by himself, and each class of persons on the platform proper to them, which is shared by no others. The Shaikh then takes his seat in his hall and sends for the qāḍī, who sits down on his left; thereafter the jurists enter, and the principal men amongst them sit down in front of the Shaikh, while the remainder salute and withdraw. Next the sharīfs come in, their principal men sit down in front of him, and the remainder salute and withdraw. If they are guests, they sit on the Shaikh's right. Next the shaikhs and pilgrims come in, and their principal men sit, and the rest salute and withdraw.
190 Then come | the viziers, then the amīrs, then the officers of the troops, group after group, and they salute and withdraw. Food is brought in; the qāḍī and sharīfs and all those who are sitting in the hall eat in the presence of the Shaikh, and he eats with them. If he wishes to honour one of his principal amīrs, he sends for him, and the latter eats with them. The rest of the people eat in the dining-hall, and the order of eating is the same as their order of entry into the Shaikh's presence. The Shaikh then goes into his residence, and the qāḍī, with the viziers, the private secretary, and four of the principal amīrs, sits for deciding cases among the population and petitioners. Every case that is concerned with the rulings of the Divine Law is decided by the qāḍī, and all cases other than those are decided by the members of the council, that is to say, the viziers and amīrs. If any case calls for consultation of the sultan, they write to him about it, and he sends out the reply to them immediately on the reverse of the document
191 as | determined by his judgement. And this too is their fixed custom.

I then sailed from the city of Maqdashaw, making for the country of the Sawāḥil [Coastlands], with the object of visiting the city of Kulwā in the land of the Zinj people. We came to the island of Mambasā, a large island two days' journey by sea from the Sawahil country.[56] It has no mainland territory, and its trees are the banana, the lemon, and the citron. Its people have a fruit which they call *jammūn*, resembling an olive and with a stone like its stone.[57] The inhabitants of this island sow no grain, and it has to be transported to them from the Sawāḥil. Their food consists mostly of bananas and fish. They are Shāfi'ites in rite, pious, honourable, and upright, and their mosques are of wood, admirably constructed. At each of the gates | of the mosques there are one or two wells 192
(their wells have a depth of one or two cubits), and they draw up water from them in a wooden vessel, into which has been fixed a thin stick of the length of one cubit. The ground round the well and the mosque is paved; anyone who intends to go into the mosque washes his feet before entering, and at its gate there is a piece of thick matting on which he rubs his feet. If one intends to make an ablution, he holds the vessel between his thighs, pours [water] on his hands and performs the ritual washings. All the people walk with bare feet.

We stayed one night in this island and sailed on to the city of Kulwā, a large city on the seacoast,[58] most of whose inhabitants are Zinj, jet-black in colour. They have tattoo marks on their faces, just as [there are] on the faces of the

[56] *Sāḥil*, literally 'coastland', meant in maritime usage a port serving as an entrepôt for the goods of its hinterland; see Dozy, s.v. Mombasa (in Arabic spelling also Manfasa) is separated from the mainland only by a narrow strait, but Ibn Baṭṭūṭa apparently means that it is two days sailing time from the 'Coastlands' properly so called, i.e. the trading ports to the southward.

[57] The *jammūn* or *jumūn* is, as indicated in later passages, the Indian *jāmun* (*Eugenia jambolata*), incorrectly identified by the French translators with the *jambu* or rose-apple; see H. Yule and A. C. Burnell, *Hobson-Jobson* (London, 1886), s.v.

[58] Kilwa (*Kulwā* is not otherwise attested), Quiloa of the Portuguese chronicles, now Kilwa Kisiwāni in Tanganyika (8° 57′ S., 39° 34′ E.), 340 miles south of Mombasa: see M. H. Dorman, 'The Kilwa civilization and the Kilwa ruins' in *Tanganyika Notes* (Dar-es-Salaam, 1938), no. 6, 61–71; J. Walker, 'The Coinage of the Sultans of Kilwa' in *Numismatic Chronicle* (London, 1936), 43–81. The journey from Mogadishu towards the end of the north-east monsoon in February or early March might take from six to ten days.

Līmīs of Janāwa.[59] I was told by a merchant that the city of Sufāla[60] lies at a distance of half a month's journey from the
193 city of Kulwā, and that between | Sufāla and Yūfī, in the country of the Līmīs, is a month's journey; from Yūfī gold dust is brought to Sufāla.[61] The city of Kulwā is one of the finest and most substantially built towns; all the buildings are of wood, and the houses are roofed with *dīs* reeds.[62] The rains there are frequent. Its people engage in *jihād*, because they are on a common mainland with the heathen Zinj people and contiguous to them, and they are for the most part religious and upright, and Shāfi'ites in rite.

Account of the Sultan of Kulwā. Its sultan at the period of my entry into it was Abu'l-Muẓaffar Ḥasan, who was called also by the appellation of Abu'l-Mawāhib, on account of the multitude of his gifts and acts of generosity. He used to engage frequently in expeditions to the land of the Zinj people, raiding them and taking booty, and he would set aside the fifth part of it to devote to the objects prescribed for it in the Book of God Most High.[63] He used to deposit the portion for the relatives [of the Prophet] in a separate treasury;

[59] *Līmī* is a variant form of *Lamlam*, applied by the Arab geographers to the (supposedly cannibal) tribes of the interior (cf. Ibn Khaldūn, *Muqaddima*, trans. F. Rosenthal (New York, 1958), I, 118). Janāwa (this reading is supported by two MSS. against *Janāda* and *Janāra*) was the name given to the country of the pagan tribes south of the Muslim lands in West Africa, which passed into Portuguese and thence into English as Guinea (cf. Yāqūt, *Geogr. Dict.*, s.v. Kināwa).

[60] Sofāla, at 20° 10′ S., 34° 42′ E., was the southernmost trading station of the Arabs in Africa, founded by colonists from Mogadishu; see also Guillain, I, 337 f. On the gold production and trade of Sofala see Devic, 173–7.

[61] Yūfī is the kingdom of Nupe in West Africa (cf. vol. IV, p. 395, Arabic). This confusion between the gold dust of the Niger and the mined gold ore of Sofala and the assumption of a connection between them are probably due to some misunderstanding on Ibn Baṭṭūṭa's part.

[62] 'Substantial', i.e. by comparison with the hutments in other settlements. The *dīs* reed is identified by Guillain (I, 295) with *ampelodesmos tenax*. (The suggested corrections of G. S. P. Freeman-Grenville, 'Ibn Baṭṭūṭa's visit to East Africa' in *Uganda Journal* (Kampala, 1955), XIX, 1–6, to read *bi'l-ḥasab* for *bi'l-khashab* and to translate *saqf* as 'concrete roof laid over mangrove poles' are more than dubious.)

[63] The Arabic *History of Kilwa* (ed. S. A. Strong in *JRAS* (1895), 385–430) dilates on the piety and warlike prowess of this Abu'l-Mawāhib Ḥasan b. Sulaimān. This text is very corrupt and omits many lines, but can be utilized with the summary made by João de Barros in his work *Asia*, translated by G. Ferrand, 'Les sultans de Kilwa' in *Mémorial Henri Basset* (Paris, 1928),

whenever he was visited by | sharīfs he would pay it out to 194
them, and the sharīfs used to come to visit him from al-'Irāq and al-Ḥijāz and other countries. I saw at his court a number of the sharīfs of al-Ḥijāz, amongst them Muḥammad b. Jammāz, Manṣūr b. Lubaida b. Abū Numayy, and Muḥammad b. Shumaila b. Abū Numayy,[64] and at Maqdashaw I met Tabl b. Kubaish b. Jammāz, who was intending to go to him. This sultan is a man of great humility; he sits with poor brethren, and eats with them, and greatly respects men of religion and noble descent.

An anecdote illustrating his generosity. I was present with him on a Friday, when he had come out [of the mosque] after the prayer and was proceeding to his residence. He was accosted by a poor brother, a Yamanite, who said to him 'O Abu'l-Mawāhib;' he replied 'At your service, O faqīr—what do you want?' The man said, 'Give me those robes that you are wearing.' He said 'Certainly I shall give you them.' The man said 'Now,' and he said 'Yes, now,' went back to the mosque and into the khaṭīb's chamber, where he dressed in
other garments, and having taken off | those robes he called 195
to the poor brother 'Come in and take them.' So the faqīr came in, took them, made a bundle of them in a kerchief, placed them on his head and went off. The population were loud in their gratitude to the sultan for the humility and generosity that he had displayed, and his son, who was his designated heir, took the clothing from the poor brother and gave him ten slaves in exchange. When the sultan learned of the gratitude expressed by the people to him for that action, he too ordered the faqīr to be given ten head of slaves and two loads of ivory, for most of their gifts consist of ivory and it is

---

242–56, and summarized also by Guillain (I, 180); but Ferrand erroneously identifies Abu'l-Mawāhib with no. 8 instead of no. 21 in Barros's list. His *jihād* against the heathen tribes is obviously slave-raiding, and his piety in 'setting aside the fifth' is contrasted with the disregard by other rulers of the injunction in Qur'ān, viii, 42: 'Whatsoever you take in booty, the fifth of it belongs to God, the Apostle, the relative, the orphans, the poor and the traveller'. By traditional interpretation the term 'relative' was taken to mean those persons related to the Prophet by descent, i.e. the sharīfs.

[64] I.e., of the Ḥusainid sharīfs of al-Madīna, from the house of Jammāz b. Shīḥa (see vol. I, p. 259, n. 55), and of the Ḥasanid sharīfs of Mecca, from the house of Abū Numayy (see above, p. 361, n. 7).

seldom that they give gold.[65] When this worthy and open-handed sultan died (God have mercy on him), he was succeeded by his brother Dā'ūd, who was of the opposite line of conduct.[66] When a petitioner came to him he would say to him 'He who gave is dead, and left nothing behind to be given.' Visitors would stay at his court for many months, and finally he would make them some small gift, so that at last solicitors gave up coming to his gate.

196 We sailed | from Kulwā[67] to the city of Ẓafāri'l-Ḥumūḍ, which is at the extremity of the land of al-Yaman, on the coast of the Indian Sea.[68] From it thoroughbred horses are exported to India,[69] and the sea between it and the land of India can be crossed with the aid of the wind in a full month. I myself crossed it once from Qāliqūṭ in the land of India to Ẓafāri in twenty-eight days with a favouring wind, sailing continuously by night and by day. Between Ẓafāri and 'Adan by land it is a month's journey through desert country, from Ẓafāri to Ḥaḍramaut sixteen days, and from Ẓafāri to 'Omān twenty days.[70] The city of Ẓafāri lies in an isolated desert region, in which there is not a village,[71] and it has no

[65] On the importance of the ivory trade of East Africa, see Devic, 179–81.

[66] Dā'ūd (who had previously reigned for two years during Ḥasan's absence on pilgrimage) reigned again for twenty-four years after his death (see the ref above in n. 63; the text translated in *JRAS* absurdly says '24 days'), and is described as 'ascetic and pious'. Note that Ibn Baṭṭūṭa here relates at second-hand events which took place after his visit.

[67] As the south-west monsoon sets in on the African coast during March and reaches the Arabian Sea in April, Ibn Baṭṭūṭa's departure from Kilwa is probably to be dated about the end of March, and the direct journey to Dhafār can be reckoned at from three to four weeks; cf. Villiers, 297.

[68] The small enclave of Dhafār on the southern coast of Arabia, backed by a high ridge (Jabal Qara) which receives the summer monsoon rains and is covered by tropical vegetation in consequence on its southern face. See T. Bent, *Southern Arabia* (London, 1900), 233–43; for ancient Dhafār, *Periplus of the Erythraean Sea*, 107. The addition of al-Ḥumūḍ (to distinguish it from several other places in al-Yaman called Ẓafār) is an error or re-cast from the term al-Ḥabūḍī, the ethnic of the dynasty from whom it was seized by the Rasūlids of al-Yaman in 1278 (al-Khazrajī, III, 60); cf. below, n. 71, and p. 390, n. 86.

[69] On the horse-trade between Dhafār and India see Yule's *Marco Polo*, II, 340, 444.

[70] Ibn al-Mujāwir gives the stages on the land routes from Dhafār to 'Adan (268–70), Shibām in Ḥaḍramaut (256–60), and Qalhāt (270–2).

[71] The Ḥabūḍī ruler Aḥmad b. 'Abdallāh removed the town from inland to the coast in 1223 to protect it from attack (presumably by the bedouins), and named the new city al-Manṣūra (Ibn al-Mujāwir, 260). This was ap-

dependencies.[72] The bazaar is outside the city in a suburb called al-Ḥarjā', and it is one of the dirtiest, most stinking and fly-ridden of bazaars, because of the quantity | of fruit 197
and fish sold in it.[73] Most of the fish in it are the species called *sardīn*, which are extremely fat there.[74] It is a strange fact that their beasts have as their sole fodder these sardines, and likewise their flocks,[75] and I have never seen this in any other place. Most of the sellers [in the bazaar] are female slaves, who are dressed in black.

The grain grown by its inhabitants is millet, which they irrigate from very deep wells. Their method of irrigation is that they make a large bucket and attach it to a number of ropes, each one of which is tied round the waist of a male or female slave; these draw up the bucket over a large beam fixed above the well, and pour the water into a tank from which they water [the crop]. They have also a wheat-grain, which they call *'alas*, but it is in reality a kind of barley. Rice is brought to them from India, and forms their principal food. The dirhams of this city are made of brass and tin, and are not accepted as currency anywhere else.[76]

The population of Ẓafāri are engaged in trading, and have no | livelihood except from this. It is their custom that when 198
a vessel arrives from India or elsewhere, the sultan's slaves go down to the shore, and come out to the ship in a *sumbuq*, carrying with them a complete set of robes for the owner of the vessel or his agent, and also for the *rubbān*, who is the captain, and for the *kirānī* who is the ship's writer.[77] Three

---

parently situated on the ruined site now called al-Balad or al-Bilād, two miles east of Salāla, on the ruins of an ancient Sabaean city, with a citadel some 100 feet in height (Bent, 240; cf. *Red Sea Pilot*, 443).

[72] The other township of Mirbāṭ was destroyed by Aḥmad al-Ḥabūḍī (Ibn al-Mujāwir, 270).

[73] Al-Ḥarjā' lay to the west of the city, 'a pleasant town on the sea-coast'; Ibn al-Mujāwir, 261–2.

[74] The surprising identity of this term (almost certainly non-Arabic) with that of the European languages is probably to be explained by common derivation from Greek.

[75] Cf. Ibn al-Mujāwir (265): 'The fodder of their animals is dried fish, which is [called] *'aid*, and they manure their lands with fish only.'

[76] There are several other instances of such debased local currencies, probably with the object of preventing the export of silver.

[77] 'The *karrānī* (or *kirānī*) is a writer who keeps the accounts of the ship': Ā'īn-i Akbarī, tr. H. Blochmann (Calcutta, 1939), I, 290.

horses are brought for them, on which they mount [and proceed] with drums and trumpets playing before them from the seashore to the sultan's residence, where they make their salutations to the vizier and amīr jandār. Hospitality is supplied to all who are in the vessel for three nights, and when the three nights are up they eat in the sultan's residence. These people do this in order to gain the goodwill of the shipowners, and they are men of humility, good dispositions, virtue, and affection for strangers. Their clothes are made of
199 cotton, which is brought to them from | India, and they wear wrappers fastened round their waists in place of drawers. Most of them wear [only] one wrapper tied round the waist and put another over their backs, because of the violent heat, and they bathe several times a day. The town has many mosques, and in each mosque there are a number of lavatories equipped for them to bathe in. In it are manufactured fabrics of silk, cotton and linen, of very good quality. There is prevalent among the inhabitants, both men and women, the disease called elephantiasis, which is a swelling of both feet, and most of the men suffer from hernia—God preserve us! One of their good customs is to shake hands with one another in the mosque after the morning and the afternoon prayers; those in the front row [of worshippers] turn their backs to the [wall containing the] *qibla*, and those [in the row] next to them shake hands with them. They do the same thing after the noon-prayer on Friday, all of them shaking hands with one another.

200 One of | the special properties and marvels of this city is that no one approaches it with an evil design but his guile turns on himself and he is prevented from attaining it. It was told me that the sultan Quṭb al-Dīn Tamahtan b. Tūrān-Shāh, the ruler of Hurmuz, invested it once by land and sea; but God (magnified be He) sent against him a violent wind which broke up his vessels, and he desisted from his siege of it and made peace with its king. So also it was told me that al-Malik al-Mujāhid, the sultan of al-Yaman, appointed a cousin of his to the command of a powerful force with the object of seizing it from the hand of its king, who was also his paternal cousin.[78] But when that commander came out of his

[78] No record of either of these expeditions is found in any of the contemporary sources relating to the Persian Gulf or southern Arabia.

house, a wall fell down upon him and upon a number of those with him, so that they all perished, and the king desisted from his project and abandoned [all thought of] besieging and laying claim to it.

Another strange thing is that the people of this city of all men most closely resemble the people of the Maghrib in | their 201
ways. I lodged in the house of the khaṭīb in its principal mosque, who was 'Īsā b. 'Alī, a man of great distinction and a generous soul. He had a number of slavegirls, who were called by the same names as the female slaves in the Maghrib; one was named Bukhait and another Zād al-Māl,[79] and I have never heard these names in any other country. Most of its inhabitants leave their heads uncovered, and do not wear a turban. In every one of their houses there is a prayer-mat of palm leaves hung up inside the house, on which the master of the house performs his prayers, exactly as the people of the Maghrib do, and their food [also] is millet. All of this similarity between them is of a nature to strengthen the opinion that the Ṣanhāja and other tribes of the Maghrib originate from Ḥimyar.[80]

In the vicinity of this city and among its groves is the hospice of the pious shaikh and devotee Abū | Muḥammad b. 202
Abū Bakr b. 'Īsā, of the people of Ẓafāri. This hospice is held in great veneration by them; they come out to it in the mornings and evenings and seek asylum in it, and when the suppliant for asylum has entered it, the sultan has no power over him. I saw there one person, who, I was told, had been in it for a period of years as a refugee, without any violence being offered to him by the sultan. During the days that I spent in Ẓafāri, the sultan's secretary took refuge in it and remained there until a reconciliation was effected between them. I went out to this hospice and spent a night in it, enjoying the hospitality of the two shaikhs Abu'l-'Abbās Aḥmad and Abū 'Abdallāh Muḥammad, sons of the shaikh Abū Bakr mentioned above, and I found them to be men of

[79] Bukhait is the diminutive of *bakht*, 'good luck'. Zād al-Māl appears to be a phrase, 'May wealth increase'.

[80] This belief is based on the legend that the Tubba's, the pre-Islamic Ḥimyarite kings of al-Yaman, conquered North-West Africa and that their Yamanite troops settled there.

great benevolence. When we washed our hands after the meal, one of them, Abu'l-'Abbās, took that water in which we had washed, drank some of it, and sent the servant with the rest of it to his wives and children, and they too drank it. This is what they do with all visitors to them in whom they per-
203 ceive indications of goodness. | In the same way I was entertained by its pious qāḍī Abū Hāshim al-Zabīdī; he himself undertook the office of serving me and of washing my hands, and would not delegate it to any other person.

In the neighbourhood of this hospice is the mausoleum of the ancestors of the sultan al-Malik al-Mughīth.[81] It is held in great veneration by them; anyone who has a petition to make puts himself under its protection and his petition is granted. It is the custom of the soldiery, if the month comes to an end and they have not been paid their allowances, to seek the protection of this mausoleum, and they remain under its protection until they receive their allowances.

Half a day's journey from this city is al-Aḥqāf where [the people of] 'Ād dwelt.[82] There is a hospice there and a mosque on the sea-coast, with a village of fishermen surrounding it. In the hospice is a tomb over which is inscribed 'This is the
204 tomb of Hūd b. 'Ābir, | upon whom be most copious blessing and peace'. I have already related that in the mosque of Damascus there is a place over which is inscribed 'This is the tomb of Hūd b. 'Ābir', but it is more likely that his tomb should be in al-Aḥqāf, since it was his country, but God knows best.[83]

[81] See below, p. 390.

[82] Al-Ahqāf, mentioned in the Qur'ān (xlvi, 20) as the land of the ancient tribe of 'Ād, to whom the prophet Hūd was sent, is commonly taken to mean all or part of the sand deserts of southern Arabia. But an early Islamic tradition locates it in 'a *wādī* between 'Omān and Mahra', and Ibn Baṭṭūṭa may well be repeating a local tradition. His statement, however, seems to confuse two places; the city of the 'Ādites is probably the ruined Sabaean city below a cave on the edge of Jabal Qara, some ten miles north of al-Balad, visited by the Bents in 1895 (*Southern Arabia,* 265–6); and the village of fishermen on the coast is probably Raisūt, ten miles west of al-Balad.

[83] This again is evidently a local ascription. The accepted tradition places the grave of Hūd at a well-known site (see *E.I.*, s.v. Barahūt) 40 miles east of Tarīm in Ḥaḍramaut, and over 300 miles west of Dhafār. Note that in his earlier reference (vol. I, 129) Ibn Baṭṭūṭa states that he had himself seen this grave, but does not actually say so here.

This city [of Ẓafāri] has groves in which grow large numbers of bananas of great size; one of them was weighed in my presence and its weight was twelve ounces. They are pleasant to the taste and very sweet. There too are betel and coconut (known as 'Indian nut'), which are to be found only in the land of India and in this city of Ẓafāri, because of its similarity and proximity to India—except, however, that in the city of Zabīd, in the sultan's garden, there are some few coconut trees. Since the mention of betel and coconuts has come up, I shall now proceed to describe them and give an account of their properties.

Account of the Betel Tree.[84] The betel is a tree which is cultivated in the same manner as the grape-vine; | trellises of 205
cane are made for it, just as for grape-vines, or else the betel trees are planted close to coconut trees, so that they may climb upon them in the same way that vines climb, and as the pepper climbs. The betel has no fruit, and is grown only for the sake of its leaves, which resemble the leaves of the bramble, and the best ones are the yellow. Its leaves are picked every day. The Indians attach immense importance to betel, and when a man comes to the house of his friend and the latter gives him five leaves of it, it is as though he had given him the world, especially if he is an amīr or some great man. The gift of betel is for them a far greater matter and more indicative of esteem than the gift of silver and gold. The manner of its use is that before eating it one takes areca nut; this is like a nutmeg but is broken up until it is reduced to small pellets, and one places these in his mouth and chews them. Then | he takes the leaves of betel, puts a little chalk on 206
them, and masticates them along with the betel. Their specific property is that they sweeten the breath, remove foul odours of the mouth, aid digestion of food, and stop the injurious effect of drinking water on an empty stomach; the

[84] The Arabic (or Perso-Arabic) word is *tanbūl* (cf. Yule's *Marco Polo*, II, 371, 374), derived from the Sanskrit name of the betel-shrub, the common European term *betel* being derived from the Malayalam language of south-west India through Portuguese (see *Hobson-Jobson*, s.v.). On the use of betel leaf in India, see *The Ocean of Story*, ed. N. M. Penzer, London, 1927, VIII, 237–319, and Mrs Meer Hasan Ali on 'the dear delightful pawn' (*Observations on the Mussulmauns of India* (*1832*), ed. W. Brooke (London, 1917), 57).

eating of them gives a sense of exhilaration and promotes cohabitation, and a man will put some by his head at nights so that, if he wakes up or is awakened by his wife or slave-girl, he may take a few of them and they will remove any foul odour there may be in his mouth. I have been told, indeed, that the slave-girls of the sultan and of the amīrs in India eat nothing else. I shall speak of this [again] in describing the land of India.

Account of the Coconut, which is the 'Indian nut'. These
trees are among the most peculiar trees in kind and most
astonishing in habit. They look exactly like date-palms,
207 without any difference between them | except that the one
produces nuts as its fruits and the other produces dates. The
nut of a coconut tree resembles a man's head, for in it are
what look like two eyes and a mouth, and the inside of it
when it is green looks like the brain, and attached to it is a fibre
which looks like hair. They make from this cords with which
they sew up ships instead of [using] iron nails, and they [also]
make from it cables for vessels. The coconut, especially that
in the islands of Dhībat al-Mahal [Maldives], is the size of a
human head, and they tell [this story]: A certain philosopher
in India in past ages was in the service of one of the kings and
was held by him in high esteem. The king had a vizier, between whom and this philosopher there was enmity. The
philosopher said to the king, 'If this vizier's head is cut off
and buried, there will grow out of it a palm that will produce
large dates which will bring advantage to the people of India
208 and other peoples in the world.' | The king said to him 'And
what if this that you have stated does not come from the head
of the vizier?' He replied 'If it does not, do with my head as
you have done with his.' So the king gave orders to cut off
the vizier's head, and the philosopher took it, planted a date-
stone in his brain, and tended it until it grew into a tree and
produced this nut as its fruit. This story is a fiction, but we
have related it because of its wide circulation among them.

Among the properties of this nut are that it strengthens the body, fattens quickly, and adds to the redness of the face. As for its aphrodisiac quality, its action in this respect is wonderful. One of the marvellous things about it is that at the beginning of its growth it is green, and if one cuts out a piece

of its rind with a knife and makes a hole in the head of the nut, he drinks out of it a liquid of extreme sweetness and coolness, but whose temperament is hot and aphrodisiac. | After drinking this liquid, he takes a piece of the rind and 209
fashions it like a spoon, and with this he scoops out the pulp which is inside the nut. The taste of this is like that of an egg which has been broiled but not fully cooked, and one uses it for food. This was what I lived on during my stay in the islands of Dhībat al-Mahal for a period of a year and a half.

Another marvellous thing about it is that there are made from it oil, milk and honey. The way in which honey is made from it is as follows. The servants who have the care of the coconut palms, and who are called *fāzānīya*, climb up a palm-tree in the morning and the evening, when they intend to take its sap, from which they make the honey (which they call *aṭwāq*).[85] They cut the stalk on which the fruit grows, leaving of it two fingers' length, and on this they tie a small bowl, into which there drips the sap which flows out of the stalk. If he ties it on in the morning, | he climbs up to it in 210
the evening, carrying with him two cups made from the rind of the nut mentioned above, one of which is filled with water. He pours out the sap that has collected from the stalk into one of the cups, washes the stalk with the water in the other cup, cuts a small piece off it, and ties the bowl on it again. He then repeats in the morning what he did the previous evening. When a large quantity of this sap has collected for him, he cooks it in the same way that grape-juice is cooked when *rubb* is made from it. It then makes a delicious honey of great utility, and this is bought by the merchants of India, al-Yaman and China, who transport it to their countries and manufacture sweetmeats from it.

The way in which milk is made from it is as follows. There is in every house a kind of chair upon which a woman sits, having in her hand a stick with a protruding ferrule at one end of it. They make a hole in the nut just large enough to admit that | ferrule and mash its contents, and all that comes 211
out of it is gathered on a plate, until nothing is left inside the nut. This mash is then steeped in water, so that it becomes

[85] Neither of these terms has been traced.

just like the colour of milk in whiteness and has the same taste as milk, and the people use it as a sauce. The method of making the oil is that they take the nuts when they are ripe and have fallen from the trees, peel off their rinds and cut them up into pieces. These are placed in the sun, and when they are dried they cook them in cauldrons and extract their oil. They use it for lighting and also as a sauce, and the women put it on their hair. It too is of great utility.

Account of the Sultan of Ẓafāri. He is the sultan al-Malik al-Mughīth, son of al-Malik al-Fā'iz, cousin of the king of al-
212 Yaman.[86] His father was governor of Ẓafāri on behalf of | the ruler of al-Yaman, and was under obligation to send the latter a present every year. Subsequently al-Malik al-Mughīth made himself independent as king of Ẓafāri, and refused to send the present. This was the occasion for the decision of the king of al-Yaman to go to war with him, his appointment of his cousin for that purpose, and the falling of the wall upon him, as we have related above. The sultan has a palace inside the city which is called the Castle, a large and extensive building, and the cathedral mosque is alongside it.[87]

It is his custom to have drums, trumpets, bugles and fifes sounded at his gate every day after the afternoon prayer, and every Monday and Thursday the troops come to his gate and stand outside the audience-hall for an hour, then withdraw. The sultan himself does not go out, nor is he seen by anyone except on Fridays, when he goes out for the [midday] prayer, and then returns to his residence, but he prevents no one from entering the audience-hall. The amīr jandār sits at its
213 gate, and it is to him that every | person with a petition or a grievance presents his case; he sends it for the sultan's consideration, and the reply comes to him at once. When the sultan desires to ride out, his riding-beasts, along with his arms and mamlūks, come out of the palace and go outside the city; then a camel is brought, bearing a litter covered with a white curtain embroidered in gold, and the sultan and

[86] Dhafār was captured in 1278 from the last of the Ḥabūḍī amīrs, Sālim b. Idrīs, by al-Malik al-Muẓaffar Yūsuf, second sultan of the Rasūlid dynasty of al-Yaman (al-Khazrajī, I, 190 sqq.). Al-Malik al-Fā'iz was a brother of his (al-Khazrajī, I, 120); al-Malik al-Mughīth (not otherwise known) would thus be an uncle or cousin of al-Malik al-Mujāhid.

[87] See above, p. 382, n. 71.

his familiar ride in the litter in such a manner as not to be seen. When he has gone out to his garden and wishes to ride a horse he does so, and dismounts from the camel. It is his custom also that no one may accost him on his way, nor stand to look at him or to make a complaint or for any other purpose. Anyone who ventures to do so is most severely beaten; consequently you find the inhabitants, when they hear that the sultan has come out, make a practice of running away from his route and avoiding it.

The vizier of this sultan is the jurist Muḥammad al-'Adanī. He was a teacher of school-children, and taught this sultan
to read and write. | He made a compact with him that he 214
would appoint him vizier if he became king, so that when he became king, he appointed this man vizier. But he was not competent for this office; consequently, while he had the title, the authority was in other hands.

From this city we sailed towards 'Omān in a small vessel belonging to a man called 'Alī b. Idrīs al-Maṣīrī, an inhabitant of the island of Maṣīra. On the day following our embarkation we alighted at the roadstead of Ḥāsik, on which there are a number of Arabs, who are fishermen and live there.[88] They possess incense trees; these have thin leaves, and when a leaf is slashed there drips from it a sap like milk, which then turns into a gum. This gum is the incense, and it is very plentiful there. The only means of livelihood for the inhabitants of this port is from fishing, and the fish that they catch is called *lukham*, which is like a dogfish. It is cut open, dried in the
sun, and used for food; their huts also are built with | fish 215
bones, and roofed with camel hides. We continued our journey from the roadstead of Ḥāsik for four days, and came to the Hill of Lum'ān, in the midst of the sea.[89] On top of it is a hermitage built of stone, with a roofing of fish bones, and with a pool of collected rainwater outside it.

[88] Bandar Ḥāsik, 80 miles east of Dhafār (*Red Sea Pilot*, 447). It is surprising that this is the first mention that Ibn Baṭṭūṭa makes of incense trees in this region although Dhafār was the main centre for the production and trade in incense; see Yule's *Marco Polo*, II, 445–9.

[89] This can only be the island of al-Ḥallānīya, one of the Khūriya Mūriya group, an island of granite peaks terminating at the northern end in an almost perpendicular bluff, 1,645 feet in height (*Red Sea Pilot*, 451). The island, however, is only 20 miles east of Ḥāsik.

Account of a Saint whom we met on this Hill. When we cast anchor under this hill, we climbed up to this hermitage, and found there an old man lying asleep. We saluted him, and he woke up and returned our greeting by signs; then we spoke to him, but he did not speak to us and kept shaking his head. The ship's company offered him food, but he refused to accept it. We then begged of him a prayer [on our behalf], and he kept moving his lips, though we did not know what he was saying. He was wearing a patched robe and a felt bonnet, but
216 had no | skin bag nor jug nor staff nor sandals. The ship's company declared that they had never [before] seen him on this hill. We spent that night on the beach of the hill and prayed the afternoon and sunset prayers with him. We offered him food, but he refused it and continued to pray until the hour of the last night-prayer, when he pronounced the call to prayer and we prayed along with him. He had a beautiful voice in his reciting of the Qur'ān and in his modulation of it. When he ended the last night-prayer, he signed to us to withdraw, so, bidding him farewell, we did so, with astonishment at what we had seen of him. Afterwards, when we had left, I wished to return to him, but on approaching him I felt in awe of him; fear got the better of me, and when my companions returned for me, I went off with them.

We resumed our voyage and after two days reached the Island of Birds, which is uninhabited. We cast anchor and
217 went ashore | on it, and found it full of birds like blackbirds, except that these were bigger.[90] The sailors brought some eggs of those birds, cooked and ate them, and also caught and cooked some of the birds themselves without slitting their throats, and ate them. There was sitting alongside me a merchant, of the people of the island of Maṣīra, but living in Ẓafāri, named Muslim; I saw him eating these birds along with them, and reproved him for it.[91] He was greatly abashed and said to me, 'I thought that they had slaughtered them,'

[90] A small island close to the western coast of the Gulf of Maṣīra, about 30 miles north of Ra's Markaz, called in the *Red Sea Pilot* (458) Hamar an-Nafūr (? 'Wild Doves'), and described as frequented by 'myriads of wild fowl'.

[91] In Islamic law and practice no animal is lawful for food unless its throat has been cut before death.

but he kept aloof from me thereafter out of shame and would
not come near me until I called him. My food during those
days on that ship was dried dates and fish. Every morning
and evening [the sailors] used to catch fish called in Persian
shīr māhī, which means 'lion of fish', because *shīr* is a lion and
māhī is fish; it resembles the fish called by us *tāzart*.[92] | They 218
used to cut them in pieces, broil them, and give every person
on the ship a portion, showing no preference to anyone over
another, not even to the master of the vessel nor to any other,
and they would eat them with dried dates. I had with me
some bread and biscuit, which I brought from Ẓafāri, and these
were exhausted I had to live on those fish with the rest of them.
We celebrated the Feast of Sacrifice at sea;[93] on that very day
there blew up against us a violent wind after daybreak and it
lasted until sunrise and almost sunk us.

A miraculous grace. There was accompanying us in the
vessel a pilgrim, a man from India named Khiḍr, but he was
called *Mawlānā* because he knew the Qur'ān by heart and
could write excellently.[94] When he saw the storminess of the
sea, he wrapped his head in a mantle that he had and pre-
tended to sleep. When God gave us relief from what | had 219
befallen us, I said to him 'O Mawlānā Khiḍr, what kind of
thing did you see?' He replied 'When the storm came, I kept
my eyes open, watching to see whether the angels who
receive men's souls had come. As I could not see them I said
"Praise be to God. If any of us were to be drowned, they
would come to take the souls." Then I would close my eyes
and after a while open them again, to watch in the same
manner, until God relieved us'. A ship belonging to one of the
merchants had gone ahead of us, and it sank, and only one
man escaped from it—he got out by swimming after suffering
severely.

[92] *Shīr māhī* is defined in the Persian lexica as 'a fish with white scales', and is presumably the fish described in the *Red Sea Pilot* (462) as 'of very excellent quality'.

[93] According to Ibn Baṭṭūṭa's chronology this would be 10 Dhu'l-Ḥijja 731 = 14 September 1331. I suspect, however, that the true year was 729, and that the Feast was not that of the Sacrifice but of the Fast-Breaking on 1st Shawwāl = 29 July 1329. Note that in speaking of his journey to Qalhāt a few days later (below, p. 396), Ibn Baṭṭūṭa says that it was the hot season, and cf. also below, p. 404, n. 130.

[94] See above, p. 293, n. 71.

I ate on that vessel a kind of dish which I have never eaten before or after. It was prepared by one of the merchants of 'Omān from millet, which he cooked without grinding, and poured over it *sailān*, that is honey made from dates,[95] and we ate it [so].

We came next to the island of Maṣīra, to which the master
220 of the ship that we were sailing on belonged. | It is a large island, whose inhabitants have nothing to eat but fish.[96] We did not land on it, because of the distance of the anchorage from the shore; [besides] I had taken a dislike to these people when I saw them eating the birds without proper slaughtering. We stayed there one day, while the master of the ship went ashore to his home and came back to join us.

We continued our voyage for a day and a night and came to the roadstead of a large village on the seashore called Ṣūr,[97] from which we saw the city of Qalhāt on the slope of a hill, and seeming to us to be close by.[98] We had arrived at the anchorage just after noon or before it, and when the city appeared to us I felt a desire to walk to it and spend the night there, since I had taken a dislike to the company of the ship's
221 folk. I made enquiries about the way to it | and was told that I should reach it by mid-afternoon, so I hired one of the sailors to guide me on the road. I was accompanied by Khiḍr the Indian, who has been already mentioned, and I left my associates with my possessions on the ship to rejoin me on the following day. I took some pieces of clothing of mine and gave them to the man I had hired as a guide, to spare me the fatigue of carrying them, and myself carried a spear in my hand. Now that guide wanted to make off with my garments, so he led us to a channel, an inlet from the sea in which there was a tidal flow and ebb, and was about to cross it with my garments, but I said to him, 'You cross over by yourself and

[95] See above, p. 276, n. 22.

[96] See G. de Gaury, 'A Note on Masira Island' in *GJ* (London, 1957), CXXIII, 499–502 (with map). The island is 40 miles long, 10 miles broad, and contains a few date plantations. Already in the *Periplus* (35) its inhabitants are described as *ichthyophagi*, 'fish-eaters'.

[97] For the village and anchorage of Ṣūr, at the southern end of 'Omān, see *Red Sea Pilot*, 476.

[98] The distance is 13 miles in a direct line. The author of *Tuḥfat al-A'yān* (see below, p. 398, n. 111) identifies the inlet mentioned immediately below with Khōr Rasāgh.

leave the clothes with us; if we can cross, we shall, but if not we shall go up higher to look for a ford.' He drew back and afterwards we saw some men who crossed it by swimming, so we were convinced that he had meant to drown us and make away with the garments. Thereupon I made a show of vigour and took a firm attitude; I girt up my waist and kept brandishing the spear, so that the guide went in awe of me. | We went up higher until we found a ford, and then came 222
out into a waterless desert, where we suffered from thirst and were in a desperate plight. But God sent us a horseman with a number of his companions, one of whom had in his hand a waterskin and gave me and my companion to drink. We went on, thinking that the city was close at hand, whereas [in reality] we were separated from it by nullahs through which we walked for many miles.

When the evening came the guide wanted to lead us down towards the shore, where there was no road, for the coast there is [nothing but] rocks. He wanted us to get stuck amongst them and to make off with the garments, but I said to him 'We shall just keep walking along this track that we are following,' there being a distance of about a mile between us and the sea. When it became dark he said to us 'The city is no distance from us, so come, let us walk on so that | we can 223
stop overnight in its outskirts.' But I was afraid that we might be molested by someone on our road, and was not sure how far we still had to go, so I said to him 'The right course is to turn off the track and sleep, and in the morning we shall reach the town, if God will.' I had observed a party of men on a hillside thereabouts, and fearing that they might be robbers said [to myself] 'It is preferable to go into hiding.' My companion was overcome by thirst and did not agree to this, but I turned off the road and made for a tree of Umm Ghailān. Although I was worn out and suffering from exhaustion, I made a show of strength and vigour for fear of the guide; as for my companion, he was ill and incapacitated. So I placed the guide between him and me, put the garments between my robe and my skin, and held the spear firmly in my hand. My companion went to sleep and so did | the guide, but I 224
stayed on watch, and every time the guide moved I spoke to him and showed him that I was awake. We remained thus

till daybreak, when we came out to the road and found people going to the town with various kinds of produce. So I sent the guide to fetch water for us, and my companion took the garments. There were still some steep slopes and nullahs between us and the city, but the guide brought us water and we drank, this being the season of heat.

Finally we reached the city of Qalhāt, arriving at it in a state of great exhaustion. My feet had become so swollen in my shoes that the blood was almost starting under the nails. Then, when we reached the city gate, the finishing touch to our distress was that the gatekeeper said to us, 'You must go with me to the governor of the city, that he may be informed of what you are doing and where you have come from.' So I went with him to the governor, and found him to be an
225 excellent man | and of good disposition. He asked me about myself and made me his guest, and I stayed with him for six days, during which I was powerless to rise to my feet because of the pains that they had sustained.

The city of Qalhāt is on the seacoast; it has fine bazaars and one of the most beautiful mosques.[99] Its walls are tiled with *qāshānī*, which is like *zalīj*, and it occupies a lofty situation from which it commands a view of the sea and the anchorage. It was built by the saintly woman Bībī Maryam, *bībī* meaning in their speech 'noble lady'.[100] I ate in this city fish such as I have never eaten in any other region; I preferred it to all kinds of flesh and used to eat nothing else. They broil it on the leaves of trees, place it on rice, and eat it [thus]; the rice is brought to them from India. They are traders, and make a livelihood by what come to them on the Indian Sea. When a vessel arrives at their town, they show the greatest
226 joy. Their speech is incorrect although they are | Arabs, and every sentence that they speak they follow up with *lā* ['no']. So, for example, they say 'You eat, no; you walk, no; you do

[99] Marco Polo (Yule, II, 449—51) calls Calatu 'a great city', 'a noble city'. In Arabic also the form Qalātū is found.

[100] Bībī Maryam, wife of Ayāz, a former ruler of Qalhāt and Hurmuz, continued to rule Hurmuz for some years after his death in 1311/12. Both were Turkish slaves of a former usurper at Hurmuz, Maḥmūd Qalhātī (Aubin, *JA* (1953) 97, 99). *Bībī* is a word of Turkish origin, glossed in Persian lexica as 'good woman, lady of the house'.

so-and-so, no.'[101] The majority of them are Kharijites,[102] but they cannot make an open profession of their tenets because they are subject to the sultan Quṭb al-Dīn Tamahtan, king of Hurmuz, who is a Sunni.[103]

In the vicinity of Qalhāt is the village of Ṭībī, one of the loveliest of villages and most striking in beauty, with flowing streams and verdant trees and abundant orchards.[104] Fruits of various kinds are brought from it to Qalhāt. There is there the banana called *marwārī*, which in Persian means 'pearly';[105] it grows plentifully there and is exported from it to Hurmuz and other places. There is also the betel but it is small-leaved. Dried dates are imported into | these parts from 'Omān. 227

We set out thereafter for the land of 'Omān,[106] and after travelling for six days through desert country we reached it on the seventh. It is fertile, with streams, trees, orchards, palm groves and abundant fruit of various kinds. We came to the capital of this land, which is the city of Nazwā[107]—a city at the foot of a mountain, enveloped by orchards and streams, and with fine bazaars and splendid clean mosques. Its inhabitants make a practice of eating [meals] in the courts of the mosques, every man bringing what he has and all assembling together to eat in the mosque courtyard, and the way-

[101] In *Tuḥfat al-A'yān* (I, 312–13; see below, n. 111) this practice is said to be limited to phrases of invitation and the like. A somewhat similar usage is recorded by Bertram Thomas for the speakers of the mountain dialect on the Musandam peninsula.

[102] The Khārijites were a sect who broke away from 'Alī when, after the indecisive battle at Ṣiffīn (A.D. 657) against Mu'āwiya, then governor of Syria, he agreed to put the question of the lawfulness of the killing of 'Othmān to arbitration. They subsequently erupted in a series of revolts against the Umayyad and 'Abbāsid caliphs on the charge of corrupting the primitive tenets and practices of Islam. Of their many sub-sects, the most lasting were the Ibāḍīya, who acquired a dominant position in 'Omān in the eighth century, and have maintained it to the present day.

[103] See below, p. 401.

[104] Called Ṭaiwā by Ibn al-Mujāwir (280, 284), but more commonly known as Ṭiwī (cf. *Tuḥfat al-A'yān*, 313). It lies 10 miles north of Qalhāt, and is described as 'with a date-grove in a gorge (and) many fruit-trees' (*Sailing Directions for the Persian Gulf* (Washington, U.S. Navy, 1931, 52).

[105] An Arabic formation from Persian *marwārīd*, 'pearl'.

[106] I.e. 'Omān proper, an area of oasis villages on the slopes of Jabal Akhḍar, in the interior.

[107] At the foot of the western flank of Jabal Akhḍar, 130 miles from Qalhāt in a direct line; general view in J. Morris, *Sultan into Oman* (London-New York, 1957), 20, plate.

farers eat along with them. They are pugnacious and brave, and there is continual warfare among them. They are Ibāḍīs in rite, and they make the congregational prayer on Friday [an ordinary] noon prayer with four 'bowings';[108] after they have finished these, the imām reads some verses from the
228 Qur'ān and delivers an address in prose, resembling | the *khuṭba*, in the course of which he uses the formula 'God be pleased with him' in respect of Abū Bakr and 'Omar, but makes no mention of 'Othmān and 'Alī.[109] These people, when they wish to speak of 'Alī (God be pleased with him), allude to him [simply] as 'the man'; thus they say 'It is related of the man' or 'The man said'. [On the other hand] they use the formula 'God be pleased with him' of the accursed wretch Ibn Muljam,[110] and refer to him as 'the pious servant [of God], the suppressor of the sedition'. Their womenfolk are much given to corruption, and the men show no jealousy nor disapproval of such conduct.[111] We shall relate an anecdote later on which bears witness to this.

Account of the Sultan of 'Omān. Its sultan is an Arab of the tribe of Azd b. al-Ghawth, and is called Abū Muḥammad Ibn Nabhān.[112] 'Abū Muḥammad' is among them an appellation

[108] See above, n. 102. The canonical Sunnī rule is to make two 'bowings' before the *khuṭba* at the congregational prayer on Friday. According to the author of *Tuḥfat al-A'yān* (1,314), the omission of the congregational prayer was for the reason that in Khārijite doctrine the presence of an imām is required for its validity, and the Nabhānī rulers were not regarded as imāms (see below, n. 112).

[109] For the mention of the first four caliphs in the Sunnī *khuṭba* see vol. I, p. 252. The Khārijites rejected 'Othmān as an innovator and evildoer and rejected 'Alī on the issue of the arbitration (see above, n. 102).

[110] The Khārijite assassin of 'Alī; see above, p. 323, n. 164.

[111] The modern Khārijite historian of 'Omān, the imām Nūr al-Dīn 'Abdallāh b. Ḥumaid al-Sālimī, and his commentator Ibrāhīm Aṭfīsh (*Tuḥfat al-A'yān*, Cairo, A.H. 1350, I, 314–18) criticize Ibn Baṭṭūṭa's statements in this paragraph as exaggerations motivated by sectarian prejudice, but do not positively deny any of them except the total avoidance of the name of 'Alī and the imputation in the last sentence (see below, however, p. 400, n. 116).

[112] The Banū Nabhān belonged to the 'Atīk branch of the great south-Arabian tribe of Azd, and ruled Inner 'Omān from 1154 to 1406. In the Khārijite tradition they are regarded as impious tyrants, who usurped the rights of the legitimate Imāms. For this reason, no precise chronological narrative of this period has survived. The author and commentator of *Tuḥfat al-A'yān* (316), however, express disbelief in the statement that every sultan of the dynasty was called Abū Muḥammad, and this was certainly not the practice in its earlier years (cf. *ibid.*, 303–4).

given to every sultan who governs 'Omān, just like the appellation 'Atābek' among the kings of the Lūrs. It is his custom to sit outside the gate of his residence in a place of audience there. He has no chamberlain nor | vizier, and no 229
one is hindered from appearing before him, whether stranger or any other. He receives a guest honourably, after the custom of the Arabs, assigns him hospitality, and makes gifts to him according to his standing, and he is of excellent character. At his table there is eaten the flesh of the domestic ass, and it is also sold in the market, because they maintain that it is lawful for food, but they conceal the fact from one who comes to their country and do not produce it openly in his presence.[113] Among the cities of 'Oman is the city of Zakī[114]—I did not enter it, but according to what was told me it is a large city— and al-Qurayyāt, Shabā, Kalbā, Khawr Fakkān, and Ṣuhār,[115] all of them with streams, groves, and palm trees. Most of this country is under the government of Hurmuz.

Anecdote. One day I was in the presence of this sultan, Abū Muḥammad Ibn Nabhān, when a woman came to him, young, pretty and with unveiled face. She stood | before him 230
and said to him, 'O Abū Muḥammad, the devil is in revolt in my head.' He said to her 'Go and drive out the devil.' She said 'I cannot, and I am under your protection, O Abū Muḥammad.' Then he said to her 'Go and do what you want.' I was told that this girl and anyone who does as she did are under the sultan's protection, and engage in debauchery.

[113] This statement also is strongly disputed in the *Tuḥfa* (317). The authors argue that the flesh of the donkey is not prohibited in the Qur'ān, that its prohibition was disputed among the early scholars of Islam, and that although some Khārijite doctors may have declared it lawful this doctrine has never been followed in practice. The general Muslim doctrine is that it is prohibited by a Tradition of the Prophet. It is reported, however, that the wild ass is eaten by some tribesmen of Inner 'Omān (W. Thesiger, *Arabian Sands* (London-New York, 1959), 147).

[114] More commonly known as Azkī or Izkī, 30 miles east of Nazwā.

[115] These are all townships on the coast, roughly from south to north: al-Qurayyāt is a group of villages 25 miles south-east of Masqaṭ; Ṣuhār is 125 miles north-west of Masqaṭ; Kalbā and Khōr Fakkan (or Fukkan) are 60 and 75 miles north of Ṣuhār. No place called Shaba (or Shabba) has been identified in 'Omān. From its order in this list it seems to correspond to Sīb, 25 miles west of Masqaṭ, the mediaeval name of which is uncertain (see *Kashf al-Ghumma*, ed. H. Klein (Hamburg, 1938), 62). Masqaṭ is omitted in this list, but is mentioned on his return journey in 1347 (vol. IV, p. 310, Arabic).

Neither her father nor any of her relatives can punish her, and if they kill her they are put to death in retaliation for her, because she is under the sultan's protection.[116]

I travelled next from the land of 'Omān to the land of Hurmuz. Hurmuz is a city on the sea-coast, and is also called Mūghistān.[117] Opposite it in the sea is New Hurmuz, and between them is a sea passage of three farsakhs. We came to New Hurmuz, which is an island whose city is called Jarawn.[118]
231 It is a fine large city, with magnificent bazaars, as it is | the port of India and Sind, from which the wares of India are exported to the two 'Irāqs, Fārs and Khurāsān. It is in this city that the sultan resides, and the island in which it is situated is a day's march in size. Most of it is salt marshes and hills of salt, namely the *dārābī* salt;[119] from this they manufacture ornamental vessels and pedestals on which they place lamps. Their food is fish and dried dates exported to them from al-Baṣra and 'Omān. They say in their tongue *Khurmā wamāhī lūtī pādishānī*, which means 'Dates and fish are a royal dish'. On this island water is an article of price; it has water-springs and artificial cisterns in which rain-water is collected, at some distance from the city. The inhabitants go there with waterskins, which they fill and carry on their backs to the sea [shore], load them on boats, and bring them to the
232 city. I saw | a remarkable thing [there]—near the gate of the cathedral mosque, between it and the bazaar, the head of a fish

[116] The author of the *Tuḥfa* admits that this story is perhaps credible, but only in view of the tyrannical and ungodly character of the government of the Nabhānids.

[117] Old Hurmuz was situated on the mainland, some six to eight miles up the Mināb creek; see Yule's *Marco Polo*, I, 110–11, and A. T. Wilson, *The Persian Gulf* (Oxford, 1928), 100–4. Mughistān was the name of the district of Kirmān adjoining the coast: see Pedro Teixeira, *Travels*, trans. W. F. Sinclair (London, Hakluyt Society, 1902), 156, 186; Wilson, *ibid.*, 126. (One MS. reads 'a region' instead of 'a city'.) Ibn Baṭṭūṭa strangely omits to say where he sailed from.

[118] New Hurmuz was founded on the island of Jarūn by Ayāz (see above, p. 396, n. 100) shortly after 1300 (Schwarz, III, 242, 245). According to Mustawfī (177) the ferry-port for Jarūn on the mainland was called Tūsar. The island is actually about six miles long.

[119] *Dārābī* (for *dārānī* in the printed text), i.e., like the salt of Dārābjird, to the south-east of Shirāz, where there were hills of salt of different colours from which platters were made (Schwarz, II, 95). The island of Jarawn is in fact a salt-plug, and almost all its water had to be brought from neighbouring islands or the mainland (cf. Wilson, 108).

as large as a hillock and with eyes like doors, and you would see persons going in by one eye and coming out by the other.[120]

I met in this city the pious shaikh and follower of the Ṣūfī path Abu'l-Ḥasan al-Aqṣarānī, from the land of al-Rūm by origin, who received me hospitably, visited me, and presented me with a robe. He gave me also the 'girdle of companionship', which is used for tying up the ends of one's robes; it supports one who is sitting and serves as something to lean on.[121] Most of the Persian poor brethren wear this girdle.

At a distance of six miles from this city is a place of visitation called by the name of al-Khiḍr and Ilyās (on both of whom be peace).[122] It is related that they used to pray there, and there have been obtained at it blessings and evidentiary miracles. There is at the same place a hospice inhabited by a shaikh, who maintains the service [of food] at it for wayfarers. We stayed with him for a day, and from there went to visit | a pious man who lives as a recluse at the end of this 233
island. He has carved out for his habitation a cave, in which is a hermitage, a sitting-room, and a small chamber in which he keeps a slave-girl. He has slaves outside the cave, who tend cattle and sheep of his. This man was one of the principal merchants, then he went on pilgrimage to the [Holy] House, renounced all attachments, and devoted himself to religious exercises at this spot, having transferred his wealth to one of his brethern to use in trading for him. We spent one night with him, when he treated us with exceeding hospitality (God be pleased with him), and the marks of goodness and of pious exercises were plainly visible on him.

Account of the Sultan of Hurmuz. He is the sultan Quṭb al-Dīn Tamahtan [Tahamtan] b. Tūrān-Shāh,[123] one of the

[120] There are relatively few references to the whale (called *bāl* or *wāl*) in Arabic writings. The most vivid are the seamen's stories at the beginning of *The Chain of Histories* (M. Reinaud (ed.), *Relation des Voyages faits dans l'Inde et à la Chine* (Paris, 1845), I, 2); cf. also al-Damīrī, *Ḥayāt al-Ḥayawān* (Cairo, A.H. 1306), I, 102.

[121] See vol. I, p. 121, n. 201.

[122] For the association of al-Khiḍr and Elijah, see below, p. 466, n. 193.

[123] Tahamtan, a descendant of the former ruling house of Hurmuz, reconquered Hurmuz in 1319, in company with his brother Niẓām al-Dīn Kaiqubād, and in 1330 or 1331 added the islands of Qais and Baḥrain and the ports of Qaṭīf and Māchūl to his dominions (Aubin, *JA* (1953), 103–5). During this period, and for some years later, complete harmony prevailed between the two brothers.

most generous of princes, exceedingly humble, and of excel-
234 lent character. It is his custom to visit in person every | jurist or pious man or sharīf who comes to his court, and to give to each one his due. When we entered his island, we found him occupied in preparations for war with the sons of his brother Niẓām al-Dīn, and on every night he would make ready for battle.[124] Meanwhile the island was in the grip of famine. We were met by his vizier, Shams al-Dīn Muḥammad b. ʻAlī, his qāḍī ʻImād al-Dīn al-Shawankārī, and a number of distinguished persons, who presented their excuses on the ground of their present situation of engagement in war. We stayed with them for sixteen days, and when we were about to leave I said to one of my associates 'How can we go away without seeing this sultan?' So we went to the vizier's residence, which was in the neighbourhood of the hospice where I lodged, and I said to him 'I wish to salute the king.' He replied 'In the name of God,' took me by the hand and went with me to his residence, which was on the shore, with ships
235 of war [125] | drawn up on the beach beside it. And lo and behold, [there was] an old man, wearing long cloaks, both skimpy and dirty, with a turban on his head, and a kerchief for a waist girdle; the vizier saluted him and I saluted him too, not knowing that he was the king. At his side was his sister's son, ʻAlī Shāh b. Jalāl al-Dīn al-Kījī,[126] with whom I was already acquainted, so I began to converse with him, not knowing the king. When the vizier informed me of the fact, I was covered with confusion before him, because of addressing my conversation to his sister's son instead of to him, and I made my excuses to him. The king then rose and went into his residence, followed by the amīrs, viziers, and officers of state;

[124] Ibn Baṭṭūṭa suddenly transports his narrative to the year 1347, when he passed through Hurmuz on his way back from India to Baghdād, probably just before Tahamtan's death in the spring of that year (vol. IV, p. 311, Arabic). See also below, p. 403, n. 128. In a later passage he vividly illustrates the disastrous effect of this conflict upon commerce in the Persian Gulf (vol. III, p. 248, Arabic).

[125] The Arabic term *ajfān* is used almost indiscriminately of merchant vessels and war galleys, but the second seems to be the more appropriate rendering in this context.

[126] This person was probably related to the ruling house of Makrān (for Kīj see above, p. 342, n. 238), which was closely connected with the princes of Hurmuz.

I entered along with the vizier and we found him sitting on his throne, wearing the same clothes without any change, and with a rosary in his hand made of pearls such as eyes have never seen, because the pearl fisheries are under his authority.[127] One of the amīrs sat down at his side, and I sat down | at the side of that amīr. The king asked me about 236
myself and my arrival, and about the kings that I had met, and I answered him on these matters. Food was served, and those present ate, but he did not eat with them; after a time he rose and I said farewell to him and went away.

The reason for the war between him and his brother's sons is that once upon a time he sailed from his new city for a pleasure outing in Old Hurmuz and its gardens, the distance between them by sea being three farsakhs, as we have already mentioned. His brother Niẓām al-Dīn revolted against him and proclaimed himself king, and the people of the island, as well as the troops, gave him their oath of allegiance.[128] Quṭb al-Dīn, fearing for his life, sailed to the city of Qalhāt (which has been mentioned above, and is included in his dominions); he stayed there for some months, equipped ships, and came to the island, but its people fought against him on his brother's side and put him to flight. He returned to Qalhāt and renewed his attack | several times, but could find no stratagem 237
[to succeed] until he sent an emissary to one of his brother's wives, whereupon she poisoned his brother and he died. He

[127] In the next paragraph Ibn Baṭṭūṭa defines the pearl fisheries as those of Qais Island, and in a later passage (vol. IV, 168, Arabic) speaks of having seen the pearl fisheries 'in the island of Qais and the island of Kish [*read* Kishm], which belong to Ibn al-Sawāmilī'. This statement seems to define fairly closely the date of this journey. (Ibn) al-Sawāmilī was the popular designation of the celebrated merchant Jamāl al-Dīn Ibrāhīm b. Muḥammad of Ṭīb, entitled Malik al-Islām (d. 1306; see *Durar*, I, 59–60), who founded a short-lived dynasty of princes of Qais. His sons held the island until 1329, and it was captured by Tahamtan from their sons in 1330 or 1331 (see Aubin, *JA* (1953), 89 sqq., 138, Table II). Ibn Baṭṭūṭa, if he visited Qais Island, must thus have done so during the government of the Sawāmilī house, and presumably before the lengthy hostilities broke out with Tahamtan in 1330.

[128] Niẓām al-Dīn seized Jarūn in 1344/5, while Tahamtan was on a hunting expedition, and in a battle on the mainland defeated Tahamtan, who, however, recovered Hurmuz and Jarūn after Niẓām al-Dīn's death in 1346. He died in the spring of 1347, and only under his son and successor Tūrānshāh was control regained over Qais and Baḥrain (Aubin, *JA* (1953), 106–9).

now came to the island and entered it, while his brother's sons fled with the treasuries, moneys and troops to the island of Qais, where the pearl fisheries are. They set about intercepting the merchants of India and Sind who were making for the island and raiding his coastal territories, with the result that the greater part of them have been devastated.

We travelled next from the city of Jarawn with the object of visiting a saintly man in the town of Khunju Pāl. After crossing the strait, we hired mounts from the Turkmens;[129] they are the inhabitants of that country, and no travelling can be done through it except in their company, because of their bravery and knowledge of the roads. In these parts there is a desert extending over four nights' journey, which
238 is the haunt of Arab brigands and in which | the samūm wind blows up in the two months of June and July. All those whom it overtakes there it kills; indeed, I was told that when a man is killed by that wind and his friends attempt to wash him [for burial] all his limbs fall apart.[130] There are many graves in it of those who have succumbed there in this wind. We used to travel by night, and when the sun rose we would halt in the shade of the Umm Ghailān trees, resuming our journey in the late afternoon [and going on] until sunrise. It was in this desert and the adjoining regions that Jamāl al-Lūk, whose name is famous in those parts, used to hold up travellers.

Anecdote. Jamāl al-Lūk was a man of Sijistān, of Persian

[129] Probably the tribesmen now called Qashqā'īs. The Arab brigands mentioned below are most probably the Qufs or Qufṣ, supposedly of south-Arabian origin but perhaps Kurds, inhabitants of the highlands of this region from pre-Islamic times. They were notorious brigands, whose haunts extended from Hurmuz far to the east (Schwarz, III, 261–6). Cf. Mustawfi (117), who describes the population of this region as 'brigands, highwaymen, and footpads'.

[130] 'They call these deadly pestiferous Storms *Bad Sammoun*, that is to say, the Winds of Poison . . . . It rises only between the 15th of June and the 15th of August, which is the time of the excessive Heats near that Gulph. That wind runs whistling through the Air, it appears red and inflamed, and kills and blasts the People; it strikes in a manner, as if it stifled them, particularly in the Day time. Its surprising Effects is not the Death it self, which it causes; what's most amazing is, that the Bodies of those who die by it, are, as it were, dissolved, but without losing their Figure and Contour; insomuch that one would only take them to be asleep; but if you take hold of any piece of them, the Part remains in your Hand' (J. Chardin, *Travels in Persia*, ed. N. M. Penzer, London, 1927, 136).

origin;[131] *al-Lūk* means 'having a hand cut off', his hand having been cut off in one of his battles. He had under him a large band of Arab and Persian horsemen, with whom he engaged | in highway robbery. He would build hospices and 239
supply food to wayfarers with the money that he robbed from people, and he is said to have claimed that he never employed violence except against those who did not give tithes on their property in alms. He continued in this way for a considerable time, he and his horsemen making raids, crossing wildernesses unknown to others and burying in them large and small waterskins, so that when they were pursued by the sultan's troops they would make off into the desert and dig out the water [they had stored], while the troops would give up pursuit of them for fear of perishing. He persisted in this conduct for a time, while neither the king of al-'Irāq nor any other could do anything against him; but afterwards he repented and gave himself up to religious devotions until his death, and his grave is a place of visitation in his country.

We travelled through this desert until we came to Kawristān, a small town with running streams and gardens, and extremely hot.[132] From there we continued our march | for 240
three days through [another] desert like the former, and came to the city of Lār, a large city with many springs and perennial streams and gardens, and with fine bazaars.[133] We stayed there in the hospice of the ascetic shaikh Abū Dulaf Muḥammad[134]—he was the person that we had in mind to visit at Khunju Pāl. In this hospice was his son Abū Zaid 'Abd al-Raḥmān, and along with him a company of poor

[131] Ibn Ḥajar (*Durar*, IV, 260) relates that this man (incorrectly called al-Ḥammāl Lūk) terrorized the caravans between Yazd and Shīrāz, but was eventually caught in an ambush by Muḥammad b. Muẓaffar and executed, before Ibn Muẓaffar occupied Yazd (see above, p. 309, n. 124). *Lūk* is glossed in the Persian lexica as 'one who crawls on hands and knees'.

[132] This is apparently Kūristān, a village on the Rūd-i Kūristān, a western affluent of the Rūd-i Shūr, and on the direct westward route from the vicinity of the later town of Bandar 'Abbās. The spelling Kawrāstān in the text is an error; cf. vol. IV, p. 311 (Arabic).

[133] This is the earliest mention of a town of Lār; the contemporary Persian geographer Mustawfī (138) mentions Lār only as a district near the seacoast (adding, strangely, 'Its population are Muslims'), but twice mentions the town of Lāghir, on the main road to Shīrāz, twelve farsakhs northwest of Khunj (176, n. 2).

[134] Not identified.

brethren. It is part of their regular practice to assemble in the hospice after the afternoon prayer every day, and then make a circuit of the houses in the city; at each house they are given one or two loaves, and from these they provide food for wayfarers. The householders are used to this practice, and include [the extra loaves] in their [daily] provision in readiness for the faqīrs, as a contribution to their distribution of food. On the eve of every Friday the poor brethren and devout men of the city assemble in this hospice, each bringing as
241 many dirhams as he can afford, | and they put them together and spend them the same night. They then pass the night in religious exercises, including prayers and recitation of the *dhikr* and of the Qur'ān, and disperse after the dawn prayer.

Account of the Sultan of Lār. In this city is a sultan named Jalāl al-Dīn, a Turkmen by origin.[135] He sent us a hospitality gift but we did not meet him nor see him.

We went on next to the city of Khunju Pāl (sometimes pronounced Hunju Pāl),[136] in which is the residence of the shaikh Abū Dulaf, whom we had set out to visit, and in whose hospice we lodged. When I entered the hospice, I saw him sitting in a corner of it on the bare earth, and wearing a dilapidated green woollen tunic, with a black woollen turban on his head. When I saluted him, he warmly returned my
242 salutation, asked me about my arrival | and my country, and assigned me a lodging. He used to send me food and fruit by a son of his, himself a pious devotee, exceedingly modest and humble, who fasted continuously and was assiduous in prayer. This shaikh Abū Dulaf is a man of remarkable character and strange ways, for his outlay in this hospice is very large; he makes immense gifts, gives presents of garments and horses to [many] persons, is generous to every wayfarer, and I saw none to compare with him in that country; yet he is not known to possess any income except

[135] Not identified.

[136] Khunj-u Pāl is a double name, for the towns of Khunj and Fāl. Khunj lies 40 miles north-west of Lār, and is often confused with Hunj, about 50 miles south of Lār. The ruins of Fāl lie 4 miles south of Gallah-Dār, some 60 miles west of Khunj, at 27° 38′ N., 52° 39′ E.; see Sir M. Aurel Stein, *Archaeological Reconnaissances in North-West India and South-Eastern Iran* (London, 1937), 220. There seems to be no explanation for Ibn Baṭṭūṭa's conjunction of the two names.

what comes to him as gifts from brethren and associates. Many persons, consequently, assert that he is able to draw on the resources of creation. In this hospice of his is the tomb of the shaikh, the pious saint and pole Dāniyāl, whose name is widely famed in that country, and of great eminence in sainthood.[137] Over his tomb is a vast cupola, built by the sultan Quṭb al-Dīn Tamahtan [Tahamtan] b. Tūrān-Shāh. | I 243
stayed with the shaikh Abū Dulaf only one day, on account of the urgency of the caravan in whose company I was travelling to press on.

I heard that in this city of Khunju Pāl there was a hospice in which there were a number of pious devotees, so I went to it in the evening and saluted their shaikh and them. [In them] I found a blessed company upon whom assiduous devotions had left their mark, for they were pale in colour, lean in body, much given to weeping and profuse in tears. When I arrived among them they brought food, and their chief said 'Call my son Muḥammad to me,' as he was engaged in solitary exercises in some part of the hospice. So the boy came to us, and he was as though he had come out of a tomb, so emaciated was he by his devotions. He said a greeting and sat down, then his father said to him 'My son, join these newcomers in the meal and you will gain the advantage of their blessings,' and although he was fasting at the time he broke his fast with us. They are Shāfi'ites | in rite, and when we had finished 244
eating they pronounced a blessing on us and we went away.

We travelled on from there to the city of Qais, also called Sīrāf.[138] It is on the coast of the Indian Sea, which connects

[137] Shaikh Dāniyāl was instrumental in the acquisition of Jarūn by Ayāz (see above, p. 396, n. 100), and his mosque still exists in Khunj (Aubin, *JA* (1953), 95).

[138] The confusion of Qais with Sīrāf here arises from Ibn Baṭṭūṭa's habit of occasionally combining literary reminiscences with his personal experiences. As is clear from above, n. 127, he was well aware that Qais was an island, and it was still relatively flourishing at this time. His description, in fact, applies much more accurately to Qais than to Sīrāf, where there were scarcely any trees or cultivation and most of its water had to be carried in (Schwarz, II, 59–64, 88–9). Down to the tenth century, however, Sīrāf had been the richest trading port on the Persian Gulf; it was destroyed by an earthquake in 977, and never recovered. Its site, near the modern Ṭāhirī, 20 miles west of Gallah-Dār, has been examined by Sir Aurel Stein (202–12, with plan). Schwarz suggests that Ibn Baṭṭūṭa confused Sīrāf with Chārak, on the coast, north-east of Qais, but it is doubtful whether Chārak existed

with the sea of al-Yaman and [that of] Fārs, and it is reckoned as one of the districts of Fārs. [It is] a city of wide extent, commodious, in a rich country-side, and with wonderful gardens of scented herbs and leafy trees amongst its houses. Its people draw their water from springs that gush out from its hills; they are Persians of noble stock, and among them is a body of Arabs of the Banū Saffāf.[139] It is these latter who dive for pearls.

Account of the Pearl Fishery.[140] The pearl fishery is situated between Sīrāf and al-Baḥrain, in a calm channel like a great river. When the month of April and the month of May come round, large numbers of boats come to this place with divers
245 and merchants of Fārs, | al-Baḥrain and al-Quṭaif. The diver, when he makes ready to dive, puts over his face a covering made of the shell of the *ghailam*, that is the tortoise, and makes of this same shell a sort of thing like scissors which he fastens on his nose, then ties a rope round his waist and submerges. They differ in their endurance under water, some of them being able to stay under water for an hour or two hours or less. When the diver reaches the bottom of the sea he finds the shells there, stuck in the sand among small stones, and pulls them out by hand or cuts them loose with a knife that he has for that purpose, and puts them in a leather bag slung round his neck. When his breath becomes restricted he pulls on the rope, and the man who is holding the rope on the

---

by name at that time, and the route from Khunj to Qais (Mustawfī, 176) ran not to Chārak, but to Hūzū, identified by Le Strange with modern Chiru. Indeed, no major town is known to have existed at this time on the Lār coast (see the next note).

139 One section of the coastal region called Irāhistān is called by the Arab geographers Sīf Bani'l-Ṣaffāq; this was apparently the coast of Lār (Schwarz, II, 75–6). The Banu'l-Ṣaffāq (or Ṣaffāf or Ṣaffār) were Arabs from 'Omān, long established on the coast of Fārs (*Bibl. Geog. Arab.*, I, 141).

140 This account is obviously at secondhand, since Ibn Baṭṭūṭa seems never to have been in the region at the pearling season, and there is a characteristic mixture of exact fact and exaggerations or misinformation in his statement. His location of the pearl beds is so vague as to be unidentifiable, and was indeed probably as vague in his own mind. On the east shore of the Gulf the principal pearl-fisheries at this time appear to have been in the vicinity of Lār (or Lārān) Island and at Khōr Shīf (Aubin, *JA* (1953), 101), but the location of this place in turn is not precisely known. The term *khōr* may, however, underlie Ibn Baṭṭūṭa's picture of 'a calm channel like a great river'.

shore[141] feels the movement and pulls him up to the boat. The bag is then taken from him and the shells are opened. Inside them are found pieces of flesh which are cut out with a knife, and when they come into contact with the air they solidify and turn into | pearls. All of these are collected, 246
whether small or large; the sultan takes his fifth and the remainder are bought by the merchants who are there in the boats. Most of them are creditors of the divers, and they take the pearls in quittance of their debts, or so much of them as is their due.[142]

We then travelled from Sīrāf to the city of al-Baḥrain, a fine large city with gardens, trees and streams.[143] Water is easy to get at there—one digs with one's hands [in the sand] and there it is. The city has groves of date-palms, pomegranates, and citrons, and cotton is grown there. It is exceedingly hot there and very sandy, and the sand often encroaches on some of its dwellings. There was formerly a road between al-Baḥrain and 'Omān, which has been overwhelmed by the sands and become impassable, so that the city cannot be reached from 'Omān except by sea. In its vicinity are two large hills, one of which is called | Kusair, which lies to the 247
west of it, and the other called 'Owair, which is to the east of it. There is a proverbial saying derived from them, 'Kusair and 'Owair, and either is no good'.[144]

[141] This presumably means, from the context, 'on the surface', but the use of the term *sāḥil* in this sense is not attested elsewhere.

[142] The statements on the disposal of the pearls are entirely accurate. See, on the industry and its processes, Ameen Rihani, *Around the Coasts of Arabia* (London, 1930), 275–81; A. Villiers, 373 ff.

[143] Al-Baḥrain in old Arabic usage meant the coastal area on the Arabian mainland now called al-Ḥasā, but Mustawfī (135) shows that already by this time it was used for the island, properly called Uwāl, and that its inhabitants were already noted for piracy. The older usage still survived, however, and may explain the apparent confusion implied in Ibn Baṭṭūṭa's statement about the road to 'Omān. The underground water-bearing beds of eastern Arabia discharge into the sea around al-Baḥrain, and are also captured on the islands.

[144] Ibn Baṭṭūṭa gives both a most confused statement and an incorrect version of a seamen's jingle: *Kusair wa-'Uwair wa-thālith laisa fīhi khair*, i.e. 'Kusair and 'Owair and a third one, in which [*sc.* in each of which] is no good'. From the precise indications given by al-Mas'ūdī (*Murūj al-Dhahab* [*Prairies d'Or*], trans. B. de Meynard (Paris, 1861), I, 240), who places them in the vicinity of Hanjām Island, and Yāqūt (*Geogr. Dict.*, svv.), who describes them as 'two large hills which project prominently at the far end of the Sea of 'Omān', it would appear that they are the group of islets called by

We then travelled to the city of al-Quṭaif, a fine large city with many date-palms, inhabited by different clans of Arabs who are extremist Rāfiḍīs, and display their recusant heresy openly, without fear of anyone.[145] Their mu'adhdhin says in his call to prayer, after the two words of witness, 'I witness that 'Alī is the friend of God', and after the two bidding formulas ['Come to prayer, come to salvation'] he adds 'Come to the best of works.'[146] He also adds after the final *takbīr* ['God is most great'] 'Muḥammad and 'Alī are the best of mankind; whoso opposes them has become an infidel.'

We went on from there to the city of Hajar, which is now
248 called al-Ḥasā.[147] | This is the place which has become proverbial in the saying 'Like the carrier of dates to Hajar', since there are such quantities of date-palms there as are not to be found in any other place, and they even feed their beasts on them. Its population are Arabs, mostly of the tribe of 'Abd al-Qais b. Afṣā.[148]

From there we travelled next to the city of al-Yamāma, also called Ḥajr, a fine and fertile city with running streams and trees, inhabited by different clans of Arabs, most of whom are of the Banū Ḥanīfa, this being their land from of old.[149] Their amīr is Ṭufail b. Ghānim. I continued my journey from there in the company of this amīr to make the

---

English seamen 'the Quoins' and in modern Arabic 'Salama and her daughters', lying 4–6 miles north and north-west of Ra's Musandam (*Sailing Directions for the Persian Gulf*, 81, views 2, 3). Mustawfī (166, 226) even more strangely defines Kusair and 'Owair as 'hidden mountainous reefs below sea-level', between al-Baḥrain and either al-Baṣra or Qais Island.

[145] Usually pronounced al-Qaṭīf, on the mainland, north-west of Baḥrain Island. The ruling family at this time was founded by a man of Quraish, Jarwān al-Mālikī, who seized it from its former Qarmaṭī ('Carmathian') rulers in 1305/6 and established a Shī'ite government in al-Ḥasā (*Durar*, I, 73–4). See also p. 401, n. 123.

[146] These are standard Shī'ite formulas; see *E.I.*², s.v. adhān.

[147] Now called al-Hofhūf or al-Hufūf; for a description of the town and its oasis see *GJ* (1924), LXIII, 189–207.

[148] One of the major tribes of the north-eastern group called Rabī'a, established in this area since the sixth century A.D.; see *E.I.*², s.v.

[149] Formerly the chief town of Najd, the sand-buried ruins of which lie 58 miles south-east of the present capital al-Riyāḍ, at 24° 07′ N., 47° 25′ E.; see H. St. J. Philby, *The Heart of Arabia* (London, 1922), II, 31–4. The Banū Ḥanīfa of al-Yamāma are famous in Islamic history for their desperate resistance to the Muslim forces in 633 (see *E.I.*², s.v. Abū Bakr). Little is known of their later history in this area.

Pilgrimage, that being in the year 32, and so came to Mecca (God ennoble her).

In this same year al-Malik al-Nāṣir, sultan of Egypt (God's mercy on him), came on pilgrimage with a number of his amīrs. This was the last Pilgrimage that he made, and he lavished largesse on the inhabitants and sojourners in the two noble sanctuaries [Mecca and al-Madīna]. | In this year 249
also al-Malik al-Nāṣir put to death Amīr Aḥmad, who is said to have been his son, as well as the chief of his amīrs, Baktumūr the cupbearer.[150]

Anecdote. It was said that al-Malik al-Nāṣir made a present of a slave-girl to Baktumūr the cupbearer. When he was about to approach her she said to him 'I am pregnant by al-Malik al-Nāṣir,' so he kept away from her and she bore a son whom he called Amīr Aḥmad. The boy grew up under his care, gave evident signs of his noble origin, and was widely known as al-Malik al-Nāṣir's son. In the course of this pilgrimage, these two made a compact to assassinate al-Malik al-Nāṣir, and that Amīr Aḥmad should succeed to the throne. Baktumūr carried with him standards, drums, [official] robes and quantities of money. The report was divulged to al-Malik al-Nāṣir, who sent for Amīr Aḥmad on a very hot day; when he came into the king's presence there were some goblets with drinks before him, and al-Malik | al-Nāṣir drank one 250
goblet and handed Amīr Aḥmad another goblet, which was poisoned. As soon as he had drunk it, the king gave orders for departure, to occupy the time, so the cortège set out and before they reached the next station Amīr Aḥmad was dead. Baktumūr was greatly perturbed by his death, rent his garments, and abstained from food and drink. The report of this was brought to al-Malik al-Nāṣir, who came to him in person, spoke kindly to him, and condoled with him, then took a goblet which had been poisoned, handed it to him and said to him 'I adjure you by my life to drink and cool the fire

150 Al-Malik al-Nāṣir's pilgrimage in 732 (the Festival in this year fell on 2 September 1332) is confirmed by the historical sources, together with the deaths of Amīr Aḥmad and Baktumūr during the journey back to Cairo (see, e.g. Zettersteen, 186; and for Baktumūr also vol. I, p. 53, n. 167, where 1335 is to be corrected to 1333). Ibn Baṭṭūṭa's 'anecdote' is apparently a popular version of the events, derived from hearsay, the main points of which are, however, cautiously indicated in the more formal sources.

in your heart.' So he drank it and died on the spot, and there were found in his possession royal robes of honour and stores of money, and thus there was verified the intention with which he was credited of assassinating al-Malik al-Nāṣir.

CHAPTER VIII

Asia Minor

WHEN the Pilgrimage ended, I went to Judda,[1] with
the intention of sailing to al-Yaman and India. But
that was not decreed for me; | I was unable to find 251
a companion[2] and I stayed in Judda about forty days. There was a ship there belonging to a man called 'Abdallāh al-Tūnisī, who was intending to go to al-Quṣair,[3] in the government of Qūṣ, so I boarded it to see what state it was in, but it did not please me and I disliked the idea of travelling by it. This was an act of providence of God Most High, for the ship sailed and when it was in the open sea it foundered at a place called Ra's Abū Muḥammad.[4] Its master and some merchants escaped in a ship's boat[5] after severe distress and were on the point of death; [even] some of these perished, and all the rest were drowned, including about seventy of the pilgrims who were on it.

Some time later I sailed in a *sumbuq* for 'Aidhāb but the
wind drove us back to a roadstead called Ra's Dawā'ir,[6] and
from there we travelled | by land with the Bujāh.[7] We made 252
our way through a desert full of ostriches and gazelles and

[1] Judda, now Jedda, see above, p. 360.

[2] *Rafīq*, 'companion', seems to be used here in the Arabian sense of 'guide, conductor'.

[3] As the nearest port to the Nile valley (five days' journey to Qūṣ), al-Quṣair was throughout the mediaeval period and up to the nineteenth century the principal Egyptian port on the Red Sea.

[4] Ra's Abū Muḥammad appears to be no longer identifiable by that name.

[5] Arabic *'ushārī*, a rowing boat for landing passengers, wares, etc., from ships (see Kindermann, 64–5).

[6] For 'Aidhāb see vol. I, p. 68, n. 218, and for Ra's Dawā'ir, p. 362, n. 9, above. But Marsā Durūr is about 190 miles south of the site of 'Aidhāb, and it seems more probable that on this occasion Ibn Baṭṭūṭa means Ra's Rawaiya and its anchorage called Dukhana bay, about 100 miles south of 'Aidhāb (see *Red Sea Pilot*, 135–6).

[7] On the Bujāh (Bejas) see vol. I, p. 69, n. 219, and p. 363 above.

inhabited by Arabs of Juhaina and Banū Kāhil,[8] who are subject to the Bujāh, and reached a waterpoint called Mafrūr and another called al-Jadīd. Since our provisions were exhausted we purchased sheep from some of the Bujāh whom we found in the wilderness, and prepared a store of their flesh. I saw in this wilderness an Arab boy who spoke to me in Arabic and told me that the Bujāh had captured him; he declared that for a whole year he had eaten no meat and had had no other food than camel's milk. Later on that meat that we had bought ran out on us and we had no provisions left. But I had with me about a load of dried dates [of the kinds called] *ṣaihānī* and *barnī*,[9] intended as presents to my friends, so I distributed them to the company and we lived on them for three nights' journey.

After a passage of nine days from Ra's Dawā'ir we reached
253 'Aidhāb. Some members of the caravan had gone ahead | to it, and [on their indications] its people came out to meet us with bread, dates, and water. We stayed there for some days, and having hired camels went out in company with a party of Arabs of Dughaim. After watering at a place called al-Khubaib, we halted at Ḥumaithirā,[10] the site of the grave of the saint of God Most High, Abu'l-Ḥasan al-Shādhilī, being granted thus the favour of visiting it a second time, and sojourned for the night at his sanctuary. Thereafter we reached the village of al-Aṭwānī, which is on the bank of the Nile opposite the city of Adfū in the upper Ṣa'īd.[11] We crossed the Nile to the city of Asnā, thence to the city of Armant, then to al-Aqṣur, where we visited the [tomb of the] shaikh Abu'l-Ḥajjāj al-Aqṣurī for the second time, thence to the city of Qūṣ, thence to the city of Qinā, where we visited

[8] See above, p. 363, nn. 12, 14.

[9] Two species of dates which are highly esteemed in Arabia (see R. F. Burton, *Personal Narrative of a Pilgrimage to El-Medinah and Mecca* (London, 1855), II, 200; (1857), I, 384 and J. L. Burckhardt, *Travels in Arabia* (London, 1829), II, 213), the *barnī* (*birnī*) because it is regarded as a specific against sickness, and the *ṣaiḥānī* ('outcrier') because a palm of this kind on one occasion saluted the Prophet and 'Alī.

[10] For Ḥumaithirā see vol. I, p. 68, n. 217. Al-Khubaib or al-Junaib is not indicated by J. Bell (see his map of water-points in *The Geography and Geology of South-Eastern Egypt* (Cairo, 1912), facing p. 26).

[11] From al-Aṭwānī to Cairo Ibn Baṭṭūṭa repeats in reverse order the journey described in vol. I, pp. 60–8. Al-Aṭwānī is a village two miles north of Asnā.

[the tomb of] shaikh ʿAbd al-Raḥīm al-Qināwī a second time, thence in succession to the cities of Hū, Akhmīm, Asyūṭ, Manfalūṭ, Manlawī, Ushmūnain, | Munyat al-Qā'id, 254
all of which cities have been previously described by us. Thence we came to Cairo, and after staying there for some days I set out for Syria by the way of Balbais,[12] accompanied by al-Ḥājj ʿAbdallāh b. Abū Bakr b. al-Farḥān of Tūzar. He continued to accompany me for many years, until we quitted the land of India, when he died at Sandabūr, as we shall relate in due course. We then came to the city of Ghazza, thence to the city of al-Khalīl [Abraham] (upon whom be peace) and renewed our visitation to his tomb, thence to Bait al-Maqdis [Jerusalem], and thence in succession to the cities of al-Ramla, ʿAkkā, Ṭarābulus, Jabala, where we visited again [the tomb of] Ibrāhīm b. Adham (God be pleased with him), and al-Lādhiqīya, all of which places we have described previously.

From al-Lādhiqīya we embarked on a large vessel[13] belonging to the Genoese, | the master of which was called 255
Martalamīn, and made for the country of the Turks, known as *Bilād al-Rūm*. Why it is called after the Rūm is because it used to be their land in olden times, and from it came the ancient Rūm and the Yūnānīs [Greeks].[14] Later on it was conquered by the Muslims, but in it there are still large numbers of Christians under the protection of the Muslims, these latter being Turkmens.[15] We travelled on the sea for ten nights with a favouring wind, and the Christians treated us

[12] For his previous journey from Cairo to Hebron and Jerusalem see vol. I, pp. 71–7, Ramla and ʿAkka pp. 82–3, Tripoli p. 88, Jabala and the tomb of Ibrāhīm ibn Adham p. 109, and Latakiya p. 113.

[13] Arabic *qurqūra*, used generally to denote a large merchant vessel, propelled by sails and with two or three decks (Kindermann, 79–81). The Genoese were at this time at the apogee of their commercial activity and power in the Levant (see Yule's *Marco Polo*, Intro., 41–51). The French translators conjecture that *Martalamīn* stands for Bartolomeo.

[14] *Rūm* is the traditional name for the Byzantine Greeks, but was applied also to the Romans (presumably the 'ancient Rūm' of this passage), as *Yūnānī* (sc. Ionian) was applied to the ancient Greeks (especially in the term *ṭibb yūnānī*, 'Greek medicine'); cf. Sāʿid al-Andalusī, *Ṭabaqāt al-Umam*, trans. Régis Blachère (Paris, 1935), 35, 57 ff., 83 ff.

[15] Anatolia was gradually occupied by Turkish tribes from Central Asia ('Turkmens') after the defeat of the Emperor Romanus IV at Malāzgird in 1171 by the Seljuk sultan Alp Arslān; see *A History of the Crusades* (Philadelphia, 1955), I, ch. IV. For the term *dhimma*, here translated 'protection' but in effect meaning 'government', see below, p. 425, n. 50.

honourably and took no passage-money[16] from us. On the tenth day we arrived at the city of al-'Alāyā, which is the beginning of the land of al-Rūm.[17] This country called *Bilād al-Rūm* is one of the finest regions in the world; in it God has brought together the good things dispersed through other lands. Its inhabitants are the comeliest of men in form, the cleanest in dress, the most delicious in food, and the kindliest of God's creatures. This is why the saying goes 'Blessing in
256 Syria and kindliness in al-Rūm', since what | is meant by the phrase is the people of this land. Wherever we stopped in this land, whether at hospice or private house, our neighbours both men and women (who do not veil themselves) came to ask after our needs. When we left them to continue our journey, they bade us farewell as though they were our relatives and our own kin, and you would see the women weeping out of grief at our departure. One of their customs in that country is that they bake bread on only one day each week, making provision on that day for enough to keep them for the rest of the week. Their men used to bring us warm bread on the day it was baked, together with delicious viands to go with it, as a special treat for us, and would say to us 'The women have sent this to you and beg of you a prayer.'

All of the people of this land belong to the school of the Imām Abū Ḥanīfa (God be pleased with him) and are firmly attached to the Sunna—there is not a Qadarī, nor a Rāfiḍī, nor a Mu'tazilī, nor a Khārijī, nor any innovator amongst them.[18]

[16] The term used is *naul*, which has in Arabic the meaning of 'gift', but is evidently used here in the technical sense of *nolo*, i.e. freight charge; cf. F. B. Pegolotti, *La Pratica della Mercatura*, ed. A. Evans (Cambridge, Mass., 1936), 16.

[17] 'Alāyā (properly 'Alā'iyya), on a small rocky promontory on the eastern rim of the Bay of Adalia, so called after the Seljuk sultan 'Alā al-Dīn Kaiqubād I, who captured it in 1220 and fortified it. From the Greek name of his citadel, *Kalon Oros*, the port derived the name of Candelore, commonly used by the Mediterranean traders. See *E.I.*[2], s.v. Alanya; Seton Lloyd and D. S. Rice, *Alanya* (*Alā'iyya*), (London, 1958).

[18] The Ḥanafī rite and school of law has always predominated among the Turks, and became the official rite in the Ottoman empire. The other groups mentioned were heretics or dissenters from Sunnite 'orthodoxy': the Qadarīs as partisans of the doctrine of freewill, the Rāfiḍīs as partisans of 'Alī (Shī'ites, see vol. I, p. 83, n. 62), the Mu'tazilites as rationalists in dogmatics, and the Khārijites as self-righteous exclusivists, excommunicating all Muslims who did not share their particular views. 'Innovator' carried in Sunni Islam the implication of 'heretic'.

This is a virtue | by which God Most High has distinguished 257
them, but they consume *ḥashīsh* and think nothing wrong in that.[19]

The city of al-'Alāyā that we have mentioned is a large place on the sea coast. It is inhabited by Turkmens, and is visited by the merchants of Cairo, Alexandria, and Syria. It has quantities of wood, which is exported from there to Alexandria and Dimyāṭ, and thence carried to the other parts of Egypt. There is at the top of the town a magnificent and formidable citadel, built by the illustrious sultan 'Alā al-Dīn al-Rūmī.[20] I met in this city its qāḍī Jalāl al-Dīn al-Arzanjānī; he went up to the citadel with me on a Friday, when we performed the prayers there, and treated me with generous hospitality. I was hospitably entertained there also by Shams al-Din Ibn al-Rajīḥānī, whose father 'Alā al-Dīn died at Māllī, in the Negrolands.[21]

Account of the Sultan of al-'Alāyā. On the Saturday the
qāḍī Jalāl al-Dīn rode out with me | and we went to meet the 258
king of al-'Alāyā, who is Yūsuf Bak, son of Qaramān,[22] [the term] *bak* meaning 'king'. His residence is at a distance of ten miles from the city. We found him sitting on the shore, by himself, on the top of a little hillock there, with the amīrs and viziers below him and the troops on his right and left. He has his hair dyed black. After I saluted him, he asked me about my arrival; I answered his questions and took leave of him, and he sent me a present [of money].

From there I went on to the city of Anṭāliya[23] (the city in

[19] *Ḥashīsh*, literally 'dry grass', is the intoxicating conserve or drug made from Indian hemp (*cannabis indica*) or from henbane (*hyoscyamus niger*). The latter is commonly known in Turkey, Persia and India by the Persian name *bang*, and is probably the variety meant here (see *Hobson-Jobson*, s.v. Bhang). See also vol. III, p. [79 Ar.], n. 175.

[20] The complex of fortifications on the upper part of the promontory was reconstructed by Sultan 'Alā al-Dīn (see above, n. 17) on the foundations of the Greek buildings; see Lloyd and Rice, plates III, X.

[21] Māllī, capital of the Negro kingdom on the Niger, was visited by Ibn Baṭṭūṭa in 1352; see *Selections*, 323–31.

[22] 'Alāyā was occupied by the Qaramān-oghlu, princes of Laranda (see below, p. 432, n. 73), at the end of the thirteenth century. According to the informant of Ibn Baṭṭūṭa's contemporary al-'Omarī, Yūsuf was governor of 'Alāyā on behalf of the Qaramān-oghlu, but no relationship is indicated (*Al-'Umarī's Bericht über Anatolien*, ed. F. Taeschner (Leipzig, 1929), 23).

[23] Anṭālya, in Turkish Adalya and in the mediaeval portolans Satalia, at the head of the Gulf of Adalya, is the ancient Attaleia, and the city walls

Syria is Anṭākiya, pronounced in the same way, but with a *k* instead of an *l*). It is one of the finest of cities, enormous in extent and bulk, [among] the most handsome of cities to be seen anywhere, as well as the most populous and best organized. Each section of its inhabitants live by themselves,
259 separated from | each other section. Thus the Christian merchants reside in a part of it called al-Mīnā[24] and are encircled by a wall, the gates of which are shut upon them [from without] at night and during the Friday prayer-service; the Rūm [Greek Christians], who were its inhabitants in former times, live by themselves in another part, also encircled by a wall; the Jews in another part, with a wall round them; while the king and his officers and mamlūks live in a [separate] township, which also is surrounded by a wall that encircles it and separates it from the sections that we have mentioned. The rest of the population, the Muslims, live in the main city, which has a congregational mosque, a college, many bath-houses, and vast bazaars most admirably organized. Around it is a great wall which encircles both it and all the quarters which we have mentioned. The city contains many orchards and delicious fruits, [especially] the wonderful apricots |
260 called by them *qamar al-dīn*, in whose kernel there is a sweet almond.[25] This fruit is dried and exported to Egypt, where it is regarded as a great luxury. In the city also there are springs of excellent water, sweet and very cold in the summertime. We stayed in the college in this city, the shaikh of which was Shihāb al-Dīn al-Ḥamawī. One of their customs is that a company of boys with beautiful voices recite every day, after the afternoon prayer in the congregational mosque and also in the college, the *sūra* of Victory, the *sūra* of Sovereignty, and the *sūra* *'Amma*.[26]

Account of the Young Akhīs (*Akhīyya*). The singular of *akhīyya* is *akhī*, pronounced like the word *akh* ('brother') with

are of Roman construction. It was captured by the Seljuk sultan Kaikhusraw I in 1207, and later occupied by Turkmens under the princes of the Teke-oghlu (see below, p. 421, n. 34).

[24] 'The Harbour', the traditional name in the Levant for the trading quarter by the port. The 'Christian' merchants are those from the western countries, outside the Byzantine Empire.

[25] See vol. I, p. 91, n. 92; p. 117, n. 178.

[26] Sūras 48, 67, and 78 of the Qur'ān.

the possessive pronoun of the first person singular.[27] They exist in all the lands of the Turkmens of al-Rūm, | in every 261
district, city, and village. Nowhere in the world are there to be found any to compare with them in solicitude for strangers, and in ardour to serve food and satisfy wants, to restrain the hands of the tyrannous, and to kill the agents of police[28] and those ruffians who join with them. An Akhī, in their idiom, is a man whom the assembled members of his trade, together with others of the young unmarried men and those who have adopted the celibate life, choose to be their leader. That is [what is called] *al-futuwwa* also.[29] The *Akhī* builds a hospice and furnishes it with rugs, lamps, and what other equipment it requires. His associates work during the day to gain their livelihood, and after the afternoon prayer they bring him their collective earnings; with this they buy fruit, food, and the other things needed for consumption in the hospice. If, during that day, a traveller alights at the town, they give him

[27] The guild organizations under leaders called Akhis were a special feature in the social life of Anatolia in this century, and Ibn Baṭṭūṭa's narrative is one of the principal sources of information about them. The term *Akhi* appears to be an original Turkish word meaning 'generous', but was readily associated with the Arabic *akhī*, 'my brother'. These corporations were in principle religious associations, but in the disturbed conditions of the fourteenth century they frequently played a political role. After the establishment of the Ottoman Empire the term *Akhi* survived only in a few traditional names, notably that of *Akhi Baba*, the head of the tanners' guild; see *E.I.*^{2}, s.v.

[28] Arabic *al-shuraṭ*. The police in the mediaeval Muslim cities were found from the governor's guard (*shurṭa*), under command of a chief of police (*ṣāḥib al-shurṭa*). In later times the singular *shurṭī* became a term of abuse, colloquially applied to a thief or pickpocket. Ibn Baṭṭūṭa probably means the ill-regulated and venal squads by which the local chiefs attempted to control (or hold to ransom) the townsmen in the cities that they had seized.

[29] *Futuwwa* is an Arabic term meaning 'youthfulness', 'the quality of a *fatā* or young man'. *Fatā* (pl. *fityān*) acquired, however, the sense of 'warrior, hero, generous man', and was adopted by the members of half-secret (and sometimes subversive) clubs in the cities, with a graded series of initiations. Under Ṣūfī influence the term acquired a religious association, and *futuwwa* organizations were set up under Sūfī auspices; but in spite of an attempt by a caliph, al-Nāṣir (1180–1225), to create a 'knightly' order of *futuwwa*, they remained confined largely to artisan and other city populations. Ibn Baṭṭūṭa occasionally uses *fatā* as a kind of synonym or adjective to *akhi* (as in the title of this paragraph); in this translation the combination is rendered by 'Young Akhī'. Strictly, however, the term *akhi* was given only to initiates in the higher grades of the *futuwwa*. For literature on the moral teachings of the *futuwwa* see *E.I.*, s.v., and F. Taeschner, *Der anatolische Dichter Nasiri und sein Futuvvetname* (Leipzig, 1944).

lodging with them; what they have purchased serves for their hospitality to him and he remains with them until his departure. If no newcomer arrives, they assemble themselves
262 to partake of | the food, and after eating they sing and dance. On the morrow they disperse to their occupations, and after the afternoon prayer they bring their collective earnings to their leader. The members are called *fityān*, and their leader, as we have said, is the *Akhī*. Nowhere in the world have I seen men more chivalrous in conduct than they are. The people of Shīrāz and of Iṣfahān can compare with them in their conduct, but these are more affectionate to the wayfarer and show him more honour and kindness.

On the day after that of our arrival in this city one of these *fityān* came to the shaikh Shihāb al-Dīn al-Ḥamawī and spoke with him in Turkish, which I did not understand at that time.[30] He was wearing shabby clothes and had a felt bonnet on his head. The shaikh said to me 'Do you know what this man is saying?' 'No' said I, 'I do not know what he said.' Then he said to me' He is inviting you to a meal with him,
263 you and your companions.' I was surprised at this, | but I said to him 'Very well,' and when the man had gone I said to the shaikh 'This is a poor man, and he has not the means to entertain us and we do not like to impose a burden on him.' Whereupon the shaikh burst out laughing and said to me' He is one of the shaikhs of the Young Akhīs. He is a cobbler, and a man of generous disposition. His associates number about two hundred men of different trades, who have elected him as their leader and have built a hospice to entertain guests in, and all that they earn by day they spend at night.'

So, after I had prayed the sunset prayer, the same man came back for us and we went with him to the hospice. We found it to be a fine building, carpeted with beautiful Rūmī rugs, and with a large number of lustres of 'Irāqī glass. In the chamber there were five [candelabra of the kind called] *baisūs*; this resembles a column of brass, having three feet and on top of it a kind of lamp, also of brass, in the centre of which is a tube for the wick. It is filled with melted grease, |

[30] There is a slight element of fanfaronnade in this statement, since Ibn Baṭṭūṭa shows no evidence of ever having learned Turkish; cf. below, p. 455, n. 157.

and alongside it are vessels of brass also filled with grease, in 264
which are placed scissors for trimming the wicks. One of their company is put in charge of them; he is called in their language the *jarājī*.[31] Standing in rows in the chamber were a number of young men wearing long cloaks, and with boots on their feet. Each one of them had a knife about two cubits long attached to a girdle round his waist, and on their heads were white bonnets of wool with a piece of stuff about a cubit long and two fingers broad attached to the peak of each bonnet.[32] When they take their places in the chamber, each one of them removes his bonnet and puts it down in front of him, but retains on his head another bonnet, an ornamental one, of silk taffeta or some other fabric.[33] In the centre of their hall was a sort of platform placed there for visitors. When we had taken our places among them, they brought in a great banquet, with fruits and sweetmeats, after which they began their singing and dancing. Everything about them
filled us with admiration | and we were greatly astonished at 265
their generosity and innate nobility. We took leave of them at the end of the night and left them in their hospice.

Account of the Sultan of Anṭāliya. Its sultan is Khiḍr Bak, son of Yūnus Bak.[34] When we arrived in the city we found him ill, but we visited him in his residence, while he was on his sick-bed, and he spoke to us in the most affable and agreeable manner, and when we took leave of him he sent us a gift [of money].

We continued our journey to the town of Burdūr,[35] which

[31] I.e. *chirāghjī*, from Persian *chirāgh*, 'lamp', with the Turkish suffix *jī*. *Baisūs* is the Persian *paisūz* (derived from *pīh* = 'tallow'), about three feet in height and with a platter some six inches in diameter at the top.

[32] The cloth tube attached to the bonnet became, later on, a feature of the uniform of the Ottoman janissaries.

[33] *Zard-khāna* (from Persian *zard*, 'yellow') is not found as a name for any known Persian textile, but appears to be a silk taffeta of local Turkish make; cf. W. von Heyd, *Histoire du Commerce du Levant au moyen-âge* (Leipzig, 1885–6), II, 674; R. P. A. Dozy, *Dictionnaire détaillé des noms des vêtements chez les Arabes* (Amsterdam, 1845), 369, note.

[34] This Turkmen dynasty of Adalia is commonly known as Teke-oghlu (see *E.I.*, s.v.), presumably from the Turkmen tribe of Teke (Tekke). They were related to the neighbouring dynasty of Ḥamīd-oghlu (see below, p. 423, n. 40), Yūnus being usually described as the brother of Dundār of the latter family.

[35] One hundred and sixty km. north of Antalya, the Greek Polydorion (see V. Cuinet, *La Turquie d'Asie* (Paris, 1892), I, 803 ff.; *Murray's Handbook for Travellers in Asia Minor, etc.*, ed. Sir Charles Wilson (London, 1895), 150).

is a small town with many orchards and streams. It has a castle with soaring walls on the top of a hill. We lodged in the house of its *khaṭīb*. The *akhīs* came in a body and desired us to lodge with them, but the *khaṭīb* refused their request, so they prepared a banquet for us in a garden belonging to one of them and conducted us to it. It was marvellous what joy they
266 showed at our presence, | what gratification and delight, although they were ignorant of our language and we of theirs, and there was no one to interpret between us. We stayed with them one day and then took our leave.

We went on next from this town to the town of Sabartā,[36] a well-built township with fine bazaars and many orchards and streams, and with a fortress on a steep hill. We reached it in the evening and lodged with its qāḍī.

From there we travelled to the city of Akrīdūr,[37] a great and populous city with fine bazaars and running streams, fruit-trees and orchards. It has a lake of sweet water, on which a vessel plies in two days to Aqshahr and Baqshahr
267 and other towns and villages.[38] We lodged | there in a college opposite the main congregational mosque, and occupied by the learned professor, the worthy pilgrim and sojourner [at the Holy Cities] Muṣliḥ al-Dīn. He had studied in Egypt and Syria, and lived for a time in al-'Irāq; he was elegant in speech and eloquent in expression, a prodigy among the rare spirits of the age, and he received us with the utmost generosity and lavishly supplied our needs.[39]

Account of the Sultan of Akrīdūr. Its sultan is Abū Isḥāq Bak, son of al-Dundār Bak, one of the great sultans of that

[36] Isparta, the ancient Baris, 22 km. east of Burdur, first captured in 1203 by the Seljuks (whose historian declares it to surpass in water and climate all the cities in Anatolia; Ibn Bībī, *Histoire des Seljoucides de l'Asie Mineure* (Leiden, 1891), 62), and subsequently occupied by the Ḥamīd-oghlu (see below, n. 40).

[37] Egerdir (Eğridir), 30 km. north-east of Isparta, at the southern end of the lake called after it. It was the capital of Dundār Bak (see below, n. 40), who gave it the name of Falakābād (from his own title Falak al-Dīn). See *E.I.*, s.v., and *Murray's Handbook*, 151.

[38] Akshehir lies some 125 km. north-east of Eğridir, and behind a range of mountains (Sultan-dagh); Beyshehir is somewhat further to the south-east and on the separate lake called by its name (*Murray's Handbook*, 132, 154). Ibn Baṭṭūṭa may have meant that by crossing the lake to the north-east the traveller reaches the most practicable roads to these cities.

[39] Literally 'performed what was due to us in the most excellent manner'.

land.[40] He lived in Egypt during his father's lifetime and made the Pilgrimage. He is a man of upright conduct, and makes a practice of attending the afternoon prayers in the congregational mosque every day. When the *'aṣr* prayers are concluded, he sits with his back to the wall of the *qibla*; the Qur'ān-readers take their seats in front of him on a high wooden platform and recite the suras of Victory, Sovereignty and *'Amma*[41] with beautiful voices, that work upon | men's 268
souls and at which hearts are humbled, skins creep, and eyes fill with tears. After this he returns to his residence.

The month of Ramaḍān came round while we were in his city.[42] On every night of the month he used to take his seat on a rug laid on the floor, without any couch, and lean his back against a large cushion. The jurist Muṣliḥ al-Dīn would sit alongside him, and I would sit alongside the former, and next to us would be his officers of state and the amīrs of the court. Food would then be brought in, and the first dish with which the fast was broken was *tharīd*, served in a small platter and topped with lentils soaked in butter and sugar. They begin the meal with *tharīd* as a source of blessing, and say 'The Prophet (God bless and give him peace) preferred it to every other dish, so we too begin with it because of the Prophet's preference for it.'[43] After that the other dishes are brought in, and this they do on all the nights of Ramaḍān.

On one day during this period the Sultan's son died, but they observed no | ceremonies other than the lamentations of 269
[entreaty for] the divine mercy, exactly as is done by the people of Egypt and Syria, and in contrast to what we have described above about the conduct of the Lūrs when their

[40] The third of the dynasty of the Ḥamīd-oghlu, who made themselves masters of the highlands of Pisidia about 1300. Ḥamīd's son, Dundār, entitled Falak al-Dīn, had a considerable local reputation (the Egyptian chancery called the dynasty *Banū Dundār*) but was in 1324 defeated and killed by Timurtāsh, the son of Choban (see above, p. 339, n. 225). After the flight of Timurtāsh, Abū Isḥāq recovered the northern part of the principality, which continued through Ottoman times to be called Ḥamīd-eli.

[41] See above, n. 26.

[42] 1 Ramaḍān 733 fell on 16 May 1333 (in 731, 8 June 1331).

[43] *Tharīd* is crumbled or broken bread, served with a seasoning of some sort. There is a famous saying attributed to the Prophet concerning his favourite wife 'Ā'isha: 'The superiority of 'Ā'isha over all other women is as the superiority of *tharīd* to all other food.'

sultan's son died.[44] After he was buried the sultan and the students of religion continued for three days to go out to his grave after the dawn prayers. On the day after his burial I went out with the others, and the sultan, seeing me walking on foot, sent me a horse with his apologies. When I reached the college [on my return], I sent back the horse but he re-returned it saying 'I gave it as a gift, not as a loan,' and sent me [also] a gift of clothing and money.

We left there for the city of Qul Ḥiṣār,[45] a small town surrounded on every side by water in which there is a thick growth of rushes. There is no way to reach it except by a path
270 like a bridge constructed | between the rushes and the water, and broad enough only for one horseman. The city is on a hill in the midst of the waters and is formidably protected and impregnable. We lodged there in the hospice of one of the Young Akhīs.

Account of the Sultan of Qul Ḥiṣār. Its sultan is Muḥammad Chalabī (*chalabī* in the language of the Rūm means 'my lord') who is the brother of the sultan Abū Isḥāq, the king of Akrīdūr.[46] When we reached his city he was away from it, but after we had stayed there for some days he arrived and treated us generously, supplying us with horses and provisions. We left by the way of Qarā Aghāj (*qarā* meaning 'black' and *aghāj* meaning 'wood'),[47] which is a verdant plain inhabited by Turkmens. The Sultan sent a number of horse-
271 men with us to escort us to the city of Lādhiq, because | this plain is infested by a troop of brigands called al-Jarmiyān.[48]

[44] See above, p. 291.

[45] Gül-Hisar, a castle on an islet in a small lake 90 km. south-west of Burdur, connected by causeway with the shore (*Murray's Handbook*, 121).

[46] *Chelebi*, of unknown origin, was a title applied to Ṣūfī leaders in Anatolia (see *Ural-Altäische Jahrbücher*, Wiesbaden, 1955, 97–9), as well as to princes and high officials.

[47] Formerly 'Āṣī Kara-Aghāch, now Garbi Kara-Aghaç, a plateau region whose chief town is Acipayam, 45 km. south-south-east of Denizli: see F. Taeschner, *Das anatolische Wegenetz nach Osmanischen Quellen* (Leipzig, 1924), 170; A. Philippson, *Reise und Forschungen in westlichen Kleinasien*, IV, 78; V, 126 and maps (in *Petermanns Mitteilungen*, Ergänzungshefte, 180, 183, Gotha, 1914–15).

[48] This reflects the attitude of the lesser princes towards Germiyān-Khān, ruler of a principality centred on Kutahya. Thanks to the allegiance of a powerful Oghuz tribe, the Chavuldur, Germiyān-Khān (d. *c.* 1330) and his successor Muḥammad were able to exercise an effective suzerainty over their neighbours and even to exact tribute from them. Al-'Omarī (30, 34–7)

They are said to be descendants of Yazīd b. Muʻāwiya and they have a city called Kūtāhiya. God preserved us from them, and we arrived at the city of Lādhiq, which is also called Dūn Ghuzluh, which means 'town of the swine'.[49]

This is one of the most attractive and immense cities. In it there are seven mosques for the observance of Friday prayers, and it has splendid gardens, perennial streams, and gushing springs. Its bazaars are very fine, and in them are manufactured cotton fabrics edged with gold embroidery, unequalled in their kind, and long-lived on account of the excellence of their cotton and strength of their spun thread. These fabrics are known from the name of the city [as *lādhiqī*]. Most of the artisans there are Greek women, for in it there are many Greeks who are subject to the Muslims and who pay dues to the sultan, including the *jizya*,[50] and other taxes. The distinctive mark of the Greeks there | is their 272
[wearing of] tall pointed hats, some red and some white, and the Greek women for their part wear capacious turbans.

The inhabitants of this city make no effort to stamp out immorality—indeed, the same applies to the whole population of these regions.[51] They buy beautiful Greek slave-girls and put them out to prostitution, and each girl has to pay a regular due to her master. I heard it said there that the girls go into the bath-houses along with the men, and anyone who wishes to indulge in depravity does so in the bath-house and nobody tries to stop him. I was told that the qāḍī in

---

confirms their reputation as savage warriors; see also *E.I.*, s.v. Germianoghlu, and P. Wittek, *Das Fürstentum Mentesche* (Istanbul, 1934), 18–20.

[49] The ruins of Lādhiq, the ancient Laodicaea-on-Lykos (whose Christian inhabitants were reproved in Revelation iii) lie 5 km. north of Denizli (*Murray's Handbook*, 103; Philippson, IV, 86 ff.). The alternative name mentioned by Ibn Baṭṭūṭa is derived from Turkish *duñuz*, 'swine', with the suffix *-lu*; it is not (as the French translators opine) a popular perversion of *deñiz-li*, 'with flowing waters', but the latter (still in use) is a later 'improvement' on the former. Its many streams and luxuriant gardens earned it the name of 'the Damascus of Anatolia', and it was at one time chosen by the Īlkhān Ghāzān Khān for his summer residence (*Letters of Rashīd al-Dīn*, 183–4, where the name is spelled in the same way).

[50] *Jizya* is the canonical poll-tax on Jews and Christians living under the protection of a Muslim sovereign by virtue of an assumed 'covenant' (*dhimma*; see *E.I.*, s.v.). The legal rates were 48, 24, and 12 silver dirhams for the rich, middling and poor respectively.

[51] Reading, with MS. 2289, *hādhihi'l-aqālīm kulluhum*.

this city himself owns slave-girls [employed] in this way.

On our entry into this city, as we passed through one of the bazaars, some men came down from their booths and seized the bridles of our horses. Then certain other men quarrelled with them for doing so, and the altercation between them grew so hot that some of them drew knives. All this time we
273 had no idea what | they were saying, and we began to be afraid of them, thinking that they were the Jarmiyān [brigands] who infest the roads, and that this was their city, and reckoning that they were out to rob us. At length God sent us a man, a pilgrim, who knew Arabic, and I asked what they wanted of us. He replied that they belonged to the *Fityān*, that those who had been the first to reach us were the associates of the Young Akhī Sinān, while the others were the associates of the Young Akhī Ṭūmān, and that each party wanted us to lodge with them. We were amazed at their native generosity. Finally they came to an agreement to cast lots, and that we should lodge first with the one whose lot was drawn. The lot of Akhī Sinān won, and on learning of this he came to meet us with a body of his associates. They greeted us and we were lodged[52] in a hospice of his, where we were served with a variety of dishes. The Akhī then conducted us to the bath and came in with us; he himself took over the
274 office | of serving me, while his associates undertook the service of my companions, three or four of them waiting on each one of the latter. Then, when we came out of the bath, they served us a great banquet with sweetmeats and quantities of fruit, and after we finished eating and the Qur'ān-readers had recited verses from the Exalted Book they began their singing and dancing. They sent word about us to the sultan, and on the following day he sent for us in the evening, and we went to visit him and his son, as we shall relate shortly.

After this we returned to the hospice, and there we found[53] the Akhī Ṭūmān and his associates awaiting us. They conducted us to their hospice and did as their confrères had done in the matter of the food and the bath, but went one better than they in that they gave us a good sprinkling with rose-water when we came out of the bath. They then went with us to the hospice, and they also, in their lavish hospitality with

[52] Reading with MS. 2289 *wa'unzilnā*. [53] Reading with MS. 2289 *alfainā*.

varieties of food, sweetmeats and fruit, | and in recitation of 275
the Qur'ān after the end of the meal, followed by singing and dancing, did just as their confrères had done or even better. We stayed with them in their hospice for several days.[54]

Account of the Sultan of Lādhiq. He is the sultan Yananj Bak, and is one of the great sultans of the land of al-Rūm.[55] When we took up our lodging in the hospice of Akhī Sinān, as we have related above, he sent to us the learned preacher and admonisher 'Alā al-Dīn al-Qaṣṭamūnī, and sent in company with him a horse for each one of our number. This was [still] in the month of Ramaḍān, and we went to visit him and saluted him. It is the custom of the kings of this land to make a show of humility to visiting scholars, and to give them soft speech and trifling donations. So we prayed the sunset prayer with him, and when his food was served broke our fast in his presence, then took leave, and he sent us a little money.
Later on | his son Murād Bak sent an invitation to us. He was 276
living in a garden outside the city, this being in the season of [ripening of] the fruit. He too sent horses, one for each of us, as his father had done, so we went to his garden and stayed that night with him. He had with him a doctor of the law to act as interpreter between us, and we took our leave the next morning.

The Feast of Fast-breaking[56] overtook us in this city, so we went out to the *muṣallā*; the sultan also came out with his troops, and the Young Akhīs too, all of them fully armed. The members of each trade carried flags, trumpets, drums and fifes, all aiming to rival and outdo one another in magnificence and in perfection of their weapons. Every group of these artisans would come out with cattle, sheep, and loads of bread, and after slaughtering the animals in the cemetery give them away in alms, along with the bread. On coming out they went first to the cemetery, and from there on to the

[54] According to the Turkish *Islâm Ansiklopedisi*, the traveller Evliyā Chelebi, passing through Denizli about 1650, found the tombs of Akhī Sinān and Akhī Ṭumān still venerated.

[55] Īnanch Beg, son of 'Alī Beg, the founder of the minor dynasty of Denizli, was apparently related to the Germiyān family. He was succeeded by his son Murād about 1335; cf. Ismail Hakki, *Kitabeler* (Istanbul, 1929), 198, and Aflākī (tr. Huart), II, 389.

[56] See vol. I, p. 14, n. 27. The date was 15 June in 1333 (8 July in 1331). For the *muṣallā* see vol. I, p. 13, n. 20.

277 *muṣallā*. | When we had prayed the festival prayer we went in with the sultan to his residence, and the food was brought. A separate table was set for the doctors of the law, the shaikhs, and the Young Brethren, and another separately for the poor and destitute; and no one, whether poor or rich, is turned back from the sultan's door on that day.

We stayed in this town for some time in view of the dangers of the road; then, as a caravan had been organized, we travelled with them for a day and part of a night and reached the castle of Ṭawās.[57] It is a large fortress, and it is said that Suhaib (God be pleased with him), the Companion of the Apostle of God (God bless and give him peace), was of its folk.[58] We made our overnight camp outside it, and next morning, on coming to the gate, were interrogated by its inhabitants from the top of the wall as to why and whence we had come. We answered their questions, and at that moment the commander of the castle, Ilyās Bak, came out with his squadron of troops to explore the environs of the castle and
278 the road as a precaution against | the raiding of the herds by robbers. When they completed the circuit of its neighbourhood, their animals came out, and this is their regular practice. We lodged in the hospice of a poor brother in the suburb of this castle, and the commander sent us a hospitality-gift and provisions.

From there we went on to Mughla,[59] where we lodged in the hospice of a shaikh there. He was a generous and worthy man, who used to visit us frequently in his hospice, and never came in without bringing food or fruit or sweetmeats. We met in this city Ibrāhīm Bak, son of the sultan of the city of Mīlās, whom we shall mention presently, and he treated us honourably and sent us robes.

We travelled next to the city of Mīlās,[60] one of the finest

[57] Ṭawās or Davās (in modern Turkish Tavas), in a steep valley 25 km. south of Denizli; see Philippson, V, 119 ff., plate 9. It is mentioned by al-'Omari (38) as an emirate, later absorbed by Menteshe, and the amīr is there called 'Alī(y)azbeh(= Ilyās Bek); cf. Aflākī (tr. Huart), II. 331.

[58] Ṣuhaib's origin was disputed in his lifetime; he himself claimed to be an Arab who had been captured by the Greeks as a child, but Muslim tradition claims him as 'the firstfruits of the Greeks'.

[59] Mugla, 75 km. south-west of Tavas; see Philippson, V, 53 ff., plate 3 For Ibrāhīm Beg see below, p. 429, n. 62, and Hakki, 150.

[60] The ancient Mylasa, capital of Caria; see *E.I.*, s.v.

and most extensive cities in the land of al-Rūm, with quantities of fruits, gardens, and waters. We lodged there in the hospice of one of the Young Akhīs, | who outdid by far all 279
that those before him had done in the way of generosity, hospitality, taking us to the bath, and such other praiseworthy and handsome acts. We met, too, in the city of Mīlās a pious and aged man named Bābā al-Shushtarī, who, so they said, was more than a hundred and fifty years old.[61] He was still vigorous and active, of sound mind and unimpaired faculties. He prayed for us and we were favoured with his blessing.

Account of the Sultan of Mīlās. He is the most honourable sultan Shujā' al-Dīn Urkhān Bak, son of al-Mantashā,[62] and one of the best of princes, handsome in both figure and conduct. His intimates are the doctors of the law, who are highly esteemed by him. At his court there is always a body of them, including the jurist al-Khwārizmī, a man versed in the sciences and of great merit. The sultan, | at the time of my 280
meeting with him, was displeased with al-Khwārizmī because he had journeyed to Ayā Sulūq[63] and had associated with its sultan and accepted his gifts. Now this jurist begged of me to speak to the sultan about him in a manner which would remove his resentment, so I praised him in the sultan's presence, and continued to relate what I knew of his learning and merit, until at length the sultan's ill-feeling against him was dissipated. This sultan treated us generously and supplied us with horses and provisions. His residence is in the city of Bārjīn,[64] which is close to Mīlās, there being two miles between them. It is a new place, on a hill there, and has fine buildings and mosques. He had built there a congregational mosque, which was not yet completed.[65] It was in this town

[61] The Turkish traveller Evliyā Chelebi (seventeenth century) mentions among other sanctuaries in Milas the mausoleum of Shaikh Shushtarī.

[62] On the principality of Menteshe see Wittek, *Mentesche*. Of this eponym of the family, nothing is known; Orkhān Beg, son of Mas'ūd, ruled from 1319 to before 1344, and in 1320 attacked Rhodes. He was succeeded by his son Ibrāhīm (d. before 1360).

[63] See below, p. 444.

[64] Pechin in later Turkish texts, 5 km. south of Milas. The castle is described by Wittek, *Mentesche*, 128; see also Hakki, plate 55.

[65] The building inscription of this mosque is quoted by Evliyā Chelebi (see above, n. 61), with the date 7(3)2; Wittek, *Mentesche*, 135–7. A.H. 732 began 4 October 1331, and as the inscription probably gives the date of its completion, Ibn Baṭṭūṭa's statement would indicate a date in 1331 for his visit.

that we visited him, and we lodged in it at the hospice of the Young Akhī 'Alī.

281 We took our departure after the sultan's gift to us, as | we have related above, making for the city of Qūniya,[66] a great city with fine buildings and abundant watercourses, streams, gardens and fruits. The apricot called *qamar al-dīn* (which we have described previously) grows there and is exported from it too to Egypt and Syria. The streets of the city are exceedingly wide, and its bazaars admirably organized, with the members of each craft in a separate part. It is said that this city was founded by Alexander. It is now in the territories of the sultan Badr al-Dīn Ibn Qaramān, whom we shall mention presently, but the ruler of al-'Irāq has seized it at various times, owing to its proximity to his territories in this region.

We lodged there in the hospice of its qāḍī, who is known as Ibn Qalam Shāh; he is one of the *Fityān*, and his hospice is among the largest of its kind. He has a large body of disciples, and they have a chain of affiliation in the *Futuwwa*
282 which goes back | to the Commander of the Faithful 'Alī b. Abū Ṭālib (God be pleased with him). The [distinctive] garment of the *Futuwwa* in their system is the trousers, just as the ṣūfīs wear the patched robe [as their distinctive dress].[67] The entertainment with which this qāḍī honoured us and his hospitality to us were even greater and more handsome than the entertainment of his predecessors, and he sent his son to take us to the bath in his place.

In this city is the mausoleum of the shaikh and pious imām, the pole Jalāl al-Dīn, known as *Mawlānā*.[68] He was a saint of

---

[66] At this point begins the divagation of Ibn Baṭṭūṭa's journey through central and eastern Anatolia. Konya, the ancient Iconium, was the capital of the Seljuk sultans of Rūm until the extinction of the dynasty in 1307. For their successors, the Qaramānoghlu, see below, p. 432, n. 73.

[67] See p. 434, n. 82, below. The qāḍī Tāj al-Dīn Ibn Qalam Shāh is mentioned by Aflākī (tr. C. Huart, *Les Saints des Derviches tourneurs*, Paris, 1918–22, II, 423).

[68] Jalāl al-Dīn al-Rūmī, the most famous of the Persian mystical poets, d. in Konya 1273. See the edition and translation (with commentary) of his *Mathnawī* (referred to below) by R. A. Nicholson (London, 1925–40), 8 vols. and the same editor's *Selected Poems from the Dīvāni Shamsī Tabrīz* (Cambridge, 1898). Shamsī Tabrīz is the sweetmeat-seller of Ibn Baṭṭūṭa's story, and the Mevlevī fraternity, or 'dancing dervishes' (Ibn Baṭṭūṭa's *Jalālīya*) was instituted by Jalāl al-Dīn in his memory.

high rank, and in the land of al-Rūm there is a brotherhood who claim affiliation to him and are called Jalālīya, after his name, in the same way that the Ahmadīya in al-'Irāq are called [after Aḥmad al-Rifā'ī] and the Ḥaidarīya in Khurāsān [after Quṭb al-Dīn Ḥaidar].[69] Over his mausoleum there is a vast hospice in which food is served to all wayfarers.

Anecdote.[70] It is related that in early life Jalāl al-Dīn was a
legist and professor, | to whom students used to flock at his 283
college in Qūniya. One day there came into the college a man selling sweetmeats, who carried on his head a trayful of them, cut up into pieces which he would sell for a copper apiece. When he came into the lecture-hall the shaikh said to him 'Bring your tray here.' The sweet-seller took a piece of his wares and gave it to the shaikh, the latter took it with his hand and ate it, whereupon the sweet-seller went out without offering anything to anyone other than the shaikh. The shaikh, abandoning his lecture, went out to follow him up; and the students, when he delayed to return and they had waited a long time, went out to seek for him, but they could not discover where he was living. Subsequently he came back to them, after many years, but he had become demented and would speak only in Persian rhymed couplets which no one could understand. His disciples used to follow him and write down that poetry as it issued from him, and they collected it into a book called the *Mathnawī*. The inhabitants of that |
country greatly revere that book, meditate on its contents, 284
teach it and recite it in their hospices on Thursday nights. In this city there is also the grave of the jurist Aḥmad, who is said to have been the teacher of this Jalāl al-Dīn.[71]

We travelled next to the city of al-Lāranda, a fine town with many watercourses and gardens.[72]

[69] For the Aḥmadīya see above, p. 273, and for the Ḥaidarīya vol. III, p. 79 (Arabic).

[70] This is apparently a variant of the traditional story of the meeting of Jalāl al-Dīn with his spiritual director Shamsī Tabrīz in 1244 (see above, n. 68).

[71] A pupil of Jalāl al-Dīn's father Bahā al-Dīn: Aflākī (see n. 67 above), I, 31, 328. Ibn Baṭṭūta seems to have transferred some details relating to his conversion to Jalāl al-Dīn.

[72] Now called Karaman (from the name of the ruling dynasty—see the following note), 100 km. south-east of Konya: see *Murray's Handbook*, 157–8; *E.I.*, s.v.

Account of the Sultan of al-Lāranda. Its sultan is the king Badr al-Dīn b. Qaramān. It belonged formerly to his uterine brother Mūsā, but he ceded it to al-Malik al-Nāṣir, who gave him another place in exchange and sent an amīr with troops to govern it. Later on the sultan Badr al-Dīn captured it, established it as the capital of his kingdom and consolidated his power there.[73] I met this sultan outside the city as he was
285 coming back from | hunting, and when I dismounted to him he also dismounted from his horse, and on my saluting him he came forward to meet me. It is the custom of the kings of this country to dismount to a visitor if he dismounts to them. They are pleased when he does so to them and redouble their consideration for him, whereas if he salutes them while on horseback this arouses their ill-will and displeasure, and leads to the visitor's exclusion [from their bounty]. This happened to me once with one of them, as I shall relate in due course. After I had saluted him and we were again mounted, he asked me about myself and my coming, and I entered the city in his company. He gave orders to treat me with the greatest hospitality and used to send quantities of food, fruit and sweetmeats in silver platters, as well as candles, robes and horses, and [altogether] he was most generous.

Our stay with him was not prolonged, and we left for the
286 city of Aqsarā, | which is one of the most beautiful and substantial towns of al-Rūm, surrounded by flowing streams and gardens on every side.[74] The city is traversed by three rivers and there is running water in its houses: it has many trees and vines and there are numbers of gardens inside it. There are manufactured there the rugs of sheep's wool called after it, which have no equal in any country and are exported

[73] The Qaramān-oghlu were the most powerful of the amīrs of Asia Minor. Originally Turkmen chiefs in Armenak, in the Cilician highlands, Qaramān's son Badr al-Dīn Maḥmūd seized Konya on the fall of the Seljuks and sought Egyptian protection against the Īlkhāns of 'Irāq. He was succeeded by his son Badr al-Dīn Ibrāhīm, the sultan mentioned in this text, who abdicated in 1333 in favour of his brother Khalīl. There is no reference in the Egyptian sources to an occupation of Laranda by Mamlūk troops; for Ibrāhīm's brother Mūsā see above, p. 357, n. 300.

[74] Aksaray, 155 km. north-east of Laranda; see *Murray's Handbook*, 162, where its luxuriant gardens and streams are noted. It is obviously misplaced here, as it lies on the direct route from Konya to Kayseri which runs roughly parallel to the route Karaman-Niğde-Kayseri.

from it to Syria, Egypt, al-'Irāq, India, China and the lands of the Turks.[75] This city is subject to the king of al-'Irāq. We lodged there in the hospice of the sharīf Ḥusain, the deputy governor of the city for the amīr Artana, Artana being the lieutenant of the king of al-'Irāq in [all] the districts of al-Rūm that he has occupied.[76] This sharīf is one of the *Fityān*, and is head of a numerous brotherhood. He entertained us with unbounded consideration, and acted in the same manner as those who preceded him.

We travelled next to the city of Nakda, which is one of | the 287
towns belonging to the king of al-'Irāq, a large and thickly-populated city, part of which is in ruins.[77] It is traversed by a river called the Black River, a large river over which there are three bridges, one inside the city and two outside it. There are norias on it, both inside and outside the city, to water the gardens, and it has quantities of fruit. We lodged in it at the hospice of the Young Akhī Jārūq,[78] who is the governor of the city, and he entertained us according to the custom of the *Fityān*.

We stayed there three nights, and then went on from it to the city of Qaisarīya, which is also in the territories belonging to the ruler of al-'Irāq, and one of the chief cities in this land.[79] In it are [quartered] the troops of the government of al-'Irāq and [there resides] one of the Khātūns of the amīr 'Alā al-Dīn Artana mentioned above. She is one of the most generous and excellent of princesses, and is related to the king of
al-'Irāq | and called *Aghā*, which means 'great', as are all 288

[75] The carpets made in this region were famous; cf. Yule's *Marco Polo*, bk. I, ch. 2. As Konya was the exporting centre they are usually called by its name, but Ibn Baṭṭūṭa's statement that Aksaray was the centre of their production is confirmed by other contemporary sources; see G. Wiet, 'Tapis égyptienne' in *Arabica* (Leiden, 1959), VI/1, 19.

[76] Ertena (Eretna), a Mongol officer under the Chobānid Timurtāsh (see above, p. 339, n. 225), was appointed governor of Anatolia after the latter's rebellion in 1327. On Abū Sa'īd's death (1335), he recognized al-Malik al-Nāṣir of Egypt as suzerain, but became independent in 1341, and founded a line of princes of Sivas.

[77] Nigde (Niğde), 70 km. south-east of Akseray, on the Kara Su (Black River); *Murray's Handbook*, 164.

[78] Or Jārūz.

[79] Kayseri, 110 km. north-east of Niğde; *Murray's Handbook*, 50–2. It was captured by the Mongols in 1244, and briefly held by the Egyptian sultan Baibars in 1277.

those related to the sultan.[80] Her name is Ṭaghī[81] Khātūn; we were admitted to her presence and she rose to meet us, greeted and spoke to us graciously, and ordered food to be served. We ate the meal, and after we took leave she sent us a horse with saddle and bridle, a robe of honour and some money by one of her slave-boys, together with her apologies [for not sending more].

We lodged in this city at the hospice of the Young Akhī Amīr 'Alī, who is a great amīr and one of the chiefs of the Akhīs in this country. He is head of a brotherhood of his disciples, which includes some of the leading men and notables of the city, and his hospice is one of the most magnificent in its furnishings and chandeliers, and in quantity of food served and excellence of organization. The notables and others of his
289 associates assemble every night | in his company, and in generosity towards the visitor far outdo all the generous actions of the other brotherhoods.[82] It is one of the customs in this land that in any part of it where there is no sultan, it is the Akhī who acts as governor; it is he who gives horses and robes to the visitor and shows hospitality to him in the measure of his means, and his manner of command and prohibition and riding out [with a retinue] is the same as that of the princes.

We travelled next to the city of Sīwās, which is in the territories of the king of al-'Irāq and the largest of the cities that he possesses in this country.[83] In it resides his amīrs and his functionaries. It is a city with fine buildings and wide streets, and its markets are choked with people. There is there a building resembling a college, which is called *Dār al-Siyāda*.[84] No person lodges in it except sharīfs, whose

[80] This use of *agha* is derived from Mongol *aqa*, 'elder, elder brother, chief', adopted by the Turks as a title, and in Ottoman use became a military term.

[81] Probably to be read Ṭoghā, as the name is spelled with *alif* in MS. 2289.

[82] In the former Seljuk territories the *futuwwa* organization appears to have remained generally on the aristocratic basis established by the caliph al-Nāṣir (see above, p. 419, n. 29), is contrast to the artisan or middle-class *Akhi* organization previously described by Ibn Baṭṭūṭa.

[83] Sivas, 175 km. north-east of Kayseri, the ancient Sebasteia; *Murray's Handbook*, 42–3. For this and the following routes see Taeschner, *Anatolische Wegenetz*, I, 182–3, 212 sqq.

[84] *Siyāda* is here a collective term for the Sayyids, i.e. the descendants of Muḥammad (=sharīfs, *ashrāf*), for whom and their Marshal (*naqīb*) see

naqīb lives in it; during their stay in it there is supplied to them furnishing, food, | candles, etc., and when they leave 290
they are furnished with travelling provisions.

When we arrived in this city there came out to meet us the associates of the Young Akhi Bichaqchī. (*Bichaq* means in Turkish 'knife' and this name [*bichaqchi*] is its relative noun).[85] They were a large company, some riding and some on foot. Then after them we were met by the associates of the Young Akhī Chalabī, who was one of the chiefs of the Akhīs and whose rank was higher than that of Akhī Bichaqchī.[86] These invited us to lodge with them, but I could not accept their invitation, owing to the priority of the former. We entered the city in the company of both parties, who were boasting against one another, and those who had met us first showed the liveliest joy at our lodging with them. They showed in due course the same munificence in the matters of food, bath, and accommodation as their predecessors, and we stayed with them for three nights, enjoying the most perfect hospitality.

After this we were visited by | the qāḍī and a company of 291
students of religion, bringing with them horses from the amīr 'Alā al-Dīn Artana, the king of al-'Irāq's lieutenant in the land of al-Rūm. So we rode to visit him, and he came out to the ante-chamber[87] of his residence to greet us and bid us welcome. He spoke in an educated Arabic speech, and questioned me about the two 'Irāqs, Iṣbahān, Shīrāz, Kirmān,[88] the sultan Atābek, the countries of Syria and Egypt, and the sultans of the Turkmens. His idea was that I would praise those of them who had been generous and find fault with the

---

vol. I, p. 258, n. 50. The *Dār al-Siyāda* at Sivas was one of several founded by Ghāzān Khān (see above, p. 344). The endowments were dilapidated after his death by the local notables and later restored by the vizier Rashīd al-Dīn (see above, p. 336, n. 215); *Letters of Rashīd al-Dīn*, 156 sq.

[85] Presumably = 'cutler', which would indicate an artisan corporation, but the word also means 'one who uses his knife freely'.

[86] For *chelebi* as a title see above, p. 424, n. 46. Ibn Baṭṭūṭa's phrase suggests that his corporation was associated with the aristocratic *futuwwa* (see above, n. 82). See also Taeschner, *Der anatolische Dichter Nasiri und sein Futuvvetname*, 64.

[87] Or 'entrance'.

[88] The mention of Kirmān here is explained by the fact that Hormuz is included in the province of Kirmān by all the Arab geographers.

miserly, but I did nothing of the kind, and, on the contrary, praised them all. He was pleased with this conduct on my part and commended me for it, and then had food served. After we had eaten he said 'You will be my guest,' but the Young Akhī Chalabī said to him 'They have not yet lodged at my hospice, so let them stay with me and receive your hospitality-gifts there.' The governor agreed, so we transferred to his hospice and stayed there for six nights, enjoying his
292 hospitality and that | of the governor. After our visit the governor sent a horse, a set of robes and some money, and wrote to his deputies in the [other] towns to give us hospitality and honourable treatment and to furnish us with provisions.

We continued our journey to the city of Amāṣiya, a large and fine city with streams and gardens, trees and abundance of fruits.[89] There are norias on its rivers to supply water to its gardens and houses, and it has spacious streets and bazaars. It belongs to the king of al-'Irāq. In its vicinity is the township of Sūnusā; it too belongs to the king of al-'Irāq and in it reside the descendants of the saint of God Most High, Abu'l-'Abbās Aḥmad al-Rifā'ī. Among them are the shaikh 'Izz al-Dīn, who is now the head of the convent and the inheritor
293 of the prayer-rug | of al-Rifā'ī, and his brothers the shaikh 'Alī, the shaikh Ibrāhīm, and the shaikh Yaḥyā, [all] sons of the shaikh Aḥmad Kuchuk (*kuchuk* means 'the little'), son of Tāj al-Dīn al-Rifā'ī.[90] We lodged in their hospice and found them superior to all other men in merit.

We travelled next to the city of Kumish, in the territories of the king of al-'Irāq, a populous city which is visited by merchants from al-'Irāq and Syria, and in which there are

[89] Amasya, 140 km. north-west of Sivas; 'it lies in a deep gorge . . . such a wealth of gardens above and below the town that it was called by the Seljuks the "Baghdād of Rūm" ' (*Murray's Handbook*, 39).

[90] Sonusa (Sunisa), 50 km. east of Amasya, at the northward bend of the Yeshil Irmak; *Murray's Handbook*, 39. Aḥmad Kuchuk was mentioned by Ibn Baṭṭūṭa in connection with his visit to Umm 'Ubaida in 1327 (above, p. 273, n. 10); he had presumably died in the interval, if his son 'Izz al-Dīn was now head of the order. No other reference has been found to this branch of the Rifā'ī family, nor to their connection with Sunisa. Evliyā Chelebi mentions only a tomb of Shaikh Aḥmad al-Rifā'ī at Ladik, near Tokat, and of an otherwise unknown 'fraternal cousin' of his, Shaikh Ḥaẓret-i Ḥusain, at Tokat. Ibn Baṭṭūṭa may have obtained this information from his meeting with 'Izz al-Dīn at Izmīr (see below, p. 445).

silver-mines.[91] At a distance of two days' journey from it there are lofty and steep mountains, which I did not go to. We lodged there in the hospice of the Akhī Majd al-Dīn, staying for three nights as his guest. He treated us in the same way as his predecessors, and the deputy of the amīr Artanā visited us and sent us a hospitality-gift and provisions.

After our departure from these parts we came to Arzanjān, in the territories of | the ruler of al-'Irāq, a large and populous 294 city, most of whose inhabitants are Armenians.[92] The Muslims there speak Turkish. It has well-organized bazaars, and there are manufactured in it fine fabrics which are called by its name.[93] In it are mines of copper,[94] from which they make utensils and the [lampstands called] *baisūs* that we have already described, which resemble the lampstands in our country.[95] We lodged there in the hospice of the Young Akhī Nizām al-Dīn; it is one of the finest hospices, and he too is one of the best and chief of the *fityān*, and he showed us the most perfect hospitality.

We left there for the city of Arz al-Rūm, in the territories of the king of al-'Irāq,[96] a place of vast extent, but mostly in ruins in consequence of a factional feud which broke out between two groups of Turkmens there. It is traversed by

[91] Gümüşane (Gümüsh-khāne, i.e. 'Silver House'), over 60 km. south of Trabzon (Trebizond); *Murray's Handbook*, 203. It lies 260 km. east of Sunusa, and could be reached only from Trebizond or from Baiburt, 70 km. further east. To the north-east the Anatolian ranges begin with Kolat Dagh. See also Yule's note in *Marco Polo*, I, 49, n. 3.

[92] Erzinjan, on the Kara Su, one of the headwaters of the Euphrates, 80 km. south of Gümüşane: *Murray's Handbook*, 249–50; *E.I.*, s.v. This is in the region called by Marco Polo 'Greater Armenia'.

[93] According to Marco Polo (I, 45) 'the best buckram in the world'; cf. also Pegolotti, 36. Yule, in his note to *Marco Polo*, concludes that 'buckram' was a quilted material.

[94] Not mentioned elsewhere, but the copper industry of Arzinjan has remained celebrated up to modern times, the raw metal being imported from Europe (Cuinet, I, 216).

[95] See above, p. 421, n. 31.

[96] Erzurum (Erzerum), 150 km. east of Erzinjan: *Murray's Handbook*, 204–6; *E.I.*, s.v. Formerly called Qālīqalā, the name Erzerum (Arzan al-Rūm, 'Byzantine Arzan') was given to it by the Armenians of Arzan who moved to it after the destruction of Arzan by the Seljuks in 1049; the local name is Karin. No other source mentions flowing streams in the city, but only fountains fed from springs, and there are no vines at Erzerum itself (Cuinet, I, 146; cf. *Selections from Ibn Battuta*, trans. (in Armenian) A. Ajarian (Yerevan, 1940), 44).

three rivers, and most of its houses have gardens in which there are fruit trees and vines. We lodged there in the hospice
295 of the Young | Akhī Ṭūmān, who is of great age, and reputed to be more than a hundred and thirty years old. I saw him going about on his feet, supported by a staff, with his faculties unimpaired, and assiduous in praying at the stated times. He had no complaint to make against himself except that he could no longer sustain the fast [of Ramaḍān]. He himself served us at the meal and his sons served us in the bath. We intended to take leave of him on the day after our arrival, but he was shocked by our proposal and refused it, saying 'If you do so, you will show disrespect for me, for the shortest period of hospitality is three nights.'

So we stayed with him for three nights and then left for the city of Birgī,[97] where we arrived in the late afternoon. We met one of its inhabitants and enquired of him for the hospice of the Akhī there. He replied 'I will guide you to it,' so we followed him and he conducted us to his own residence, in a garden that he had, and put us up on the roof of his house,
296 overshadowed by trees, | for this was the season of extreme heat. He brought us all kinds of fruit, and gave us excellent hospitality and fodder for our beasts, and we spent that night with him.

We had already learned that there was in this city an eminent professor named Muḥyī al-Dīn. Our host for the night, who was a student of religion, took us to the college, and there was the professor just arriving, mounted on a lively mule and wearing magnificent robes, open in front and embroidered with gold, with his slaves and servants to right and left of him and preceded by the students. When we saluted him he bade us welcome, greeted us and spoke to us most graciously, and, taking me by the hand, made me sit beside him. Later on the qāḍī 'Izz al-Dīn Firishtā arrived; *firishtā* means 'angel' [in Persian], and this nickname was given to him on account of his piety, purity of life, and virtue. He

[97] At this point Ibn Baṭṭūṭa resumes his journey through south-eastern Anatolia, interrupted above, on p. 430. Birgi lies to the north-east of Ödemish in the valley of the Cayster (Küçük Menderes), 105 km. north of his last stop at Milas: *Murray's Handbook*, 91; Philippson, II, 68–9. The name is derived from the Greek Pyrgion.

took his seat on the right of the professor, who began to lecture on the sciences, both fundamental | and accessory.[98] 297
When he had finished his lecture, he went to a small chamber[99] in the college, ordered it to be furnished, put me up in it, and sent a superb meal.

Later on, after the sunset prayer, he sent an invitation to me, and I went to him. I found him in a reception chamber in a garden of his, where there was an ornamental pool into which the water was flowing down from a white marble basin edged with enamelled tiles. In front of him were a number of the students, and his slaves and servants were standing on either side of him, while he himself was sitting on a dais covered with beautiful embroidered rugs. When I saw him [in so stately a setting] I took him for a prince. He rose up and came forward to welcome me, took me by the hand, and made me sit beside him on the dais. Food was then brought, and after we had eaten we returned to the college. One of the students told me that all of the students who were present at the professor's that night were regular attendants |
at his meal every night. This professor wrote to the sultan a 298
letter, composed in laudatory terms, to inform him about us. The sultan was at the time living on a mountain thereabouts, passing the summer there on account of the severe heat; this mountain was cool, and it was his practice to pass the summer there.[100]

Account of the Sultan of Birgī. He is the sultan Muḥammad, son of Āydīn,[101] one of the best, most generous, and worthiest of sultans. When the professor sent to inform him about me, he despatched his deputy to me with an invitation to visit him, but the professor advised me to wait until the sultan

[98] The traditional division of the Muslim schoolmen between 'basic' sciences, i.e. those which deal with the principles of law, theology, etc., and the 'subsidiary' disciplines which deal with the application of these principles to specific problems.

[99] The term (*duwaira*) probably means a separate pavilion.

[100] Tmolos, in Turkish Bos-dagh (2157 m.), the higher valleys of which have often been inhabited as summer residences; see Philippson, II, plates 11, 12.

[101] Founder of the house of Aydîn (Aydîn-oghlu), which gave its name to the city formerly called Tralles, in the Maeander (Büyük Menderes) valley (see *Murray's Handbook*, 101–2), and known to contemporaries as the kingdom of Birgi. He died early in 1334; P. Lemerle, *L'Emirat d'Aydin* (Paris, 1957).

sent for me again. He himself was at the time suffering from a boil that had broken out on his foot, on account of which he was unable to ride and had ceased to go to college. Later on the sultan sent for me again. This gave great distress to the professor and he said 'It is impossible for me to ride on horseback, although it was my intention to go with you in order to
299 reaffirm | to the sultan what is due to you.' He braced himself, however, wrapped his foot in bandages, and mounted, without putting his foot in the stirrup. I and my companions mounted also and we climbed up to the mountain by a road that had been hewn [in its side] and evened out. We arrived at the sultan's place just after noon, alighted by a stream of water under the shade of walnut trees, and found the sultan agitated and preoccupied on account of the flight from him of his younger son Sulaimān to his father-in-law, the sultan Urkhān Bak.[102] On hearing of our arrival he sent his two sons Khiḍr Bak and 'Omar Bak to us. These saluted the doctor of the law, and on his instructions to salute me also they did so, and asked me about myself and my coming. After they had gone, the sultan sent me a tent [of the kind] which is called by them *kharqa*, and consists of wooden laths put together in the
300 shape of a cupola and covered with pieces of felt.[103] | The upper part of it can be opened to admit light and air, like a ventilation pipe, and can be closed when required. They also brought rugs and furnished it. The doctor sat down, and I sat down with him, together with his companions and my companions, outside the tent under the shade of walnut trees. It was very cold in that place, and on that night a horse of mine died from the sharpness of the cold.

On the following morning the professor rode to visit the sultan and spoke about me in terms dictated by his own generous qualities. He then returned to me and told me about this, and after a while the sultan sent to summon both of us. On reaching his place of residence we found him standing up;

[102] Sulaimān Shāh, later sultan of Tīra (see below, p. 444), d. 1349. This Orkhān is the sultan of Menteshe (Milas): see above, p. 429, n. 62; see also Wittek, *Mentesche*, 68; Lemerle, 35–6). For Khiḍr and 'Omar see below, p. 445.

[103] Persian *khargāh*, used for the tents of the Turkmens; a fuller description is given by William of Rubruck (*Contemporaries of Marco Polo*, ed. M. Komroff (London, 1928), 58–61).

we saluted him and sat down, the doctor on his right and I next to the doctor. He enquired of me about myself and my coming, and then questioned me about al-Ḥijāz, Egypt, Syria, al-Yaman, the two 'Irāqs, and the lands of the Persians. Food was then served, and we ate | and with- 301
drew. He sent presents of rice, flour, and butter in sheep's stomachs,[104] this being a practice of the Turks. We continued in this way for several days, being sent for every day to join in his meal. One day he came to visit us after the noon prayer; [on that occasion] the doctor sat in the place of honour, with me on his left, and the sultan sat on his right—this being due to the prestige enjoyed by doctors of the law among the Turks. He asked me to write down for him a number of *ḥadīths*, of the sayings of the Apostle of God (God bless and give him peace),[105] and when I had written them for him and the doctor presented them to him in the same hour, he commanded the latter to write an exposition of them for him in the Turkish language. He then rose and went out, and observing that our servants were cooking food for us under the shade of the walnut trees without any spices or greens, commanded that his store-keeper should be punished, and sent spices and butter.

Our stay on this mountain lasted so long | that I began to 302
weary and wished to take my leave. Since the doctor also had had enough of staying there he sent word to the sultan that I desired to continue my journey. On the morning after, therefore, the sultan sent his deputy who spoke with the professor in Turkish (which at that time I did not understand),[106] and withdrew after the latter had answered his talk. The professor said to me 'Do you know what he said?' I replied, 'I don't know what he said.' 'Well' he said, 'the sultan sent to me to ask me what he should give you, so I said to him "He has at his disposal gold and silver and horses and slaves—let him give whatever of these he likes".' So the deputy went off to the sultan and then came back to us saying 'The sultan com-

[104] Cf. Yule's *Marco Polo*, I, 262.

[105] The ability to recite extempore a collection of relevant *ḥadīths* (i.e. sayings of the Prophet) was regarded as one of the chief accomplishments of the religious scholar (*'ālim*); cf. above, p. 312.

[106] See above, p. 420, n. 30.

mands you both to remain here today, and to go down with him tomorrow to his residence in the city.'

Next morning he sent a fine horse from his own stud, and went down to the city, and we with him. The population came out to welcome him, with the above-mentioned qāḍī
303 and others among them, | and the sultan made his entry, we being still with him. When he dismounted at the gate of his residence, I made off with the professor towards the college, but he called to us and bade us come into his palace with him. On our arrival at the vestibule of the palace, we found about twenty of his servants, of surpassingly beautiful appearance, wearing robes of silk, with their hair parted and hanging loose, and in colour of a resplendent whiteness tinged with red. I said to the doctor 'What are these beautiful figures?' and he replied 'These are Greek pages.' We climbed a long flight of stairs with the sultan and came eventually into a fine audience-hall, with an ornamental pool of water in the centre and the figure of a lion in bronze at each corner of it, spouting water from its mouth.[107] Round this hall there was a succession of benches covered with rugs, on one of which was the
304 sultan's cushion. When | we came up to this bench, the sultan pushed away his cushion with his hand and sat down alongside us on the rugs. The doctor sat on his right, the qāḍī next to him, and I next to the qāḍī. The Qur'ān-readers sat down below the bench, for there are always Qur'ān-readers in attendance on him in his audiences, wherever he may be. The servants then brought in gold and silver bowls filled with sherbet [of raisins][108] steeped in water, into which citron juice had been squeezed, with small pieces of biscuit in it, along with gold and silver spoons. At the same time they brought some porcelain bowls containing the same beverage and with wooden spoons, and any who felt scruples [about using the gold and silver vessels] used the porcelain bowls and wooden spoons.[109] I made a speech of thanks to the sultan and

[107] The lions, although a traditional palace decoration in Anatolia, had sumably been taken over in this instance from a Byzantine fountain.

[108] *Jullāb*, literally 'rose-water', but applied to any kind of sherbet (see Lane, ch. V, *ad fin.*); hence the English *julep*.

[109] Muslim piety extended the Prophet's traditional reprobation of gold rings and ornaments (cf. W. Muir, *The Life of Mahomet*, 3rd ed. (London, 1894), 515) to the use of gold and silver vessels generally.

eulogized the doctor, sparing no efforts in doing so, and this gave much pleasure and satisfaction to the sultan. |

Anecdote. While we were still sitting with the sultan there 305 came in an elderly man, wearing on his head a turban with a tassel, who saluted him. The qāḍī and the doctor stood up as he came in, and he sat down in front of the sultan, on the bench, with the Qur'ān-readers beneath him. I said to the doctor 'Who is this shaikh?' He just laughed and said nothing, but when I repeated the question he said to me 'This man is a Jew, a physician. All of us need his services, and it was for this reason that we acted as you saw in standing up at his entry.' At this my old feeling of indignation flared up anew,[110] and I said to the Jew 'You God-damned son of a God-damned father, how dare you sit up there above the readers of the Qur'ān, and you a Jew?' and went on berating him in loud tones. The sultan was surprised and asked what I was saying. The doctor told him, while the Jew grew angry and left the chamber in the most crestfallen state. When we took our leave, the doctor said to me 'Well done, | may God 306 bless you. Nobody but you would dare to speak to him in that way, and you have let him know just what he is.'

Another anecdote. In the course of this audience the sultan asked me this question: 'Have you ever seen a stone that fell from the sky?' I replied, 'I have never seen one, nor ever heard tell of one.' 'Well,' he said, 'a stone did fall from the sky outside this town of ours,' and then called some men and told them to bring the stone. They brought in a great black stone, very hard and with a glitter in it—I reckoned its weight to amount to a hundredweight. The sultan ordered the stone-breakers to be summoned, and four of them came and on his command to strike it they beat upon it as one man four times with iron hammers, but made no impression on it. I was astonished at this phenomenon, and he ordered it to be taken back to its place.

[110] The Arabic phrase, 'what just occurred and what was of old', is taken from a well-known Tradition concerning the Prophet. The physicians of Muslim rulers were very frequently Jews, whose wealth and influence were deeply resented in Muslim religious circles (see A. S. Tritton, *The Caliphs and their non-Muslim Subjects* London, 1930), 95, 155 sqq.). Hence Ibn Baṭṭūṭa's indignation at the physician's action in sitting 'above the Qur'ān-readers'.

307 Two | days after our entry into the city with the sultan, he gave a great banquet and invited the legists, shaikhs, superior officers of the army, and notables among the citizens. After they had eaten, the Qur'ān-reciters recited the Qur'ān with beautiful modulations, and we returned to our lodging in the college. Every night he used to send food, fruit, sweetmeats and candles, and finally sent to me a hundred mithqāls of gold,[111] a thousand dirhams, a complete set of garments, a horse, and a Greek slave called Mikhā'īl, and to each of my companions a robe and some dirhams—all this owing to the friendly offices of the professor Muḥyī al-Dīn, God Most High reward him with good. He bade us farewell and we left, having spent fourteen days with him on the mountain and in the city.

We proceeded next to the city of Tīra,[112] which is in the territories of this sultan, a fine town with running streams,
308 gardens | and fruits. We lodged there in the hospice of the Young Akhī Muḥammad,[113] a most saintly man, who fasts continually and has a number of followers of his Way. He treated us hospitably and gave us his blessing.

We went on to the city of Ayā Sulūq, a large and ancient city venerated by the Greeks, in which there is a great church built with huge stones, each measuring ten or less cubits in length and most skilfully hewn.[114] The congregational mosque in this city is one of the most magnificent mosques in the world and unequalled in beauty. It was formerly a church of the Greeks, greatly venerated among them, which they used to visit from all parts, and when the Muslims captured the city they made it a congregational mosque.[115] Its walls are of

[111] The *mithqāl* is a measure for precious metals, equal to 4.25 grammes (the standard weight of the gold dinar).

[112] Tire, 30 km. south-west of Birgī.

[113] Doubtfully identified with the 'amīr' Muḥammad b. Qalamān, founder of a mosque in Tire in 1338 (*Repertoire chron. d'épigraphie arabe*, XV, 117).

[114] Aya Soluk (on modern Turkish maps Selçuk), at the mouth of the Cayster river, is Ephesus (the older Turkish name being derived from Hagios Theologos); see Murray, 94 sqq., and Philippson, II, 87 sqq. The church here described is apparently the Church of Mary (or of the Council), built on the foundations of the ancient Musaion; see *Forschungen in Ephesos* (Vienna, 1932), IV, pt. 1.

[115] The mention below of eleven domes shows that this was the Church of St. John, which had six large domes over the main building and five over

marble | of different colours, and it is paved with white marble 309
and roofed with lead. It contains eleven domes, differing in size, with a water pool in the centre of [the area under] each dome. The city is traversed by the river, which has on either side of it trees of different species, grapevines, and trellises of jasmine, and it has fifteen gates.

The governor of this city is Khiḍr Bak, son of the sultan Muḥammad b. Āydīn.[116] I had already seen him at his father's place in Birgī, and I met him again at this city, in its outskirts. I saluted him while on horseback, and this act on my part displeased him and was the cause of depriving me of his generosity. For it is their custom when a visitor dismounts to them, to dismount (in turn) to him and to be pleased with his action. He sent me nothing but a single robe of silk woven with gold thread [of the kind] that they call *nakh.*[117] I bought in this city a Greek slavegirl, a virgin, for forty gold dinars.

We went on next to the city of Yazmir, | a large city on the 310
sea-coast, mostly in ruins, with a citadel adjoining its upper end.[118] We lodged there in the hospice of the shaikh Ya'qūb, who belongs to the Aḥmadīya brotherhood,[119] a pious and worthy man. In the outskirts of the city we met the shaikh 'Izz al-Dīn b. Aḥmad al-Rifā'ī, who had with him Zāda al-Akhlāṭī, one of the great shaikhs, together with a hundred poor brethren, all of them demented. The governor had set up tents for them and the shaikh Ya'qūb gave them a feast at which I was present and so met with them.

The amīr of this city is 'Omar Bak, son of the sultan

---

the narthex; see *Forschungen in Ephesos* (Vienna, 1951), IV, pt. 3. It was replaced shortly afterwards by the mosque of 'Īsā Beg, nephew of Khiḍr Beg, and the church itself was reputedly destroyed by Timur in 1402.

[116] He was the eldest son of Muḥammad (see above, p. 439, n. 101). On him and the general situation at Ephesus at this time see Lemerle, 28–34.

[117] *Nakh* (*nakhkh*) is a Persian term for gold brocade, which passed into the trading vocabulary of the Mediterranean area as *nacchi*, *nac*, etc.; cf. Yule's *Marco Polo*, I, 65, n. 4.

[118] A description of Smyrna (modern Turkish Izmir) at this period is given by Lemerle, 40 sqq. The citadel mentioned in the text was the ancient Acropolis on Mons Pagus, captured by Sultan Muḥammad in 1317 from the Genoese. The port and its citadel were invested by 'Omar Beg in 1327 and captured in 1329; this probably accounts for the ruined condition of the city.

[119] I.e. the Rifā'īya; see above, p. 273. For 'Izz al-Dīn Aḥmad see above, p. 436, n. 90.

Muḥammad b. Āydīn mentioned above,[120] and his residence
is in the citadel. At the time of our arrival there he was with
his father, but he returned after we had stayed in it for five
nights. He gave an example of his generous qualities in
coming to visit me in the hospice, and greeting me with
apologies [for his absence]. He sent an immense hospitality-
311 gift, and in addition gave me | a Greek slave, a dwarf[121]
named Niqūla, and two robes of *kamkhā*, which are silken
fabrics manufactured at Baghdād, Tabrīz, Naisābūr, and in
China.[122] The jurist who acts as his imām told me that the
amīr had no other slave left than the slave that he gave me, on
account of his generosity—God have mercy on him. To the
shaikh 'Izz al-Dīn also he gave[123] three horses with their equipment, several large silver vessels [of the kind] that they call
mishraba ['goblet'], filled with dirhams, garments of woollen
cloth,[124] *qudsī* and *kamkhā*, and slavegirls and slaveboys.

This amīr was a generous and pious prince, and continually
engaged in *jihād* [against the Christians]. He had war-galleys
with which he used to make raids on the environs of Constantinople the Great and to seize prisoners and booty, then
after spending it all in gifts and largesse he would go out
again to the *jihād*. Eventually his pressure became so galling
to the Greeks that they appealed to the Pope, who ordered
312 the Christians | of Genoa and France to attack him, and
attack him they did.[125] The Pope sent an army from Rome,

[120] 'Omar (in old Turkish Umur) Beg was governor of Smyrna from about 1327, and succeeded his father as sultan of Birgi. One of the oldest Anatolian Turkish epics is devoted to his exploits and death (*Le Destan d'Umur Pacha*, ed. I. Mélikoff-Sayar (Paris, 1954)).

[121] Or 'not yet fullgrown' (literally 'five spans tall'), probably one of the children captured by 'Omar in his raid on Chios about the beginning of 1330.

[122] *Kamkhā* was apparently a gold (or silver) brocade made with metal thread on different foundations, called by Pegolotti *cammocca* and in modern India *kincob*. The first element in the term is the Chinese *kin*, 'gold'. See *Hobson-Jobson*, s.v. Kincob; Pope, III, 2006; and Cordier's note in Yule's *Marco Polo*, II, 238.

[123] MS. 2289 reads 'The shaikh 'Izz al-Dīn also gave me'.

[124] Arabic *milf*, generally read as *milaff*, but apparently derived from the name of Amalfi, one of the earliest Italian cities to engage in the Levant trade. *Qudsi* is 'Jerusalem stuff', but of what kind is not known.

[125] 'Omar's first expedition to the Dardanelles was made in conjunction with a son of Ṣarukhān (see below, p. 447, n. 129) in 1332 (probably, therefore, after Ibn Baṭṭūṭa's visit). Subsequently, more or less in alliance with Byzantium, he harassed the Latin possessions in Greece, and so exposed himself to counterattack.

and [the combined forces] made an assault on the city by night with a large number of galleys, capturing the harbour and the town. The amīr 'Omar came down from the citadel to engage them, but died a martyr's death together with a great number of his men.[126] The Christians established themselves in the town, but could not capture the citadel because of its impregnability.

We continued our journey from this city to the city of Maghnīsīya,[127] where we lodged on the evening of the Day of 'Arafa[128] in the hospice of one of the *fityān*. It is a large and fine city on a mountain slope, and its plain abounds in rivers, springs, gardens and fruits. |

Account of the Sultan of Maghnīsīya. Its sultan is called 313
Ṣārū-khān,[129] and when we arrived in this town we found him at the mausoleum of his son, who had died some months before. He and the boy's mother spent the eve of the festival and the following morning at the tomb. The boy had been embalmed and placed in a coffin of wood with a lid of tinned iron; the coffin was raised on high trestles in a domed chamber without a roof, so that its odour should escape, and after this the dome would be roofed in and the boy's coffin placed where it could be seen on ground level, and his garments laid upon it. This same practice I have seen done by other kings also.[130] We saluted him in this place, prayed with him the festival prayers, and returned to the college.

The slaveboy who belonged to me took our horses and

[126] The port and its castle were captured in a surprise attack by Venetian, Rhodian and Papal vessels in 1344. 'Omar was unable to recapture the castle, and was killed in an attack on it in May 1348: see Lemerle, 218 sqq.; A. S. Atiya, *The Crusade in the Later Middle Ages* (London, 1938), 290–7. Ibn Baṭṭūṭa presumably heard of this event during his return journey through Syria in 1348.

[127] Magnesia ad Sipylum, in modern Turkish Manisa, 35 km. north-east of Smyrna (*Murray's Handbook*, 80; Philippson, II, 23, plate 8).

[128] I.e. of the Mecca Pilgrimage, preceding the Feast of Sacrifice on 10th Dhu'l-Ḥijja (see vol. I, pp. 243–6). In 731 this fell on 13 September 1331; in 733 on 21 August 1333.

[129] Chief of a Turkmen tribe, who captured Magnesia from the Catalans about 1313 and occupied the greater part of Lydia; d. 1345 and was succeeded by his direct descendants until the Ottoman conquest in 1391 (see *E.I.*, s.v.).

[130] This appears to be an Islamized modification of an old Siberian practice of placing the bodies of the dead in trees to desiccate; see J. Hastings (ed.), *Encyclopaedia of Religion and Ethics* (Edinburgh, 1912), IV, 421.

went to water them, in company with a slave of one of my companions. He was absent for a long time, and by the
314 afternoon no trace of them had appeared. | There was in this town [at the time] the excellent jurist and professor Muṣliḥ al-Dīn, and he rode with me to the sultan. We informed him of the event, but although he sent in search of them they were not found. While all the inhabitants were occupied with their feast, they made for a city belonging to the infidels on the sea-coast, called Fūja, a day's journey distant from Maghnīsīya. These infidels are in a strongly fortified town, and every year they send a gift to the sultan of Maghnīsīya, so he is content with this gift from them [and leaves them alone] because of the strength of their town.[131] In the afternoon [of the next day] the fugitives were brought in, along with the horses, by some Turks, who said that the pair of them had passed by them the previous evening, and that they, becoming suspicious about them, had used pressure on them until they confessed their design of escaping.

We continued our journey from Maghnīsīya and spent one
315 night with a body of | Turkmens who had encamped in a pasturage of theirs, but we could not obtain from them anything with which to feed our animals that night. Our party spent that night standing guard by turns, for fear of being robbed. When the turn of the jurist 'Afīf al-Dīn al-Tūzarī came round, I heard him reciting the *sūra* of the Cow[132] and said to him 'When you want to go to sleep let me know, so that I may see who is keeping guard.' I then went to sleep and he woke me only at dawn, by which time the robbers had gone off with a horse of mine—the one that 'Afīf al-Dīn had been riding—saddle, bridle, and all. It was a good horse, too, which I had bought at Ayā Sulūq.

We set off again in the morning, and came to the city of Barghama, a city in ruins, with a great and formidable fort-

[131] Eski Foja, the ancient Phocaea, at the western edge of the promontory, 60 km. west of Manisa (*Murray's Handbook*, 89; Philippson, II, 3–4, plates 2, 3), was at this time possessed by the Genoese family of Zaccaria, who controlled the alum mines there and the mastic trade of Chios. They built a new port, closer to the mines, on the northern edge of the promontory, called 'New Phocaea' (Yeni Foja), and this is probably the place to which Ibn Baṭṭūṭa refers: see Heyd, index; Lemerle, 51 sqq.

[132] The long second sūra of the Qur'ān.

ress on top of a hill.[133] It is related that the philosopher Aflāṭūn [Plato] was an inhabitant of this city, and his house is known by his name to the present day.[134] We lodged there in the hospice | of a poor brother of the Aḥmadīya, but after- 316
wards one of the chief men of the city came and took us over to his residence, where he entertained us right royally.

Account of the Sultan of Barghama. Its sultan is named Yakhshī Khān.[135] *Khān* in their language means 'sultan', and *Yakhshī* means 'excellent'. When we arrived he was away in a summer camp, but he was informed of our coming and sent a hospitality gift and a robe of *qudsī*.

We now hired a man to guide us on the road, and travelled over steep and rugged mountains until we came to the city of Balī Kasrī,[136] a fine and populous city with pleasant bazaars, but it has no mosque for congregational Friday prayers. They proposed to build a congregational mosque outside the town |
and adjoining it, but after building its walls they left it 317
without a roof, and now they pray in it and hold the Friday service under the shade of the trees. We lodged in this city at the hospice of the Young Akhī Sinān, one of their eminent men, and were visited by its qāḍī and khaṭīb, the legist Mūsā.

Account of the Sultan of Balī Kasrī. He is named Dumūr Khān, and is a worthless person.[137] It was his father who built this city, and during the reign of this son of his it acquired a large population of good-for-nothings, for 'Like king like people'. I visited him and he sent me a silk robe. I bought in this city a Greek slavegirl named Marghalīṭa.

We went on next day to the city of Burṣā, a great and im-

[133] Bergama, the ancient Pergamon, 60 km. north of Manisa: *Murray's Handbook*, 85 sqq.; Philippson I, 87 sqq., plate 1.

[134] As the French translators point out, Plato's name has been substituted in error for Galen.

[135] The dynasty is known as Qarasī, from its founder Qara-'Īsā, who occupied Pergamon about 1306. His son Yakhshī-Khān is mentioned in both Greek and Latin sources as a notable corsair: see *E.I.*, s.v.; Wittek, *Mentesche*, 21; Lemerle, 96.

[136] Balikesir, 80 km. north-east of Bergama: *Murray's Handbook*, 61; Philippson, III, 1–9. The region was famous for its silk products: 'Omarī, 43. For the route from Bergama to Brusa via Balikesir, see Taeschner, *Anatolische Wegenetz*, I, 161.

[137] Demir-Khān is variously called the brother or the son of Yakhshī-Khān, and his principality is called Akīrā by the contemporary source of al-'Omarī (43). It was annexed by the Ottomans about 1345.

318 portant city | with fine bazaars and wide streets, surrounded on all sides by gardens and running springs.[138] In its outskirts there is a river of exceedingly hot water which flows into a large pond; beside this have been built two [bath] houses, one for men and the other for women. Sick persons seek a cure in this hot pool and come to it from the most distant parts of the country. There is a hospice there for visitors, in which they are given lodging and food for the period of their stay, that is three days, and which was built by one of the kings of the Turkmens.[139]

We lodged in this city at the hospice of the Young Akhī Shams al-Dīn, one of the leaders of the *fityān*, and happened to be staying with him on the day of 'Ashūrā'.[140] He made a great feast to which he invited the principal officers of the army and leading citizens during the night, and when they had broken their fast the Qur'ān-readers recited with beauti-
319 ful voices. The jurist and preacher Majd al-Dīn | al-Qūnawī attended the gathering, and delivered an eloquent homily and exhortation, after which they began to sing and dance. It was a truly sublime night. This homiletic preacher is a man of saintly life; he fasts continually, and breaks his fast only every three days, he eats nothing but [what he has earned] by the labour of his hand, and he is reputed never to have eaten food [offered to him by] any person. He has no dwelling place, nor possessions other than clothes enough to cover his nakedness, and he sleeps only in the cemetery. He delivers homilies at assemblies and warns [men of the torments of hell fire, with such eloquence] that a number of persons repent at his hands in every assembly. I sought him out after this night but could not find him; even when I went to the cemetery I did not find him, and it was reported that he used to repair to it only when everyone else was asleep.

[138] Burṣā (Brusa), 120 km. north-east of Balikesir. It was captured from the Byzantine Greeks by Orkhan in 1326, just before the death of his father 'Othmān; for descriptions see *Murray's Handbook, Constantinople, Brusa, and the Troad* (London, 1900), 130–1—for its hot springs and baths, still famed—and A. Gabriel, *Une capitale turque, Brousse* (Paris, 1958).

[139] I.e. before the Ottoman conquest in 1326.

[140] The tenth day of Muḥarram, commonly observed as a fast day; see *E.I.*^{2}, s.v. In 732 the date was 13 October 1331; in 734, 21 September 1333. Akhī Shams al-Dīn has been identified with the father of Akhī Ḥasan, noted in the Ottoman chronicles as the spiritual advisor of Sultan Orkhan;

Anecdote. When we were attending [the celebration of] the night of 'Ashūrā' in the hospice of Shams al-Dīn, Majd al-Dīn delivered a homily there at the end of the night, and one of the poor brethren gave a loud cry | and fainted. They poured 320
rose-water over him, but he showed no signs of life, nor did he when they repeated the treatment. Those present expressed different opinions about him, some saying that he was dead, others that he had fainted. The preacher finished his discourse, the Qur'ān-readers recited, we prayed the dawn prayer, and the sun rose; then they investigated the man's condition and found that he had quitted the world—God's mercy on him—so they busied themselves with washing him and wrapping him in his shroud. I was among those who attended his funeral prayers and burial.

This poor brother was called 'the shrieker', and they related that he used to engage in devotional exercises in a cave in those parts on a mountain. When he heard that the preacher Majd al-Dīn was to preach [anywhere] he would go there to attend his sermon, but without accepting food from anyone. During Majd al-Din's discourse he would cry out and faint; then after a time he would revive, perform his ablutions and pray | two bowings. But on hearing the preacher again, 321
he would cry out, [and go on] doing this several times in the course of the night. He was called 'the shrieker' for this reason. He was mutilated in the arm and the leg and unable to do any work, but he had [at first] a mother who procured food for him by her spinning, and when she died he lived on wild plants.

I met in this city the pious shaikh 'Abdallāh al-Miṣrī, the traveller, and a man of saintly life. He journeyed through the earth, but he never went into China nor the island of Ceylon, nor the Maghrib, nor al-Andalus, nor the Negrolands, so that I have outdone him by visiting these regions.

Account of the Sultan of Burṣā. Its sultan is Ikhtiyār al-Dīn Urkhān Bak, son of the sultan 'Othmān Chūq (*chūq* in Turkish means 'the little').[141] This sultan is the greatest of

---

see F. Taeschner, 'Beiträge zur Geschichte der Achis in Anatolien' in *Islamica* (Leipzig, 1931), IV, 25, n. 3.

[141] Orkhan (reigned 1326–59), second sultan of the Ottoman ('Othmānli) dynasty, so named after its first sultan, 'Othmān. The Turkish suffix *-jik*

322 the kings of the Turkmens and the richest in wealth, | lands and military forces.[142] Of fortresses he possesses nearly a hundred, and for most of his time he is continually engaged in making the round of them, staying in each fortress for some days to put it into good order and examine its condition. It is said that he has never stayed for a whole month in any one town. He also fights with the infidels continually and keeps them under siege. It was his father who captured the city of Burṣā from the hands of the Greeks, and his tomb is in its mosque, which was formerly a church of the Christians.[143] It is told that he besieged the city of Yaznīk for about twenty years, but died before it was taken.[144] Then this son of his [Urkhān] whom we have mentioned besieged it for twelve years before capturing it; it was there that I met him and he sent me a large sum of money.

We continued our journey to the city of Yaznīk, and spent a night before reaching it at a village called Kurluh,[145] in the
323 hospice of one of | the Young Akhīs. From this village we travelled for a whole day through [countryside with] flowing rivers bordered with pomegranates, both sweet and acid, and eventually came to a rushy lake, at a distance of eight miles from Yaznīk.[146] This city is surrounded on all sides by the lake, and cannot be entered except by one road like a dyke, that can be traversed by only one horseman at a

is said to have been added to his name in order to distinguish him from the caliph 'Othmān (see vol. I, p. 180, n. 91); another suggestion is that it was derived from the town of 'Othmānjiq (Osmanjik), on the Kizil Irmak river, west of Amasya; see *E.I.*, s.vv. and 'Othmāndjiḳ.

[142] The contemporary sources of al-'Omarī (22, 42) give him 25,000 or 40,000 cavalry troops, but are critical of their military qualities. His territories at this time extended to Eskishehir in the south-east.

[143] Traditionally placed in the church of St. Elias (*Murray's Constantinople, etc.*, 126), but some Turkish sources assert that 'Othmān was buried in Sögüt, 60 km. south-east of Iznik, the original centre of the dynasty (*Murray's Handbook for Asia Minor*, 15).

[144] This is apparently a confusion with the capture of Brusa (above, n. 138). Iznik (Nicaea) was captured by Orkhan in March 1331 (Lemerle, 54, n. 6; G. G. Arnakis, *Oi Prōtoi Othōmanoi* (Athens, 1947), 187, n. 155).

[145] So vocalized in MS. 2289; not identified on modern maps.

[146] See *Murray's Constantinople, etc.*, 133–5, for the fertility of the plain and its swamps. The Arabic text that follows is in some disorder and has been slightly rearranged.

time.[147] It is for this reason that it held out so long, but it is now in a mouldering condition and uninhabited except for a few men in the sultan's service.[148] In it lives also his wife Bayalūn Khātūn, who is in command of them, a pious and excellent woman.[149]

The city is surrounded by four walls with a moat between every two of them,[150] and can be entered only over wooden drawbridges that they raise up when they wish to do so. Inside it there are orchards, homesteads, land and cultivated fields, and every man has his homestead, his field and
orchard, all together. Its drinking water | is obtained from 324
shallow wells inside the town, and it has all sorts of fruits. Walnuts and chestnuts are exceedingly plentiful and very cheap with them; they call the chestnut *qasṭana* and the walnut *qauz*.[151] In it grow also 'virgin' grapes,[152] the like of which I have never seen elsewhere, of the utmost sweetness, large in size, clear in colour, and thin-skinned, with only one stone to each grape.

We were given lodging in this city by the jurist and imām, the pilgrim and sojourner [in the Holy Cities] 'Alā al-Dīn al-Sulṭanyūkī, a worthy and generous man. I never went to

[147] This statement is puzzling, since the city was built on the eastern edge of the lake (Ascania, now Iznik Gölü). The outer wall was protected by a ditch, and the entrance in the south wall (the Yenishehir gate) is approached by a causeway; this may perhaps account for Ibn Baṭṭūṭa's repetition of his earlier description of Gül-Ḥiṣār (above, p. 424), but he may possibly have found the city flooded by the rise of the river.

[148] According to the early Turkish sources the majority of the inhabitants of Nicaea left the city after Orkhan's conquest; O. Turan, 'L'Islamisation dans la Turquie du Moyen Age' in *Studia Islamica* (Paris, 1959), X, 152.

[149] As will be seen below (p. 488), the name Bayalūn is given by Ibn Baṭṭūṭa to one of the wives of Sultan Muḥammad Özbek also. Although the reading is apparently attested by all MSS. it may possibly be an error for Nīlūfar, the correct name of Orkhan's wife (the difference in Arabic script being minimal); see *E.I.*, s.v. Nīlūfar Khātūn.

[150] These details are dubious; the city had only an outer and an inner wall, with a ditch protecting the latter, but the defences may have been temporarily strengthened during the siege.

[151] Literally 'they call the *qasṭal qasṭana* with an *n*, and the *jawz* the *qawz* with a *q*'. The Greek *kastana* passed into Arabic in the form *qasṭal* (*qasṭall*). *Qoz* is ordinary Turkish for 'walnut'.

[152] '*Adhārā* or '*adhārī*, so called because they resemble the fingers of young girls. The term is commonly applied to the white grapes of Ṭā'if, near Mecca, but also to dark grapes (from the practice of dyeing girls' fingers with henna).

visit him but he served up food. He was of handsome appearance and still more handsome character. He went with me to the Khātūn mentioned above, and she treated me honourably, gave me hospitality, and sent gifts. Some days after our arrival the sultan Urkhān Bak whom we have men-
325 tioned came to this city. I stayed in it about | forty days, on account of the illness of a horse of mine, but when I became impatient at the delay I left it behind and set out with three of my companions, and a slavegirl and two slaveboys. We had no one with us who could speak Turkish and translate for us. We had a translator previously but he left us in this city.

After our departure from it we spent the night at a village called Makajā[153] with a legist there who treated us well and gave us hospitality. On continuing our journey from this village we were preceded by a Turkish woman on a horse, and accompanied by a servant, who was making for the city of Yanijā,[154] while we followed her up. She came to a great river which is called Saqarī, as though it took its name from *Saqar* (God preserve us from it).[155] She went right on to ford the river, but when she was in the middle of it the horse nearly sank with her and threw her off its back. The servant who
326 was with her tried | to rescue her, but the river carried them both away. There were some men on the opposite bank who threw themselves in and swam after them; they brought out the woman with a spark of life still in her, but the man had perished—God's mercy on him. These men told us that the ford was below that place, so we went down to it. It consists of four balks of wood, tied together with ropes, on which they place the horses' saddles and the baggage; it is pulled over by men from the opposite bank, with the passengers riding on it, while the horses are led across swimming, and that was how we crossed.

We came the same night to Kāwiya,[156] where we lodged in the hospice of one of the Akhīs. We spoke to him in Arabic,

[153] Mekece, about 30 km. east of Iznik.

[154] I.e. Tarakli, 20 km. south-east of Geyve; see Taeschner, *Anatolische Wegenetz*, I, 193, n. 4.

[155] The Sakarya river. *Saqar* (apparently meaning 'vehement heat') is one of the names of Hell in the Qur'ān (sūra liv. 48).

[156] Geyve, 50 km. east of Iznik (also called Ṭorbali); *Murray's Constantinople, etc.*, 121. Ibn Baṭṭūṭa indicates his spelling of the name by adding 'on the pattern of the feminine participle from *kayy* (i.e. "cauterization")'.

and he did not understand us; he spoke to us in Turkish, and we did not understand him. Then he said 'Call the doctor of the law, for he knows Arabic,' | so the legist came and spoke 327
to us in Persian. We addressed him in Arabic, but he did not understand us, and said to the Young Brother ***Īshān 'arabī kuhnā miqūwān waman 'arabī naw mīdānam. Īshān*** means 'these men', ***kuhnā*** means 'old', ***miqūwān*** 'they say', ***naw*** 'new', and ***mīdānam*** 'I know'.[157] What the legist intended by this statement was to shield himself from disgrace, when they thought that he knew the Arabic language, although he did not know it. So he said to them 'These men speak the ancient Arabic speech and I know only the new Arabic.' However, the Young Brother thought that matters really were as the man of law said, and this did us good service with him. He showed us the utmost respect, saying 'These men must be honourably treated because they speak the ancient Arabic language, which was the language of the Prophet (God bless and give him peace) and of his Companions.' I did not understand what the legist said at that time, | but I retained the 328
sound of his words in my memory, and when I learned the Persian language I understood its meaning.

We spent the night in the hospice, and the Young Brother sent a guide with us to Yanijā, a large and fine township.[158] We searched there for the Akhī's hospice, and found one of the demented poor brothers. When I said to him 'Is this the Akhī's hospice?' he replied ***na'am*** [yes] and I was filled with joy at this, [thinking] that I had found someone who understood Arabic. But when I tested him further the secret came to light, that he knew nothing at all of Arabic except the word ***na'am***. We lodged in the hospice, and one of the students brought us food, since the Akhī was away. We became on friendly terms with this student, and although he knew no Arabic he offered his services and spoke to the deputy

[157] This passage again betrays Ibn Baṭṭūṭa's use of the North African colloquial form ***na'raf*** for 'I know', and a second time below in ***lam nafham***, 'I did not understand'. The faculty of memorizing phrases in a foreign language is not uncommon among Arabs; a parallel case is quoted by Yāqūt (***Irshād al-Arīb***, ed. D. S. Margoliouth (London, 1907), I, 173). But it is a little surprising that the doctor of the law should speak to the Turk in Persian.

[158] See above, n. 154. The full name of the place was Tarakli-Yenijesi; *Murray's Handbook*, 14.

[governor] of the town, who supplied us with one of his mounted men.

329 This man went with us to Kainūk, | which is a small town inhabited by infidel Greeks under the government of the Muslims.[159] There is only one household of Muslims in the place, and they are the governors of the Greeks, the town being in the territories of the Sultan Urkhān Bak. We lodged in the house of an old woman, an infidel; this was the season of snow and rain,[160] so we gave her some money and spent that night in her house. This town has no trees or grape-vines nor is anything cultivated there but saffron, and this old woman brought us a great quantity of saffron, thinking we were merchants and would buy it from her.

In the morning when we mounted our horses, the horseman whom the Young Brother had sent with us from Kainūk came to us and sent with us another horseman to conduct us to the city of Muṭurnī. There had been a heavy fall of snow during the night, which obliterated the road, so that the horseman went ahead of us and we followed in his tracks
330 until | we reached about midday a village of Turkmens. They brought food, of which we ate, and the horseman spoke with them, whereupon one of them rode on with us. He led us over steep slopes and mountains, and by a watercourse which we crossed again and again, more than thirty times. When we got clear of this, the [Turkmen] horseman said to us 'Give me some money,' but we replied 'When we reach the town we shall give you all that you want.' He was not satisfied with our answer, or else did not understand us, for he took a bow belonging to one of my companions and went off a little way, then returned and gave the bow back to us. I gave him some money then, and he took it and decamped, leaving us with no idea which way to go, and with no road visible to us. We made an effort to find traces of the road under the snow and to follow it, until about sunset we came to a hill where the track was shown by a great quantity of stones. I was afraid |

[159] Göynük, 25 km. east of Tarakli; *Murray's Handbook*, 14.

[160] *Shitā'*, which in classical Arabic means 'winter', is often used in North African for 'rain' (certainly for 'winter', however, on p. 459, l. 32 below). For the next phrase, MS. 2289 reads 'and she treated us well' (*aḥsanat 'ilainā*. For the use of *aḥsana 'ilā* in the sense of 'give money to', cf. p. 459, l. 14 below)

that both I and my companions would perish, as I expected 331
more snow to fall in the night, and the place was uninhabited; if we dismounted we were doomed, and if we continued on through the night we should not know which way to go. I had a good horse, however, a thoroughbred, so I planned a way of escape, saying to myself, 'If I reach safety, perhaps I may contrive some means to save my companions,' and it happened so. I commended them to God Most High and set out.[161] Now the people of that country build over their graves wooden chambers, which anyone who sees them would take to be habitations, but finds to be graves. I saw a large number of these, but after the hour of the night prayer I came to some houses and said 'O God, grant that they be inhabited.' I found that they were inhabited, and God Most High guided me to the gate of a certain building. I saw by it an old man
and spoke to him in Arabic; he replied to me in Turkish | and 332
signed to me to enter. I told him about my companions, but he did not understand me. It happened by the providential goodness of God that that building was a hospice of some poor brethren, and that the man standing by the gate was its shaikh. When the brethren inside the hospice heard me speaking with the shaikh, one of them came out; he was a man with whom I had an acquaintance, and when he greeted me I told him the tale of my companions, and advised him to go with the brethren to rescue them. They did so and went with me to rejoin my companions, and we came back together to the hospice, praising God Most High for our safety. This was on the eve of Friday, and the inhabitants of the village assembled and occupied the night with liturgies to God Most High. Each one of them brought what food he could, and our distress was relieved.

We rode on at dawn and reached the city of Muṭurnī[162] at
the hour of the congregational prayer. | On alighting at the 333
hospice of one of the Young Akhīs we found a company of travellers already there, and no stabling [available] for our animals. So we prayed the Friday prayer in some anxiety, on account of the quantities of snow, the cold, and the lack of stabling. Then we met one of the inhabitants who had made

[161] Two MSS. read 'set out in the dark' (*saraitu*).

[162] Mudurnu or Mudurlu, 35 km. east of Goynuk; *Murray's Handbook*, 14.

the Pilgrimage and who greeted us, knowing Arabic. I was heartily glad to see him and asked him to direct us to some place where we could hire stabling for the animals. He replied 'To tether them inside any place of habitation could not be managed, because the doors of the houses in this town are small, and horses could not be got through them; but I shall guide you to a covered arcade in the bazaar, where travellers and those who come to do business in the bazaar tie up their horses.' So he guided us to the place and we tethered our horses in it, and one of my companions settled himself in an empty shop alongside it, to guard the animals. |

334 *Anecdote.* There was a strange thing happened to us [there]. I sent one of the servants to buy chopped straw for the beasts, and one of them to buy ghee. Number one came back with the straw, but number two came back empty-handed and laughing. We asked him what he was laughing at, and he replied 'We stopped at a stall in the bazaar and asked him for *samn* [ghee]. He signed to us to wait, and spoke to a boy with him, to whom we then gave the money. He was away for a long time, and came back with some straw. We took it from him and said "We want *samn*," whereupon he said "This is *samn*".' It came to light that they say *samn* for chopped straw in Turkish, and ghee is called by them *rughan.*[163]

When we met in with this pilgrim who knew Arabic, we besought him to travel with us to Qaṣṭamūniya, which is ten days' journey from this town. I presented him with an
335 Egyptian robe, | one of my own, gave him also ready money, which he left to meet the expenses of his family, assigned him an animal to ride, and promised him a good reward. When he set out with us it became evident from his conduct that he was a man of substantial wealth, who had made loans to a number of persons, but of mean ambitions, base character, and evil actions. We used to give him money for our expenses and he would take what bread was left over and trade it for spices, vegetables and salt, and appropriate the money that he got by selling these. I was told too that he used to steal some of the money for our expenses as well. We had to put up

[163] *Semen* in Persian and Turkish means 'clover'. *Rawghan* also is a Persian word, colloquially pronounced *rūghan* in Turkish.

with him because of our difficulties through not knowing Turkish, but the thing went so far that we openly accused him and would say to him at the end of the day 'Well, Hajji, how much of the expense-money have you stolen today?' He would reply 'So much,' and we would laugh at him and make the best of it.

One of his base actions was that, when a horse of ours died at one of the halts of our journey, he did the job of | skinning 336
it with his own hands and sold the hide. Another occurred when we lodged for the night with a sister of his in a village. She brought us food and fruit, namely pears,[164] apples, apricots and peaches, all of them dried and [then] cooked in water until they soften, when they are eaten and their juice drunk. We wanted to pay her, but when he learned of this he said 'Don't give her anything, but give that amount to me.' So we gave the money to him to satisfy him, but we also gave her something secretly, in such a way that he did not know of it.

We came next to the city of Būlī.[165] When we were nearly there, we came upon a river which seemed, to all appearances, a small one, but when some of my companions got into the stream, they found it exceedingly fast and impetuous. They all crossed it, however, except for a young slavegirl whom they were afraid to take across. | Since my horse was a better 337
one than theirs, I mounted her behind me and started to cross the river. But when I was in the middle of it, my horse stumbled with me and the girl fell off. My companions got her out with a spark of life still in her, and I for my part came out safely.

On entering the city, we sought out the hospice of one of the Young Akhīs. One of their customs is to keep a fire always alight in their hospices during the winter. At each angle of the hospice they put a fireplace, and they make vents for them by which the smoke rises, so that it does not incommode [those in] the hospice. They call these [chimneys] *bakhārī*, the singular being *bakhīrī*.

[164] *Ijjāṣ* in classical Arabic means 'plums', but in Maghribine usage 'pears' (adopted also by the French translators).

[165] Bolu, 45 km. north-east of Mudurnu, on the northern side of the Bolu Su, a tributary of the Filyos (Filiyas) river; *Murray's Handbook*, 5.

Ibn Juzayy remarks: [The poet] Ṣafī al-Dīn 'Abd al-'Azīz b. Sarāyā al-Ḥilli[166] showed an excellent skill in the use of concealed allusion in his verse, which was recalled to my mind by the mention of the *bakhīrī*:

Since you left it, our chimney-place in the morning light
Stands cold, with the ashes strewn over the dusty grate. |
338 If you wish to revive it as 'father of flame' tonight,
Let your mules, as 'carriers of firewood', return to our gate.[167]

(*To return*). When we entered the hospice we found the fire alight, so I took off my clothes, put on others, and warmed myself at the fire; and the Akhī not only brought food and fruit but lavished them. What an excellent body of men these are, how nobleminded, how unselfish and full of compassion for the stranger, how kindly affectionate to the visitor, how magnanimous in their solicitude for him! The coming of a stranger to them is exactly as if he were coming to the dearest of his own kin.

We passed that night in an agreeable way, and having resumed our journey in the morning, came to the city of
339 Garadai Būlī.[168] | It is a large and fine city situated in a plain, with spacious streets and bazaars, one of the coldest towns in the world, and divided into separate quarters, each inhabited by a particular community, the members of which are not mixed with those of any other.

Account of its Sultan. He is the sultan Shāh Bak, one of the middling class of sultans in this country,[169] a man of good figure and conduct, of fine character, but not liberal. We prayed the Friday prayers in this city and lodged in a hospice there. I met in it the khaṭīb, who was the Ḥanbalī jurist Shams al-Dīn al-Dimashqī; he had been resident in it for many years and had children there. He is the religious adviser

[166] A celebrated contemporary poet; see above, p. 353, n. 286.

[167] The allusions are to sūra cxi of the Qur'ān, in which Muḥammad's uncle is called Abū Lahab, 'father of flame', and his wife satirized as a 'carrier of firewood'; see vol. I, p. 209, n. 92.

[168] Gerede, 37 km. east of Bolu, the ancient Crateia; *Murray's Handbook*, 6. A little to the east of this town Ibn Baṭṭūṭa leaves the main Anatolian highway to make for the Black Sea coast.

[169] Little is known of this principality. Al-'Omarī (22) calls the sultan Shāhīn (probably an error for Shāh Bak), and puts his army at about 5,000 horse. Gerede was occupied by the Ottomans in 1354.

and khaṭīb of this sultan and enjoys great authority with him. This jurist came into my room in the hospice and informed us that the sultan had come to visit us. So I thanked him for | his action and went out to welcome the sultan. After 340
I had saluted him he sat down and asked me about myself and my journey, and whom I had met of sultans; I answered all his questions, and after a short stay he went away and sent a horse with its saddle and a robe.

We left there for the city of Burlū, a small town on a hill, with a valley below it, and a citadel on the top of a steep eminence.[170] We lodged there in a fine college whose professor and students were known to the ḥājjī who travelled with us. He would attend the instruction along with them, for in spite of everything he was a student of religion, a Ḥanafī by rite. On invitation from the amīr of this town, who was 'Alī Bak, son of the esteemed sultan Sulaimān Pādshāh, the king of Qaṣṭamūniya (whom we shall mention later[171]), we went up to visit him in the citadel. He greeted us, bade us welcome, treated us with courtesy, and asked me about my journeys and myself; | when I answered him on these matters, he bade 341
me sit beside him. His qāḍī and secretary, the pilgrim[172] 'Alā al-Dīn Muḥammad, one of the most distinguished of secretaries, was in attendance. Food was served, and after we had eaten, the Qur'ān-readers recited with voices to draw tears and with wonderful modulations, and we withdrew.

We continued our journey next day to the city of Qaṣṭamūniya,[173] one of the largest and finest of cities, where commodities are abundant and prices low. We lodged there in the hospice of a shaikh called al-Uṭrush ['the deaf'],[174] because of his hardness of hearing, and I witnessed an astonishing thing in connection with him, namely that one of the students would write for him with his finger in the air, or sometimes on the

[170] On modern Turkish maps Safranbolu, 65 km. north-east of Bolu; in old Turkish texts Za'farān Burlu (so called from the cultivation of saffron in the district: *Murray's Handbook*, 6, under Zafaranboli; cf. Taeschner, *Anatolische Wegenetz*, I, 219–20).

[171] See below, p. 463, n. 179.

[172] The French editors note that in two MSS. the term 'pilgrim' is replaced by 'chamberlain' (*al-ḥājib*).

[173] Kastamonu, 90 km. east of Safranbolu (therefore at least two days' journey): *Murray's Handbook*, 6–7; *E.I.*, s.v. Ḳasṭamūnī.

[174] In MS. 2289 vocalized al-Aṭrash.

ground, and he would understand what he meant and reply. Long stories were told to him in this way, and he would grasp them.

342 We stayed in this city | about forty days. We used to buy a quarter of fat mutton for two dirhams and bread for two dirhams—this would satisfy our needs for a day, and there were ten of us. We would buy sweetmeats made of honey for two dirhams, and they would be enough for us all, and walnuts for a dirham or chestnuts at the same price, and after all of us had eaten of them there would be some left over. We used to buy a load of firewood for a single dirham, and this in the season of extreme cold. I have never in any country seen a city where prices were lower than there.

I met there the shaikh, the learned imām, the muftī and professor Tāj al-Dīn al-Sulṭānyūkī, one of the great scholars. He had studied in the two 'Irāqs and Tabrīz, where he made his home for a time, and also in Damascus, and had sojourned long ago at the two Holy Cities. I met there also the scholar and professor Ṣadr al-Dīn Sulaimān al-Fanīkī, of the people of Fanīka in the land of al-Rūm,[175] who gave me hos-
343 pitality in his college, which | is in the horse-market,[176] and the aged and pious shaikh Dādā Amīr 'Alī. I visited this man in his hospice, in the vicinity of the horse-market, and found him lying on his back. One of his servants assisted him to sit up and one of them raised his eyelids from his eyes; on opening them he addressed me in pure Arabic, saying 'You are heartily welcome.' I asked him his age and he said 'I was an associate of the caliph al-Mustanṣir billāh, and at his death I was thirty years old, and my age now is one hundred and sixty three years'.[177] I asked him to invoke a blessing on me; he did so, and I withdrew.

Account of the Sultan of Qaṣṭamūniya. He is the esteemed sultan Sulaimān Pādshāh, a man of great age, more than
344 seventy years old, with a fine face and long beard,[178] | a

[175] Finike, on the south coast, to the south-west of Antalya.

[176] Kastamonu was famous for its breed of fast geldings (gelding is forbidden in Islam, but these were 'Greek' horses), valued at up to a thousand dinars each ('Omarī, 23).

[177] Since al-Mustanṣir Billāh, the penultimate caliph of Baghdād, died in A.H. 640 (5 December 1242), the shaikh's age could not have been more than 123 (lunar) years.

[178] Two MSS. read 'long side-lock'.

stately and venerable figure.[179] Students of religion and devotees have entry to his private circle. I visited him in his audience-hall, and he bade me sit beside him and asked me about myself and my journey, and about the Holy Sanctuaries, Egypt and Syria. When I answered his questions, he commanded me to be lodged near him and gave me on the same day a thoroughbred horse, parchment-coloured, and a robe, besides assigning me money for my expenses and forage. Later on he ordered for me [an assignment of] wheat and barley, which was delivered to me[180] from a village dependent on the city, and half a day's journey from it, but I could not find anyone to buy it because of the cheapness of prices, so I gave it to the ḥājjī who was in our company.

It is the custom of this sultan to take his seat in his audience-hall every day after the afternoon prayer; food is brought in and the doors are opened, and no one, whether townsman or nomad, stranger or traveller, is prevented from partaking. He also sits during the early part | of the day in 345
private session; his son comes, kisses his hands, and withdraws to an audience-chamber of his own, and the officers of state come and eat in his presence, and then retire. It is his custom also on Fridays to ride to the mosque, which is at some distance from his residence. This mosque is a wooden building of three stories; the sultan, the officers of state, the qāḍī and the jurists, and the chief officers of the army pray in the lowest story; 'Afandī,'[181] who is the Sultan's brother, together with his entourage and attendants, and some of the townspeople, pray in the middle story; and the sultan's son and heir (he is his youngest son, and is called al-Jawād),[182] with his retinue, slaves and attendants, and the rest of the

[179] Shujā' al-Dīn Sulaimān, son of Timur-Jāndār, feudatory of Aflāni (north-east of Safranbolu), seized Kastamonu from its hereditary Seljuk governors, the Chupānids, in 1310 or 1320, and established there his own dynasty, the Jāndār-oghlu or Isfandiyārids. He captured also Burlu and Sinope, and appointed his sons 'Alī (above, p. 461) and Ibrāhīm (below, p. 465) as their governors. In the other contemporary sources he is always styled 'Sulaimān Pasha'.

[180] The complement *li* clearly indicates that the verb is to be read ***nuffidha***; cf. vol. III, p. 436 (Arabic).

[181] One of the earliest examples of the use among Turks of this Greek honorific (*afthéntēs*).

[182] Otherwise unknown. Sulaimān was succeeded on his death (about 1339) by Ibrāhīm.

population, pray in the top story. The Qur'ān-readers assemble and sit in a circle in front of the *miḥrāb*, and along with them sit the khaṭīb and the qāḍī. The sultan has his place in line with the *miḥrāb*. They recite the *Sūra* of 'The
346 Cave' with beautiful intonations, | and repeat the verses[183] in a marvellous arrangement. When they finish the recital of this, the khaṭīb mounts the *mimbar* and delivers the address. He then prays, and after finishing this prayer they perform further additional prayers. The reader[184] now recites one-tenth of the Qur'ān in the sultan's presence, after which the sultan and his suite withdraw. The reader proceeds to recite before the sultan's brother; he also withdraws with his attendants at the end of this recital, and the reader then recites before the sultan's son. When he finishes this recital, the *mu'arrif* stands up (he is the remembrancer[185]), and praises the sultan in Turkish verse, and praises also his son, calling down blessings on both, and retires. The king's son proceeds to his father's residence, after first kissing his uncle's hand on his way (his uncle in the meantime standing to await him), after which they enter the sultan's presence together; his brother advances, kisses his hand, and sits down in front of him, then his son comes forward, kisses his hand
347 and withdraws to | his own hall, where he takes his seat with his own suite. When the hour of afternoon prayer arrives they all pray it together; the sultan's brother then kisses his hand and leaves him, and does not return to him until the following Friday. As for his son, he presents himself every morning, as we have related.

We travelled on thereafter from this city and lodged in a large hospice at a certain village—one of the finest hospices that I saw in that country. It was built by a great amīr called Fakhr al-Dīn, who repented before God Most High of his sins.[186] He assigned to his son the control of the [income of

[183] This is the literal translation, but the meaning may be that they trill or give a choral rendering of the verses.

[184] One MS. reads 'the qāḍī'.

[185] His function is described in a later passage (below, p. 473).

[186] This can hardly be other than the madrasa founded at Tashköprü (40 km. east-north-east of Kastamonu; *Murray's Handbook*, 7) by the Chupānid amīr of Kastamonu, Muẓaffar al-Dīn Yūluq Arslān (d. 1304/5), and re-endowed by Sulaimān Pādshāh in 1329; the inscription recording this is

the] hospice and the supervision of the poor brethren who resided in it, and all the revenues derived from the village are constituted an endowment for it. Alongside the hospice he built a bath-house *ad majorem Dei gloriam*, which may be entered by every wayfarer without any obligation of payment, and he built also a bazaar in the village and made it an endowment for the congregational mosque. From the endowments of this hospice he assigned to every poor brother who should come from | the two Holy Cities or from Syria, Egypt, 348
the two 'Irāqs, Khurāsān, and other parts, a complete set of clothing and one hundred dirhams on the day of his arrival, three hundred dirhams on the day of his departure, and maintenance for the days of his stay, consisting of meat, rice cooked in ghee, and sweetmeats. To each poor brother from the land of al-Rūm he assigned ten dirhams and hospitality for three days.

After leaving this hospice we spent a second night in a hospice on a lofty mountain without any habitations.[187] It was established by one of the Young Akhīs called Niẓām al-Dīn, an inhabitant of Qaṣṭamūniya, and he gave it as endowment a village, the revenue from which was to be spent for the maintenance of wayfarers in this hospice.

We continued our journey from this hospice to the city of Ṣanūb,[188] a superb city which combines fortification with beautification. It is encompassed by sea on all sides except one, namely the east,[189] and it has | on that side a single gate- 349
way through which no one may enter except by permission of its governor; he is Ibrāhīm Bak, son of the sultan Sulaimān Pādshāh whom we have mentioned.[190] When permission for us had been obtained from him, we entered the town and lodged in the hospice of 'Izz al-Dīn Akhī Chalabī, which is outside the Sea-Gate. From there one can climb up to a

---

reproduced in *Répertoire chron. d'épigraphie arabe*, XIV, no. 5573. 'Fakhr al-Dīn' is probably a slip of memory.

[187] For the route over the Changal Dagh between Tashköprü and Sinop see *Murray's Handbook*, 11.

[188] Sinope, in modern Turkish Sinop, 95 km. north-east of Tashküprö; *Murray's Handbook*, 2.

[189] Erroneously for the west, as often in mediaeval descriptions.

[190] Above, p. 463, n. 179.

mountain projecting into the sea,[191] like Mīna at Sabta [Ceuta],[192] on which there are orchards, cultivated fields and streams, most of its fruits being figs and grapes. It is an inaccessible mountain that cannot be taken by escalade. On it there are eleven villages inhabited by Greek infidels under the government of the Muslims, and on top of it is a hermitage called after al-Khiḍr and Ilyās (on both of them be peace),[193] which is never without a resident devotee. Beside it is a spring of water, and prayer made in it is answered. At the foot of this mountain is the tomb of the pious saint,
350 the Companion Bilāl | al-Ḥabashī,[194] over which there is a hospice at which food is supplied to wayfarers.

The congregational mosque in the city of Ṣanūb is one of the most beautiful mosques. In the centre of it is a pool of water, over which is a cupola supported by four pilasters, each pilaster accompanied by two marble pillars, and on top of the cupola is a rostrum to which one ascends by a wooden staircase. This was constructed by the sultan Barwāna, son of the sultan 'Ala al-Dīn al-Rūmī, and he used to perform the Friday prayer on top of this cupola. He was succeeded as sultan by his son Ghāzī Chalabī, and on his death the abovementioned sultan Sulaimān took possession of the city.[195]

This Ghāzī Chalabī was a brave and audacious man, endowed by God with a special gift of endurance under water

[191] Boz Tepe, a projecting bluff about 6 km. in length, joined to the land by a low and narrow peninsula, on which the city was situated; see the plan and old print in M. I. Maksimova, *Antichnye Goroda Yugo-vostochnago Prechernomor'a* (Moskva-Leningrad, 1956), 32–3.

[192] Jabal Mīna commands the eastern end of the peninsula upon which the city of Ceuta was built.

[193] For al-Khiḍr, see vol. I, p. 123, n. 203. Ilyās is Elijah, in Greek Elias, and frequently identified with al-Khiḍr, especially on hill-top sites; see *E.I.*, s.vv., also above, p. 401, and F. W. Hasluck, *Christianity and Islam under the Sultans* (Oxford, 1929), I, 319 sqq.

[194] See vol. I, p. 139, n. 239, for the presumed tomb of Bilāl at Damascus.

[195] The complex of errors in this statement is noted by the French editors. *Perwāna* ('chamberlain') was the designation of the dynasty of princes of Sinope under suzerainty of the Mongol Ilkhāns of Persia (Sinope being a valuable outpost for protection of the trade-route via Trebizond to Tabrīz). The dynasty was established about 1260 by a relative by marriage of the Seljuk sultans of Rūm, and ousted in 1301 by Ghāzī Chelebi, son of the Seljuk sultan Mas'ūd II (d. 1304). In 1322 the city was captured by Sulaimān. To add to the confusion, one of al-'Omarī's sources (23) states that Ghāzī Chelebi was governor of Sinope under Sulaimān's successor Ibrāhīm (*c.* 1340–2).

and power of swimming. He used to make expeditions in war galleys to fight the Greeks,[196] and when the fleets met and everybody was occupied with the fighting he would dive under | the water, carrying in his hand an iron tool with 351
which to hole the enemy's galleys, and they would know nothing of what had befallen them until the foundering [of their ships] took them unawares. On one occasion a fleet of galleys belonging to the enemy made a surprise attack on the harbour of Ṣanūb, and he holed them and captured all the men who were on board.[197] He possessed indeed a talent that was unmatched, but they relate that he used to consume an excessive quantity of *ḥashīsh*,[198] and it was because of this that he died. He went out one day hunting (to which he was passionately addicted) and pursued a gazelle, which led him on among some trees; he spurred his horse on too hard and was intercepted by a tree, which struck and crushed in his head. So he died,[199] and the sultan Sulaimān seized the town and placed his son Ibrāhīm in it [as governor]. It is said that he too consumes as much as his predecessor did, but the people of all the districts of al-Rūm show no disapproval of consuming it. Indeed, I passed one day by the gate of the congregational mosque in Ṣanūb, outside of which there are benches | where the inhabitants sit, and I saw several of the 352
superior officers of the army with an orderly of theirs in front of them holding in his hand a bag filled with something resembling henna. One of them took a spoonful of it and ate it, as I was looking at him; I had no idea what there was in the bag, but I enquired of the person who was with me, and he told me that it was *ḥashīsh*. We were hospitably entertained in this city by its qāḍī, as well as by the governor's deputy in it and the local professor; his name was Ibn 'Abd al-Razzāq.[200]

196 This probably refers to his exploits against the Genoese at Kaffa; Heyd, I, 551.

197 The episode presumably referred to is somewhat differently presented in the Genoese sources, which relate that in 1324 'Zarabi' treacherously attacked a flotilla of ten Guelph ships while their leaders were being entertained by him in the city; Jacobus de Voragine 'Iacopo da Voragine anonimi Giorgio Stella', *Annali Genovesi* (Genova, 1941), I, 174–6.

198 See above, p. 417, n. 19.

199 As indicated above in nn. 195, 197, it would appear that Ghāzī Chelebi survived Sulaimān's occupation for at least twenty years.

200 The text appears to imply the identity of the three functionaries, but the next paragraph refers to 'the sultan's deputy' separately.

Anecdote. When we entered this city, its people observed that we performed the prayers with our arms hanging down. They are Ḥanafīs, who know nothing of the rite of Mālik nor of his manner of prayer, the preferred practice according to his school being to let the arms hang down.[201] Now some of
353 them were accustomed to see | the Rāfiḍīs in the Ḥijāz and al-'Irāq praying with their arms hanging down, so they suspected us of following their doctrine, and interrogated us on the point. We told them that we belonged to the school of Mālik, but they remained unconvinced by our statement. The suspicion became so firmly fixed in their minds that the sultan's deputy sent us a hare, and instructed one of his servants to remain with us in order to see what we should do with it. We slaughtered it ritually, cooked it and ate it, and the servant returned to him and informed him accordingly. Consequently the suspicion was removed from us and they sent us the [usual] hospitality-gifts, for the Rāfiḍīs do not eat the hare.[202]

Four days after our arrival at Ṣanūb, the mother of the amīr Ibrāhīm died there, and I went out in her funeral procession. Her son went out on foot and with bare head, and so
354 also did the amīrs and mamlūks, | with their robes inside out.[203] As for the qāḍī, the khaṭīb, and the jurists, they too reversed their robes, but they did not bare their heads, and covered them instead with kerchiefs of black wool, in place of turbans. They continued to serve food for forty days, this being the period of mourning in their usage.

Our stay in this city lasted for about forty days, while we were awaiting an occasion to travel by sea to the city of al-Qiram.[204] We then hired a vessel belonging to the Greeks and remained eleven days [more] waiting for a favourable wind. At length we began the voyage, but when we were out in the open sea, after three nights, a storm blew up against us and

[201] Instead of bending them upwards from the elbow at the first invocation, as in the Ḥanafī rite (see 'Prayer' in T. P. Hughes's *Dictionary of Islam* (London 1885, reprint 1935)).

[202] The Shī'ites adopted the Mosaic prohibition of the hare (Leviticus, xi, 6).

[203] See above, p. 291, n. 69.

[204] For the trade between Sinope and the Crimea see Heyd, I, 298; G. I. Bratianu, *Recherches sur le commerce génois dans la Mer Noire au XIIIe siècle* (Paris, 1929), 172.

we were in sore straits, with destruction visibly before our
eyes. I was in the cabin,[205] along with a man from the
Maghrib named Abū Bakr, and I bade him go up on deck to
observe the state of the sea. He did so and came back to me
in the cabin saying | to me 'I commend you to God.' The 355
storm raged against us with unparalleled fury, then the wind
changed and drove us back nearly to the very city of Ṣanūb
from which we had started. One of its merchants wanted to
go down to its harbour, but I prevented the master of the
ship from disembarking him.[206] Afterwards the wind fell,
and we resumed our journey, but when we were in the open
sea a storm blew up [again] and the same thing happened to
us as before; then eventually the wind became favourable
and we saw the mountains on the mainland.

We made for a harbour called Karsh,[207] intending to put
in there, but some persons who were on the mountain made
signs to us not to enter, so, fearing that we might run into
danger and thinking that there were galleys[208] of the enemy
in the port, we turned back along the coast. As we approached
the land, I said to the master of the ship 'I wish to descend
here' so he put me ashore. I saw a church so we made to-
wards it. In it I found a monk, and on one of | the walls of the 356
church I saw the figure of an Arab man wearing a turban,
girt with a sword, and carrying a spear in his hand, and in
front of him a lamp, which was alight. I said to the monk
'What is this figure?' and when he replied 'This is the figure
of the prophet 'Alī'[209] I was filled with astonishment. We spent
the night in that church, and cooked some fowls, but we
could not eat them because they were among the provisions
that we had taken with us on the ship, and everything that
had been on board was impregnated with the smell of the
sea.

[205] Arabic *ṭārima*, apparently of Persian origin, meaning a shed or portico.

[206] MS. 2289 reads 'the master of the ship prevented him from bringing this about (?)'.

[207] Kerch, on the strait of Yeni-kale, at the entrance to the Sea of Azov, in classical times called the 'Cimmerian Bosphorus' and hence Vospro in the Italian portolans. It became a metropolitan see in 1332 (Heyd, II, 184–5).

[208] *Ajfān*, sing. *jafn*, a North African term meaning 'galley' in general, but here obviously implying 'war-galleys'; cf. p. 402, n. 125.

[209] This looks like a natural confusion with Elias, the Greek genitive of which is *Elía*.

This place where we landed was in the wilderness known as
Dasht-i Qifjaq (*dasht* in the language of the Turks means
'wilderness').[210] This wilderness is green and grassy, with no
trees nor hills, high or low, nor narrow pass nor firewood.
What they use for burning is animal dung (which they call
tazak),[211] and you can see even their men of rank gathering
357 it up | and putting it in the skirts of their robes. There is no
means of travelling in this desert except in waggons, and it
extends for six months' journey, three of them in the territories of the sultan Muḥammad Ūzbak, and three in those of
other princes. On the day after our arrival at this roadstead,
one of the merchants in our company went to some of the
tribesmen known as Qifjaq who inhabit this desert and pro-
fess the Christian religion, and hired from them a waggon
drawn by horses.[212] We rode in this, and came to the city of
al-Kafā, which is a great city along the sea coast inhabited
by Christians, most of them Genoese, who have a governor
called al-Damdīr.[213] We lodged there in the mosque of the
Muslims.

Anecdote. When we alighted at this mosque and stayed in
358 it for an hour or so, we heard the sounds | of clappers[214] on
every side, and never having heard them before I was
alarmed at this and bade my companions ascend the minaret
and chant the Qur'ān and praises to God, and recite the call

[210] *Dasht* is the Persian equivalent of the Arabic *ṣaḥrā'*, i.e. desert, wilderness, open country. After the occupation of South Russia by the Qipchaq (=Comans), this name became current among Arabic geographers for the Russian steppes: see *E.I.*, s.v. Ḳipčaḳ; W. Barthold, *Histoire des Turcs d'Asie Centrale* (Paris, 1945), 90.

[211] The ordinary Turkish term.

[212] Many Comans were converted to Christianity in South Russia: *E.I.*, s.v. Ḳipčaḳ; cf. Bratianu, 210.

[213] Kaffa, the ancient Theodosia (modern Feodosia), was rebuilt by the Genoese in the thirteenth century as their trading centre in the Crimea (Heyd, II, 157 sqq.), destroyed by the Mongols in 1308, and later rebuilt (B. Spuler, *Die Goldene Horde* (Leipzig, 1943), 84). That al-Damdīr conceals the name Demetrio (as suggested by the French translators) is uncertain in the absence of evidence, nor can it be said what Ibn Baṭṭūṭa meant by the 'governor' (*amīr*) of the Genoese. There is an eighteenth-century 'view' of Kaffa in Bratianu, plate IV.

[214] *Nāqūs*, plural *nawāqīs*, is strictly the term for the wooden clappers or church-gongs (called in Greek *sēmantra*) used by the Greek churches, but here must mean the bells of the Latin churches. Muslims held the ringing of bells in the greatest abhorrence, and a Prophetic Tradition says, 'The angels will not enter any house in which bells are rung.'

to prayer. They did so, when suddenly a man came in wearing breastplate and weapons and saluted us. We asked him what was his business, and he told us that he was the qāḍī of the Muslims there, and said 'When I heard the chanting and the call to prayer, I feared for your safety and came as you see.' Then he went away, but no evil befell us.

On the following day the governor[215] came to visit us and prepared a banquet, which we ate in his residence. We made a circuit of the city and found it provided with fine bazaars, but all the inhabitants are infidels. We went down to its port, where we saw a wonderful harbour with about two hundred vessels in it, both ships of war and trading vessels, small and large, for it is one of the world's celebrated ports.

We then hired | a waggon and travelled to the city of al- 359
Qiram,[216] a large and fine city in the territories of the illustrious sultan Muḥammad Ūzbak Khān. There is an amīr who governs it on his behalf, named Tuluk-tumūr. One of the subordinates of this amīr, who had accompanied us on our journey, informed him of our arrival, and he sent me a horse by the hand of his imām, Sa'd al-Dīn. We lodged in a hospice, whose shaikh, Zāda al-Khurāsānī, welcomed us and treated us honourably and generously. He is held in great veneration among them; I saw many persons come to salute him, of the rank of qāḍī, khaṭīb, doctor of law, etc. This shaikh Zāda told me that outside this city there was a Christian monk living in a monastery, who devoted himself to ascetic exercises and
used frequently to fast, and that he eventually reached | the 360
point of being able to fast for forty days at a stretch, after which he would break his fast with a single bean; also that he had the faculty of revealing secret things. He desired me to go with him to visit the man, but I refused, although after-

215 Two MSS. read 'the Akhī', but the existence of a Muslim qāḍī does not necessarily imply the presence of a resident Muslim colony at this time, which is, indeed, implicitly denied in the following sentence.

216 Al-Qiram (from which the name Crimea is derived), later called Stary Krim, 42 km. west of Feodosia, in mediaeval texts Solgat; see Heyd, II, 174 sqq. The Crimea was included in the empire of the so-called 'Golden Horde', the apanage of Chingiz Khān's eldest son Juchi and his descendants, called by the Arabs the Khanate of Qipchaq. Sultan (Muḥammad) Özbeg (reigned 1312–41) was one of the most powerful Khāns of its ruling group, the Blue Horde; but the governor of the Crimea exercised a largely independent authority; see Spuler, *Die Goldene Horde*, 75–99, and for the Crimea, 314.

wards I regretted not having seen him and found out the truth of what was said about him.

I met in this city its chief qāḍī, Shams al-Dīn al-Sāyilī,[217] who is the qāḍī of the Ḥanafīs, and the qāḍī of the Shāfi'īs, who is named Khiḍr, as well as the jurist and professor 'Alā al-Dīn al-Āṣī,[218] the khaṭīb of the Shāfi'īs, Abū Bakr (it is he who pronounces the *khuṭba* in the congregational mosque that al-Malik al-Nāṣir (God's mercy on him) erected in this city),[219] the pious shaikh and sage Muẓaffar al-Dīn (he was a Greek who embraced Islam and became a sincere Muslim), and the pious and ascetic shaikh Muẓhir al-Dīn, who was a highly respected doctor of law. The amīr Tuluktumūr was ill, but we visited him and he received us honourably and made
361 gifts to us. He was on the point of setting out for the city | of al-Sarā, the capital of the sultan Muḥammad Ūzbak, so I planned to travel in his company and bought some waggons for that purpose.

Account of the waggons in which one journeys in this country. These people call a waggon '*araba*.[220] They are waggons with four large wheels, some of them drawn by two horses, and some drawn by more than two, and they are drawn also by oxen and camels, according to the weight or lightness of the waggon. The man who services the waggon rides on one of the horses that draw it, which has a saddle on it, and carries in his hand a whip with which he urges them to go and a large stick by which he brings them back to the right direction when they turn aside from it. There is placed upon the waggon a kind of cupola made of wooden laths tied together with thin strips of hide; this is light to carry, and covered with
362 felt | or blanket-cloth, and in it there are grilled windows. The person who is inside the tent can see [other] persons

[217] I cannot place this appellative.

[218] I.e. the Ossete (see below, p. 516, n. 349); one MS. reads Ābī (=Āwī).

[219] A mosque was built in Qrim with the aid of the Egyptian sultan Baibars in 1288, but the chief mosque at this time was that built by order of Özbeg Khān in 1314: see V. D. Smirnov in the *Zapiski* of the Oriental Section of the Russian Archaeological Society (St. Petersburg, 1887), I, 280–1. It appears, however, that the name of the sultan of Egypt was mentioned in the *khuṭba* at this mosque; Spuler, *Die Goldene Horde*, 255.

[220] This was a new word, recently introduced by the Qipchaqs, although not necessarily of Turkish derivation. Ibn Baṭṭūṭa, naturally, does not observe the method of harnessing; see *E.I.*², s.v.

without their seeing him, and he can employ himself in it as he likes, sleeping or eating or reading or writing, while he is still journeying. Those of the waggons that carry the baggage, the provisions and the chests of eatables are covered with a sort of tent much as we have described, with a lock on it.[221] When I decided to make the journey, I prepared for my own conveyance a waggon covered with felt, taking with me in it a slavegirl of mine, another small waggon for my associate 'Afīf al-Dīn al-Tūzarī, and for the rest of my companions a large waggon drawn by three camels, one of which was ridden by the conductor of the waggon.

We set out in company with the amīr Tuluktumūr, his brother 'Īsā, and his two sons Quṭlūdumūr and Ṣārūbak. With him also travelled on this journey his imām Sa'd al-Dīn, the khaṭīb Abū Bakr, the qāḍī | Shams al-Dīn, the jurist 363
Sharaf al-Dīn Mūsā, and the remembrancer 'Alā al-Dīn. The office of this remembrancer is to take his place in front of the amīr in his audience hall, and when the qāḍī comes in he rises up for him and says in a loud voice '*Bismillāh*, our lord and master, the qāḍī of qāḍīs and magistrates, the elucidator of cases and rules of law, *bismillāh*.' When a respected jurist or man of consequence comes in, he says, '*Bismillāh*, our lord so-and-so al-Dīn, *bismillāh*,' whereupon those who are present prepare for the entry of the visitor, rise up to salute him, and make room for him in the chamber.

The habit of the Turks is to organize the journey through this desert in the same way as that of the pilgrims [to Mecca] on the Ḥijāz road. They set out after the dawn prayer and halt in the mid-forenoon, then set out again after noon and halt in the evening. When they halt they loose the horses, camels and oxen | from the waggons and drive them out to 364
pasture at liberty, night and day. No one, whether sultan or any other, gives forage to his beast, for the peculiar property of this desert is that its herbage takes the place of barley for animals; this property belongs to no other land, and for that reason there are large numbers of animals in it. Their animals [pasture] without keepers or guards; this is due to the

[221] A fuller description of the waggons, the manner of carrying the huts upon them, and the chests is given by William of Rubruck (Komroff, 58–61).

severity of their laws against theft. Their law in this matter is that any person found in possession of a stolen horse is obliged to restore it to its owner and to give him along with it nine like it; if he cannot do that, his sons are taken instead, and if he has no sons he is slaughtered just as a sheep is slaughtered.[222]

These Turks do not eat bread nor any solid food, but they
prepare a dish made from a thing in their country like millet,
365 which they call *dūgī*.[223] | They put water over a fire; when it
boils they pour into it some of this *dūgī*, and if they have any
meat they cut it in small pieces and cook it along with the
dūgī. Then every man is given his portion in a dish, and they
pour over it curdled milk and sup it. [Sometimes] they sup
with it mares' milk, which they call *qumizz*.[224] They are
powerful and hardy men, with good constitutions. At certain
times they make use of a dish that they call *būrkhānī*.[225] It is
a paste which they cut into very small pieces, making a hole
in the middle of each, and put into a pot; when they are
cooked, they pour over them curdled milk and sup them.
They have also a fermented drink which they make from the
grain of the *dūgī* mentioned above. They regard the eating of
sweetmeats as a disgrace. [To give an instance of this] I went
one day to the audience of the sultan Ūzbak during [the
366 month of] Ramaḍān. There was served horse-flesh (this is | the
meat that they most often eat) and sheep's flesh, and *rishtā*,[226]
which is a kind of macaroni cooked and supped with milk. I
brought for him that night a plate of sweetmeats made by one
of my companions, and when I presented them before him he
touched them with his finger and put it to his mouth, and
that was all he did. The amīr Tuluktumūr told me of one of
the high-ranking mamlūks of this sultan, who had between
sons and sons' sons about forty descendants, that the sultan

[222] Cf. Yule's *Marco Polo*, I, 266, and V. A. Riasanovsky, *Fundamental Principles of Mongol Law* (Tientsin, 1937), 35–6.

[223] *Dugu* in Ottoman Turkish is pounded rice; the term probably therefore means pounded millet or spelt. For 'millet' Ibn Baṭṭūṭa uses the Berber word *anlī*.

[224] The well-known curdled milk of the Tatars and Turks; for details of its preparation and varieties see Spuler, *Die Goldene Horde*, 429 sqq.

[225] Not otherwise known; the Persian and Turkish *būrānī* is made with egg-plant or spinach and yoghurt.

[226] Persian for 'spun thread', hence 'macaroni', etc.

said to him one day 'Eat sweetmeats, and I free you all,' but he refused, saying 'If you were to kill me I would not eat them.'

When we moved out of the city of al-Qiram we halted at the hospice of the amīr Tuluktumūr, at a place known as Sajijān, and he sent for me to present myself before him. So I rode to him (for I had a horse ready for me to ride, which was led by the conductor of the waggon, and when I wanted to ride it I did so), came to the hospice, and found that the amīr had prepared there a great banquet, including bread.[227]| 367
They then brought in a white liquid in small bowls and those present drank of it. The shaikh Muẓaffar al-Dīn was next to the amīr in the order of sitting and I was next to him, so I said to him 'What is this?' He replied 'This is *duhn* juice.' I did not understand what he meant, so I tasted it and finding a bitter taste in it left it alone. When I went out I made enquiry about it and they said 'It is *nabīdh* [a fermented drink] which they make from *dūgī* grain.' These people are Ḥanafīs and *nabīdh* is permissible according to their doctrine. They call this *nabīdh* which is made from *dūgī* by the name of *būza*.[228] What the shaikh Muẓaffar al-Dīn said to me was [meant to be] '*dukhn* juice' [i.e. millet juice], but since his [Arabic] speech was mispronounced, as commonly among foreigners, I thought he was saying '*duhn* juice' [i.e. oil juice].

After travelling eighteen stations from the city of al-Qiram we reached a great [expanse of] water, through which we continued to ford for a whole day.[229] When a large number | of beasts and waggons have to pass through this water, 368
it becomes very muddy and more difficult, so the amīr, thinking of my comfort, sent me on ahead of him with one of his subordinates, and wrote a letter for me to the governor of Azāq, informing him that I was proposing to proceed to the king and urging him to treat me honourably. We con-

[227] As Ibn Baṭṭūṭa has noted above, bread was a rarity among the Tatars.

[228] *Būza* is millet beer, improved in later times by malting. Although 'wine' (*khamr*) is forbidden in the Qur'ān (sūra v. 90), some jurists of the Ḥanafī school held *nabīdh* (properly 'date juice, more or less fermented') to be permitted; see *E.I.*, s.v.

[229] I take this to be the estuary of the Miuss river, west of Taganrog. See the map to ch. XII in E. D. Clarke, *Travels in Various Countries of Europe, Asia and Africa* (London, 1810), pt. I; inserted in ch. XV of the American editions, 1811, 1813.

tinued our journey until we came to a second [expanse of] water, which we took half a day to ford, and after travelling for three nights more we arrived at the city of Azāq.[230]

This city is on the seacoast, with fine buildings, and visited by the Genoese and others with merchandise. One of the *Fityān* there is Akhī Bichaqchī; he is one of the important personages and supplies food to wayfarers. When the letter of the amīr Tuluktumūr was delivered to the governor of Azāq, who was Muḥammad Khwāja al-Khwārizmī,[231] he came out to meet me, accompanied by the qāḍī and students
369 of religion, and had | food sent out as well. After saluting him, we halted at a certain place, where we ate; we then came to the city, and encamped outside it in the vicinity of a hermitage there called after al-Khiḍr and Ilyās (on both be peace).[232] A shaikh, one of the inhabitants of Azāq, named Rajab al-Nahr Malakī—a name derived from a village in al'Irāq[233]—came out and entertained us with fine hospitality in a hospice of his.

Two days after our arrival the amīr Tuluktumūr arrived; the governor Muḥammad went out to meet him, accompanied by the qāḍī and students of religion, and the citizens made preparations to receive him with banquets and gifts.[234] They erected three pavilions next one another, one of them of parti-coloured silk, a marvellous thing, and the other two of linen, and put up round them a *sarācha* [i.e. cloth enclosure], which is what is called among us *āfrāg*,[235] with an antechamber outside it in the shape of a *burj* among us.[236] When the amīr dis-

[230] Now Azof, called by the mediaeval merchants Tana, 30 km. west of Rostov, and on the southern bank of the estuary of the Don (which was presumably the second river forded). It was the starting point for caravans to the Volga and beyond; H. Yule (ed.), *Cathay and the Way Thither* (London, Hakluyt Society, 1918), III, 146 sqq.

[231] He is mentioned as governor of Tana in a Venetian report of the same period; Heyd, II, 183–4.

[232] See above, p. 466, n. 193.

[233] Nahr al-Malik, about 20 miles south of Baghdād, on the old 'King's Canal' from Fallūja to the Tigris.

[234] The term *ḍiyāfāt* implies more than 'banquets'. By custom or regulation, the population was frequently required to furnish food and other gifts and necessaries to governors and emissaries on their passage (cf. below, p. 499), and these were also euphemistically called 'hospitality-gifts'.

[235] A Berber term, used in Morocco for the royal enclosure.

[236] The 'shape' meant by Ibn Baṭṭūṭa is not at all clear, since *burj* is any kind of tower, whether for military defence or private residence or pigeon-loft.

mounted pieces of silk were spread before him | to walk on, 370
and one of his acts of generosity and benevolence was that he made me precede him, in order that the governor should see the high esteem that he had for me.

We then came to the first tent, the one that had been prepared for his [public] sitting. At the place of honour in it there was a wooden settee for him to sit on, large and inlaid with woods of different colours,[237] and with a beautiful cushion on it. The amīr made me walk ahead of him and bade the shaikh Muẓaffar al-Dīn also go on ahead, then he himself came up and sat between us, all [three] of us being on the cushion. His qāḍī, his khaṭīb, and the qāḍī and students of religion of this city sat on the left on magnificent rugs, and the two sons of the amīr Tuluktumūr, his brother, the governor Muḥammad and his sons stood in respectful attendance. The servants then brought in the dishes, consisting of the flesh of horses, etc., and also brought mares' milk. Afterwards they brought the *būza*, and when the meal was finished the Qur'ān-readers
recited with beautiful voices. A pulpit was then set up | and 371
the preacher mounted it, the Qur'ān-readers sitting in front of him, and he delivered an eloquent address and prayed for blessings on the sultan, the amīr, and all those present, saying that [first] in Arabic and then translating it for them in Turkish. During the intervals of this [ceremony], the Qur'ān-readers would start again to recite verses from the Qur'ān in a wonderful harmony then they began to sing, singing [first] in Arabic (this they call *qaul*) and then in Persian and Turkish (this they call *mulamma'*).[238] Afterwards more food was served, and they continued in this fashion until the evening, and every time that I made a move to leave the amīr stopped me. They then brought a robe for the amīr and robes for his sons and his brother, for the shaikh Muẓaffar al-Dīn

[237] Ibn Baṭṭūṭa uses the term *muraṣṣa'* to indicate almost any kind of decoration, by gold, jewels, or inlay. The French translators have 'incrusted with gold', which is certainly the correct interpretation in some passages (cf. p. 485, l. 23), but in relation to a wooden object it seems more likely to mean 'inlay-work', as the technical term for which the Arabic *tarṣī'* passed into the languages of Europe ('intarsia').

[238] *Qaul* in Arabic means 'speech', but is glossed in Persian dictionaries as 'a kind of song'. *Mulamma'*, meaning a brindled or piebald horse, was applied to poetry composed of alternate verses or strophes in Persian and Turkish.

and for me, after which they presented ten horses to the amīr, six horses to his brother and his sons, one horse to each notable in his suite and one horse to me.

The horses in this country are exceedingly numerous and
372 their price is negligible. A good horse costs fifty | or sixty of their dirhams, which equals one dinar of our money or thereabouts. These are the horses known in Egypt as *akādīsh*,[239] and it is from [the raising of] them that they make their living, horses in their country being like sheep in ours, or even more numerous, so that a single Turk will possess thousands of them. It is the custom of the Turks who live in this country and who raise horses to attach a piece of felt, a span in length, to a thin rod, a cubit in length, for every thousand horses [possessed by each man]. These rods are put on the waggons in which their women ride, each being fixed to a corner of the waggon, and I have seen some of them who have ten pieces [of felt] and some with less than that.

These horses are exported to India [in droves], each one numbering six thousand or more or less. Each trader has one or two hundred horses or less or more. For every fifty of them
373 he hires | a drover, who looks after them and their pasturage, like sheep; and this man is called by them *alqashī*.[240] He rides on one of them, carrying in his hand a long stick with a rope on it, and when he wishes to catch any horse among them he gets opposite to it[241] on the horse that he is riding, throws the rope over its neck and draws it to him, mounts it and sets the other free to pasture. When they reach the land of Sind with their horses, they feed them with forage, because the vegetation of the land of Sind does not take the place of barley, and the greater part of the horses die or are stolen. They are taxed on them in the land of Sind [at the rate of] seven silver dinars a horse, at a place called Shashnaqār,[242] and pay a further tax at Multān, the capital of the land of Sind. In former times they paid in duty the quarter of what they imported, but the king of India, the Sultan Muḥammad, abolished this [prac-

[239] I.e. horses with no pedigree or of mixed breed.

[240] Eastern Turkish (Uighur) *ulaqchi*, 'groom', 'stable-boy' (Radloff, *Wörterbuch*, I, 1680). The word is not vocalised in the Arabic text.

[241] Probably rather 'gets alongside it'.

[242] Probably Hashtnagar, 16 miles north-west of Peshawar; see vol. III, p. 90 (Arabic).

tice] and ordered that there should be exacted from the Muslim traders | the *zakāt*[243] and from the infidel traders the 374
tenth. In spite of this, there remains a handsome profit for the traders in these horses, for they sell the cheapest of them in the land of India for a hundred silver dinars (the exchange value of which in Moroccan gold is twenty-five dinars), and often sell them for twice or three times as much. The good horses are worth five hundred [silver] dinars or more. The people of India do not buy them for [their qualities in] running or racing, because they themselves wear coats of mail in battle and they cover their horses with armour, and what they prize in these horses is strength and length of pace. The horses that they want for racing are brought to them from al-Yaman, 'Omān and Fārs, and each of these horses is sold at from one to four thousand dinars.[244]

When the amīr Tuluktumūr set out from this city [Azāq], I stayed behind for three days, until the governor Muḥammad Khwāja provided me with the equipment for my journey. | I 375
then set out for the city of al-Māchar, a large town, one of the finest of the cities of the Turks, on a great river, and possessed of gardens and fruits in abundance.[245] We lodged in it at the hospice of the pious shaikh and aged devotee Muḥammad al-Baṭā'iḥī, from the *baṭā'ih* [marsh-lands] of al-'Irāq, who was the delegate of the shaikh Aḥmad al-Rifā'ī (God be pleased with him). In his hospice were about seventy poor brethren, Arabs, Persians, Turks and Greeks, some married and some single, whose livelihood came solely from alms. The people of that country have a firm belief in the [virtues of the] poor brethren, and come to the hospice every night bringing horses, cattle, and sheep. The sultan and the khātūns also come to visit the shaikh and to obtain blessing by him, and they are lavish with their charity and donate large sums—especially the women, for they bestow alms profusely | and 376
seek to do all manner of good works.

243 The annual canonical tax (properly 'alms-tax') on the property of Muslims, generally calculated at 2½ per cent of total possessions. On animals of different kinds the calculation is a more complicated one, the normal for horses being 5 per cent of the total value (see Hughes's *Dictionary of Islam*, s.v.).

244 See above, p. 382 and n. 69.

245 Identified with Burgomadzhary, on the Kuma river, at 44° 50′ N., 44° 27′ E.; see Yule's *Marco Polo*, II, 491.

We prayed the Friday prayers in the city of al-Māchar, and when the prayers were over the preacher 'Izz al-Dīn[246] ascended the *mimbar*. He was one of the jurists and eminent doctors of Bukhārā, and had a company of students and Qur'ān-readers who would recite in front of him. He delivered a homily and exhortation in the presence of the governor and principal personages of the city, then the shaikh Muḥammad al-Baṭā'ihī rose and said 'The learned preacher is about to set out and we wish to furnish him with means for his journey.' He then took off a robe of goats' hair that he was wearing, saying 'This is for him from me,' and of those present some took off a robe, some gave a horse, and some gave money, and from all this a large provision was collected for him.

In the *qaisārīya*[247] of this city I saw a Jew who saluted me and spoke to me in Arabic. I asked him what country he came from and he told me that he was from the land of al-
377 Andalus and had come from it over | land, without travelling by sea, but by way of Constantinople the Great, the land of al-Rūm and the land of the Jarkas, and stated that it was four months since he had left al-Andalus.[248] The travelling merchants who have experience of this matter assured me of the truth of his statement.

I witnessed in this country a remarkable thing, namely the respect in which women are held by them, indeed they are higher in dignity than the men. As for the wives of the amīrs, the first occasion on which I saw them was when, on my departure from al-Qiram, I saw the khātūn, the wife of the amīr Salṭīya, in a waggon of hers. The entire waggon was covered with rich blue woollen cloth, the windows and doors of the tent were open, and there were in attendance on her four girls of excelling beauty and exquisitely dressed. Behind her were a number of waggons in which were girls belonging to her suite. When she came near the encampment of the amīr, she descended from the waggon to the ground and with
378 her alighted | about thirty of the girls to carry her train. Her

[246] One MS. reads 'Majd al-Dīn'.

[247] I.e., main bazaar; see vol. I, p. 97, n. 115.

[248] The Jarkas are the Circassians (Cherkess), who inhabited the lands at the eastern end of the Black Sea and the Kuban territory. Presumably the merchant followed the regular route to Trebizond and then turned north-eastwards. One MS., however, has *al-Rūs* for *al-Rūm*.

robes were furnished with loops of which each girl would take one, and altogether they would lift the skirts clear of the ground on every side. She walked thus in a stately manner until she reached the amīr, when he rose before her, saluted her, and sat her beside him, while her maidens stood around her. Skins of *qumizz* were brought and she, having poured some of it into a bowl, went down on her knees before the amīr and handed the bowl to him. After he had drunk, she poured out for his brother, and the amīr poured out for her. The food was then served and she ate with him, he gave her a robe and she withdrew. Such is the style of the wives of the amīrs, and we shall describe [that of] the wives of the king later on. As for the wives of the traders and the commonalty, I have seen them, when one of them would be in a waggon, being drawn by horses, and in attendance on her three or four girls to carry her train, | wearing on her head a *bughtāq*, which 379
is a conical headdress decorated with precious stones and surmounted by peacock feathers.[249] The windows of the tent would be open and her face would be visible, for the womenfolk of the Turks do not veil themselves. One such woman will come [to the bazaar] in this style, accompanied by her male slaves with sheep and milk, and will sell them for spicewares. Ṣometimes one of the women will be in the company of her husband and anyone seeing him would take him to be one of her servants; he wears no garments other than a sheepskin cloak and on his head a high cap to match it, which they call a *kula*.[250]

We made preparations to travel from the city of al-Māchar to the sultan's camp, which was four days' march from al-Māchar at a place called Bish Dagh.[251] *Bish* in their language means 'five' and *dagh* means 'Mountain'. In these Five Mountains there is a hot spring | in which the Turks 380
bathe, and they claim that anyone who bathes in it will not be attacked by disease.[252] We set out for the site of the

[249] A kind of golden headdress, ornamented with jewels, to which was attached a train reaching to the ground (Dozy, s.v.). It is described in detail by William of Rubruck, by the name of *botta* (Komroff, 69).

[250] Persian *kulāh*, 'cap'.

[251] Called in Russian P'atigorsk (a literal translation of the Turkish name), in the sub-Caucasian region, and still noted for its sulphur springs.

[252] The term is used particularly of skin diseases.

maḥalla and reached it on the first day of Ramaḍān,[253] but found that the *maḥalla* had left, so we returned to the place from which we started, because the *maḥalla* was encamping in its vicinity. I set up my tent on a low hill thereabouts, fixed my flag in front of the tent, and drew up my horses and waggons behind. Then the *maḥalla* came up—they call it the *urdū*[254]—and we saw a vast city on the move with its inhabitants, with mosques and bazaars in it, the smoke of the kitchens rising in the air (for they cook while on the march), and horse-drawn waggons transporting the people. On reaching the camping place they took down the tents from the waggons and set them on the ground, for they are light to
381 carry, and so likewise they did with the mosques | and shops. The sultan's khātūns passed by us, each one separately with her retinue. The fourth of them (she was the daughter of the amīr 'Īsā, and we shall speak of her presently), as she passed, saw the tent on top of the hill with the flag in front of it as the sign of a new arrival, so she sent pages and girls who saluted me and conveyed her salutations to me, while she halted to wait for them. I sent her a gift by one of my companions and the remembrancer of the amīr Tuluktumūr. She accepted it as a token of blessing, and gave orders that I should be taken under her protection, then went on. [Afterwards] the sultan came up and encamped separately in his *maḥalla*.

Account of the exalted Sultan Muḥammad Ūzbak Khān.[255] His name is Muḥammad Ūzbak, and Khān in their language means 'sultan'. This sultan is mighty in sovereignty, ex-
382 ceedingly | powerful, great in dignity, lofty in station, victor over the enemies of God, the people of Constantinople the Great, and diligent in the *jihād* against them. His territories are vast and his cities great; they include al-Kafā, al-Qiram, al-Māchar, Azāq, Surdāq and Khwārizm, and his capital is al-Sarā.[256] He is one of the seven kings who are the great and

[253] In 732, 27 May 1332; in 734, 6 May 1334.

[254] Turkish *ordu*, 'residence of a [nomadic] prince': Kāshgharī, I, 112, 5; distinct from *yurt*, 'apanage of a prince': Juwainī, *History of the World-Conqueror*, trans. J. A. Boyle (Manchester, 1958), I, 42–3. The *ordu* included all the individual *maḥallas* or camps described above. To William of Rubruck also, the *horda* of Batu 'seemed like a mighty city' (Komroff, 98).

[255] See above, p. 471, n. 216.

[256] For Surdāq see p. 499, and for al-Sarā p. 515 below.

mighty kings of the world, to wit: our Master, the Commander of the Faithful, the Shadow of God on His earth, the Imām of the victorious company who shall never cease to defend the Truth till the advent of the Hour, may God aid his cause and magnify his victory [i.e. the sultan of Morocco], the sultan of Egypt and Syria, the sultan of the two 'Irāqs, this sultan Ūzbak, the sultan of the land of Turkistan and the lands beyond the river [Oxus], the sultan of India, and the sultan of China. This sultan when he is on the march, travels in a separate *maḥalla*, accompanied by his mamlūks and his officers of state, and each one of | his khātūns travels 383
separately in her own *maḥalla*. When he wishes to be with any one of them, he sends to her to inform her of this, and she prepares to receive him.

He observes, in his [public] sittings, his journeys, and his affairs in general, a marvellous and magnificent ceremonial. It is his custom to sit every Friday, after the prayers, in a pavilion, magnificently decorated, called the Gold Pavilion. It is constructed of wooden rods covered with plaques of gold, and in the centre of it is a wooden couch covered with plaques of silver gilt, its legs being of pure silver and their bases encrusted with precious stones.[257] The sultan sits on the throne, having on his right hand the khātūn Ṭaiṭughlī and next to her the khātūn Kabak, and on his left the khātūn Bayalūn and next to her the khātūn Urdujā. Below the throne, to his right, stands the sultan's son Tīna Bak, and to his left his second son Jāni Bak, and in front of him sits his daughter Īt Kujujuk. As each of the khātūns comes in the sultan rises before her, | and takes her by the hand until she 384
mounts to the couch. As for Ṭaiṭughlī, who is the queen and the one of them most favoured by him, he advances to the entrance of the pavilion to meet her, salutes her, takes her by the hand, and only after she has mounted to the couch and taken her seat does the sultan himself sit down. All this is done in full view of those present, without any use of veils. Afterwards the great amīrs come and their chairs are placed for them to right and left, each man of them, as he comes to the sultan's audience, being accompanied by a page carrying

[257] A somewhat similar account of an audience is given by William of Rubruck (Komroff, 99).

his chair. In front of the sultan stand the scions of the royal house,[258] i.e. his nephews, brothers, and relatives, and parallel to them, at the entrance to the pavilion, stand the sons of the great amīrs, with the senior officers of the troops standing behind them. Then the [rest of the] people are admitted to make their salute, in their degrees of precedence and three at
385 a time, and after saluting | they retire and sit at a distance. After the hour of afternoon prayer the queen-khātūn withdraws, whereupon the rest of them also withdraw and follow her to her *maḥalla*. When she has entered it, each of them retires to her own *maḥalla*, riding in her waggon, each one accompanied by about fifty girls, mounted on horses. In front of the waggon there are about twenty elderly women[259] riding on horses between the pages and the waggon. Behind the whole cortège there are about a hundred young mamlūks, and in front of the pages about a hundred adult mamlūks on horseback and an equal number on foot carrying staves in their hands and swords girt on their waists, who walk between the horsemen and the pages. Such is the ceremonial of each of the khātūns both on her withdrawal and on her arrival.

My camping place was in the *maḥalla*, in the vicinity of the sultan's son Jāni Bak, of whom an account will be given later.
386 On the morrow of | the day of my arrival I made my entrance to the sultan after the afternoon prayer.[260] He had assembled the shaikhs, qāḍīs, jurists, sharīfs and poor brethren and prepared a great banquet, and we broke our fast in his presence. The sayyid and sharīf, the Marshal of the Sharīfs,[261] Ibn ʿAbd al-Ḥamīd, and the qāḍī Ḥamza spoke favourably about me and made recommendations to the sultan to show honour to me. These Turks do not know the practice of giving hospitable lodging to the visitor or of supplying him with money for his needs. What they do is to send him sheep and horses for slaughtering and skins of *qumizz*, and this is their

[258] Literally 'the sons of the kings'.

[259] Literally 'retired women' (*qawāʿid*), above child-bearing age or widows, but distinguished in a later passage (p. 512) from 'aged women'.

[260] For the favour shown by Özbeg Khan to 'Saracen faqirs', see William of Adam, 'De modo Sarracenos extirpandi' in *Recueil des historiens des Croisades*, Documents arméniens (Paris, 1906), II, 530.

[261] For the office and its holders see vol. I, p. 258, n. 50.

[manner of] honourable treatment. Some days after this I prayed the afternoon prayer in the sultan's company and when I was about to withdraw he bade me be seated. They brought in dishes of the various soups, like that made from *dūgī*, then roasted fleshmeats, both of sheep and of horses. It was on that night that I presented to the sultan | a plate of 387
sweetmeats, when he did no more than touch it with his finger and put that to his mouth.[262]

Account of the Khātūns and their Ceremonial. Each of the khātūns rides in a waggon, the tent that she occupies being distinguished by a cupola of silver ornamented with gold or of wood encrusted with precious stones. The horses that draw her waggon are caparisoned with cloths of silk gilt, and the conductor of the waggon who rides on one of the horses is a page boy called *qashī.*[263] The khātūn, as she sits in her waggon, has on her right hand an elderly woman called *ūlū khātūn*, which means 'lady vizier', and on her left another elderly woman called *kujuk khātūn*, which means 'lady chamberlain'.[264] In front of her are six young slavegirls called 'girls', of surpassing beauty and the utmost perfection, and behind her two more like them[265] on whom she leans. On | the 388
khātūn's head is a *bughtāq* which resembles a small 'crown' decorated with jewels and surmounted by peacock feathers,[266] and she wears robes of silk encrusted with jewels, like the mantles worn by the Greeks. On the head of the lady vizier and the lady chamberlain is a silk veil embroidered with gold and jewels at the edges, and on the head of each of the girls is a *kulā*, which is like an *aqrūf*,[267] with a circlet of gold encrusted with jewels round the upper end, and peacock feathers above this, and each one wears a robe of silk gilt, which is called *nakh.*[268] In front of (the waggon of) the khātūn are ten

[262] See above, p. 474.

[263] *Qoshi*, from Qipchaq **qoshchi*, 'slave, man-servant, page', derived from middle Turkish *qosh*, 'tent, herd' (W. Radloff, *Wörterbuch*, II, 646). The word passed into old Russian as *koshchey*.

[264] Literally 'great lady' and 'little lady'.

[265] This translation, like that of the French translators (see their note *ad loc.*), combines two readings.

[266] See above, p. 481, n. 249. 'Crown' (*tāj*), in Arabic usage, denotes a headdress like a conical turban.

[267] *Kulā* for Persian *kulāh*, 'cap'. *Aqrūf* or *uqrūf* is a Maghribine term for a high conical headdress (Dozy, s.v.).

[268] See above, p. 445.

or fifteen pages,[269] Greeks and Indians, who are dressed in robes of silk gilt, encrusted with jewels, and each of whom carries in his hand a mace of gold or silver, or maybe of wood veneered with them. Behind the khātūn's waggon there are about a hundred waggons, in each of which there are four |
389 slavegirls, fullgrown and young, wearing robes of silk and with the *kulā* on their heads. Behind these waggons [again] are about three hundred waggons, drawn by camels and oxen, carrying the khātūn's chests, moneys, robes, furnishings and food. With each waggon is a slaveboy who has the care of it and is married to one of the slavegirls that we have mentioned, for it is the custom that none of the slaves may set foot among the girls except one who has a wife among their number. Every khātūn enjoys the honour of this style, and we shall now describe each one of them separately.

Account of the Principal Khātūn. The principal khātūn is the queen, the mother of the sultan's two sons Jāni Bak and Tīna Bak, of whom we shall speak later. She is not the mother of his daughter Īt Kujujuk; her mother was the queen
390 before this one. This khātūn's name is Ṭaiṭughlī[270] | and she is the favourite of this sultan, with whom he spends most of his nights. The people hold her in great honour because of his honouring her; otherwise, she is the most close-fisted of the khātūns. I was told for a fact by one in whom I have confidence, a person well acquainted with matters relating to this queen, that the sultan is enamoured of her because of a peculiar property in her, namely that he finds her every night just like a virgin. Another person related to me that she is of the lineage of that queen on whose account, it is said, the kingdom was withdrawn from Solomon (on whom be peace),[271] and whom, when his kingdom was restored to him, he

[269] Presumably in this instance 'eunuchs', but the term *fatā* is applied almost indiscriminately to 'page' and 'eunuch'.

[270] This name is spelled out by Ibn Baṭṭūṭa, following his usual custom with proper names, but seems to stand for Taï-Dula; see P. Pelliot, *Notes sur l'histoire de la Horde d'Or* (Paris, 1950), 101–5.

[271] This alludes to the legendary development of Qur'ān, xxxviii. 34: 'And verily We tried Sulaimān and put upon his throne a [phantom] body, thereafter he repented.' One of his wives, deceived by a demon, is said to have given the latter Solomon's magic ring, by virtue of which he occupied Solomon's throne for forty days: see *E.I.*, s.v. Sulaimān; D. Sidersky, *Les Origines des légendes musulmanes* (Paris, 1933), 120–1.

commanded to be placed in an uninhabited desert, so she was deposited in the desert of Qifjaq. [He related also] that the vagina of this khātūn has a conformation like a ring, and likewise all of those who are descendants | of the 391
woman mentioned. I never met, whether in the desert of Qifjaq or elsewhere, any person who said that he had seen a woman formed in this way, or heard tell of one other than this khātūn—except, however, that one of the inhabitants of China told me that in China there is a class of women with this conformation. But nothing like that ever came into my hands nor have I learned what truth there is in it.

On the day after my meeting with the sultan, I visited this khātūn. She was sitting in the midst of ten elderly women, who seemed to be attendants waiting on her, and in front of her were about fifty young slavegirls, whom the Turks call 'girls' and before whom there were gold and silver salvers filled with cherries which they were cleaning. In front of the khātūn also there was a golden tray filled with cherries, and she was cleaning them. We saluted her, and among my companions there was a Qur'ān-reader who recited the Qur'ān according to the method of the Egyptians, | in a pleasing 392
manner and agreeable voice, and he gave a recitation. She then ordered *qumizz* to be served, and it was brought in light and elegant wooden bowls, whereupon she took a bowl in her hand and offered it to me. This is the highest of honours in their estimation. I had never drunk *qumizz* before, but there was nothing for me to do but to accept it. I tasted it and [finding] it disagreeable passed it on to one of my companions. She asked me many questions concerning our journey, and after answering her we withdrew. We went to visit her first because of the great position she has with the king.

Account of the second Khātūn, who comes after the Queen. Her name is Kabak Khātūn, *kabak* in Turkish meaning 'bran'.[272] She is the daughter of the amīr Naghatay, and her father is still living, [but] suffering from gout, and I | saw him. On the 393
day following our visit to the queen we visited this khātūn, and found her sitting on a divan, reading in the Holy Book. In front of her were about ten elderly women and about

[272] See C. Brockelmann, *Mitteltürkischer Wortschatz* (Budapest-Leipzig, 1928), 100 (kābāk).

twenty girls embroidering pieces of cloth. We saluted her, and she gave us gracious salutations and speech. Our Qur'ān-reader recited and she commended his recital, then ordered *qumizz*, and when it was brought she offered me a bowl with her own hand, just as the queen had done and we took leave of her.

Account of the third Khātūn. Her name is Bayalūn,[273] and she is the daughter of the king of Constantinople the Great, the Sultan Takfūr.[274] When we visited this khātūn, she was sitting on an inlaid couch with silver legs; before her were |
394 about a hundred slavegirls, Greek, Turkish and Nubian, some standing and some sitting, and pages[275] were [standing] behind her and chamberlains in front of her, men of the Greeks. She asked about us and our journey hither and the distance of our native lands, and she wept in pity and compassion and wiped her face with a handkerchief that lay before her. She then called for food, which was brought, and we ate before her, while she looked on at us. When we made to withdraw, she said 'Do not stay away from us, but come to us and inform us of your needs.' She showed herself to be of a generous nature, and sent after us food, a great quantity of bread, ghee, sheep, money, a fine robe, three horses of good breed and ten of ordinary stock. It was with this khātūn that my journey to Constantinople the Great was made, as we shall relate below. |

395 *Account of the fourth Khātūn.* Her name is Urdujā. *Urdu* in their language means *maḥalla*, and she was so called because of her birth in the *maḥalla*.[276] She is the daughter of the great amīr 'Īsā Bak, *amīr al-ulūs*, which means 'amīr of amīrs'.[277] He was still alive at the time of my journey, and married to

[273] This is a Turkish name, probably the feminine of *bayan*, 'rich' (Pelliot, 83–5), presumably given to the Greek princess after the name of Özbeg Khān's mother. The marriage of a daughter of the Emperor to the Khan is confirmed by a letter of Gregory Akindynos, dated 1341: Lemerle, 265.

[274] The traditional Arabic title of the Byzantine emperor, said to be derived from Armenian *tagavor*.

[275] See above, n. 269.

[276] This etymology is questioned by Pelliot (32, n. 1).

[277] *Ulūs* is the Mongol term for a major tribe, i.e. an association of clans and lineages under a superior chief; see B. Vladimirtsov, *Le régime social des Mongols* (Paris, 1948), 124 sqq., where he translates it by 'peuple-patrimoine'.

the sultan's daughter Īt Kujujuk. This khātūn is one of the most virtuous, most amiable in manners, and most sympathetic of princesses, and it was she who sent to [enquire about] me when she noticed my flag on the hill during the passage of the *maḥalla*, as we have previously related. We visited her and she showed us a beauty of character and generosity of spirit that cannot be surpassed. She ordered food to be served, then when we had eaten in her presence she called for *qumizz*, and our companions drank. She asked about us and we answered her questions. We visited also her sister, the wife of the amīr 'Alī b. Arzaq (Arzan).[278] |

Account of the Daughter of the exalted Sultan Ūzbak. Her 396
name is Īt Kujujuk, which means 'little dog', for *īt* means 'dog' and *kujujuk* means 'little'.[279] We have mentioned above that the Turks give names by chance of omens, as do the Arabs. We went to visit this khātūn, the sultan's daughter, who was in a separate *maḥalla* about six miles from that of her father. She gave orders to summon the jurists, the qāḍīs, the sayyid and sharīf Ibn 'Abd al-Ḥamīd, the body of students of religion, the shaikhs and poor brethren. Her husband, the amīr 'Īsā, whose daughter was the sultan's wife, was present, and sat with her on the same rug. He was suffering from gout, and was unable for this reason to go about on his feet or to ride a horse, and so used to ride only in a waggon. When he wished to present himself before the sultan, his servants lifted him down and carried him into the audience-hall. | In 397
the same state too, I saw the amīr Naghatay, who was the father of the second khātūn, and this disease is widespread among the Turks. By this khātūn, the sultan's daughter, we were shown such generosity and good qualities as we had seen in no other, and she loaded us with surpassing favours—may God reward her with good.

Account of the Sultan's two Sons. They are uterine brothers, the mother of both being the queen Ṭaiṭughlī, whom we have mentioned above. The elder is named Tīna Bak, *bak* meaning 'amīr' and *tīna* meaning 'body', so that he is called, as it

[278] The last name is uncertain.

[279] *Īt* is common Turkish for 'dog', and *küchük* in middle Turkish had the special meaning of 'little dog' (confused by Ibn Baṭṭūṭa with *kichik*, 'little'), *jak* being the common Turkish diminutive suffix.

were, 'amīr of the body'.[280] His brother is named Jāni Bak, and as *jāni* means 'spirit' he is called as it were, 'amīr of the spirit.' Each one of them has his own separate *maḥalla*. Tīna
398 Bak was one of the most beautiful of God's creatures | in form, and his father had designated him [to succeed him] in the kingship, and gave him the preference and superior honour. But God willed otherwise, for when his father died he ruled for a brief space and was then killed for certain disgraceful things that happened to him, and his brother Jāni Bak, who was better and worthier than he, succeeded to the rule.[281] The sayyid and sharīf Ibn 'Abd al-Ḥamīd was the tutor who had supervised the education of Jāni Bak, and he himself, as well as the qaḍī Ḥamza, the imām Badr al-Dīn al-Qiwāmī, the imām and professor of Qur'an-reading Ḥūsam al-Dīn al-Bukhārī and other persons, advised me on my arrival to make my residence in the *maḥalla* of the abovementioned Jāni Bak because of his superior merit, and I did so.

Account of my journey to the city of Bulghār.[282] I had heard of the city of Bulghār and desired to go to it, to see for myself what they tell of the extreme shortness of the night there, and the shortness of the day, too, in the opposite season.[283]
399 Between it and the sultan's camp | was a ten nights' journey, so I requested him to furnish me with a guide to it, and he sent with me a man who escorted me there and brought me back again. I reached it during [the month of] Ramaḍān, and when we had prayed the sunset prayer we broke our fast;

[280] Ibn Baṭṭūṭa was evidently misled, since his interpretation would require *Tani* (from Persian *tan*, 'body') instead of *Tina*. Pelliot (96–8) has shown that the prince's name was *Tīnī* (*tīnī*), from Turkish *tīn*, 'spirit', the name being thus the equivalent in Turkish of the Persian name of his brother Jāni Beg (from Persian, *jān*, 'spirit').

[281] In 1341/2.

[282] The ruins of the city of Bulghār lie 'near the village Bolgarskoye, or Uspenskoye, in the Spassk district, 115 km. south of Kazan and at 7 km. from the left bank of the Volga' (V. Minorsky, *Ḥudūd al-'Ālam* (London, 1937), 461). It was the capital of the Volga Bulgars (who had been converted to Islam by the tenth century), and although captured by the Mongols in 1237, remained a commercial centre throughout this period.

[283] This was a frequent theme of Arabic and Persian geographical lore; see J. Markwart, 'Ein arabischer Bericht über die arktischen (uralischen) Lander aus dem 10. Jahrhundert' in *Ungarische Jahrbücher* (Berlin-Leipzig, 1924), IV, 261–334.

the call to the night prayer was made during our eating of this meal, and by the time that we had prayed that and had prayed also the *tarāwīḥ* prayers, the 'even' and the 'odd', the dawn broke.[284] So too the daytime becomes as short there in the season of its brevity. I stayed there three days.[285]

Account of the Land of Darkness. I had intended to enter the Land of Darkness, which is reached from Bulghār after a journey of forty days.[286] But I renounced this project in view of the immense effort and expense that it required and the small profit to be got from it. The journey to it can be made
only in small waggons drawn by large dogs, for in that |
desert there is ice, so that neither the foot of man nor the 400
hoof of beast has a firm hold on it, whereas the dogs have claws and so their feet remain firm on the ice. No one can go into this desert except merchants with great resources, each of whom will have a hundred waggons or thereabouts loaded with his food, drink, and firewood, for there are no trees in it, nor stones, nor habitations. The guide in that land is the dog that had already made the journey in it many times, and its price is as high as a thousand dinars or so. The waggon is fastened to its neck, and three other dogs are yoked with it; it is the leader and all the other dogs follow it with the waggons and stop when it stops. This dog is never beaten nor berated by its owner, who, when food is prepared, feeds the dogs first before the humans, otherwise the dog is angered and escapes, leaving its owner to perish. When the travellers
have completed forty stages in this desert they alight | at the 401
Darkness. Each one of them leaves thereabouts the goods that he has brought and they return to their usual camping-ground. Next day they go back to seek their goods, and they find alongside them skins of sable, minever, and ermine. If

[284] For the *tarāwīḥ* prayers in Ramaḍān, and the 'even' and 'odd', see vol. I, p. 239.

[285] S. Janicsek ('Ibn Baṭṭūṭa's Journey to Bulghār: is it a Fabrication?' in *JRAS* (1929), 791–800), has shown that this narrative is drawn from literary sources. The distance from Majar to Bulghār is 800 miles, an impossible journey to make twice within one month.

[286] Markwart has shown (*Ungarische Jahrbücher* (1924), IV, 288–301) that Ibn Baṭṭūṭa has put together here the traditional reports on the land of the Yughrā, the northern trans-Ural steppes, twenty days' journey from Bulghār, and the legendary 'Land of Darkness' beyond it. Cf. also Yule's *Marco Polo*, II, 484–6.

the owner of the goods is satisfied with what he has found alongside his goods he takes it, but if it does not satisfy him he leaves it, and then they add more skins, and sometimes they (I mean the people of the Darkness) take away their goods and leave those of the merchant. This is their method of selling and buying, and those who go to those parts do not know who it is who do this trading with them, whether they are of the jinn or of men, for they never see anyone.[287]

Ermine is of the best of the varieties of furs. One mantle of this fur is valued in the land of India at a thousand dinars (which are worth two hundred and fifty in our gold). It is exceedingly white [and comes] from the skin of a small
402 animal of the length | of a span, and with a large tail which they leave in the mantle in its natural state. Sable is less valuable; a mantle made from it is worth four hundred dinars or less. A special property of these skins is that lice do not enter into them. The amīrs and dignitaries of China use a single skin, attached to their fur mantles round the neck, and so do the merchants of Fārs and the two 'Irāqs.[288]

I returned from the city of Bulghār with the amīr whom the sultan had sent to accompany me, and found the sultan's *maḥalla* by the place known as Bish Dagh on the twenty-eighth of Ramaḍān. I attended in his company the festival prayers, and the day of the festival happened to be a Friday.[289]

Account of their ceremonial on the Festival. On the morning of the day of the festival the sultan rode out on horseback among his huge bodies of troops, and each khātūn rode in her
403 waggon, accompanied by | her troops. The sultan's daughter rode with a crown on her head, since she is the queen in

[287] This passage on dumb trade with the fur-trappers agrees almost literally with that of the contemporary geographer Abu'l-Fidā (*Taqwīm al-Buldān*, ed. M. Reinaud (Paris, 1840), I, 284; quoted also by al-Qalqashandī, 421–2).

[288] For the fur trade of the Arabs through Bulghār see Bruno Schier, *Wege und Formen des ältesten Pelzhandels in Europe* (Frankfurt, 1951), 21–45; and for the skins J. Klein, *Der sibirische Pelzhandel* (Bonn, 1906), 10–13, 63–7.

[289] By Ibn Baṭṭūṭa's dating this should be 1 Shawwāl 734, but this fell on a Sunday, 5 June 1334. The only year between 731 and 734 in which 1 Shawwāl fell on a Friday was in 732, viz. Friday, 26 June 1332.

reality, having inherited the kingdom from her mother.[290] The sultan's sons rode, each one with his troops. The Grand Qāḍī Shihāb al-Dīn al-Sāyilī had come to attend the festival, having with him a body of legists and shaikhs, and they rode, as did also the qāḍī Ḥamza, the imām Badr al-Dīn al-Qiwāmī, and the sharīf Ibn 'Abd al-Ḥamīd. These doctors of the law rode in the procession with Tīna Bak, the designated heir of the sultan, accompanied by drums and standards. The qāḍī Shihāb al-Dīn then led them in the [festival] prayers and delivered a most excellent *khuṭba*.

The sultan mounted [again] and [rode until he] arrived at a wooden pavilion, which is called by them a *kushk*,[291] in which he took his seat, accompanied by his khātūns. A second pavilion was erected beside it, in which sat his heir and daughter, the lady of the crown. | Two [other] pavilions 404
were erected beside these two, to right and left of them, in which were the sons and relatives of the sultan. Chairs (which they call *ṣandalīya*)[292] were placed for the amīrs and the scions of the royal house to the right and left of the [Sultan's] pavilion, and each one of them sat on his own chair. Then archery butts were set up, a special butt for each *amīr ṭūmān*. An *amīr ṭūmān* in their usage is a commander under whose orders there ride ten thousand [horsemen],[293] and there were present seventeen of such amīrs, leading one hundred and seventy thousand, yet the sultan's army is even larger than this. There was set up for each amīr a kind of pulpit and he sat on this while his soldiers engaged in archery exercises before him. They continued thus for a time, after which robes of honour were brought; each amīr was invested with a robe, and as he put it on he would come to the bottom of the sultan's pavilion and do homage. His manner

290 Her mother was presumably the earlier wife of Özbeg Khan, called in a Russian chronicle Baalin (? Bayalun), who died in 1323 (Pelliot, 84), but it is difficult to understand what Ibn Baṭṭūṭa means by saying that this daughter 'inherited the kingship' from her.

291 Persian *kūshak, kushk*, whence our 'kiosk'.

292 Persian *ṣandalī*, 'chair, throne, bench', said to be so called because made of sandalwood.

293 Turkish *tümen*, 'ten thousand'. For commanders of tümens in the army of Chingiz Khan see W. Barthold, *Turkestan down to the Mongol Invasion* (London, 1928), 386. Ibn Baṭṭūṭa's figure of seventeen of these in Özbeg's army seems exaggerated.

of doing homage is to touch the ground with his right knee
405 and to extend his leg | underneath it,[294] while the other leg
remains upright. After this a horse is brought, saddled and
bridled, and its hoof is lifted; the amīr kisses this, then leads
it himself to his chair and there mounts it and remains in his
station with his troops. Each amīr among them performs the
same act.

The sultan then descends from the pavilion and mounts a
horse, having on his right his son, the heir designate, and next
to him his daughter, the queen Īt Kujujuk, and on his left
his second son. In front of him are the four khātūns in waggons covered with silk fabrics gilded, and the horses that
draw them are also caparisoned with silk gilded. The whole
body of amīrs, great and small, scions of the royal house,
viziers, chamberlains and officers of state alight and walk on
foot in front of the sultan until he comes to the *wiṭāq*, which
is an *āfrāg*.[295] At this place there has been erected a huge
bārka, a *bārka* in their language being a large tent[296] sup-
406 ported by four | wooden columns covered with plaques of
silver coated with gold, each column having at its top a
capital of silver gilt that gleams and flashes. This *bārka*, seen
from a distance, looks like a hummock. To right and left of
it are awnings of cotton and linen cloth, and the whole of this
is carpeted with silken rugs. In the centre of the *bārka* is set
up an immense couch which they call the *takht*,[297] made of
inlaid wood, the planks of which are covered with a large rug.
In the centre of this immense couch is a cushion, on which sit
the sultan and the principal khātūn. To the sultan's right is
a cushion, on which his daughter Īt Kujujuk took her seat,
and with her the khātūn Urdujā, and to his left a cushion on
which the khātūn Bayalūn took her seat, and with her the
khātūn Kabak. To the right of the couch was placed a chair,
on which sat Tīna Bak, the sultan's son, and to the left of it a
407 chair, on which sat Jāni Bak, his second son. | Other chairs
were placed to right and left on which sat the scions of the

[294] Two MSS. read 'upon the ground' (*'alaihā*), but this reading is corrected in the margin of MS. 2289.

[295] Turkish *utaq*, 'tent'. For the *āfrāg* see p. 476.

[296] Persian *Bārgāh, bārgah*, 'audience hall, tribunal'.

[297] Persian for 'throne'.

royal house and the great amīrs, then after them the lesser amīrs such as [those called] *amīr hazāra*, who are those who lead a thousand men.[298]

The food was then brought in on tables of gold and silver, each table being carried by four men or more. Their food consists of boiled horse-meat and mutton, and a table is set down in front of each amīr. The *bāwarjī*, i.e. the carver of the meat,[299] comes, wearing silken robes on top of which is tied a silken apron, and carrying in his belt a number of knives in their sheathes. For each amīr there is a *bāwarjī*, and when the table is presented he sits down in front of his amīr; a small platter of gold or silver is brought, in which there is salt dissolved in water, and the *bāwarjī* cuts the meat up into small pieces. They have in this matter a special art of cutting up the meat together with the bones, for the Turks do not eat any meat unless the bones are mixed with it. |

After this, drinking-vessels of gold and silver are brought. 408
The beverage they make most use of is fermented liquor of honey, since, being of the Ḥanafite school of law, they hold fermented liquor to be lawful.[300] When the sultan wishes to drink, his daughter takes the bowl in her hand, pays homage with her leg, and then presents the bowl to him. When he has drunk she takes another bowl and presents it to the chief khātūn, who drinks from it, after which she presents it to the other khātūns in their order of precedence. The sultan's heir then takes the bowl, pays homage, and presents it to his father, then, when he has drunk, presents it to the khātūns and to his sister after them, paying homage to them all. The second son then rises, takes the bowl and gives it to his brother to drink paying homage to him. Thereafter the great amīrs rise, and each one of them gives the cup to the sultan's heir and pays homage to him, after which the [other] member of the royal house rise and each one of them gives the cup to this second son, paying homage to him. The lesser amīrs

[298] Persian *hazār*, 'thousand'.

[299] Mongol *bao'urchin*, 'army cook', an office regarded by Chingiz Khān as of special importance; see also Barthold, *Turkestan*, 382; Spuler, *Die Mongolen in Iran*, 273.

[300] See above, p. 475, n. 228. On the drink called hydromel, see M. Canard, 'Relation du Voyage d'Ibn Faḍlān', in *Annales de l'Institut d'Études Orientales* (Algiers, 1958), XVI, 89, n. 180.

then rise and give the sons of the kings to drink. During all
409 this [ceremony], they sing | [songs resembling the] chants sung by oarsmen.

A large pavilion had been erected also alongside the mosque for the qāḍī, the khaṭīb, the sharīf, and all the other legists and shaikhs, including myself. We were brought tables of gold and silver, each one carried by four of the leading men of the Turks, for no one is employed in the sultan's presence on that day except the principal men, and he commands them to take up such of the tables as he wishes [and carry them] to whomsoever he wishes. There were some of the legists who ate and some who abstained from eating [out of scruples at doing so] on tables of silver and gold.[301] To the limit of vision both right and left I saw waggons laden with skins of *qumizz*, and in due course the sultan ordered them to be distributed among those present. They brought one waggon to me, but I gave it to my Turkish neighbours.

After this we went into the mosque to await the Friday prayers. The sultan was late in coming, and some said that he
410 would not come because | drunkenness had got the better of him, and others said that he would not fail to attend the Friday service. When it was well past the time he arrived, swaying, and greeted the sayyid Sharīf, smiled to him, and kept addressing him as Āṭā, which means 'father' in the Turkish language. We then prayed the Friday prayers and the people withdrew to their residences. The sultan went back to the *bārka* and continued as before until the afternoon prayers, when all those present withdrew, [except that] his khātūns and his daughter remained with the king that night.

After this, when the festival had ended, we set out in company with the sultan and the *maḥalla* and came to the city of al-Ḥājj Tarkhān. *Tarkhān* in their usage means 'a place exempted from taxes'. The person after whom this city is named was a Turkish pilgrim, a saintly man, who made his residence at its site and for whom the sultan gave exemption
411 to that place.[302] | So it became a village, then grew in size and

[301] See above, p. 442, n. 109.

[302] This is a popular derivation. *Tarkhān* (*tärkän*), well known as a Turkish sovereign title, here represents Mongol *darqan*, meaning a person or place exempt from taxation. The name al-Hājj Tarkhān appears also on the

became a city, and it is one of the finest of cities, with great bazaars, built on the river Itil, which is one of the great rivers of the world.[303] It is there that the sultan resides until the cold grows severe and this river freezes over, as well as the waters connected with it. The sultan gives orders to the people of that land, and they bring thousands of loads of straw, which they spread over the ice congealed upon the river. Straw is not eaten by the animals in those parts, because it is injurious to them, and the same applies in the land of India; they eat nothing but green herbage, because of the fertility of the country. The inhabitants travel in waggons over this river and the adjacent waters for a space of three days' journey, and sometimes caravans cross over it at the end of the winter season and perish by drowning.

When we reached the city of al-Ḥājj Tarkhān, the khātūn Bayalūn, the daughter of the king of the Greeks, begged | of 412
the sultan to permit her to visit her father, that she might give birth to her child at the latter's residence, and then return to him. When he gave her permission I too begged of him to allow me to go in her company to see Constantinople the Great for myself. He forbade me, out of fear for my safety, but I solicited him tactfully and said to him 'It is under your protection and patronage that I shall visit it, so I shall have nothing to fear from anyone.' He then gave me permission, and when we took leave of him he presented me with 1500 dinars, a robe, and a large number of horses, and each of the khātūns gave me ingots of silver (which they call *ṣawm*, the singular being *ṣawma*).[304] The sultan's daughter gave me more than they did, along with a robe and a horse, and alto-

---

coins of the Golden Horde, but is apparently derived from Astarkhān, whether from the name of a particular Khazar ruler or as a title connected with the Ās (Ossetes): cf. Markwart, *Ungarische Jahrbücher* (1924), IV, 271; Minorsky, 451.

[303] *Ātil* or *Itil* is the traditional name in Arabic geography for the Volga, or rather for the Kama above Kazan and then the Volga from the point of their junction; Minorsky, 216.

[304] These were small bars of silver, called by Pegolotti *sommo*, and defined by him (21–2) as weighing eight and a half ounces of Genoa and worth five gold florins; see also Yule, *Cathay and the Way Thither*, III, 148–9. *Ṣawm* is the Old Bulgar *sōm* (itself derived from Old Turkish *sān*, 'number'), which passed into general use through the role of the Volga Bulgars in mediaeval trade, and is still used in some Eastern Turkish languages for 'rouble'.

gether I had a large collection of horses, robes, and furs of miniver and sable.

Account of my journey to Constantinople. We set out on the
413 tenth of Shawwāl[305] | in the company of the khātūn Bayalūn and under her protection. The sultan came out to escort her for one stage, then returned, he and the queen and his heir designate; the other khātūns travelled in her company for a second stage and then they returned. The amīr Baidara, with five thousand of his troops, travelled along with her, and the khātūn's own troops numbered about five hundred, some two hundred of whom were slaves and Greeks in attendance on her, and the remainder Turks. She had with her about two hundred slavegirls, most of them Greeks, and about four hundred waggons with about two thousand horses to draw them and for riding, as well as some three hundred oxen and two hundred camels to draw them. She also had ten Greek pages with her, and the same number of Indian pages, whose leader in chief was named Sumbul the Indian; the leader of the Greeks was named Mīkhā'īl (the Turks used to call him
414 Lu'lu'), and was a man of | great bravery. She left most of her slavegirls and of her baggage in the sultan's *maḥalla*, since she had set out with the intention [only] of paying a visit and of giving birth to her child.

We made for the city of Ukak,[306] a city of middling size, with fine buildings and abundant commodities, and extremely cold. Between it and al-Sarā, the sultan's capital, it is ten nights' march, and one day's march from this city are the mountains of the Rūs, who are Christians; they have red hair, blue eyes, and ugly faces, and are treacherous folk.[307] In their country are silver mines, and from it are imported the *ṣawm*, that is, the ingots of silver with which selling and

[305] In 732 (see above, n. 289) this fell on 5 July 1332.

[306] It is pointed out in Yule's *Marco Polo* (II, 488) that this Ukak is not the well-known mediaeval town of that name situated on the Volga about six miles below Saratov, but a small place mentioned in the portolans as Locachi or Locaq, on the Sea of Azof.

[307] Ibn Baṭṭūṭa's statement no doubt reflects the information given to him by the Turks, and refers to the real Russians (as distinct from the earlier Scandinavian *Rūs* or Varangians). The silver mines mentioned below are 'certain mines of argentiferous lead-ore near the river Miuss (see above, p. 475, n. 229). . . . It was these mines which furnished the ancient Russian *rubles* or ingots' (Yule's *Marco Polo*, II, 488).

buying are done in this land, each *ṣawma* weighing five ounces.

Next we came, after ten nights' journey from this city, to the city of Surdāq, which is | one of the cities of the Qifjaq 415
desert, situated on the sea-coast.[308] Its port is one of the greatest and finest of harbours. Outside it are orchards and streams, and it is inhabited by Turks and a number of Greeks under their dominion. These Greeks are artisans, and most of their houses are built of wood. This city was formerly a big one, but most of it was laid in ruins in consequence of a feud that broke out between the Greeks and the Turks. The Greeks got the upper hand [at first], but the Turks received assistance from their fellows, killed the Greeks remorselessly, and drove most of them out [of the city], but some of them remain to this day as a subject community.[309] At every halting-place in this land there was brought to the khātūn a hospitality-gift of horses, sheep, cattle, *dūgī*, *qumizz*, and cows' and sheep's milk. In these regions travelling is done in the forenoon and in the evening, and every amīr would accompany the khātūn with his troops right to the limit of his territories, |
to show her honour, not out of fear for her safety, for those 416
regions are quite secure.

We came to the town known by the name of Bābā Salṭūq.[310] *Bābā* in their language has exactly the same meaning as among the Berbers [i.e. 'father'], but they pronounce the *b* more emphatically. They relate that this Salṭūq was an ecstatic devotee, although things are told of him which are

[308] Surdāq or Soldaia, now Sudak, in the Crimea, was, until the rise of Kaffa (see above, p. 470, n. 213), the principal trading port on the northern coast of the Black Sea: see Heyd, I, 298–301; Yule's *Marco Polo*, I, 2–4. It seems improbable that the party should have made a detour through the Crimea, and presumably Ibn Baṭṭūṭa, if he visited Surdaq, did so during his previous stay in the Crimea (above, pp. 470–2).

[309] This apparently relates to the seizure of Sughdāq by a force sent by Özbeg Khan in 1322, during and after which the churches were closed or destroyed; see *E.I.*, s.v. Sughdāḳ.

[310] According to a Turkish tradition, the saint Sarī Saltīq joined a group of Turkmens who settled under Seljuk leadership in the Dobruja after 1260, and died there after 1300; see P. Wittek, 'Yazijioghlu 'Alī on the Christian Turks of the Dobruja' in *BSOAS* (London, 1952), XIV/3, esp. 648–9, 658. His tomb is shown in the town of Babadāgh (see *E.I*[2]., s.v.), in the northern Dobruja. Since, however, he is said to have lived for a time in the steppes (*dasht*; see above, p. 470, n. 210), it is probable that the place called after him was in Southern Russia, somewhere near the lower Dnieper, and about 1200 km. from Astrakhan.

reproved by the Divine Law. This town is the last of the towns possessed by the Turks, and between it and the beginning of the territory of the Greeks is [a journey of] eighteen days through an uninhabited waste, for eight days of which there is no water. A provision of water is laid in for this stage, and carried in large and small skins on the waggons. Since our entry into it was in the cold weather, we had no need of much water, and the Turks carry milk in large
417 skins, mix it with cooked *dūgī*, and drink that, | so that they feel no thirst.

At this city we made our preparations for [the crossing of] the waste. As I needed more horses I went to the khātūn and told her of my need. I used to make my salutations to her every morning and evening, and whenever a hospitality-gift was brought to her, she would send me two or three horses and some sheep. I made a practice of sparing the horses instead of slaughtering them; the slaves and attendants who were with me used to eat with our Turkish associates, and in this way I collected about fifty horses. The khātūn ordered that I should be given fifteen horses and bade her steward, the Greek Sārūja,[311] choose them fat among the horses intended for the kitchen. She said to me 'Don't be afraid, if you need others we shall give you more.' We entered the wasteland in the middle of [the month of] Dhu'l-Qa'da, our journey from the day that we left the sultan until the beginning of the waste having taken twenty-nine[312] days, and our halt [at
418 Bābā Salṭūq] five days. We marched through this | waste for eighteen days, in the forenoons and evenings, and met with nothing but good, praise be to God.

Thereafter we came to the fortress of Mahtūlī, at the beginning of the territory of the Greeks.[313] The Greeks had been

[311] This is probably a Turkish name (? *saruja*, 'yellowish').

[312] The text reads 'nineteen', but a comparison of the precise dates given for the start of the journey and the beginning of this stage shows that *'ishrī* must be read for *'ashara*.

[313] To define in detail the route followed on this journey is impossible; since Ibn Baṭṭūṭa was travelling in a large party, his information, except on the point of times, was probably never very clear and had become confused in his memory. The frontier city of the empire at this time was Diampolis, otherwise Kavúli (now Jamboli), at the southward bend of the Tunja (Tontzos) river in Bulgaria. The number of days taken from 'Baba Salṭūq' would indicate a distance of about 800 km., which corresponds very well to the distance from the lower Dnieper to Jamboli.

informed of the journey of this khātūn to their land, and there came to join her at this castle the Greek Kifālī Niqūla,[314] with a great body of troops and a large hospitality-gift, as well as the khātūns and nurses from the palace of her father, the king of Constantinople. From Mahtūlī to Constantinople it is a journey of twenty-two days, sixteen of them to the channel and six from there to Constantinople. From this castle travelling is done on horses and mules only, and the waggons are left behind there because of the roughness of the country and the mountains. The above-mentioned Kifāli had brought a large number of mules, six of which the khātūn sent to me. | She also recommended to the care of the gover- 419
nor of the fortress those of my companions and of my slaves whom I left behind with the waggons and baggage, and he assigned them a house. The amīr Baidara turned back with his troops, and none but her own people travelled on with the khātūn. She left her mosque behind at this castle and the prescription of the call to prayer was discontinued. Wines were brought to her as part of her hospitality-gift, and she would drink them, and [not only so but even] swine, and one of her personal attendants told me that she ate them. No one was left with her who observed the [Muslim] prayers except a certain Turk, who used to pray with us. Inner sentiments concealed [hitherto] suffered a change through our entry into the land of infidelity, but the khātūn charged the amīr Kifālī to treat me honourably, and on one occasion he beat one of his mamlūks when he laughed at our prayer.

We came next to the castle of Maslama ibn 'Abd al-Malik,[315] which is at the foot of a mountain beside a tumultuous river called Iṣṭafīlī.[316] Nothing is left of this fortress | except its 420
ruins, but alongside it is a large village. We continued our

[314] *Kifālī* is a transliteration of Greek *kephalê*, 'head, chief', and Niqūla is the common Arabic form of Nicholas. The term is apparently used here in the sense of 'governor'.

[315] Maslama, son of the caliph 'Abd al-Malik (685–705), was the commander of the Arab expedition which besieged Constantinople in 716–17. This episode was greatly expanded by legendary accretions in later sources (see M. Canard, 'Les Expeditions des Arabes contre Constantinople', in *JA* (Paris, 1926), 61 sqq., esp. 80–102), but no other reference is known to a fortress built by Maslama so far north of the city.

[316] This apparently renders the Greek name Astelephos, which is recorded, however, only as the name of a river on the coast of Pontus.

journey for two days and came to the channel, on the bank of which there is a large village. We found a rising tide on it and waited until the ebb set in, when we forded it, its breadth being about two miles. After marching four miles through sands, we came to the second channel and forded it, its breadth being about three miles. We then marched about two miles among rocks and sand and reached the third channel. The tide had begun to rise, so we had trouble in [fording] it, its breadth being one mile. The breadth of the entire channel, therefore, including both water and dry land, is twelve miles, and in the rainy season the whole of it becomes water and cannot be forded except in boats.

On the bank of this third channel is the city of al-Fanīka,[317] which is small but pretty and strongly fortified, and its churches and houses are beautiful. It is traversed by running
421 streams | and surrounded by orchards, and in it grapes, pears, apples and quinces are preserved from one year to the next. We halted in this city for three nights, the khātūn staying in one of her father's castles there.

After this her uterine brother, whose name was Kifālī Qarās,[318] arrived with five thousand horsemen, bristling with arms. When they were about to meet the khātūn, this brother of hers, dressed in white robes, rode on a grey horse and carried over his head a parasol ornamented with jewels. On his right hand he placed five sons of kings, and on his left the same number, all dressed in white also, and with parasols embroidered in gold over their heads. In front of him he posted a hundred foot-soldiers and a hundred horsemen, clad in long coats of mail covering both themselves and their horses, each one of whom led a horse saddled and armoured, carrying the arms of a horseman, namely a jewelled helmet, a
422 breastplate, a quiver, a bow and a sword, | and held in his hand a lance with a pennant at the point of its head. Most of these lances were covered with plaques of gold and silver,

317 The 'channel' is evidently a tidal river or estuary, and naturally suggests the mouths of the Danube, although this involves a serious misplacing, especially if, as seems probable, Fanīka stands for Agathoníke, where the main road from Diampolis crossed the river Tunja (Tontzos), at or near the modern Kizil Agach.

318 Qarās is certainly no Greek name, and it looks as if Ibn Baṭṭūṭa had got the prince's name mixed up with the Golden Horn (*Chrysokeras*). The use of *kephalé* as a title is also peculiar.

and those led horses were the riding beasts of the sultan's son. He divided his horsemen into squadrons, two hundred horsemen in each squadron. Over them was an amīr, who had preceding him ten horsemen bristling with arms, each of them leading a horse, and behind him ten particoloured standards carried by ten horsemen, and ten kettledrums slung over the shoulders of ten horsemen, who were accompanied by six others sounding trumpets and bugles and *ṣurnāyāt*, which are [the same as] *ghaiṭas*.[319] The khātūn rode out with her mamlūks, her slavegirls, pages and attendants, about five hundred, wearing robes of silk embroidered with gold and jewels. She herself was wearing a mantle [of the fabric] called *nakh*[320] (it is called | also *nasīj*) embroidered with jewels, with a crown 423
set with precious stones on her head, and her horse was covered with a saddle-cloth of silk embroidered in gold. On its forelegs and hindlegs were anklets of gold and round its neck were necklaces set with precious stones, and the saddle-frame was covered with gold ornamented with jewels. Their meeting took place on a flat piece of ground about a mile from the town. Her brother dismounted to her, because he was younger than she, and kissed her stirrup and she kissed his head. The amīrs and the scions of the royal house also dismounted and they all kissed her stirrup, after which she set out in company with her brother.

On the next day we came to a large city on the seacoast,[321] whose name I do not remember now, provided with streams and trees, and we encamped in its outskirts. The khātūn's brother, the heir to the throne, arrived in magnificent style with a vast army of ten thousand mailed men. On his head he wore a crown, and on | his right hand he had about twenty 424
of the scions of the royal house, with the like number on his left. He had disposed his horsemen exactly according to his brother's disposition, but the display was more magnificent and the concourse more numerous. His sister went out to meet him in the same array as before, and both dismounted together. A silken tent was brought and they both went into it, so I do not know how they greeted each other.

[319] See above, p. 343, n. 242.
[320] See above, p. 445, n. 117. *Nasīj* means 'woven stuff'.
[321] Most probably Selymbria or Rhegium.

We camped at a distance of ten miles from Constantinople, and on the following day its population, men, women and children, came out riding or on foot in their finest array and richest apparel. At dawn the drums, trumpets and fifes were sounded, the troops mounted, and the sultan and his wife, the mother of this khātūn, came out with the officers of state and the courtiers. Over the king's head there was a canopy, carried by a number of horsemen and men on foot, who held in their hands long staves, each surmounted by something
425 like a ball of | leather with which they hoisted the canopy. In the middle of the canopy was a sort of pavilion supported by horsemen with staves. When the sultan drew near, the troops became entangled with one another and there was much dust. I was unable to make my way in among them, so I kept with the khātūn's baggage and party, fearing for my life. I was told, however, that when the khātūn approached her parents, she dismounted and kissed the ground before them, and then kissed the two hoofs of their horses, and the principal men of her suite did the same.

Our entry into Constantinople the Great was made about noon or a little later, and they beat their church-gongs until the very skies shook with the mingling of their sounds. When we reached the first of the gates of the king's palace we found it guarded by about a hundred men, who had an officer of theirs with them on top of a platform, and I heard them
426 saying *Sarākinū, Sarākinū,* | which means 'Muslims'.[322] They would not let us enter, and when the members of the khātūn's party told them that we had come in her suite they answered 'They cannot enter except by permission,' so we stayed by the gate. One of the khātūn's party sent a messenger to tell her of this while she was still with her father. She told him about us, whereupon he gave orders to admit us and assigned us a house near the residence of the khātūn. He wrote also on our behalf an order that we should not be molested wheresoever we might go in the city, and this order was proclaimed in the bazaars. We remained indoors for three nights, during which hospitality-gifts were sent to us of flour, bread, sheep, fowls, ghee, fruit, fish, money and rugs, and on the fourth day we had audience of the sultan. |

[322] The Arabic transcription correctly renders the Greek *sarakenoi*, 'Saracens'.

Account of the sultan of Constantinople. His name is Takfūr, 427
son of the sultan Jirjīs.[323] His father the sultan Jirjīs was still in the bond of life, but had renounced the world and had become a monk, devoting himself to religious exercises in the churches, and had resigned the kingship to his son. We shall speak of him later. On the fourth day from our arrival at Constantinople, the khātūn sent her page Sumbul the Indian to me, and he took my hand and led me into the palace.[324] We passed through four gateways, each of which had porticoes in which were footsoldiers with their weapons, their officer being on a carpeted platform. When we reached the fifth gateway the page Sumbul left me, and going inside returned with four Greek pages, who searched me to see that I had no knife on my person. The officer said to me
'This is a custom of theirs; | every person who enters the 428
king's presence, be he noble or commoner, foreigner or native, must be searched.' The same practice is observed in the land of India.

Then, after they had searched me, the man in charge of the gate rose, took me by the hand, and opened the door. Four of the men surrounded me, two holding my sleeves and two behind me, and brought me into a large audience-hall, whose walls were of mosaic work, in which were pictured figures of creatures, both animate and inanimate.[325] In the centre of it was a water-channel with trees on either side of it, and men were standing to right and left, silent, not one of them speaking. In the midst of the hall there were three men standing, to whom those four men delivered me. These took hold of my garments as the others had done and so on a signal from another man led me forward. One of them was a Jew and
he said to me in Arabic, 'Don't be afraid, | for this is their 429
custom that they use with every visitor.[326] I am the inter-

[323] *Takfūr* is the designation in Arabic, not the name, of the Greek emperor (see above, p. 488, n. 274). For Jirjis see below, p. 512 and n. 342. The reigning emperor was Andronicus III, who was the grandson of his predecessor Andronicus II (abdicated 1328).

[324] The palace of the Palaeologi was the Blachernae, near the north-western angle of the city, an annexe of which is still known in Turkish as *takfūr sarāy*.

[325] As is well known, Muslim piety disapproved the representation of living creatures.

[326] See Constantinus Porphyrogenitus, *De Cerimoniis*, Bonn, 1829, 568, 584.

preter and I am originally from Syria.' So I asked him how I should salute, and he told me to say *al-salāmu 'alaikum*.

I came then to a great pavilion; the sultan was there on his throne, with his wife, the mother of this khātūn, before him, and at the foot of the throne were the khātūn and her brothers. To the right of him were six men, to his left four, and behind him four, everyone of them armed. He signed to me, before I had saluted and reached him, to sit down for a moment, so that my apprehension might be calmed, and I did so. Then I approached him and saluted him, and he signed to me to sit down, but I did not do so. He questioned me about Jerusalem, the Sacred Rock, [the Church called] al-Qumāma,[327] the cradle of Jesus, and Bethlehem, and about the city of al-Khalīl (peace be upon him) [Hebron], then about Damascus, Cairo, al-'Irāq and the land of al-Rūm, and
430 I answered him on | all of his questions, the Jew interpreting between us. He was pleased with my replies and said to his sons 'Honour this man and ensure his safety.' He then bestowed on me a robe of honour and ordered for me a horse with saddle and bridle, and a parasol of the kind that the king has carried above his head, that being a sign of protection. I asked him to designate someone to ride about the city with me every day, that I might see its wonders and curious sights and tell of them in my own country, and he designated such a guide for me. It is one of the customs among them that anyone who wears the king's robe of honour and rides on his horse is paraded through the city bazaars with trumpets, fifes and drums, so that the people may see him. This is most frequently done with the Turks who come from the territories of the sultan Ūzbak, so that they may not be molested; so they paraded me through the bazaars. |

431 *Account of the City.* It is enormous in magnitude and divided into two parts, between which there is a great river, in which there is a flow and ebb of tide,[328] just as in the wādī of Salā in the country of the Maghrib. In former times there was a bridge over it, built [of stone], but the bridge has fallen into ruin and nowadays it is crossed in boats. The name of this

[327] I.e. the Church of the Holy Sepulchre (see vol. I, p. 80, n. 43).

[328] The Golden Horn, which Ibn Baṭṭūṭa compares to the estuary of the Bou Regreg, on the Atlantic coast of Morocco, between the towns of Salā and Rabāṭ.

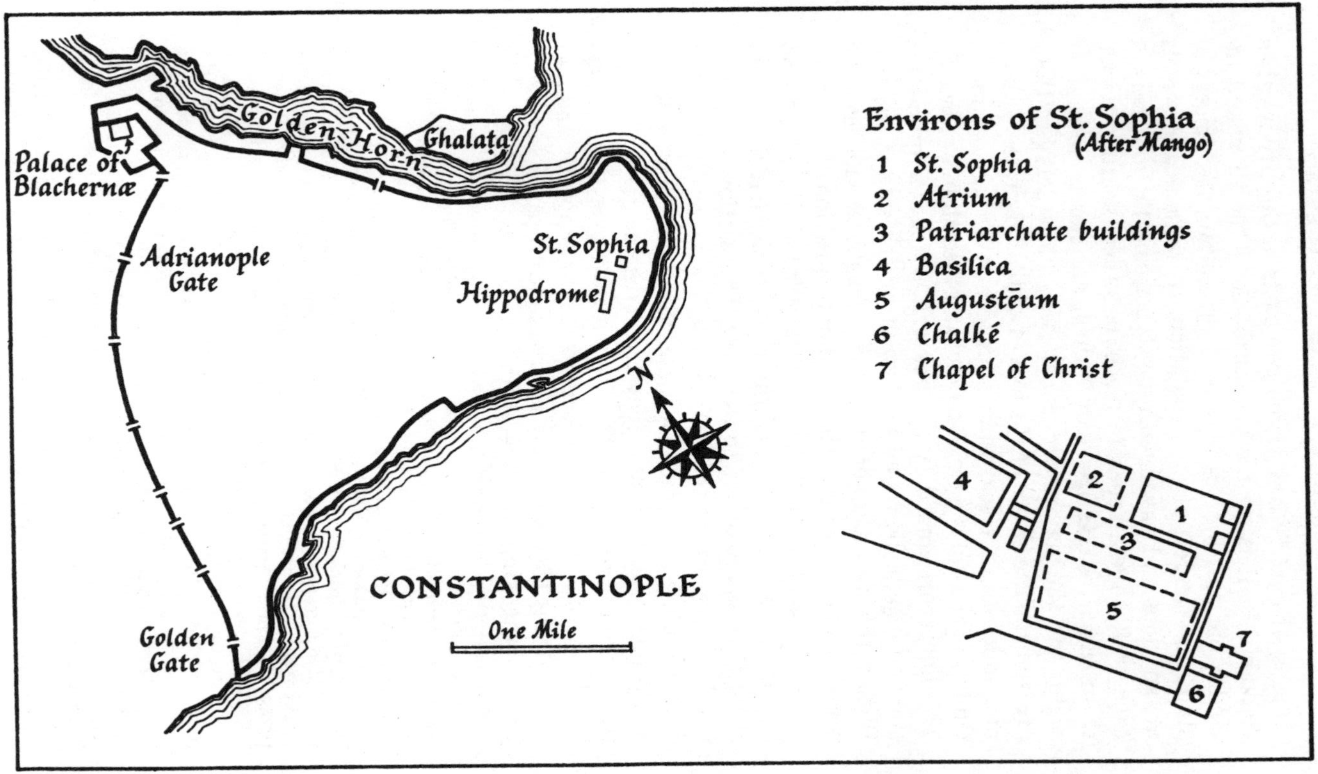
Golden Horn
Ghalata
Palace of Blachernæ
Adrianople Gate
Golden Gate
St. Sophia
Hippodrome
N
CONSTANTINOPLE
One Mile
Environs of St. Sophia
(After Mango)
1 St. Sophia
2 Atrium
3 Patriarchate buildings
4 Basilica
5 Augustēum
6 Chalké
7 Chapel of Christ
4
2
1
3
5
7
6

river is Absumī.[329] One of the two parts of the city is called Aṣṭanbūl;[330] it is on the eastern bank of the river and includes the places of residence of the sultan, his officers of state, and the rest of the population. Its bazaars and streets are spacious and paved with flagstones, and the members of each craft have a separate place, no others sharing it with them. Each bazaar has gates which are closed upon it at
432 night, and the majority of the artisans and sellers | in them are women. The city is at the foot of a hill that projects about nine miles into the sea, and its breadth is the same or more. On top of the hill is a small citadel and the sultan's palace.[331] This hill is surrounded by the city wall, which is a formidable one and cannot be taken by assault on the side of the sea. Within the wall are about thirteen inhabited villages. The principal church too is in the midst of this section of the city.

As for the other section of it, it is called al-Ghalaṭa,[332] and lies on the western bank of the river, somewhat like Ribāṭ al-Fatḥ in its proximity to the river. This section is reserved for the Christians of the Franks dwelling there. They are of different kinds, including Genoese, Venetians, men of Rome and people of France, and they are under the government of the King of Constantinople, who appoints over them [as his
433 lieutenant] one of their number | whom they approve, and him they call the *Qumṣ*.[333] They are required to pay a tax every year to the king of Constantinople, but they often rebel

[329] Apparently a deformation of Greek *potamos*, 'river'. It is doubtful whether a bridge had in fact existed over the Golden Horn; see R. Janin, 'Les Ponts byzantins de la Corne d'Or', *Ann. Inst. de Phil. et d'Hist. Orientales et Slaves* (Brussels, 1949), IX, 247–53.

[330] The name Iṣṭanbūl is used already by Yāqūt (*c.* 1220) and in several Arabic and Persian texts of the XIVth century; in some contexts it seems to be derived from the usage of the Italian merchants. (So too I have heard Mediterranean seamen speak of 'Cospoli'.) Various theories of the origin of the name are discussed by D. J. Georgacas 'The Names of Constantinople' in *Trans. American Philological Association* (Lancaster, Pa., 1947), LXXVIII, 366–7; see also *Islâm Ansiklopedisi*, s.v. Istanbul, coll. 1143–4.

[331] This apparently refers to the complex of walls which protected the palace, including the towers of Anemas and Isaac Angelus on its northern side. For the following account of the city cf. J. Ebersolt, *Constantinople byzantine et les voyageurs du Levant* (Paris, 1919).

[332] Still known by this name, and correctly described as the quarter of the Italian and French merchants, although it was strictly a Genoese colony: Heyd, I, 454 sqq., 482 sqq.

[333] I.e. *comes*, 'count'. The chief Genoese officer was, however, called Podestat, and I suspect that the term rendered by Ibn Baṭṭūṭa is 'consul'.

against his authority and then he makes war on them until the Pope restores peace between them. They are all men of commerce, and their port is one of the greatest of ports; I saw in it about a hundred galleys, such as merchant vessels and other large ships, and as for the small ships they were too numerous to be counted. The bazaars in this section are good, but overlaid with all kinds of filth, and traversed by a small, dirty and filth-laden stream. Their churches too are dirty and mean.

Account of the Great Church. I can describe only its exterior; as for its interior I did not see it. It is called in their language *Ayā Ṣūfiyā*, and the story goes that it was an erection of
Āṣaf the son of Barakhyā', who was | the son of the maternal 434
aunt of Solomon (on whom be peace).[334] It is one of the greatest churches of the Greeks; around it is a wall which encircles it so that it looks like a city [in itself]. Its gates are thirteen in number, and it has a sacred enclosure, which is about a mile long and closed by a great gate.[335] No one is prevented from entering the enclosure, and in fact I went into it with the king's father, who will be mentioned later; it is like an audience-hall, paved with marble and traversed by a water-channel which issues from the church. This [flows between] two walls about a cubit high, constructed in marble inlaid with pieces of different colours and cut with the most skilful art, and trees are planted in rows on both sides of the channel. From the gate of the church to the gate of this hall there is a lofty pergola made of wood, covered with grape-vines and at the foot with jasmine and scented herbs. Outside the gate of this hall is a large wooden pavilion containing platforms, on
which the guardians of this gate sit, | and to the right of the 435
pavilions are benches and booths, mostly of wood, in which sit their qāḍīs and the recorders of their bureaux.[336] In the

[334] The famous church of Hagia Sophia needs no description. Āṣaf b. Barakhyā' was, in Jewish and Muslim legend, the vizier of Solomon, but I have found no other reference to this story.

[335] This estimate of the open space round St Sophia is evidently exaggerated. The section of it which resembled an audience-hall is probably the Atrium, to the west of the main entrance to the church, and in which there was a fountain, although the water-channel and the pergola do not seem to be attested elsewhere.

[336] The buildings of the Patriarchate extended along the south side of the church and the Atrium, and offer a more probable location for the 'bazaar'

middle of the booths is a wooden pavilion, to which one ascends by a flight of wooden steps; in this pavilion is a great chair swathed in woollen cloth on which their qāḍī sits. We shall speak of him later. To the left of the pavilion which is at the gate of this hall is the bazaar of the druggists. The canal that we have described divides into two branches, one of which passes through the bazaar of the druggists and the other through the bazaar where the judges and the scribes sit.

At the door of the church there are porticoes where the attendants sit who sweep its paths, light its lamps and close its doors. They allow no person to enter it until he prostrates himself to the huge cross at their place, which they claim to
436 be a relic of the wood on which | the double of Jesus (on whom be peace) was crucified.[337] This is over the door of the church, set in a golden frame about ten cubits in height, across which they have placed a similar golden frame so that it forms a cross. This door is covered with plaques of silver and gold, and its two rings are of pure gold. I was told that the number of monks and priests in this church runs into thousands, and that some of them are descendants of the Apostles, also that inside it is another church exclusively for women, containing more than a thousand virgins consecrated to religious devotions, and a still greater number of aged and widowed women. It is the custom of the king, his officers of state, and the rest of the inhabitants to come to visit this church every morning, and the Pope comes to it once in the year. When he is at a distance of four nights' journey from the town the king goes out to meet him and dismounts before
437 him; | when he enters the city, the king walks on foot in front of him, and comes to salute him every morning and evening during the whole period of his stay in Constantinople until he departs.[338]

---

and pavilion of the judges and scribes than the Basilica, a porticoed building opposite the Atrium (as suggested by M. Izzeddin, 'Ibn Battouta et la Topographie byzantine' in *Actes du VI. Congrès internationale des Études byzantines* (Paris, 1951), II, 195).

[337] See vol. I, p. 80, n. 43.

[338] All these details, like many of those in the following paragraph, are evidently dragoman's inventions, but the popularity of the monastic life among the higher classes in fourteenth-century Byzantium is a fact; see R. Guilland, *Études byzantines* (Paris, 1959), ch. 2.

Account of the monasteries in Constantinople. A *mānistār* (which is pronounced like *māristān* [i.e. 'hospital'], only with the *n* and the *r* interchanged) is among them what a *zāwiya* is among Muslims. There are a great many of such monasteries in the city; among them is a monastery founded by the father of the king of Constantinople, the king George, (we shall mention him later), outside Aṣṭanbūl and opposite al-Ghalaṭa, and two monasteries outside the great Church, to the right as one enters it.[339] These two are inside a garden traversed by a stream of water, one of them for men, and the other for women. In | each of them there is a church, and round them 438
[in the interior] run the cells for the male and female devotees. Each of them has been endowed with pious foundations to supply clothing and maintenance for the devotees, and they were built by one of the kings. There are also two monasteries on the left as one enters the great church, similar to the former two and encircled by cells, one of them inhabited by blind men and the other by aged men, sixty years old or thereabouts, who are unable to work.[340] Each one of them receives clothing and maintenance from the endowments affected to that purpose. Inside each of these monasteries is a little building designed for the ascetic retreat of the king who built it, for most of these kings on reaching the age of sixty or seventy build a monastery and put on cilices, which are garments made of hair, invest their sons with the kingship, and occupy themselves with devotions | until their death. 439
They display great magnificence in building these monasteries, constructing them of marble and mosaic work, and they are very numerous in this city.

I went into a monastery with the Greek whom the king had designated to accompany me on my rides. It was traversed by a stream, and in it was a church containing about five hundred virgins wearing cilices, and with their heads shaved and covered with felt bonnets. They were of exceeding beauty and showed the traces of their austerities. A boy was sitting on a pulpit reading the gospel to them in the most beautiful voice

[339] Probably the Patriarchate and the Chapel of Our Saviour (on which see C. Mango, *The Brazen House* (Copenhagen, 1959), 149 sqq.).

[340] Identified by Izzedin (see above, n. 336) with two of the *xenodochia* known to have existed in this quarter.

that I have ever heard; round him were eight other boys on pulpits accompanied by their priest, and when this boy finished another boy began. The Greek said to me, 'These girls are kings' daughters who have given themselves to the service of this church, and the boys who are reading also [are
440 kings' sons].' They have another church of their own | outside that church. I went with him also into a church inside a garden and we found in it about five hundred virgins or more, with a boy on a pulpit reading to them and a number of other boys on pulpits, just like the former. The Greek said to me 'These are the daughters of viziers and amīrs, who engage in devotional exercises in this church.' In his company I entered churches in which were virgin daughters of the principal men of the city, and churches in which were aged and elderly women,[341] and churches where there were monks, numbering a hundred men or more or less in each church. Most of the inhabitants of this city are monks, devotees, and priests, and its churches are numerous beyond computation. The men of the city, both soldiers and others, small and great, carry over their heads huge parasols, both in winter and summer, and the women wear voluminous turbans. |

441 *Account of the King Jirjis, who became a Monk.*[342] This king invested his son with the kingdom, consecrated himself to the service of God, and built a monastery (as we have related) outside the city, on the bank [of its river]. I was out one day with the Greek appointed to ride with me when we chanced to meet this king, walking on foot, wearing hair-cloth garments, and with a felt bonnet on his head. He had a long white beard and a fine face, which bore traces of his austerities; before and behind him was a body of monks, and he had a pastoral staff in his hand and a rosary on his neck. When the Greek saw him he dismounted and said to me, 'Dismount, for this is the king's father.' When the Greek saluted him the king asked about me, then stopped and said to the Greek (who knew the Arabic tongue), 'Say to this Saracen (meaning

341 See above, p. 484, n. 259.

342 By no possible chronology can Ibn Baṭṭūṭa have visited Constantinople before the death of Andronicus II on 12/13 February 1332. Since, moreover, the monastic name of the ex-Emperor was Antonius, it is evident that he either misunderstood or was misled by his guide as to the identity of the monk 'George'.

Muslim) "I clasp the hand that has entered Jerusalem and the foot | that has walked within the Dome of the Rock and 442
the great Church called Qumāma, and Bethlehem",' and [so saying] he put his hand upon my feet and passed it over his face. I was amazed at their belief in the merits of one who, though not of their religion, had entered these places. He then took me by the hand and as I walked with him asked me about Jerusalem and the Christians living there, and questioned me at length. I entered with him into the enclosure of the church which we have described. When he approached the great door, there came out a number of priests and monks to salute him, for he is one of their great men in the monastic life, and when he saw them he let go my hand. I said to him 'I should like to go into the church with you' but he said to the interpreter 'Tell him that every one who enters it must needs prostrate himself before the great cross, | for this is a rule laid 443
down by the ancients and it cannot be contravened.' So I left him and he entered alone and I did not see him again.

Account of the Qāḍī of Constantinople. After leaving this king who had become a monk, I went into the bazaar of the scribes, where I was noticed by the qāḍī, who sent one of his assistants to question the Greek who was with me. The Greek told him that I was a Muslim student of religion, and when the man returned to the qāḍī and reported this to him, he sent one of his associates for me. They call the qāḍī *al-Najshī Kifālī,*[343] so this man said to me 'Al-Najshī Kifālī invites you,' and I went up to him in the pavilion that I have described above. I found him to be an old man with a fine face and hair, wearing the robe of the monks, which is of black woollen cloth, and with about ten of the scribes in front of him writing. He rose to meet me, his associates rising also, and said, 'You are the king's guest, and we are bound to honour you.' He asked me about Jerusalem, | Damascus 444
and Cairo, and spoke with me for a long time. A great crowd gathered round him, and he said to me 'You must come to my

[343] *Najshī* is obviously a corruption of some term, but it is difficult to relate it to any Greek word. The most probable explanation is that the word is to be read *bakhshī*, used in Mongolian and Turkish for a scribe or ecclesiastic (see Yule's *Marco Polo*, I, 314), the Arabic letters of which are the same as those of *najshī*, and which could have been used by the interpreter to indicate his office.

house that I may entertain you as my guest,' but after taking leave of him I never met him again.

Account of my departure from Constantinople. When it became clear to the Turks who were in the khātūn's company that she professed her father's religion and wished to remain with him, they asked her permission to return to their own country. She gave them permission and made them rich presents, and sent with them to escort them to their country an amīr called Sārūja the Little with five hundred horsemen. She sent for me and gave me three hundred dinars in their gold coinage (they call this *al-barbara*, and it is not good money),[344] two thousand Venetian dirhams, a length of
445 woollen cloth of the work of the girls (this is the best | kind of such cloth), ten robes of silk, linen, and wool, and two horses, this being the gift of her father. She commended me to Sārūja and I bade her farewell and left, having spent one month and six days in their city.[345]

We set out in company with Sārūja, who continued to treat me honourably, and arrived at length at the frontier of their territory, where we had left our associates and our waggons. We then rode in the waggons and entered the desert; Sārūja went on with us to the city of Bābā Salṭūq,[346] where he remained as a guest for three nights and then returned to his own country. This was in the depth of winter, and I used to put on three fur coats and two pairs of trousers, one of them quilted, and on my feet I had woollen boots, with a pair of boots quilted with linen cloth on top of them, and on top of these again a pair of boots of [the kind called] *al-burghālī*, which is horse-skin lined with bear-skin.[347] I used to perform
446 my ablutions with hot water close to | the fire, but not a drop of water fell without being frozen on the instant. When I washed my face, the water would run down my beard and freeze, then I would shake it and there would fall from it a

[344] *Barbara* is a transcription of *hyperpyra*, plural of *hyperpyron*, the Byzantine gold 'dinar', the debasement of which began in the reign of Andronicus; see A. Andréades in *Byzantion* (Liége, 1924), I, 10, n. 2, and T. Bertelé in Acc. dei Lincei, *Atti dei Convegni*, 12 (Rome, 1957), p. 253.

[345] About 24 October 1332.

[346] See above, p. 499, n. 310.

[347] *Burghālī* is the narrator's or his copyists' error for *bulghārī*, i.e. leather from Bulghār. Cf. with this passage Ibn Faḍlān, tr. M. Canard, p. 64.

kind of snow. The moisture that dripped from the nose would freeze on the moustache. I was unable to mount a horse because of the quantity of clothes I had on, so that my associates had to help me into the saddle.

After this I arrived at the city of al-Ḥājj Tarkhān, where we had parted from the sultan Ūzbak. We found that he had moved and had settled at the capital of his kingdom, so we travelled [to it] for three nights on the river Itil [Volga] and its joining waters, which were frozen over. Whenever we needed water we used to cut out pieces of ice, put the ice in a cauldron until it turned into water, and then use this for drinking and cooking. [On the fourth day] we reached the
city of al-Sarā, | known also as Sarā Baraka, which is the 447
capital of the sultan Ūzbak.[348] We had an audience of the sultan; he asked us how our journey had gone and about the king of the Greeks and his city, and after we had answered him he gave orders for our lodging and for the issue to us of [what was needed for] our maintenance.

The city of al-Sarā is one of the finest of cities, of boundless size, situated in a plain, choked with the throng of its inhabitants, and possessing good bazaars and broad streets. We rode out one day with one of its principal men, intending to make a circuit of the city and find out its extent. Our lodging place was at one end of it and we set out from it in the early morning, and it was after midday when we reached the other end. We then prayed the noon prayer and ate some food, and we did not get back to our lodging until the hour of the sunset prayer. One day we went on foot across the breadth of the town, going and returning, in half a day, this too through a continuous line of houses, among which there were
no ruins and no gardens. The city has | thirteen mosques for 448
the holding of Friday prayers, one of them being for the

[348] Özbeg Khān had shortly before this removed the capital from [Old] Sarai (situated near the modern village of Selitrennoe, 74 miles above Astrakhan), to a town, probably founded by Berke Khān (1255–67), and now called 'New Sarai', at the site of the modern town of Tsarev, 225 miles above Astrakhan. The ruins of the city cover an area of over twenty square miles and extend for a distance of more than 40 miles: see Spuler, *Die Goldene Horde*, 266–9; F. Balodis, 'Alt-Serai und Neu-Serai, die Hauptstädte der Goldenen Horde' in *Latvijas Universitates Raksti* (*Acta Universitatis Latviensis*) (Riga, 1926), XIII, 3–82.

Shāfi'ites; as for the other mosques, they are exceedingly numerous. There are various groups of people among its inhabitants; these include the Mughals, who are the dwellers in this country and its sultans, and some of whom are Muslims, then the Āṣ, who are Muslims,[349] the Qifjaq,[350] the Jarkas,[351] the Rūs, and the Rūm—[all of] these are Christians. Each group lives in a separate quarter with its own bazaars. Merchants and strangers from the two 'Irāqs, Egypt, Syria and elsewhere, live in a quarter which is surrounded by a wall for the protection of the properties of the merchants. The sultan's palace in it is called *Alṭūn Tāsh, alṭūn* meaning 'gold', and *tāsh* 'head'.[352]

The qāḍī of this capital city is Badr al-Din al-A'raj, one of
449 the best of qāḍīs. There too, among the professors | of the Shāfi'ites, is the worthy jurist and imām Ṣadr al-Dīn Sulaiman al-Lakzī,[353] a man of distinction, and of the Mālikites Shams al-Dīn al-Miṣrī, a man whose rectitude is regarded with some suspicion, also the hospice of the pious pilgrim Niẓām al-Dīn, who entertained us in it and showed us honour, and the hospice of the learned imām Nu'mān al-Dīn al-Khwārizmī, whom I met in it, one of the eminent shaikhs and a man of fine character, generous in soul, of exceeding humility but also of exceeding severity towards the possessors of this world's goods. The sultan Ūzbak comes to visit him every Friday, but the shaikh will not go out to meet him nor rise before him. The sultan sits in front of him, addresses him in the most courteous manner and humbles himself to him, whereas the shaikh's conduct is the opposite of this.[354] But in his dealings with poor brethren, with the needy and with wayfaring visitors, his demeanour is the antithesis of that which he adopts towards the sultan, for he humbles himself |
450 to them, speaks to them in the kindest way, and shows them honour. He received me honourably (God reward him well)

[349] The Ossetes, formerly known as the Alān (*E.I.*[2], s.v. Alān).

[350] See above, p. 470, nn. 210, 212.

[351] See above, p. 480, n. 248.

[352] Ibn Baṭṭūṭa has confused *ṭāsh*, 'stone' with *bāsh*, 'head'. *Alṭūn*, for Turkish *altin*, is correctly glossed as 'gold'.

[353] The Lakz were a tribe in the region of Daghestan. Their name, in the form of Lazgi, was later applied to the mountaineers of Daghestan generally (Minorsky, 455).

[354] Cf. p. 484, n. 260.

and presented me with a Turkish slaveboy. I was witness too to an example of his endowment with blessed power.

A miraculous grace of his. I had intended to set out from al-Sarā to Khwārizm, but he forbade me to do so, saying to me 'Stay here for some days, and then you may continue your journey.' I still hankered to go, however, and finding a large caravan that was making ready to set out and that included some merchants with whom I was acquainted, I made an agreement to travel in their company. When I told him of this he said to me 'You have no alternative to staying here.' Nevertheless I determined to set out, when a slaveboy of mine escaped and I had to stay because of him. This is an evident instance of miraculous grace. Three days later one of my associates found the fugitive slave in the city of al-Ḥājj Tarkhān and brought him to me, whereupon I set out for Khwārizm. Between Khwārizm and the capital city of al-Sarā is a desert | of forty days' march, in which horses cannot 451
travel owing to lack of fodder, and only camels are employed to draw the waggons.

BIBLIOGRAPHY

Oriental texts and translations

ABU'L-FAẒL 'ALLĀMĪ. *Ā'īn-i Akbarī*. Trans. H. Blochmann et al. 2nd ed. Calcutta, 1927–49. 3 vols.

ABU'L-FIDĀ. *Taqwīm al-Buldān*. Ed. M. Reinaud. Paris, 1840–8. 3 vols.

ABU'L-ḤASAN AL-DAILAMĪ. *Sīrat-i Ibn al-Ḫafīf aş-Şīrāzī*. Ed. A. Schimmel. Ankara, 1955.

AFLĀKĪ. *Manāqib al-'Ārifīn*. Trans. C. Huart, *Les Saints des Derviches tourneurs*. Paris, 1918–22. 2 vols.

Ā'īn-i Akbarī. See ABU'L-FAẒL 'ALLĀMĪ.

'ALĪ B. ABĪ BAKR AL-HARAWĪ. *Guise des Lieux des Pèlerinages*. Ed. and trans. J. Sourdel-Thoumine. Damascus, 1953–7. 2 vols.

AL-'AZZĀWĪ, 'ABBĀS. *Ta'rīkh al-'Irāq baina Iḥtilālain*. Baghdad, 1935–58. 8 vols.

'Anonym of Iskandar' (*Muntakhab al-Tawārīkh-i Mu'īnī*). Ed. J. Aubin. Tehran, 1336 Sh.

BAHMAN KARĪMĪ. *Rāhnumāyi Āthār-i Tārīkh-i Shīrāz*. Tehran, 1327 Sh.

AL-BĪRŪNĪ. *India*. Revised ed. Hyderabad, India. 1958.

Chroniken der Stadt Mekka. Ed. F. Wüstenfeld. Leipzig, 1858–61. 4 vols.

COMBE, E. *et al.* (edd.). *Répertoire chronologique d'épigraphie arabe*. Cairo, 1931—, proceeding (vols. 1–15 published).

AL-DAMĪRĪ. *Ḥayāt al-Ḥayawān*. Cairo, A.H. 1306. 2 vols.

Le Destan d'Umur Pacha. Ed. and trans L. Mélikoff-Sayar. Paris, 1954.

ḤAFIZ-I ABRŪ. *Chronique*. Trans. K. Bayani. Paris, 1936.

AL-HAMDĀNĪ. *Ṣifat Jazīrat al-'Arab*. Ed. D. H. Müller. Leiden, 1884–91. 2 vols.

AL-HARAWĪ. See 'ALĪ B. ABĪ BAKR AL-HARAWĪ.

History of Kilwa. Ed. S. A. Strong, in *JRAS*, 1895, 385–430.

AL-HUJWĪRĪ. *Kashf al-Maḥjūb*. Trans. R. A. Nicholson. London, 1911.
IBN BAṬṬŪṬA. *The Travels of Ibn Battuta*. Trans. and selected by H. A. R. Gibb. London, 1929. (Cited as *Selections*.)
—*Selections from Ibn Battuta*. Trans. (in Armenian) A. Ajarian. Yerevan, 1940. (Utilized in typescript English translation.)
—*The Rehla of Ibn Battuta*. Trans. Mahdi Husain. Baroda, 1953.
IBN BĪBĪ. *Histoire des Seljoucides de l'Asie Mineure*. Ed. Th. Houtsma. Leiden, 1891–1902. 2 vols.
IBN FAḌLĀN. *Relation du Voyage*. Trans. M. Canard. *Annales de l'Institut des Études orientales*, vol. XVI. Algiers, 1958, pp. 43–146.
IBN HAJAR AL-'ASKALĀNĪ. *Al-Durar al-Kāmina*. Hyderabad-Dn, 1929–31. 4 vols. (Cited as *Durar*.)
IBN HAUKAL. *Opus Geographicum*. 2nd ed., ed. J. H. Kramers. Leiden, 1938–9. 2 vols.
IBN AL-'IMĀD. *Shadharāt al-Dhahab*. Cairo, n.d. 8 vols.
IBN JUBAIR. *Travels* (*Riḥla*). Ed. W. Wright, 2nd ed. revised by M. J. de Goeje. Leiden and London, 1907.
—*The Travels of Ibn Jubayr*. Trans. by R. J. C. Broadhurst. London, 1952.
IBN KATHĪR. *al-Bidāya wa'l-Hidāya*. Cairo, n.d. 14 vols.
IBN KHALDŪN. *Muqaddima*. Trans. F. Rosenthal. New York, 1958. 3 vols.
IBN AL-MUJĀWIR. *Descriptio Arabiae Meridionalis*. Ed. O. Löfgren. Leiden, 1951–4. 2 vols.
IBN AL-ṢĀBŪNĪ. *Takmilat al-Ikmāl*. Baghdad, 1958.
IBN SA'D. *Kitāb al-Ṭabaqāt al-Kabīr*. Leiden, 1905–28. 9 vols.
IBN TAGHRĪBIRDĪ. [*Al-Manhal al-Ṣāfī*. Summarized translation by] G. Wiet, *Les biographies du Manhal Safi*. Cairo, 1932. (Cited as *Manhal*.)
AL-IṢFAHĀNĪ, ABŪ NU'AIM. *Ḥilyat al-Awliyā'*. Cairo, 1936. 12 vols.
AL-IṢṬAKHARĪ. *Viae Regnorum*. Ed. M. J. de Goeje. 2nd ed. Leiden, 1927.
JUNAID SHĪRĀZĪ. *Shadd al-Izār*. Tehran, 1327 Sh.
JUWAINĪ, 'AṬA-MALIK. *Ta'rīkh-i Jahāngushā*. Leiden and London, 1912–37. 3 vols.

—*History of the World-Conqueror*. Trans. J. A. Boyle. Manchester, 1958. 2 vols.

Kashf al-Ghumma. [Anonymous Chronicle] ed. H. Klein. Hamburg, 1938.

KĀSHGHARĪ, MAḤMŪD. *Dīwān Lughāt al-Turk*. Istanbul, 1333. 3 vols.

AL-KHAṬĪB AL-BAGHDĀDĪ. *Ta'rīkh Baghdād*. Cairo, 1931. 14 vols.

AL-KHAZRAJĪ. *History of the Resuliyy Dynasty of Yemen*. Ed. and trans. J. M. Redhouse. Leiden and London, 1906–8. 5 vols.

AL-MAQDISĪ. *Descriptio Imperii Moslemici*. Ed. M. J. de Goeje. 2nd ed. Leiden, 1906.

AL-MAQRĪZĪ. *Al-Sulūk fi duwal al-Mulūk*. Ed. M. M. Ziada. Cairo, 1934—, proceeding. Vols. 1, 2.

AL-MAS'ŪDĪ. *Murūj al-Dhahab* [*Prairies d'Or*]. Ed. and trans. Barbier de Meynard. Paris 1861–77. 9 vols.

MEIER, F. (ed.) *Die Vita des Scheich Abū Isḥāq al-Kāzarūnī*. Leipzig, 1948.

MUSTAWFĪ. *Nuzhat al-Qulūb*. Ed. and trans. G. Le Strange. London, 1919. 2 vols.

AL-'OMARĪ. See AL-'UMARĪ.

AL-QALQASHANDĪ. *Ṣubḥ al-A'shā*. Cairo, 1913–19. 14 vols.

QĀSIM GHANĪ. *Ta'rīkh-i 'Aṣr-i Ḥāfiẓ*. Tehran, n.d.

Rashīd al-Dīn, Letters of Faḍl Allah. Ed. M. Shafi. Lahore, 1947.

REINAUD, M. (ed.). *Relation des Voyages faits dans l'Inde et à la Chine*. Paris, 1848. 2 vols.

Répertoire chronologique d'épigraphie arabe. See COMBE, E.

RŪMĪ, JALĀL AL-DĪN. *Mathnawī*. Ed. R. A. Nicholson. London, 1925–40. 8 vols.

—*Selected Poems from the Dīvāni Shamsī Tabrīz*. Ed. R. A. Nicholson. Cambridge, 1898.

SA'DĪ. *Gulistān*. Ed. J. Platts. 2nd ed., London, 1874.

SA'ĪD AL-ANDALUSĪ. *Ṭabaqāt al-Umam*. Trans. R. Blachère. Paris, 1935.

AL-SĀLIMĪ, NŪR AL-DĪN. *Tuhfat al-A'yān*. Ed. Ibrāhīm Aṭfīsh. Cairo, A.H. 1350. 2 vols.

SIOUFI, A. [Articles in *Sumer*, vols. VI and XI.] Baghdad, 1950–5.

TĀJ AL-DĪN AL-SUBKĪ. *Ṭabaqāt al-Shāfi'īya*. Cairo, n.d. 6 vols.

Ta'rīkh-i Guzīda. Ed. E. G. Browne. Leiden and London, 1910. 2 vols.

AL-'UMARĪ. *L'Afrique moins l'Egypte*. Trans. M. Gaudefroy-Demombynes. Paris, 1927.

—*Bericht über Anatolien*. Ed. F. Taeschner. Leipzig, 1929. (Cited as 'Omari.)

AL-YA'QŪBĪ. *Le Livre des Pays*. Ed. M. J. de Goeje. Leiden, 1861. Trans. G. Wiet. Cairo, 1937.

YĀQŪT AL-RŪMĪ. *Irshād al-Arīb*. Ed. D. S. Margoliouth. London, 1907–26. 7 vols.

—*Mu'jam al-Buldān*. Ed. F. Wüstenfeld. Leipzig, 1866–73. 6 vols. (Cited as YĀQŪT.)

ZETTERSTÉEN, K. V. (ed.). *Beiträge zur Geschichte der Mamlukensultane in den Jahren* 690–741 *der Hiğra*. Leiden, 1919. (Cited as ZETTERSTEEN.)

Books and articles in western languages

ADAM, WILLIAM OF. 'De modo Sarracenos extirpandi.' *Recueil des Historiens des Croisades*, Documents Arméniens (Paris, 1906), II.

ANDRÉADES, A. 'De la monnaie . . . dans l'Empire Byzantine.' *Byzantion* (Liége, 1924), I.

ARBERRY, A. J. *Shiraz, Persian City of Saints and Poets*. Norman, Oklahoma, 1960.

ARNAKIS, G. G. *Oi Prōtoi Othōmanoi*. Athens, 1947.

ATIYA, A. S. *The Crusade in the Later Middle Ages*. London, 1938.

AUBIN, J. 'Les Princes d'Ormuz du XIIIe au XVe siècle.' *Journal Asiatique* (Paris, 1953), 77–138.

BALODIS, F. 'Alt-Serai und Neu-Serai, die Hauptstädte der Goldenen Horde.' *Latvias Universitatis Raksti* (*Acta Universitatis Latviensis*) (Riga, 1926), XIII.

BALL, J. *The Geography and Geology of South-Eastern Egypt*. Cairo, 1912.

BARTHOLD, W. *Turkestan down to the Mongol Invasions*. London, 1928.

—*Histoire des Turcs d'Asie Centrale*. Paris, 1945.

BENT, TH. *Southern Arabia*. London, 1900.

BRATIANU, G. *Recherches sur le commerce génois dans la Mer Noire au XIIIe siècle*. Paris, 1929.

BROCKELMANN, C. *Geschichte der arabischen Litteratur*. Weimar-Berlin, 1898–1902. 2 vols.

—*Mitteltürkischer Wortschatz*. Budapest-Leipzig, 1928.

BROWNE, E. G. *A Literary History of Persia*. Vol. III. Cambridge, 1920.

—*A Year among the Persians*. Reprint, London, 1950.

BURCKHARDT, J. L. *Travels in Arabia*. London, 1829.

BURTON, Sir RICHARD. *Personal Narrative of a Pilgrimage to El-Medinah and Meccah*. London, 1855–6. 3 vols.

CAETANI, L. *Annali dell'Islam*. Milan, 1905–26. 10 vols.

CANARD, M. 'Les Expeditions des Arabes contre Constantinople.' *Journal Asiatique* (Paris, 1926).

—'Relations du Voyage d'Ibn Faḍlān.' *Annales de L'Institut d'Études Orientales* (Algiers, 1958), XVI.

CHARDIN, J. *Travels in Persia*. Ed. N. M. Penzer. London, 1927.

CLARKE, E. D. *Travels in Various Countries of Europe, Asia and Africa*. London, 1810–23.

CLAVIJO, P. *Embassy to Tamerlane*. Trans. G. Le Strange. London, 1928.

CRESWELL, K. A. C. *Early Muslim Architecture*. Vol. I. Oxford, 1932.

—*A Short Account of Early Muslim Architecture*. London, 1958.

CUINET, V. *La Turquie d'Asie*. Vol. I, Paris, 1892.

DE GAURY, G. 'A Note on Masira Island.' *Geographical Journal* (London, 1957), CXXIII, 499–502 (with map).

DEVIC, L. M. *Le Pays des Zendjs*. Paris, 1883.

DORMAN, M. H. 'The Kilwa Civilization and the Kilwa Ruins.' *Tanganyika Notes* (Dar-es-Salaam, 1938), no. 6, 61–71.

DOZY, R. P. A. *Dictionnaire détaillée des noms des vêtements chez les Arabes*. Amsterdam, 1945.

—*Supplément aux dictionnaires arabes*. Leiden, 1881. 2 vols.

EBERSOLT, J. *Constantinople byzantine et les voyageurs du Levant*. Paris, 1918.

Enciclopedia Italiana. Milano, 1929–36. 36 vols.

ENCYCLOPAEDIA OF ISLAM. Ed. M. Th. Houtsma (*et al.*), Leiden, 1913–38, 4 vols. and Supplement. (Cited as *E.I.*).

—New Edition, ed. H. A. R. Gibb (*et al.*). Leiden, 1954—. Vol. I published. (Cited as *E.I.*[2].)

FARMER, H. G. 'Ṭabl-Khāna.' *E.I.*, Supplement.

—*Turkish Instruments of Music in the Seventeenth Century*. Glasgow, 1937.

FERRAND, G. 'Les sultans de Kilwa.' *Mémorial Henri Basset* (Paris, 1928), 242–56.

FISCHEL, W. J. 'The Spice Trade in Mamlūk Egypt.' *Journal of the Economic and Social History of the Orient* (Leiden, 1958), I/2.

Forschungen in Ephesos. Austrian Archaeological Institute, 1906–51. 5 vols.

FREEMAN-GRENVILLE, G. S. P. 'Ibn Batuta's visit to East Africa.' *Uganda Journal* (Kampala, 1955), XIX, 1–6.

GABRIEL, A. *Une capitale turque, Brousse*. Paris, 1958.

GEORGACAS, D. J. 'The Names of Constantinople.' *Transactions of the American Philological Association* (Lancaster, Pa., 1947), LXXVIII.

GUILLAIN, M. *Documents sur . . . l'Afrique orientale*. Paris, 1856. 3 vols.

GUILLAND, R. *Études byzantines*. Paris, 1959.

HAKKI, ISMAIL. *Kitabeler*. Istanbul, 1929.

HASLUCK, F. W. *Christianity and Islam under the Sultans*. Oxford, 1929. 2 vols.

HASTINGS, J. (ed.). *Encyclopaedia of Religion and Ethics*. Edinburgh, 1908–21. 12 vols.

HERZFELD, E. *Geschichte der Stadt Samarra*. Hamburg, 1948.

—See also SARRE, F.

HEYD, W. VON. *Histoire du commerce du Levant au moyen-âge*. Leipzig, 1885–6. 2 vols.

HINZ, W. *Islamische Masse und Gewichte*. Leiden, 1955.

A History of the Crusades. Vol. I. Philadelphia, Pa., 1955.

HOLDICH, T. H. 'Notes on Ancient and Mediaeval Makran.' *Geographical Journal* (London, 1896), VII.

HOURANI, G. F. *Arab Seafaring*. Princeton, 1951.

HUGHES, T. P. *Dictionary of Islam*. London, 1885 (reprint 1935).

JACOBUS DE VORAGINE. 'Iacopo da Voragine anonimi Giorgio Stella,' *Annali Genovesi* (Genova, 1941).

IZZEDDIN, M. 'Ibn Battouta et la Topographie byzantine.' *Actes du VI. Congrès internationale des Études byzantines* (Paris, 1951), II.

JANICSEK, S. 'Ibn Baṭṭūṭa's Journey to Bulghār: is it a Fabrication?' *JRAS* (1929), 791–800.

JANIN, R. 'Les Ponts byzantins de la Corne d'Or.' *Annuaire de l'Institut de Philologie et d'Histoire Orientales et Slaves* (Brussels, 1949), IX.

KINDERMANN, H. *'Schiff' in Arabischen.* Zwickau, 1934.

KLEIN, J. *Der sibirische Pelzhandel.* Bonn, 1906.

KOMROFF, M. *Contemporaries of Marco Polo.* London, 1928.

LANE, E. W. *An Account of the Manners and Customs of the Modern Egyptians.* London, 1836. 2 vols.

LANE-POOLE, S. *Saladin.* London and New York, 1898.

LEMERLE, P. *L'Emirat d'Aydin.* Paris, 1957.

LE STRANGE, G. *Baghdad during the Abbasid Caliphate.* Oxford, 1900.

—*Lands of the Eastern Caliphate.* Cambridge, 1905.

LLOYD, S. and RICE, D. S. *Alanya (Ala'iyya).* London 1958.

LOCKHART, L. *Famous Cities of Iran.* London, 1933.

MACMICHAEL, H. A. *History of the Arabs in the Sudan.* Cambridge, 1922. 2 vols.

MAKSIMOVA, M. I. *Antichnye Goroda Yugo-vostochnago Prechernomor'a.* Moskva-Leningrad, 1956.

MANGO, C. *The Brazen House.* Copenhagen, 1959.

MANSUROǦLU, M. 'Some Titles and Names in Old-Anatolian Turkish'; *Ural-Altäische Jahrbücher,* XXVII. Wiesbaden, 1955, pp. 94–102.

MARKWART, J. 'Ein arabischer Bericht über die arktischen (uralischen) Länder aus dem 10. Jahrhundert.' *Ungarische Jahrbücher* (Berlin-Leipzig, 1924), IV.

MASSIGNON, L. *Essai sur les origines du lexique technique de la mystique musulmane.* Paris, 1922.

—'Explication du Plan de Kufa.' *Mélanges Maspéro* (Cairo, 1935), III.

—'Explication du Plan de Basra.' *Westöstliche Abhandlungen Rudolf Tschudi überreicht* (Wiesbaden, 1954).

—'La Vie et les Oeuvres de Rûzbehân Baqlî.' *Studia Orientalia Ioanni Pedersen dicata* (Copenhagen, 1953).

MEER HASAN ALI, Mrs. *Observations on the Musselmauns of India*. 2nd ed., ed. W. Crooke. London, 1917.

MORRIS, J. *Sultan into Oman*. London and New York, 1957.

MUIR, Sir WILLIAM. *The Life of Mahomet*. 3rd ed. London, 1894.

Murray's Handbook, Constantinople, Brusa and the Troad. London, 1900.

Murray's Handbook for Travellers in Asia Minor, etc. Ed. Sir Charles Wilson. London, 1895.

MUSIL, ALOIS. *The Middle Euphrates*. New York, 1927.

OPPENHEIM, MAX FREIHERR VON. *Die Beduinen* (Wiesbaden, 1952), III.

—*Vom Mittelmeer zum Persischen Golf*. Berlin, 1900. 2 vols.

PAUL, A. *A History of the Beja Tribes of the Sudan*. Cambridge, 1954.

PEGOLOTTI, FRANCESCO BALDUCCI. *La Pratica della Mercatura*. Ed. A. Evans. Cambridge, Mass., 1936.

PELLIOT, PAUL. *Notes sur l'histoire de la Horde d'Or*. Paris, 1950.

PENZER, N. M., ed. *The Ocean of Story*. London, 1927. 10 vols.

Periplus of the Erythraean Sea. Trans. W. H. Schoff. New York, 1912.

PHILBY, H. ST. J. *The Heart of Arabia*. London, 1922. 2 vols.

PHILIPPSON, A. *Reise und Forschungen in westlichen Kleinasien* (*Petermanns Mitteilungen, Ergänzungshefte* 176, 180–3). Gotha, 1910–15. 5 pts.

PIRES, TOMÉ. *The Suma Oriental*, ed. A. Cortesão. London, Hakluyt Society, 1944. 2 vols.

POLO, MARCO. *The Book of Ser Marco Polo*. Trans. Sir H. Yule. 3rd ed. revised by H. Cordier. London, 1903. 3 vols.

POPE, A. U. (ed.). *A Survey of Persian Art*. London, 1939. 6 vols.

RADLOFF, W. *Versuch eines Wörterbuches der Türk-dialecte*. 2nd ed., ed. O. Pritsak. The Hague, 1960. 4 vols.

Red Sea and Gulf of Aden Pilot. London, Admiralty, 1900.

RIASANOVSKY, V. A. *Fundamental Principles of Mongol Law*. Tientsin, 1937.

RIHANI, AMEEN. *Around the Coasts of Arabia*. London, 1930.

RUBRUCK, WILLIAM OF. See KOMROFF, M.

SACHAU. E. *Reise in Syrien und Mesopotamien*. Leipzig, 1883.

Sailing Directions for the Persian Gulf. Washington, U.S. Navy, 1931.

SARRE, F. and HERZFELD, E. *Archäologische Reise in Mesopotamien*. Berlin, 1911–20. 3 vols.

SCHIER, B. *Wege und Formen des ältesten Pelzhandels in Europa*. Frankfurt, 1951.

SCHWARZ, P. *Iran im Mittelalter*. Leipzig-Berlin, 1896–1936. 9 parts.

SIDERSKY, D. *Les origines des légendes musulmanes*. Paris, 1933.

SMIRNOV, V. D. 'Archaeological Excursion to the Crimea' (in Russian). *Zapiski vostochnago otdyela Imper. Russk. Arkh. Obshchestva* (St. Petersburg, 1887), I.

SPULER, B. *Die Goldene Horde*. Leipzig, 1943.

—*Die Mongolen in Iran*. 2nd ed. Berlin, 1955.

STEIN, Sir M. AUREL. *Archaeological Reconnnaissances in North-West India and South-Eastern Iran*. London, 1937.

TAESCHNER, F. *Der anatolische Dichter Nasiri und sein Futuvvetname*. Leipzig, 1944.

—*Das anatolische Wegenetz nach Osmanischen Quellen*. Vol. I. Leipzig, 1924.

—'Beiträge zur Geschichte der Achis in Anatolien.' *Islamica* (Leipzig, 1931), IV.

TEIXEIRA, PEDRO. *Travels*. Trans. W. F. Sinclair. London, Hakluyt Society, 1902.

THESIGER, W. *Arabian Sands*. London and New York, 1959.

TRITTON, A. S. *The Caliphs and their non-Muslim Subjects*. London, 1930.

TURAN, O. 'L'Islamisation dans la Turquie du Moyen Age.' *Studia Islamica* (Paris, 1959), X.

VLADIMIRTSOV, B. *Le régime social des Mongols*. Paris, 1948.

VILLIERS, ALAN. *Sons of Sinbad*. London, 1940.

WALKER, J. 'The Coinage of the Sultans of Kilwa.' *Numismatic Chronicle* (London, 1936).

WIET, G. 'Les Marchands d'épices sous les Sultans mamlouks.' *Cahiers d'Histoire égyptienne* (Cairo, 1955), VII/2.

—'Tapis égyptiens.' *Arabica* (Leiden, 1959), VI/1.

WILSON, A. T. *The Persian Gulf*. Oxford, 1928.

WITTEK, P. *Das Fürstentum Mentesche*. Istanbul, 1934.

—'Yazijioghlu 'Alī on the Christian Turks of the Dobruja,' *BSOAS* (London, 1952), XIV/3.

YULE, Sir HENRY (ed.). *Cathay and the Way Thither*. London, Hakluyt Society, 1913–16. 4 vols.

—and BURNELL, A. C. *Hobson-Jobson*. London, 1886.

—See also POLO, MARCO.

APPENDIX

A Provisional Chronology of Ibn Baṭṭūṭa's Travels in Asia Minor and Russia

Ever since the publication of Defrémery and Sanguinetti's edition of the *Riḥla* of Ibn Baṭṭūṭa—already a century ago—it has been realized that the narrative of his travels in Asia Minor and South Russia involves a number of serious inconsistencies, if not indeed impossibilities. Some of them were indicated by the translators themselves in their *Avertissement* to volume II; others, relating more particularly to the itineraries in Asia Minor and the steppes, were pointed out by P. Wittek in various articles; and the journey to and from Bulghār (pp. 490–1 in this volume) has been shown to be a complete fiction by St. Janicsek (*JRAS*, 1929, 791–800). Since, however, no critical investigation has been made as yet of this section of the *Riḥla*, the following notes may be regarded as a preliminary survey of the problem.

I. CHRONOLOGY

The most important initial task is to establish as far as possible an exact chronology for this part of the Travels. The chronology furnished by Ibn Baṭṭūṭa himself, as follows, is clearly an impossible one:

II. 248: Attended the Pilgrimage of A.H. 732 (2 Sept. 1332)
261: 1 Ramaḍān [733] at Eğridir[1] (16 May 1333)
312: 9 Dhu'l-Ḥijja [733] at Manisa (21 August 1333)
319: 'Ashūrā [734] at Burṣa (21 Sept. 1333)
380: 1 Ramaḍān [734] at Bishdagh (6 May 1334)
412: 10 Shawwāl [734] left for Constantinople (5 June 1334)
417: Mid-Dhu'l-Qa'da [734] at Bābā Salṭūq (15 July 1334)

From this point no dates are cited during the whole journey to and from Constantinople, and through Turkestan and Afghanistan, until:

III. 92: 1 Muḥarram 734, crossing of Indus river (12 Sept. 1333).

[1] Place-names in Turkey are spelled in their present Turkish forms.

There can be no doubt that the entire journey through Asia Minor to India took three years, and the attempt must therefore be made to correlate Ibn Baṭṭūṭa's statements with external evidence wherever possible. The most obvious instance is furnished by his reported interview with the ex-Emperor at Constantinople (p. 512). It was already pointed out by Defrémery and Sanguinetti (*Avertissement au 2e vol.*, p. XII) that this can refer only to Andronicus II, who died 12–13 February 1332. As we shall see, however, this date is of no assistance whatever, since it cannot be fitted into any consistent chronological scheme.

The first step is to determine whether there is any supporting evidence for either the first date in the above list, that of Ibn Baṭṭūṭa's presence at the Pilgrimage of 1332, or for the last date, that of his arrival on the Indus river. So far as I am aware, no event that he relates during the narrative of his experiences in India *certainly* supports or negates the dating of his arrival on 1 Muḥarram 734 (12 Sept. 1333). But somewhat earlier, after recounting his interview with the Chagaṭāy-khān Ṭarmashīrīn, he adds (III. 39) that 'about two years' after his arrival in India the news was received of the revolt in the eastern provinces against Ṭarmashīrīn. Barthold, after reviewing the evidence, has dated this revolt 'circa 734'.[2] This would agree with the dating of the interview to the spring of 733 (1333), whereas on a chronology beginning with the Pilgrimage of 732 it would fall in the spring of 735 (1335), and the news of the revolt would have arrived in 736 or 737.[3] Ibn Baṭṭūṭa's date of 734 may also be confirmed by his meeting with Shaikh 'Alā ud-Dīn Mawj-Daryā at Ajodhan, if Mahdi Husain's correction of the narrative is justified.[4]

To return to the first date, the Pilgrimage of 732, Ibn Baṭṭūṭa appears to validate it by recounting the Pilgrimage

[2] *Enc. of Islam*, s.v. Caghatāi-khān.

[3] B. Spuler gives 1337 as the date of the revolt in *Die Mongolen in Iran*[2] (375, n. 5; 378, n. 5), but in his survey, *Die Mongolenzeit* (Handbuch d. Orientalistik, 1953, p. 50) dates the reign of Ṭarmashīrīn 1326–1334. Ibn Ḥajar, *al-Durar al-Kāmina*, i, 516–17, estimates the length of Ṭarmashīrīn's reign as six years, and places his death in 735/1334–5.

[4] *The Reḥla of Ibn Baṭṭuṭa*, Baroda 1953, p. 20, n. 4. Mawj-Daryā was the grandson of Shaikh Farīd ud-Dīn, and died in 734/1335.

of al-Malik al-Nāṣir in that year, and his subsequent execution of Baktumūr and the Amīr Aḥmad (p. 411). The statements are in their main lines correct,[5] but this in no way confirms Ibn Baṭṭūṭa's own presence on that occasion. For Ibn Baṭṭūṭa, as is well known to all those who have read the *Riḥla*, often relates historical events at secondhand, even when they occurred long after the period of their context and when Ibn Baṭṭūṭa himself was at the time in far distant lands. For example, after describing his interview with 'Omar Beg of Izmīr, he adds an account of the death of 'Omar after the capture of Izmīr by the knights of St. John, in a battle which occurred in 1348, many years later (pp. 446–7). The more striking fact is that for the Pilgrimages of 727, 728 and 729 he mentions the names of many other pilgrims and accurately gives the precise day of the 'Standing' at 'Arafāt (pp. 356–8), but for the Pilgrimages of 730 and 732 gives no other names and notes only historical incidents of common knowledge. It must be repeated, however, that this in itself proves nothing, for it is abundantly evident that the presence or absence, accuracy or inaccuracy, of his general historical statements bears little or no relation to the veracity of his travel-narrative.

A more positive line of approach is to take the period of three years for the journey from Mecca to India, accept Muḥarram 734 for its conclusion, work out a provisional chronology from Muḥarram 731, and discover how far such a chronology can be supported by external evidence.

II. 251–267 (pp. 413–22): Journey via Egypt and Latakieh to 'Alaya and Eğridir, Muḥarram–Sha'bān 731 (Oct. 1330–June 1331)

269 (p. 423): 1 Ramaḍān 731 at Eğridir (8 June 1331)

276 (p. 427): 1 Shawwāl 731 at Denizli (8 July 1331) ('Season of fruit-ripening')

295–307 (pp. 438–44): About 21 days at Birgi during great heat (August 1331)

312 (p. 447): 9 Dhu'l-Ḥijja 731 at Manisa (13 Sept. 1331)

318 (p. 450): 10 Muḥarram 732 at Burṣa (13 Oct. 1331)

325 (p. 454): Left Iznik after 40 days (end of Ṣafar 732 = end of Nov. 1331).

[5] Cf. Zetterstéen, p. 186, and note 150 ad loc.

(329 [p. 456]: Road to Mudurnu obliterated by snow)
334, 342, 354 (pp. 458, 462, 468): About three months to embarkation at Ṣanūb
380 (p. 482): 1 Ramaḍān 732 at Bishdagh (27 May 1332)
402 (p. 492): 1 Shawwāl on a Friday (26 June 1332)
412 (p. 498): 10 Shawwāl 732, departure from Astrakhan (5 July 1332)
417 (p. 500): Mid-Dhu'l-Qa'da 732 at Bābā Salṭūq (9 August 1332)[6]
417, 418 (pp. 500–1): 40 days to arrival at Constantinople (18 Sept. 1332)
445 (p. 514): After 36 days departure from Constantinople (24 Oct. 1332) and journey through the steppe in winter.
446 (p. 515): Arrival and short stay in Saray (early January 1333)
451 (p. 517): Journey to Khwārizm in 40 days

III. 8: Two or three weeks there (February 1333)
19: 18 days to Bukhārā (mid-March 1333)
(III. 20: Pond at Bukhārā frozen over)
39: 54 days in camp of Tarmashīrīn (beginning of May 1333)
83: About 40 days at Qundūz 'to await the hot weather' (to end of June, 1333)
85 sqq.: Crossing of Hindu Kush and journey through Kābul
92: 1 Muḥarram 734, crossing of Indus river (12 Sept. 1333).

So far as I have been able to discover as yet, only three details are mentioned in the course of this journey which can be checked to some extent against external evidence.

(1) Ibn Baṭṭūṭa states (p. 429) that the mosque at Bārjīn (Pechin) was in course of construction but not yet completed. The building inscription of this mosque is quoted by Evliya Chelebi with the date 7(3)2.[7] Since the inscription presumably gives the date of completion, not of starting to build, and 732 began on 4 October 1331, this would agree with the dating of Ibn Baṭṭūṭa's stay at Pechin in July 1331.

(2) Ibn Baṭṭūṭa was given a young slave by 'Omar Beg

[6] See note 312 ad loc. That this was 'in the cold season' could not possibly apply as a general rule to any month of Dhu'l-Qa'da during the relevant period of years.
[7] See note 65 ad loc.

at Izmir, and was told that this was the last in his possession (p. 446). It can be reasonably conjectured that this slave was one of the children captured in ʿOmar's raid on Chios, dated by P. Lemerle in 1330 (*L'Emirat d'Aydin*, Paris 1957, 60), since ʿOmar's later strained relations with his father and his absence on expeditions in 1332 (and 1333?) would seem to exclude a later date. On the other hand, the chronology of ʿOmar's expeditions is still too tentative to serve as a firm foundation.

(3) Ibn Baṭṭūṭa describes Iznik (Nicaea) as in a ruinous condition and depopulated (p. 453). The city was captured by Orkhān in March 1331,[8] and in November of that year would still be in the condition described. It very soon began to be repopulated, however, if the arguments of H. A. Gibbons carry any weight.[9]

Although each of these details is hardly conclusive by itself, the concordance of all three for the year 731/1331 constitutes a reasonable presumption for this dating. At all events, (1) by itself makes a date later than 732/1332 unlikely, and (3) by itself makes a date earlier than 731/1331 impossible.

II. THE JOURNEY TO CONSTANTINOPLE

If this chronology is accepted, it is obvious that the journey to Constantinople acquires at least a *prima facie* confirmation; it not only fits easily into the chronology, but is required to account for the six months' interval between midsummer on the Volga and the journey to Bukhārā in the following winter. The only really discordant statement is that the month of Dhu'l-Qaʿda fell in 'the cold weather' (p. 500), but nothing can be built upon this (see n. 6 above). The other problems are relatively minor. Although I have been unable to check the fact directly, it appears that the marriage of a Greek princess to Uzbeg Khan is confirmed by Greek sources,[10] and the name Bayalūn, given to her by Ibn Baṭṭūṭa, is explained by B. Spuler as apparently a frequent

[8] See notes 144 and 148 ad loc.

[9] H. A. Gibbons, *The Foundation of the Ottoman Empire*, Oxford 1916, 61–3; cf. also G. G. Arnakis, *Oi prōtoi othōmanoi*, Athens 1947, 187–9.

[10] See p. 488, note 273.

name (or title?) for the wife of a Khān.[11] The somewhat hazy and confused geographical details of the journey are easily enough explained by the facts of the situation, that Ibn Baṭṭūṭa was travelling in strange territory and in a large company, which precluded any need to familiarize himself with routes and names. (It is obvious that Ibn Baṭṭūṭa had very little knowledge of geography *per se.*) As for the interview with the ex-Emperor Andronicus II, the fact that he calls the person whom he met Jirjīs (p. 512) is enough to rouse the suspicion that this person was not the ex-Emperor (whose monastic name was Antonios). Either, having been informed of the ex-Emperor's abdication and adoption of the monastic life, he misunderstood what was said to him, or else his guide misled him on this point as completely as on several other features of religious practice and organization at Constantinople.

III. THE DIVAGATIONS

The most puzzling feature of Ibn Baṭṭūṭa's *Riḥla* as a whole is the existence of a number of what are obviously divagations. By this term I mean the interruption of a journey along some well-defined route at a certain point, and the insertion of a more or less lengthy excursion into a neighbouring district, ending abruptly with the resumption of the original journey from the point at which it was broken off. Such divagations occur: in the first volume, in the intercalation of a tour through Syria into a normal three-weeks' journey from Cairo to Damascus (cf. Vol. I, pp. 71, 117); in the second volume, in the intercalation of a journey through Konya and Sivas to Erzurum between his stay at Milas in July 1331 and at Birgi in August 1331 (pp. 430–8), as well as the journey to Bulghār (pp. 490–2); and in the third volume, in the intercalation of a journey through the cities of Khurāsān between his stop at Balkh and arrival at Qundūz (III. 63–82 Ar.). In all these instances it seems impossible to bring the divagations within the chronological framework required by the narrative.

Yet these facts do not of themselves prove the divagations

[11] *Die Goldene Horde*, Leipzig 1943, p. 85, n.4.

to be outright fabrications. The tour through Syria is evidently a conflation of two (or even three) journeys, a fact which partly explains its geographical irregularity.[12] The tour through Khurāsān is highly suspect, and it contains no personal details except in regard to the stay at Nīshāpūr. The tour from Konya to Erzurum, on the contrary, is a mass of personal experiences, with the names of his hosts, *akhīs* and other, and accounts of his meetings with Badr al-Dīn ibn Qaramān and other dignitaries. There are few means, unfortunately, of identifying any of these persons (in comparison with those available for the first volume), except for the Qaramān prince and the Mongol viceroy Eretna (Artana). Since, however, the former, Badr al-Dīn Ibrāhīm, abdicated in 1333, the tour in itself does not conflict with the overall dating of this part of his travels. At the same time, it is clearly impossible to fit a journey of not less than 1300 km. each way between Konya and Erzurum, with stays of about three days in each town, into the chronology proposed in § 1 above, and still less to fit it into the chronology at the point where it occurs in Ibn Baṭṭūṭa's narrative.

The impasse that seems to result is, however, not quite insoluble. Accepting the starting-point of the journey from Judda at the end of Muḥarram 731 (mid-November 1330), the journey to Cairo would occupy 40–45 days, i.e. to the end of December 1330. Allowing even sixty or more days for the journey to Latakieh and the voyage to 'Alaya and Antalya, this would bring him to the end of February or early March 1331, i.e. about the end of Jumādā I. From Antalya to Eğridir is only 212 km., but he was at Eğridir at the beginning of Ramaḍān (June 8). There are thus three months to be accounted for. In the next place, there was no reason for Ibn Baṭṭūṭa to go to Eğridir if his objective was Denizli; the direct route to the latter lay via Göl Hisar (on a small lake 90 km. south-west of Burdur), and the journey to Burdur, Isparta and Eğridir was a considerable detour. But these were on the route from Antalya to Konya. It is a not very revolutionary suggestion that Ibn Baṭṭūṭa misplaced the beginning of his 'divagation'. That, even so, he can have gone

[12] See § IV below.

all the way to Erzurum I still find difficult to credit, but within three months he could certainly have travelled through Eğridir to Konya and thence via Laranda (Karaman) and Niğde to Kayseri (or even Sivas) and back to Eğridir through Aksaray.

IV. THE SYRIAN JOURNEY OF 730

There is still another consideration, however, which bears upon this journey. Up to this point in the argument, it has been accepted that the initial chronological datum is Ibn Baṭṭūṭa's presence at the Pilgrimage of 730/1330. But this fact also appears to be doubtful. As has already been noted in para. I above, he gives no personal details regarding the Pilgrimage of that year, but related only a historical event of common knowledge, namely the conflict between the amīr of Mecca, 'Uṭaifa, and the Egyptian detachment, which resulted in the death of the amīr jāndār Aldamur and his son (pp. 358–9). That Ibn Baṭṭūṭa did not relate this incident from personal observation is indicated, not only by the trifling error of calling Aldamur 'Āydamur', but by other details of greater significance. One of these is that he goes on to relate the consequent action of al-Malik al-Nāṣir in sending a detachment under a commander, unnamed, and the subsequent events at Mecca. This detachment, commanded by Āytamush, arrived in Mecca only some three months later, when Ibn Baṭṭūṭa was certainly not in the city.[13]

A more convincing detail is that Ibn Baṭṭūṭa was evidently ignorant of the real cause of the conflict, although it was one which would certainly have interested him personally. On two occasions he relates with some emphasis his friendship with the leader of the 'Irāqī caravan, called in his text Muḥammad al-Ḥawīḥ (I, 404 [p. 249]; II, 148–9 [p. 355]). This man was an active agent on behalf of the Īlkhān Abū Sa'īd, and Ibn Baṭṭūṭa himself relates that during the Pilgrimage of 729 the name of Abū Sa'īd was included in the *khuṭba* after that of al-Malik al-Nāṣir (p. 358; in I, 404 [p. 248], he dates this with less probability in 728). These facts do not appear to be related in other available sources, but

[13] See p. 359, n. 312.

they tie up with an isolated notice of al-Maqrīzī (*Sulūk*, ed. Ziada, II, 323–4) that the conflict in 730 arose out of secret orders sent by al-Malik al-Nāṣir to 'Uṭaifa to kill the leader of the 'Irāqī caravan, 'a man of Tabrīz called Muḥammad al-Ḥajīj' (who is evidently identical with Ibn Baṭṭūṭa's Muḥammad al-Ḥawīḥ), but the plan miscarried.[14] Had Ibn Baṭṭūṭa been in Mecca at the time, he would surely have known something of this, nor can I imagine that he would have omitted to say something about the elephant which accompanied the 'Irāqī pilgrims through all the ceremonies at Mecca in that year.[15]

If Ibn Baṭṭūṭa was not in Mecca at this time, where was he? I confess that I have not been able to complete the drastic recasting of the chronology of the earlier journeys, necessitated by placing his journey in Anatolia two years earlier than his own dating, since the task calls for an intricate cross-checking of all his data relating to places and persons. But as regards the antecedents of his journey to Anatolia, it can be argued with some assurance that he spent some time in Syria in the latter months of 730.

As pointed out in a note to the translation of vol. I (p. 81, n. 48), the journey there described through northern Syria could not have been made in 726, since Ibn Baṭṭūṭa left Cairo in the middle of Sha'bān and arrived in Damascus on 7 Ramaḍān. Although he does not mention another visit to Aleppo before 749/1348, there are not a few indications that some part of the journey there described was in fact made about the last months of 730 or beginning of 731. (1) In a casual statement about a certain Manṣūr b. Shakl (I, 291 [p. 182]), not otherwise identified, he speaks of a visit to Aleppo after the Pilgrimage of 726, but in a manner that can hardly refer to his visit in 749.

(2) A more substantial proof is given by his mention of Arghūn as governor of Aleppo (I, 156 [p. 100]). As pointed out in note 129 ad loc., Arghūn left Cairo to take up his post at Aleppo only on 8 December 1326, and died in office there on 30 December 1330. Ibn Baṭṭūṭa's visit must therefore have occurred between these two dates.

14 See p. 359, note 310.

15 Wüstenfeld, *Chroniken der Stadt Mekka*, II, 280–1; IV, 250.

(3) In the description of his journey through Syria in vol. I, Ibn Baṭṭūṭa goes to Latakiya *from* Aleppo (p. 113). Against this is to be set his passing through Jabala, where he visited the tomb of Ibrāhīm b. Ad'ham, but even in his earlier description he places Jabala between Aleppo and Latakiya.

(4) Another curious detail also tends to confirm a stay in Syria just before his journey to Anatolia. In IV, 345–6, Ibn Baṭṭūṭa relates that he had left a wife of his, who was pregnant, in Damascus, and had learned, 'when in India', that she had given birth to a male child. If this child was born in 726 or 727, the statement would be totally absurd, since he was certainly in communication with Damascus during the following Pilgrimage seasons at least. But if he left the wife pregnant at Damascus in 730, it is entirely intelligible that he should not have received news of her until he reached India.

There is, consequently, every possibility that the period of Ibn Baṭṭūṭa's journey in Asia Minor could be appreciably lengthened beyond the calculations at the end of the preceding paragraph. But, in conclusion, it must be emphasized again that these reconstructions of Ibn Baṭṭūṭa's journeys are at this stage to be regarded as purely tentative, and none of the proposed datings can be accepted as final until a fuller investigation has been completed.